STRUGGLING
TO LEARN

STRUGGLING TO LEARN

An Intimate History of School Desegregation in South Carolina

June Manning Thomas

THE UNIVERSITY OF
SOUTH CAROLINA PRESS

Published by the University of South Carolina Press
Columbia, South Carolina 29208

www.uscpress.com

Manufactured in the United States of America

30 29 28 27 26 25 24 23 22 21
10 9 8 7 6 5 4 3 2 1

Library of Congress Cataloging-in-Publication Data
can be found at http://catalog.loc.gov/.

ISBN 978-1-64336-259-5 (hardcover)
ISBN 978-1-64336-260-1 (ebook)

Publication of this book is made possible in part by the
Distinguished University Professorship and the A. Alfred Taubman
College of Architecture and Urban Planning at the University of Michigan.

To Hubert and Ethel's great-grandchildren:
Mobin, Marzieh, Adib, Amil

CONTENTS

ILLUSTRATIONS

PREFACE

"Have you seen Cindy Tyler lately?" my sister Michelle asked. I laughed. Why no, I said, what do you mean, and why would I want to see her? "You should talk to her," Michelle said. "She's really quite nice. She has a shop just around the corner. We could walk there and talk to her! You'd be surprised. I've talked to her quite often."

I had not visited Orangeburg, South Carolina, frequently for a number of years, having made my home as an adult in Michigan. There, marriage, children, faith community, and work had happily filled the years. Once our father died and my invalid mother came to Michigan to live with my husband and me, there was little reason to visit Orangeburg, until my younger sister moved back there to accept a job. Orangeburg was the site of many happy memories during my childhood, such as of rare snows and school pageants and our sweet-smelling backyard peach trees laden with fruit once a year, of homecoming parades and college choirs singing glorious music. It was also, however, the site of trauma, of daily evidence of the denigration of an entire race of people, of college students jailed or shot for protests against segregation. It was the site of my own pained efforts on school mornings to get out of bed and attend Orangeburg High School, as one of several Black students enrolled in the previously all-white school because of a federal district court order. Memories of Cindy, unfortunately, connected strongly with memories of that struggle.

Just before several Black students desegregated that high school, many years after the 1954 *Brown v. Board of Education of Topeka* Supreme Court decision had ruled public school segregation unconstitutional, hopes had been high for a new, integrated reality. Instead white South Carolinians had resisted, keeping separate and unequal schools, ignoring the *Brown* decision except to insure for as long as possible that it would not change segregated practice. The hope for many of us in the 1950s and 1960s was that once Black children entered those schools, white people would see that we were just the same as them, human beings eager to learn, and that friendships would soon emerge. This was not to be.

Shortly before encouraging me to visit Cindy, Michelle had decided to attend her older sister's (my) high school reunion; she was curious about who these people were, and I had refused to travel South for this event. She attended with another Black woman who had entered that high school a year or two after several of us integrated it in 1964. It's so unusual to attend someone else's high school reunion that several people approached her asking if she was me. When a few of them found out that she was my sister, they talked to her about me, explaining why they noticed me so many years ago. At least one was in tears as she spoke. Please tell her we are sorry, they told Michelle; please tell her we are sorry for the way we treated her.

Just before the reunion, Michelle had bought a rambling ranch house on a street somewhere in town for a very reasonable price. When I visited her there, at first I could not get my bearings, although she kept showing me the middle school that replaced the high school, and I recognized a nearby commercial area. The enclosed mall that once sat across the street was now a strange amalgam of shops surrounded by mall-like parking lots, with no enclosed mall, just shops created around the outer rim of the old building, in a strange configuration that added to my confusion. In the surrounding area, everything seemed unfamiliar, even though this is a small town. Then I realized that her house was located in one of the older, formerly all-white neighborhoods arrayed around the formerly all-white high school—no wonder I was lost. Years ago, no Black people lived there, and no one would have asked any of us to enter one of those homes, except perhaps as maids. It gradually became clear that her house was located on a side street that led directly into the street I would have used to walk to high school if it had been safe to do this. Although the school was only one mile from my house, my parents had never once let me walk there after our successful court action; the route would have taken me through hostile White neighborhoods at the height of resistance to desegregation. Almost fifty years later, my sister had moved into this forbidden territory, now open but still unfamiliar.

"It's walking distance," she said on my last day visiting from Michigan. "She has a shop that we visited during the reunion. It's just around the corner from here. I talked to her. I'm sure she'd be glad to see you."

I considered the situation. I remembered Cindy quite well. She was lead soprano in our high school choir, fellow classmate in several classes, and one of the ones I had watched silently, wondering: How is it possible for us to sit in the same class, day after day, and for these people to say not even one word to me, except to hurl epithets? Cindy had been a part not of the hecklers but of the great silence; as a part of the white resistance in that town, evidently white students had created a pact to ostracize the new Black students, to ignore their presence except to heckle. I remembered a comment Cindy made in gym class, said to her friends but addressed to me, and I remembered other difficult moments as well. What would motivate people to act in this way? I'd only seen her once or twice since graduation but did not hesitate. My husband, Richard, had packed the rental car. It will just be a few minutes, I said; I have to see someone from high school.

It was indeed a short walk physically but a long walk emotionally. I trudged uphill, filled with misgivings. The shop itself was pleasant, a compendium of small items appropriate for a residential house turned into a boutique shop located in a section of the country that loves crafts, pottery, scarves, and baby clothes. Cindy and my sister chatted easily as I walked around the shop, wondering what to say, wanting to buy something if for no other reason than to show that I could. I chose a small item for purchase. After an awkward silence at the cash register, Cindy started talking about the reunion. I should have seen how everyone looked, she noted. The girls had "kept themselves up," but the boys had not; they had gained weight and gray hair. She proceeded to name several students, one by one, all white; did I know what they were doing now? This and that? Of course I didn't know, never having had a simple conversation with any of them and having no idea of what their lives were like during or after high school. More talk ensued, and then she asked questions about what I was doing, my husband, my children, my job, my children's professions. "Your sister told me you are a college professor. I'm hoping at least one of my grandchildren is smart like that," she said.

The comment stopped me. It was a moment of clear insight into my own bounties. I still thought of myself as a victim, but here was a former high school classmate, white, popular at the time, lead soprano in the choir I had to fight to get into (the choir director did not want any Black singers), expressing a clear, revealing ambition for her grandchildren. I'd had many blessings in life since leaving that town. We all had weathered the storm of the 1960s, and yet some of us had managed to make a life for ourselves. This moment was in some ways a reenactment of an age-old truth: high school is the nadir for many people, a time of ostracism and rejection, perhaps not as thoroughly as some of us had experienced, but a nadir nonetheless. The second part of the truth: those who seem to fare well in high school do not necessarily fare well in life. Yet this recognition of a truism unfolding in real time felt almost shameful. I was a college professor, a person who loved writing and had written and edited several books, a woman with plenty of confirmations in adult life, mother of an architect and a physician, grandmother to four children with great potential, acutely conscious of the implications of Cindy's clearly expressed wish.

She was asking me something else. Brought back from my reverie, I focused on what she was saying. Putting the words together, as if in a fog, I finally realized that she had asked me this: "We didn't treat you too bad in high school, did we, June?" Without thinking, I responded with the truth: "Why, of course you did, Cindy." Her face fell, darkened in some subtle way, and she mumbled: "I've always tried to treat everybody the same." Once again I checked myself, counted my blessings, summoned my humanity. Racing through my memories, I managed to fetch one redeeming encounter: "Why, Cindy, I saw you a few years after high school, when you worked at another shop as a salesperson, and you spoke to me and were very nice on that day." Her face brightened a bit, and the tension in my chest eased a bit as well. I reached out to her, and we hugged, bridging a gap nurtured by many years of distance, and with that one gesture having said all, I left, feeling sadder but wiser, and contemplated the moral terrain just navigated. For my part, the lesson concerned bounties; for her part, was some part of the lesson contrition? Repentance? What did it feel like to be part of an oppressive race, at a time and place of great oppression?

I am an academic who struggles to write personal history but with a lifelong curiosity about the fit between yesterday's lessons and today's dilemmas. This is a personal narrative in the sense that personal experiences drove the selection of themes and facts, but the book is only partially autobiographical. It instead settles into a format more comfortable for me, one with personal and family narrative but also with some distance, as it reexamines historic events now, a time when the journey away from oppression and toward social justice seems stalled in some way. This incident with my old schoolmate was one of several that led me to believe that it was time to write this story about a state not often considered in the forefront of the civil rights movement, even though it was in several ways. Battles took place over the simple right of Black children to obtain a public school education equal to that of white children and should have faded into memory as society moved on. It is important to understand why the battles were so difficult, to consider with some dispassion the apologists for oppression, to recount exploits of those who fought for desegregation, and to examine the implications of that era for the present.

Many books have focused on the civil rights movement. These narratives have recounted events in specific states, among certain organizations, and in several spheres of influence, such as the courts, schools, or public facilities. Even so, as with most big moments, many parts of the story still lie hidden, particularly from the vantage point of less-than-famous individuals and less-than-prominent localities. This book attempts to uncover aspects of this hidden narrative, focusing on the larger historical background of that simple conversation so painfully navigated a few years ago, in a small boutique located on an unfamiliar side street in Orangeburg, South Carolina.

ACKNOWLEDGMENTS

I started to write this book several times over many years and failed to move beyond a few autobiographical passages. I am especially grateful for the people who made completion possible. Legions of archivists kept and then organized crucial historical materials. It was in 2017, when I saw just how far their work had taken them over the years, that I realized this book was possible. Previously I had planned and even started a memoir, but I waited too long, as contemporaries moved away or passed on to other worlds or as my own memories faded and dissipated into the ether. Not sure of basic facts anymore, I was overjoyed to see that someone had been keeping records, particularly of South Carolina's civil rights activities and school desegregation, and that these records were fully accessible.

Amazingly, some of the best records were located at the University of South Carolina (USC). This was a surprise; I still thought of that university as "white," but I had been away from the state for many years. Meanwhile USC had taken significant steps to diversify racially in terms of faculty, staff, students, and programming, and its archivists were keenly interested in civil rights history. USC archivists put online key resources, such as the papers of Rev. I. DeQuincey Newman, and I accessed these starting in 2009, about the same time that I accessed NAACP branch records on microfilm at the University of Michigan. It was hard to continue the story with just those sources, however, and life and other writing projects intervened.

USC subsequently issued a short research guide summarizing its civil rights collections. After reading this, I began to correspond by email with Herbert Hartsook, at that time head archivist for USC's South Carolina Political Collections. When I traveled to South Carolina and we were able to meet in person, in fall 2017, it was clear that he was determined to assist this project. He not only set up a time for me to review finder's guides and archived materials but also set up a lunch with historian Bobby Donaldson, who heads the USC Center for Civil Rights History and Research and is extremely knowledgeable about the state's civil rights era. This was the beginning of an essential support system.

At that first lunch, Hartsook and Donaldson recommended that I contact M. Hayes Mizell, who had donated extensive archival materials and was very involved in supporting the school desegregation movement in the 1960s and '70s.

Mizell's archives turned out to be a treasure trove of information, voluminous and insightful, providing raw material for large sections of two chapters in this book. He and I met just once for lunch, but we then initiated an informal email correspondence that has extended now for four years. At times I would send him draft chapters, and he would respond with excellent comments or suggested additional resources. Mizell is second only to my husband in the extent of his support for this book.

Hartsook and Donaldson also recommended that I explore the South Carolina Council on Human Relations collection, housed at the South Caroliniana branch of USC's library system. This too proved valuable; I spent many days exploring those and Mizell's papers. The South Caroliniana archivists labored in challenging conditions—their own building was not open because of extensive structural problems—and they cheerfully hauled boxes of materials to and from off-site storage facilities as needed.

Several other archivists were helpful as well. Daron Calhoun and Aisha Haykal provided as many of the interviews as they could from an incompletely processed oral history collection at the Avery Research Center, College of Charleston. Although the pandemic interfered with efforts to process all interviews, their help was very useful. Many thanks to Millicent Brown, Charleston's pioneering "first" Black student, who videotaped many of us other "firsts" to create that collection and who donated other material to Avery's collection as well.

At Furman archivist Jeffrey Makala welcomed me warmly to the university's archives and greatly assisted this project. At a later point he reviewed two draft chapters about Furman, gently offering corrections, and he provided both encouragement and resources, such as camera-ready photographs and additional articles. Deborah Allen was a Furman staff member who offered critical support and read the draft epilogue as well as facilitating my reengagement with campus. She and Makala invited me back for the first Joseph Vaughn Day in 2020, and so in that sense they helped create the book's epilogue.

In Orangeburg archivist Avery Daniels provided access to South Carolina State University's annual reports, and he offered draft photographs from their small Cecil Williams collection. Eric Powell, volunteer archivist for the Orangeburg Historical Society, did fine work ferreting out vertical files and yearbooks that I had no hope of finding.

At the H. V. Manning Library at Claflin University, Marilyn Gibbs Drayton and Barbara Green happily corresponded with me, unburied materials from my father's own archives, suggested other sources that proved to be extremely helpful, and gave me plenty of room and table space—with no time limit—to explore these documents. They are the keepers of Claflin's history; the way that these librarians treasure the various H. V. Manning files, plaques, and photographs and even Dad's commencement robe is heartwarming. Future generations will benefit from that library's stewardship of much Black and civil rights history, because Cecil Williams has donated his own complete photography collection to that library. Williams has helped the library gain the grant money and equipment necessary to digitize the material.

Williams, a force unto himself, has made an extraordinary contribution to civil rights history in South Carolina and in the region at large. Our town was fortunate that he lived in our midst and snapped photographs throughout the '50s, '60s, and up to the present and that he published many of these in his own books. Williams photographed Claflin events for several decades, often giving our family a copy when we were included; this was like having our own personal family friend who was also a top-rate photographer. Our family scrapbooks, therefore, contained extremely professional images! He generously gave me permission to include many of his photographs in this book, and he identified many of the people and events that were unknown to me. In some ways, this book is his too.

One able doctoral student in urban planning helped when I sorely needed assistance. Christine Hwang was indispensable. She not only collected raw data from the smaller of two Workman collections, located at the William L. Clements Library in Ann Arbor, but she also devoted considerable time to organizing and coding information from that and other collections. What is particularly remarkable about her work is that it required her at times to sift through racist pamphlets, letters, and other offensive writings, since Workman collected and wrote such material. She became a fellow researcher and equal partner as we fought outrage and consoled each other, reminding ourselves that all human beings are equal in contradiction to what we were reading. In spite of her onerous tasks, she consistently displayed high levels of professionalism and meticulous attention to detail, for a topic other than her own dissertation research.

Another essential helper was my oldest grandchild, Mobin Olinga Mazloomian. He was a crucial part of our two-member production team in the book's final few weeks before submission. By the time he came on board, exhaustion had set in for the author, and I needed tangible assistance! Mobin, a University of Michigan engineering undergraduate student with little experience writing formal papers, nevertheless undertook a self-education crash course in the *Chicago Manual of Style* for endnotes, text, and bibliographies. He created the bibliography of published work from scratch and reformatted much of the text and endnotes, always working with enthusiasm and good cheer. He was a wonderful helpmate for this project.

Ehren Foley, acquisitions editor for the USC Press, was an important support system in and of himself. He was my first point of contact at the Press, and he consistently nudged me toward honoring my own personal and family reflections rather than overly relying on archival materials and secondary sources, which was my first inclination. He convinced me that personal experiences were important in themselves and that those combined with other sources had, upon his final reading, created an "intimate history." He surely championed this book within his own Press, but he also felt like my own personal champion. Foley watched every step of the way as we considered length, focus, photographs, and subtitle; I very much appreciate his assistance in helping this book take form.

Other helpers include the Office of Baha'i Review, headed by fellow scholar Martha Schweitz, which reviews work by Baha'i authors to check errors of fact related to the Baha'i Faith. I am grateful that they took the time to review the manuscript for this purpose, and that Martha was open to my questions about how to discuss political actors in this book. The University of Michigan's Distinguished University Professor program provided a modest annual grant 2016–20, channeled through my ever-supportive College of Architecture and Urban Planning, and this grant paid for many necessary travel expenses. Their grant also financed graduate student labor and the book's map illustrations, beautifully redrawn and designed from original sources by my university's talented Michigan Creative office.

For those giving emotional and review support, I offer sincere gratitude. One of the earliest to provide affirming comments on memoir drafts, over fifteen years ago, was Howell Baum of the University of Maryland. He consistently urged me to complete the work, even when I wanted to drop it. One evening conversation with Heather Thompson, at an urban history conference in Columbia, was more important than she could know. Other crucial support came from colleague Robert Fishman, my department chairperson Joe Grengs, Harley Etienne, Roy Jones, the late Patricia Rose, Claflin's former president Henry Tisdale and former vice-president Whittaker Middleton, and many other friends and colleagues. Four Felton elementary school classmates offered friendship when, during the intense pandemic months in 2020–21, memories of Orangeburg flooded and almost overwhelmed. Our simple Zoom sessions, so filled with laughter, helped see me through to the end. These are Juretta Wallace Dash, Frances Edwards Hamilton, Gwendolyn Thompson Hedgepath, and Janice Frederick Watts. Janice read the chapter that described our years at Felton and offered wonderful comments; Juretta during 2019 emerged as a personal tour guide for my children and grandchildren, helping them connect to Claflin's campus; Gwendolyn and Frances shared pictures of us as children and youths that had us all laughing over Zoom. My sister Michelle consistently offered cheerful encouragement and occasional anecdotes about our parents and grandparents, things that I had forgotten long ago.

I also thank two anonymous reviewers, who suggested crucial changes to earlier drafts. In addition, historians Matt Lassiter, Pero Dagbovie, and Louis Venters offered helpful marketing advice. Venters's excellent scholarship on South Carolina Baha'is provided much inspiration, as did Ricky Abercrombie's memoir on the same subject.

My husband, Richard W. Thomas, was a helper in every way for this project. He has been for all of my adult life the best possible companion, counselor, sounding board, co-parent, and husband, all rolled into one. He offered steadfast support throughout the many years of my starting and then abandoning the writing of this book; he never lost faith in it or in my other scholarship; and he remains a source of wisdom and inspiration because of his own exceptional scholarship and many other talents. Crucially, as the first reader for almost all of the chapters, he suggested changes with loving exactitude, and his wisdom, spiritual insight, historical training, and humor were essential every step of the way. It is not an exaggeration to say that his extraordinary scholarship was the inspiration for much of this book.

ABBREVIATIONS

1866 Conference	Methodist Church's South Carolina Mission Conference, founded 1866; almost completely Black
ACLU	American Civil Liberties Union
AFSC	American Friends Service Committee
CORE	Congress of Racial Equality
GEB	General Education Board, a philanthropic foundation
HBCU	Historically Black Colleges and Universities
NAACP	National Association for the Advancement of Colored People
NAACP LDF	NAACP Legal Defense Fund
PEA	Palmetto Education Association, previously PSTA
PSTA	Palmetto State Teacher's Association
SCBC	South Carolina Baptist Convention
SCCHR	South Carolina Council on Human Relations
SCLC	Southern Christian Leadership Conference
SSOC	Southern Student Organizing Committee
SNCC	Student Nonviolent Coordinating Committee

Introduction

This book is a narrative about efforts to improve Black education in South Carolina, with a focus on school desegregation as a planned strategy. Its main timeframe is the period from 1947 to 1974. It uses this timeframe to examine legal and behavioral change during a pivotal era in US history. The legal struggle is well-known and features lawyers and judges but also ordinary teachers, parents, and families willing to challenge segregationist law and practice. During that struggle, it became evident that changing attitudes of supremacy and privilege was much more difficult than changing law. This was true not just in relation to schools but also in other areas of life as well.

Studying the roots of Jim Crow–era educational segregation and attempts to dismantle it can help illuminate contemporary dilemmas of exclusion. In the view of white southerners living in the mid-twentieth century, equal access to public school education threatened familiar bastions of privilege and exclusion, because it could rearrange social, economic, and racial ordering. Civic leaders took extreme measures to assure unequal access to public education in states such as South Carolina.[1] Studying those repressive measures and efforts to dismantle them can help us understand why such systems arose as well as why their effects still linger.

The year 1947 is pivotal because it marked the filing of a petition by a Black parent living in South Carolina's Clarendon County, Levi Pearson, who asked for bus transportation for his children in a place where the school district provided transportation only for white children. His petition led to two additional suits by local Black parents, first for equal facilities and then for desegregation. The US Supreme Court considered simultaneously school desegregation cases from five different places, including Clarendon County; the five made up the landmark 1954 US Supreme Court decision in *Brown v. Board of Education of Topeka*. After that decision states throughout the South refused to desegregate public schools or universities voluntarily, and several did not *begin* to desegregate schools until forced to do so in the mid-1960s or later. The pace of active desegregation efforts slowed by 1974 because of a number of policy changes and the substantial elimination of two-race, unequal local public school systems sanctioned by law.

Numerous small actors worked for such change in hundreds of small towns and cities before, during, and after that period. We need to know more about how change in this critical era looked and felt in places out of the glare of national headlines. In this narrative, we uncover several quiet stories of heroism, adding rich complexity to standard interpretations of this aspect of the civil rights era and before.

The main purpose of the book is to help bring to life a crucial period of school desegregation and civil rights history, but also to describe how a sorely oppressed people, South Carolina's Black population, managed to protect and educate their children and youths in spite of dire oppression. The struggle in this narrative concerns their efforts to live with dignity and to gain a better education, even higher education, under Jim Crow and its aftermath. This book uses the matrix of life in one small town and in one state, and the perspective of one family, my own, to draw out larger lessons of oppression, resistance, and constructive resilience.

South Carolina is an important case study for several reasons. South Carolina had an unusually entrenched Jim Crow system because of repressive post-Reconstruction laws culminating in its 1895 state constitution. That constitution concretized racial separation and legalized the systematic marginalization of the Black public school system, such as it was. At the same time, a small portion of Black South Carolinians benefited from Black schools and colleges that provided rudimentary education and trained a small Black professional class, including teachers. This laid the groundwork for civil rights era pressure for equal education. Organized protests began in Charleston as early as 1917, and throughout the 1920s, 1930s, and 1940s, pressure arose for equalized public school facilities, never provided. Then in the 1940s a sympathetic white federal circuit court judge, Charlestonian J. Waties Waring, helped provide legal foundations and opinions in several rulings that began to loosen the chokehold of Jim Crow in South Carolina. Judge Waring's clearly worded dissenting opinion on behalf of school desegregation in *Briggs v. Elliott* was particularly important, helping to provide NAACP lawyers with arguments they later used in the composite *Brown* case.

The litigation that led to *Brown* actually started in several places in the Deep South, border states, and Midwest, as masterfully described in Devlin's *A Girl*

Stands at the Door. South Carolina with *Briggs v. Elliott,* filed well before To-peka, Kansas's *Brown* case, was one of five interconnected cases that eventually went forth before the US Supreme Court as *Brown. Briggs v. Elliott,* while not as famous as *Brown,* offered substantive experience with arguing such cases. The fight for voters' rights was also an essential part of the civil rights movement; an essential region-wide program designed to educate illiterate Blacks well enough to allow them to register to vote began in South Carolina's Sea Islands. There, Charlestonian Septima Clark helped pioneer a basic literacy / voter education project eventually adopted by the Southern Christian Leadership Conference (SCLC) and used throughout the southern United States, forming the basis for an empowered Black electorate.

South Carolina was also an important stronghold for white supremacy for much of its history. The first state to secede from the nation through its Articles of Secession (1860), it thus helped birth the Confederacy and launch the Civil War. Like other Deep South states, South Carolina resisted Reconstruction reforms that emerged after the Civil War, restoring white power after a brief period of relative freedom for Black people. The state hosted a culture of lynching that lasted for decades, all the while maintaining a supposedly genteel landed class that exploited Black labor through tenant farmer systems and pretty much ignored the reign of terror that mobs perpetrated against Black residents. The state hosted less violent vehicles of repression as well, such as disenfranchise-ment of Black voters, purposefully inferior public education for Black students, and then, beginning in the mid-twentieth century, white citizens' councils and private academies designed to fight against school integration.

The tendency now is to think of the "classical" era of the civil rights movement--perhaps 1954 to 1968, from *Brown* to the Civil Rights Act of 1968 (the "Fair Housing Act")—as a time of triumph, with southern recalcitrance yielding to high-profile public events led by national civil rights leaders. In this telling, brilliant lawyers smashed Jim Crow racial segregation laws, paving the way for reforms. In truth the movement was more complicated than that. Gains overcame major legal and political barriers, but they did not resolve structural problems of income, class, and racial inequality. Some scholars suggest that this was true in part because civil rights leaders had to pick their battles. For example, they settled for strategies, such as access to whites-only schools and voting rights, that did not question the dominant market economic system with many built-in inequities.[2]

The longer civil rights era extended further back, perhaps to Reconstruc-tion, just after the Civil War. Minor legal skirmishes dating from then and ex-tending to the mid-twentieth century gave only brief relief from the purposeful suppression of Black education. The two-race public school system was deeply entrenched in the culture and polity of the white South, with racially separate and unequal schools considered foundational for white people's way of life. School districts not only supported wildly unequal levels of expenditures for Black and white students but also harassed, drove into bankruptcy, or forced into exile those Black families that dared request equal educational facilities. Such tactics, and lack of federal enforcement, allowed white southerners to ignore the 1954 *Brown* decision for many years. By the early 1960s, when national pressure made it evident that school systems segregated by law (de jure) must fall, white people placed the burden of initiating desegregation on the backs of Black children, faculty, and staff. Their experiences, plus resisted efforts to eliminate actual (de facto) segregated schools there and in other parts of the nation, dampened national support for school desegregation. Efforts to desegregate schools in the North and southern recalcitrance led to the movement's death knell.

Telling such a rich, complex, and potentially emotional story in a way that informs but also engages the reader is no small feat. In addition, other authors have told much of the story in literature, film, and art. Here is how we will approach this task. This book draws primarily on historical research, such as published narratives or books, and on other archival material. It also uses several people's lived experiences (as expressed in autobiographies, talks, or other such means) to explain what happened. The main vehicle, however, is a combination of family and personal history set in the context of larger social events. This narrative, then, is both a history and a memoir.

Such an approach should add warmth and human interest to the telling, as well as offer complexity to common, sometimes flattened views of Black education in the Jim Crow South, the civil rights movement, and school desegregation. Just as one example, we can consider the place of Orangeburg in literature about the civil rights era. Books and articles often mention Orangeburg only as a site for a 1968 incident of violent repression known as the Orangeburg Massacre, and they may mention only the college students who endured gunfire during that event for the sake of desegregation.

This narrative will show that a civil rights movement in my hometown—and by implication in many hometowns—predated the 1960s and involved not only college students but also adults and whole families. Dating from 1955, for over a decade, Black adults, college and high school students, and even children petitioned, marched, picketed, protested, and suffered arrest. When college, high school, and junior high school students boycotted classes or cafeterias or went to jail, particularly during the period from 1955 to 1956 and then again from 1960 to 1964, Orangeburg's Black community supported them, at times providing food, blankets, bail money, and moral support. In 1955 national publicity led concerned citizens from around the country to send money, food, and clothes to Black petitioners in our county and in our state who suffered harassment because they had dared to challenge segregated and unequal schools. Telling about such protests and such support enriches views of not only Orangeburg and South Carolina but also the civil rights movement in general.

I am humbly offering myself, with the help of several observers and authors, as narrator. I spent most of my childhood and youth in Orangeburg, giving me a firsthand view of the classical civil rights era as it unfolded there. Orangeburg was a bastion of Jim Crow segregation as well as Black higher education. Railroad tracks split the town down the middle physically and racially. Black people lived mostly on the eastern side, with the campuses of two historically Black colleges, named in the 1960s Claflin College and South Carolina State College. Up until the age of seventeen, with the exception of four early childhood years in Charleston, I lived on Claflin's campus. From second to eighth grade, I attended an all-Black grade school on SC State's campus. Almost every school day, I walked twice through a rough gap in a chain-link fence from one campus to the other. The role of these two campuses in the struggle for equal education therefore is of great personal interest, but these two colleges were important for other reasons as well.

In South Carolina, Claflin is the oldest HBCU, dating back to 1869. In 1896 it split in two and gave birth to SC State as the only public college for South Carolina's Black population. Both schools have existed side by side ever since, with both striving to educate Black students. Claflin has consistently placed among the top ten HBCUs in annual rankings of US colleges over the last ten years, according to the *US News and World Report*.[3] SC State has a noble legacy as the only institution, until the mid-1960s, where the state's Black students could receive higher education at a state-supported college or university.

My family was wedded to Claflin. From 1956 until his 1984 retirement, my father, Hubert Vernon Manning, was its president. My mother, Ethel Augusta Braynon Manning, was a Claflin faculty member, teaching mathematics and educational statistics. This meant that our family, unusual but also representative of a larger Black professional class, had a unique view of one college important to the civil rights movement. Our family also helped fight for equal education for Black students, not only through Claflin but also through desegregation efforts. In 1964, under court order given in response to a lawsuit, I was one of thirteen Black students to desegregate the local all-white Orangeburg High School. This extraordinary experience shaped my life, and so this personal history brings a level of passion and intimacy with cold facts that might be harder for someone more removed from these events. In this way, this book connects with other histories of Black schools and desegregation that rely on personal stories, such as Vanessa Siddle Walker's history of one rural North Carolina high school, *Their Highest Potential,* and Devlin's excellent collection of desegregation narratives. Devlin argued that Black girls (rather than boys) often led school desegregation battles, for tactical and cultural reasons, and this was the case for Orangeburg.

Derrick Bell Jr., an NAACP Legal Defense Fund (NAACP LDF) attorney, advanced storytelling as a way for Black scholars to uncover and describe the effects of racial oppression. In addition, he was one of the first scholars to analyze the shortcomings of civil rights efforts to improve Black education by relying, too heavily, on school desegregation as a legal strategy. Thus in terms of methodology, which includes history plus memoir, and in terms of topic, school desegregation, Bell's approach helped me frame events in a broader context.[4]

Focusing on one state, South Carolina, makes it possible to expose interlinked actors, since many people important to Black education or to civil rights at that time worked together. This also helps create a longitudinal perspective on places of importance during several phases of the struggle. Sometimes those key places are surprising: Johns Island, a rural barrier island not connected by bridge to the mainland near Charleston until 1945, was important to the struggle for Black educational parity.[5] Sometimes those key places are less surprising, such as Columbia, state capitol and seedbed of NAACP state leadership. Charleston, part of the state's southeast Lowcountry and bastion of the plantation economy, hosted an early campaign for equal education, and Greenville, in the northwest Piedmont district of the state, offered lessons in both conservatism and liberalism. The pivotal location for this narrative, however, is Orangeburg, situated in the geographic center of the state, home of two HBCUs, battlefield for civil rights activists, and my hometown.

Orangeburg was a battlefield partially because of the presence of two colleges, important both for the struggle for Black education and for the civil rights movement. Each housed students who were major participants in the marches and demonstrations that challenged the state's balance of power from 1955 until 1968. Although Columbia, forty miles away, was the state capitol and thus the seat of white political power, Orangeburg had great influence among the state's Black population. At least a portion of Black teachers, ministers, and other professionals were likely to have attended one of the two Orangeburg HBCUs, and working-class Black families of more modest means aimed to send their children there as well. Orangeburg was also an important location for white resistance to Black activism, since it nurtured white citizens' councils, white boycotts, and white private academies, and in addition it hosted several incidences of white police repression. These two trends, Black activism and white reactionary suppression, occasionally collided in confrontational ways.

Several key questions drive this book, which began as pieces for a story about my own high school experience. Narratives already exist about school desegregation during that time, and these give ample evidence of the difficulties Black youth faced as they encountered hostility at their new schools.[6] Although we will address some such experiences in one chapter, choosing that approach as a focus for a whole book had little appeal. I became more interested in the less obvious questions: What was the nature of white suppression of Black education in South Carolina in the early to mid-twentieth century? How did Black South Carolinians nevertheless manage to educate their children and youth? What were signs of white racism and repression during the Jim Crow era, and how did Black people respond? How did school desegregation ramp up, and who were the key actors promoting it in this state? How did all of this feel, for at least one family that experienced it but also for others?

Clarifying some terms will help with this effort. During most of the era we are discussing, state law and social mores enforced the biologically indefensible concept of two different races, when other populations (e.g., Asian or Native American) were negligible in size. South Carolina defined people as "colored," according to the 1895 constitution, if they had at least one-eighth African blood. It is impossible to speak of this place and this era without using such a working definition for what we now call "Black." According to that constitution, a "colored" person could not marry a "white" person or attend school with one; it mentioned no other types of people.[7] Racial division is at the heart of the story, and so we will talk in terms of "Black" and "white" populations, except when using direct quotes from earlier eras. The label we will use for the racially mixed population previously defined as "colored" or "Negro" is Black.

Two terms about Black efforts are especially important. The first, "constructive resilience" refers to the fact that, even in a strongly repressive environment, marginalized people may still build the framework for a future better society, in some ways anticipating the key aspects of that future. They may indeed display higher moral values than the dominant race, class, or organization. The second term, "constructive resistance," is a very similar concept, implying positive moral values and constructive action for the future in the midst of unfair oppression, but it implies in this context overt activism. Protests, marches, and litigation filed during the civil rights era exemplified constructive resistance.

Simple resistance can take many forms, ranging from passive subterfuge, such as purposeful work slowdowns, to negotiations, civil demonstrations, or rebellions. Quiet, passive resistance, such as work slowdowns, characterized much of the Black community's response to subjugation during the South's Jim Crow era, not unlike the response of many people in oppressive circumstances, including serfs and enslaved people. Such forms of subterfuge are safer when directly confronting power. All such resistance, passive or active, seeks to challenge power.[8]

The term *constructive resistance* implies a higher moral framework and a visionary process of building a better future, a step above simple resistance. Many groups throughout human history have used "methods of nonviolent action by civilians engaged in asymmetric conflicts with opponents not averse to using violence to defend their interests."[9] Specific modern advocates of constructive resistance include Mohandas Gandhi, who combined nonviolent civil resistance with simultaneous campaigns to create alternative social systems. For example, in colonial India he urged economic self-sufficiency through home-based production of cotton clothing in addition to nonviolent protests against British rule. Gandhi inspired Dr. Martin Luther King Jr., who translated the nonviolent ethos into a civil rights rallying cry. In King's version, the constructive vision was a multiracial society characterized by equal rights for all.

Gandhi called the other part of what he was doing, building up a strong parallel society, his "constructive programme." He may have considered the constructive program, including the spinning of homespun cloth and rejection of manufacturing clothing, to be more important than his civil disobedience strategy.[10] Through such means he aimed to bridge divisions by religion and caste among Indian people and to establish a social and economic system that was a viable alternative to British colonialism.

Many historical examples exist of subjugated people who not only resisted the oppressors but also showed means of building alternative, in some ways superior, societies. Often the point of constructive resistance is not simply to build alternatives but also to do so in ways that foreshadow the desired future society. Here is Sorensen's definition: "Constructive resistance occurs when people start to build the society they desire independently of structures of power. In order to be considered constructive resistance, [efforts] necessarily have to be both constructive and provide a form of resistance, but there is a huge variety within both concepts. . . . Resistance can be either an implicit or explicitly outspoken critique of structures of power upholding the status quo. . . . Constructive resistance does not exclude conventional forms for protest, boycotts and civil disobedience, but focuses on creating, building, carrying out and experimenting with what is considered desirable."[11]

Examples of constructive effort abound in twentieth-century South Carolina. One important example is the alternative educational institutions that Black people built during the era of Jim Crow segregation. The schools that they set up in homes, churches, recreational centers, and on modest college campuses did not begin to compete with educational facilities for white students, but they represented a constructive process of creating educational venues in spite of barriers imposed by white society. They were constructive in the sense that they paralleled the desired future society. For example, historically Black Claflin never barred white students and depended for much of its history on white and international faculty, creating thereby an island of limited racial integration and tolerance amidst a hostile state. This was, however, resilience rather than resistance.

Constructive resilience is a softer version of the concept of constructive resistance. The term constructive resilience is one that worldwide leaders of the Baha'i Faith use when writing to members of their religion who live in Iran. Members of that persecuted minority have lost many civil rights under Iran's Islamic regime, including the right to hold any profession for which they are qualified or to attend universities. In a series of remarkable letters, their worldwide governing body has written open letters to these hundreds of thousands of minority-religion Iranians urging them to show forth the highest moral principles despite persecution. This means not responding in a violent or confrontational manner to injustices. Instead, adherents should find modest means of livelihood, create home-based schooling for their college-age students, and conduct themselves in a manner that is worthy of emulation. Their leaders have told Baha'i believers in that country to undertake constructive efforts and remain resilient in the face of oppression, exemplifying constructive resilience.[12]

In South Carolina, for most of the decades leading up to the 1960s, Black activist resistance to racial oppression was very difficult. Occasional efforts took place, with lawsuits and labor strikes, petitions and efforts to register to vote. Often, however, even mild strategies were dangerous. Many Black people engaged instead in constructive resilience. They went about their daily lives, perhaps building up constructive institutions in order to gain some semblance of normalcy and progress. They adapted to difficult circumstances in a quiet, persistent, even life-affirming way that made it possible to raise families and carry out community life under oppressive circumstances. The subtle, persistent, gradual, or cataclysmic ways that an oppressed people adjusted to what could have been an impossible circumstance, while educating their children and teaching spiritual nobility, shows their great courage.

It is challenging to describe this concept of constructive resilience in words, but a few personal narratives illustrate this point very well. One story comes from Mamie Garvin Fields's autobiography, *Lemon Swamp and Other Places*, published when she was in her nineties, having lived a full life. Fields was born in 1888 and lived for most of that life in Charleston, working as a schoolteacher. Those were difficult years; she was a child when the US Supreme Court's 1896 *Plessy v. Ferguson* decision legitimized separate but equal laws, just after her state had passed a new segregationist state constitution. Her graphic description of that era explains immediate repercussions Blacks felt from white neighbors but also illustrates how Black people managed nonetheless.

Fields's first teacher, her first cousin Anna Eliza "Lala" Izzard, set up a small school built by her parents and attached to their home. Izzard's father, a carpenter, built the school because public school teaching jobs in Charleston were not available to Black aspiring teachers with credentials; the school board would only hire white teachers. In a literal and material show of constructive resilience, Izzard's father built a schoolhouse so that his daughter could teach: "Uncle Izzard . . . built her a school at the back of their house: Miss Anna Eliza Izzard's School. He saw that everything was first-rate. He made benches and desks, divided the rooms, hung a blackboard—a modern thing to have in those days, since most schoolchildren only had slates. Lala kept the maps and the globe, schoolbooks of all kinds, storybooks, songbooks, magazines. . . . [Her mother] served as principal, supervising the children in the yard and helping with discipline. After a while, Ms. Izzard's was well-known around Charleston and very successful. There was no other like it in Charleston. So many parents wanted their children to be taught by Ms. Izzard that they had to enroll a year ahead of time."[13]

Fields gives detailed examples about the way this teacher taught; Izzard apparently displayed a great deal of originality and competence: "She gave us a very good basis in spelling, arithmetic, and especially in geography, which she loved. Her geography lessons made us feel we were going all around the world. We knew what rivers we would cross where, when we would have to go over the mountains, what cities we could find. Sometimes we would find the places on the maps or on the globe and then look at the pictures in *National Geographic*."[14] Izzard taught arithmetic through memorization songs and took the children on long walks for accessible field trips that taught them much about local history.

The quality of this education was such that, after three years with Miss Anna Eliza Izzard's School, Fields at age six was able to attend public school, where she immediately skipped two grades and enrolled in third grade. There Fields encountered the norm for that city. Her white teachers displayed abysmally poor teaching skills, bidding students simply to read text aloud in class, all day, every day, in never-ending rounds of mindless recitation with no attention to comprehension. They showed open contempt for their Black students, refusing even to touch or stand near them.

Such public schools for Black students existed in Charleston at the turn of the century, but they were of inferior quality, and so Black people set up alternative schools in their own homes or churches. This constructive approach allowed parents and teachers to create the kind of education they wanted their children to have, in an environment that respected their humanity. We have no way of knowing how many of Charleston's Black children had access to such schools,[15] but much data exists concerning the dismal state of Black public school education in that city and the state at large. At least one major alternative existed: Charleston's private Avery Normal Institute.[16] In Field's story about Izzard's school as well as in Avery, we clearly see the kernel of a need for all children— a good education, sensitively transmitted. In Charleston the Black community sometimes created their own institutions and sometimes pressured the white power structure to support fundamental reforms. Efforts to get Black teachers hired, for example, required mild but determined tactics of resistance such as petitions.

This book will also refer to white experiences and actions. For Black people, the two concepts I have described, constructive resistance and constructive resilience, are very similar. For white people, the two concepts I will rely upon most heavily are not so similar. They are in fact polar opposites. On the one hand, the vast majority of white South Carolinians repressed Black educational improvement, either actively or through passive complicity. They justified such repression by upholding concepts of white supremacy and privilege. On the other hand, sometimes a few white people were genuinely supportive of efforts to improve Black education or civil rights in the state. A few, in fact, were actual champions. These will arise in our story as well.

An important goal for forces of repression was the survival of a system that protected schools and other public facilities for white people by insuring worse facilities for Black citizens. The privileged white power structure arguably used racial prejudice as a way to retain power over both Black and working-class white people. During the Jim Crow era, school districts provided inadequate educational expenses for many white public schools but allayed white concerns by upholding comparative privilege, because public schools serving Black students were so much worse off. They furthermore justified inequality by arguing that Black people were inferior, dangerous if educated, not paying their fair share of taxes, or otherwise deserving of lesser education.

I will sometimes refer to this concept as some variant of "supremacist repression." This is a shorthand way to describe both the unwillingness on the part of many white South Carolinians to accept the fundamental human equality of Black people and their determination to prevent racial equality in education. Inherent within this term are several others. One of these is "white supremacy," the belief that white people are superior to Black people or other races; white racism is a variant of that, more focused on individual prejudice. As some theorists have noted, however, white people may have neither overt belief in white supremacy nor apparently racist attitudes and yet benefit from "practices, beliefs, and behaviours that serve to maintain white supremacy."[17] Some call this "white privilege."[18] Other related terms are "systemic" or institutional racism, referring to the legacy of white supremacy ingrained in social and political institutions. This is a problem that Bell pioneered analyzing in educational and legal contexts but that other authors have addressed as well.[19]

Mechanisms for resistance to Black educational equality within South Carolina's white society were more virulent than personal, or even institutional, white supremacy or racism. For years leaders made systemic efforts to purposely ensure that the vast majority of Black students did not receive the resources necessary to provide even rudimentary grade school education, much less higher education. This was an open, not hidden, process, reinforced by legitimate institutions, such as state legislatures and school boards. Active supremacist repression emerged at specific points in time, but underlying all was a less volatile steady-state system of institutional racism supported by white privilege.

Instances of white support for Black educational equality are also key to this story. I will refer to strong white supporters for Black education and civil rights, what Ibram Kendi might call white anti-racists, as "white allies." One historian has called such white allies part of "the other tradition" that included biracial efforts to support abolition, enfranchisement, and civil rights.[20] Such support ebbed and flowed but emerged at important periods. White allies will be evident in our story immediately after the Civil War, when northern missionaries and philanthropists ensured the establishment of at least some Black colleges, schools, and churches. They also emerged during the civil rights era: For example, federal district Judge J. Waties Waring; Alice Spearman Wright, South Carolina Council on Human Relations director; and M. Hayes Mizell,

American Friends Service Committee, three people who worked mostly in sequence from the 1940s to the 1970s and beyond. Although some authors have
written about the amazing Judge Waring, so vital to the battle for civil rights,[21]
less attention has flowed to other white allies that we will mention.

Black families, social activists, and leaders, of course, made the greatest
sacrifices. Parents weathered decades during which they could not assure their
children of even the most basic education, and Black teachers struggled to get
the facilities they knew those children deserved. In the 1940s and 1950s, Black
parents and community leaders, especially in Clarendon County, birthplace of
the *Briggs* case, showed uncommon heroism in challenging patently unequal
school facilities, as did the state's NAACP leaders. Those leaders—Clarendon
County's Rev. Joseph De Laine, NAACP warrior Modjeska Simkins, NAACP
president and then field secretary Rev. I. DeQuincey Newman, and many others
who worked steadfastly in their own localities—persevered and resisted in the
face of extraordinary harassment as they sought equal rights for Black people
and equal education for Black children. Some families, such as my own, made
quieter and less visible sacrifices.

1

Black Education as a Response to Jim Crow

I lived through most of my childhood on the campus of a college built through decades of efforts by diverse people striving to provide higher education to Black students living in a hostile state. Two historically Black colleges—Claflin and SC State—existed in a town that contained only fifteen thousand people in 1950. Forty miles down the road, in the capital city of Columbia, sat two other church-sponsored Black campuses, Allen and Benedict Colleges, and twenty miles in another direction lay another Black institution, Voorhees College, in the even smaller town of Denmark. Major struggles that followed the end of the Civil War birthed these entities.

In the 1950s the status of education for most Black children in South Carolina was one of chronic deprivation. Although starting in 1951 state government improved its financial support for Black public education, the fundamental inequity was strong enough to provide easy evidence for additional lawsuits filed in the 1960s. Integration of the white public school system occurred many years after the US Supreme Court's 1896 *Plessy v. Ferguson* supposedly guaranteed separate but equal public facilities and almost a decade after the 1954 *Brown* decision. In 1895 South Carolina mandated two racially separate public school systems, but it thereafter gave grossly unequal financial support to Black versus white public schools. The results: high levels of illiteracy and low educational levels among South Carolina's Black population in comparison to its white citizens. The state's HBCUs were islands of higher education in a sea of racially unequal and oppressive practices at lower educational levels.

Although establishing such Black schools accomplished much, reformers' efforts were woefully inadequate because of innate drawbacks. Lying just outside the compact spheres of Black institutions were large swatches of underserved towns and rural areas. These areas may have had no public schools open to Black students beyond a few grades or Black schools with major shortcomings. This situation was not due to accidental neglect but rather to deliberate white suppression.

This chapter describes how public education generally failed for Black southerners following the end of slavery but how Black institutions nevertheless emerged. Two forces affected Black education in the South after the Civil War. White supremacist influences tried to make sure that Black students received inferior public education compared to white students, if they received any education at all. Constructive forces included Black communities and teachers, white missionaries, and some white philanthropists. White repression explains why Black education faltered; stories of Black constructive resilience and of white allies reveal efforts to overcome such repression.

From Slavery to Post-Reconstruction Repression

It took a great deal of courage and good luck for enslaved Black people to learn how to read and write. Most planters saw literacy as dangerous, offering broader horizons and mobility for a subject race. Nevertheless, through subterfuge or the occasional action of white people, many enslaved people did become literate; by 1860 about 5 percent of them in the US South could read.[1]

Black historian Asa H. Gordon, the first SC State professor to write a book, published *Sketches of Negro Life and History in South Carolina* in 1929 as a way to highlight Black constructive resilience. He explained that enslaved people sought literacy in part because travel off the plantation required written passes. Gordon listed several pre–Civil War Black schools set up by free Black people; Charleston hosted many such schools. After the Denmark Vesey insurrection of 1822, however, increasingly restrictive laws made schooling more difficult. A 1740 law already forbade anyone to teach enslaved people to write; by 1834 the law forbade teaching them to read. This retarded the literacy movement but did not stop it.[2]

Black people yearned to become educated. As the Union gained victories during the Civil War, large numbers of them flocked to federal soldiers and pleaded for help. Such pleas led to the formation of several efforts to set up schools. Freed Black people located at South Carolina's liberated Port Royal "joyfully accepted" the northern teachers dispatched to help them learn to read and write. They showed an eagerness to learn so strong it startled and challenged their teachers, white and Black.[3]

After the Civil War, freed Black people's demand for education swept through all the former slaveholding states.[4] The Freedmen's Bureau was the major impetus behind free elementary education. This initiative was, according to W. E. B. Du Bois, the bureau's "greatest success"; it planted "the free school among Negroes, and the idea of free elementary education among all classes in the South."[5] The Reconstruction era, with the political and military support that it offered, enabled Black state legislators to get state governments to support free public schools. By 1870 each of the southern states had a constitution that provided for a public school system; perhaps one-fourth of formerly enslaved people of school age attended such schools.[6]

The fervor for education was no less in South Carolina. Several schools for Black students arose after the Civil War, including in Columbia Howard (High) School, the Baptists' Benedict College, and the African Methodist Episcopal Church's Allen University. In Orangeburg the Methodists established Claflin; in Charleston the Avery Normal Institute was founded in 1864; the Browning Industrial Home and Mather Academy for Girls emerged in Camden. In addition Black people provided financial support for many educational initiatives, and during Reconstruction they served "efficiently as teachers and administrators along with the white people."[7] These were not passive recipients of largesse but active proponents in their own right, constructive agents of their own future.

Such efforts failed, however, to quench southern white hostility toward granting freedoms to formerly enslaved people. Du Bois explained: "The opposition to Negro education in the South was at first bitter, and showed itself in ashes, insult, and blood; for the South believed an educated Negro to be a dangerous Negro. And the South was not wholly wrong; for education among all kinds of men always has had, and always will have, an element of danger and revolution, of dissatisfaction and discontent."[8] The majority of southern planters "did not believe in giving the Negro any education," according to Freedmen's Bureau staff, and white employers threatened to fire workers who sent their children to school. The planter class regained control of state legislatures between 1869 and 1877, leading up to the pivotal Compromise of 1877, which removed federal troops from the South and effectively ended Reconstruction.[9]

Nationwide, two offshoots from these developments are particularly relevant here. One was the rise of white public education as a tool for white supremacy. Another was the debate over what kind of education to offer Black children, if any.

Plans to enhance education for white children arose as a practical matter. Reconstruction politicians had argued for universal school for all children, thus benefiting low-income white people as well. One response by white leaders seeking to roll back Reconstruction reforms was to promote educating only white children, to make them "properly prepared to maintain the supremacy of the white race."[10] Southern states began to spend more money for white students than for Black.

In South Carolina in 1879–80, per pupil expenditure for Black students was approximately equal to that of white ones, under the continued influence of Reconstruction. As white conservatives gained power, using race-baiting to appeal to white voters, expenditures for Black education fell. South Carolina's 1895 state constitutional convention insured Black disenfranchisement by decentralizing voter eligibility decisions and by mandating racial segregation in public education. By 1916 South Carolina, ignoring the "separate but equal" principle mandated in *Plessy v. Ferguson,* spent 9.4 times more per white student than per Black.[11] Stripping expenditures for Black students had taken less than forty years.

The state exhibited low standards of education for all races, but much more so for Black students. In 1880, 78 percent of the state's Black citizens and 22 percent of its white citizens were illiterate. In 1890 most children went to school for fewer than ninety days a year, and some for fewer than thirty days. A 1923 study of Orangeburg County found that 81 percent of white and 71 percent of Black children attended school, but only fifty-four days a year for white students and twenty-eight days for Black.[12] In 1910 South Carolina had 166 high schools, but only 13 of these functioned at a high school level. After the Southern Association of Secondary Schools and Colleges formed in 1895, no South Carolina college or university met accreditation requirements until the white USC did in 1917. Meanwhile "in 1920 South Carolina had the lowest per pupil expenditure not only in the South but also in the United States."[13]

In one important way, however, such numbers are misleading. South Carolina's skewed expenditures by race dragged down its overall statistics. The state in 1923–24 spent $11.6 million overall for white students and only $1.4 million for Black students, although Black people were almost half (48.6 percent in 1920) of the state's population. That same academic year, the state spent $173,806 to transport white pupils and $196 for Black pupils. The list goes on; everything related to education was widely unequal by race, including teacher salaries, the value of school property, and funding for libraries.[14]

Many white people felt that even this low level of education would leave Black citizens unfit for work. A white state official commented in 1911: "The objections to negro education arise chiefly from the feeling that it unfits the negro for the place he must fill in the state. . . . And that the so-called educated negro too often becomes a loafer or a political agitator."[15] Those who tolerated some education for Black people felt that this should be minimal and should most certainly prepare them to accept white supremacy. They underfunded

Black schools and denied textbooks or mandated that they either ignore or disparage Black people. Discussions of the Civil War—never called that but something more palatable to white southerners such as "The War between the United States and the Confederate States"—lauded the Confederacy and its heroes, disparaged northerners, praised slavery as social uplift for savage Africans, and castigated abolitionists, slave rebellions, and Reconstruction. In spite of all this, Black illiteracy rates for the state dropped from 80 percent in 1869 to 29.3 percent in 1922.[16]

Education for white students improved even more. In 1924, the South Carolina General Assembly passed an act enabling all white children to receive government support for at least seven months of schooling a year. This 6-0-1 Act mandated that the state would pay for six months, counties could pay zero, and local school districts would pay for one. The state made no such provisions for Black children. Backed by philanthropic support, the state also ramped up funding for secondary schools, but only for white students. In 1929 only three public high schools for Black students existed in the state. Not surprisingly, in 1920, 745 white students received public high school diplomas, and Black students received none. In 1925 no such diplomas were awarded to Black students, but 3,716 were to white students, and in 1930 only 104 Black students received diplomas, compared to 5,542 white. In 1935, the year my dad graduated from public high school, 7,974 white and 303 Black students received public high school diplomas.[17]

An influential but problematic proposal that arose for educating Black students drew considerable philanthropic funding. Begun in 1868 by Samuel Chapman Armstrong at Virginia's Hampton Institute—and later given contested legitimacy by Armstrong's pupil Booker T. Washington, who launched a shadow initiative at Tuskegee Institute in Alabama—this Hampton-Tuskegee movement aimed to train Black teachers in so-called industrial education but also reinforce white supremacy. Armstrong's program urged Black citizens to accept marginalized employment, low social status, and political noninvolvement.[18] Hampton and Tuskegee, for a time, shackled Black youth with flawed education even as they purported to elevate them. As applicants for their teacher-training programs, the schools favored prospective students who were hard physical workers rather than those who showed academic promise. The curriculum evoked "self-help" but relied upon manual labor to train elementary-school teachers in all subjects, not just in the trades. Until the 1920s the institutes required incoming students to devote most of their daytime hours to physical labor instead of academic study.

The Hampton-Tuskegee version of industrial education emphasized preparing Black youths for jobs such as household and farm labor. The model shunned intellectual pursuits and professional training and advocated removing Black voters from political life. Booker T. Washington adopted this model and gave it credibility to the wider world, which proclaimed him the foremost Black "leader." W. E. B. Du Bois bemoaned the effects of Washington's Armstrong-influenced ideology, countering that this cut off all possible paths of advancement. Du Bois called for educating at least a portion of Black students at the university level so that they could lead the race into social progress.[19]

Several major philanthropies seized upon the Hampton-Tuskegee model as a filter for their largesse. Armstrong's supporters included the John F. Slater and Peabody Funds, Ulysses S. Grant, Theodore Roosevelt, Woodrow Wilson, Andrew Carnegie, John D. Rockefeller Jr., and Julius Rosenwald. John D. Rockefeller Sr. created the General Education Board (GEB) in 1902, and by 1921 this foundation had invested major funding in industrial education for Black students as defined by Armstrong and Washington. The Hampton-Tuskegee model soon faded in credibility, but then philanthropists began to focus on promoting secondary education for white southerners, exacerbating inequalities.[20]

What was the alternative to the Hampton-Tuskegee model? Anderson argues that the "missionary vanguard" offered a better path for Black education and for teacher training. Church-based organizations founded most institutions of higher education for Black students in the South, and these institutions resisted full adoption of the Hampton-Tuskegee model. Mission-founded colleges relied upon classical liberal education; they used industrial or agricultural education only as supplemental material. Anderson praises few actors in his detailed history of Black education in the South, but he reserves special praise for the missionary vanguard. Claflin's founders were part of this vanguard. They worked through the Methodist Church's post–Civil War relief organization, the Freedmen's Aid Society, and they saw Black people as fully capable of higher learning and intellectual development.

Constructing Two Black Colleges

Claflin's campus, where my family lived in college-supplied housing for most of my childhood and youth, was part of this complex story of destruction and construction. This little campus world lay, just as a small Russian doll lies nested within progressively bigger containers, within territories essential to the struggle for Black education in the Deep South in general and in South Carolina in particular. From my limited perspective as a child, the central "doll" was a set of sibling institutions: Claflin, where I lived, and its conjoined but fraternal, state-government-supported sibling, SC State, where I attended Felton Training School. Two historically Black, intimately connected institutions separated only by a fence, these colleges made up the core of daily life for me and for many others.

Struggles date back to the schools' origins and show how difficult it was for formerly enslaved people and their progeny to gain basic, much less advanced, education. Only because of philanthropy were Black schools such as Claflin established. At first these were neither true "universities" nor true colleges. They were underfunded and able to serve no students at the college level, operating instead at elementary and high school levels, because of the lack of Black public education able to feed high school graduates into true colleges or universities.

I grew up hearing the names of pivotal actors in Claflin's history throughout my life, usually because of a building named after one or the other. At first they seemed to be just labels, but I later realized that these names commemorated white donors who had established or supported Claflin and indirectly SC State. Little-known Black pioneers created rudimentary educational programs for freed persons, but white missionaries established the first Black university in South Carolina, Claflin, in 1869. Claflin was also the first university or college in the state technically open to all races from its very beginning.

These were some of the names associated with Claflin that I heard as a child: T. Willard Lewis, Lewis and Mary E. Dunton, Bishop Matthew Simpson, Samuel Tingley, Lee Claflin. All of them were white, either missionaries, college promoters, church leaders, or philanthropists. T. Willard Lewis was the name associated with the college's wooden chapel building, which hosted vespers as well as graduations, concerts, and lectures. The Duntons's name identified not only the Dunwalton faculty house but also the Mary E. Dunton dormitory, and most faculty and administrators worked in the classroom/administrative building named Tingley Memorial Hall, located steps from my parents' house; they both worked in Tingley. Contributions from the Massachusetts-based Claflin family had earned them the name of the college. Although our family's first residence at Claflin was a campus apartment in Dunwalton, in 1956 we moved into the Matthew Simpson Memorial Home, where I lived until leaving for college. I grew up, therefore, living in two houses named for notable white patrons, and the entire series of labels has an intimate association that extends beyond names, evoking colorful memories of events in my family's lives.

Who were these white patrons? They were all northerners, members of the Methodist Episcopal Church. They had supported Black education as an extension of abolitionist fervor, at a time when many northern white Christians did not trust southern white Christians to bring formerly enslaved people into full citizenship. Denominations such as the Methodist Church split over such issues. In the 1840s white southerners separated from the larger denomination and formed the Methodist Episcopal Church South after years of strife with their northern peers over the moral rightness of slavery. Yet both branches actively recruited Black members; by 1860 close to 208,000 Black people belonged to the pro-slavery Methodist Church South.[21]

In South Carolina this situation changed in large part because Timothy "T." Willard Lewis, eventual namesake of Claflin's chapel, helped establish a separate, self-governing conference (collection of churches and ministers) affiliated with the Methodist Church and largely composed of Black worshipers. He then joined the conference himself, as one its very few white ministers. By the time he was done with his relatively short life, Black membership in the rival Methodist Church South had plummeted, as Black Christians sought churches that better honored their freedom.

Lewis, born in Massachusetts in 1825, became a Methodist Church minister with the New England conference and then in 1862 the first missionary sent by that conference to serve Black South Carolinians. Until his death in 1871, he actively recruiting Black Methodists away from both the Methodist Church South and the AME Church. The AME Church's argument for complete racial separation was a strong enticement for Black Methodists, and so at first it was not clear which path they would take.

The position of the Methodist Church South was unequivocally clear: it supported visible white supremacy even within church buildings. During the Civil War, in Charleston, Black members had left their former places in church balconies to sit on the main floor as white members left, fleeing the war zone. Once the war ended, white members returned and told Black members to go back to the prewar practice of watching from the balcony, staying in their places both socially and physically. Lewis disrupted that mandate. At a meeting held April 10, 1866, after the other white ministers exhorted Black churchgoers to sit upstairs in what they called galleries, "Lewis leapt to his feet and cried out in resounding tones: 'There are no galleries in Heaven! Those who are willing to go to a church that makes no distinction as to race or color, follow me to the Normal School.'"[22] Lewis then led most Black church members out of the meeting, and they formed Centenary Methodist Church, with yet another white New Englander, Alonzo Webster, as pastor. Another church founded in this way was Charleston's Wesley Methodist, the family church for Mamie Garvin Fields and a church that my father pastored in the early 1950s.[23]

Lewis cofounded several Black churches as well as Claflin. A race-unity visionary, he encouraged Black Methodists in Charleston to form inclusionary churches—which very few local white Methodists joined and which therefore became all-Black—but he also organized churches in Columbia, Orangeburg, and Sumter. These formed the Methodist Church's South Carolina Mission Conference (hereafter the 1866 Conference, after the year of its origin),[24] to which my father and his father, both of whom were ordained ministers, belonged. Lewis, Webster, and several other white missionaries created other institutions designed to assist formerly enslaved people through the Methodist subsidiary Freedmen's Aid Society, which set up educational institutions throughout the South. Lewis joined forces with Webster to create a university in honor of Massachusetts governor William Claflin. Governor Claflin and his father, Lee Claflin, a leading shoe manufacturer, both contributed substantial funds toward founding the college. Claflin became one of "largest and most successful schools" for the Freedmen's Aid Society.[25]

T. Willard Lewis was but the first of four white men who pushed Claflin into survival. Webster, Claflin's first president, got a formal charter approved and recruited the first faculty members, white northerners. Lewis and Webster aimed for an interracial school by writing a constructive charter that prohibited discrimination based on race or complexion. They convinced state legislators to remit funds from the Morrill Land-Grant Act of 1862. Although Claflin was church-affiliated, making Morrill Act funds problematic, a separate South Carolina Agricultural College and Mechanics Institute, created in 1872, operated as a division within Claflin to receive Morrill Act funds. Claflin's second president, from 1874 to 1884, Edward Cooke from New Hampshire, was also white.

Lewis Dunton, the third president and fourth man in this list, was a strong white ally for Black education. He became a special agent raising funds for Claflin in 1877 and president in 1884. Dunton, who protected Claflin from rising white supremacist forces and led it until 1921, excelled at fundraising. He took groups of Claflin singers to perform in the North to solicit donations (as did schools such as Fisk University). In this task his talented wife, Mary, sometimes joined him; she was a teacher, financial agent, and capable fundraiser as well. Gordon gave the following testimony about Dunton: "The development of Claflin was greatly accelerated and long sustained under the wise leadership of Dr. L. M. Dunton, who is one of those friends of Negroes we have referred to. He labored at Claflin over forty years and really built that institution. Doctor Dunton always showed profound interest in the general welfare of the colored people of Orangeburg, and the entire state of South Carolina."[26] Dunton promoted

Laying of memorial wreath during Founders' Day at the tomb of L. M. Dunton, Claflin's fourth president and its last white president to date. Dunton offered more than four decades of service to Claflin. Pres. H. V. Manning stands behind the wreath. Family album.

building a Black public elementary school next to Claflin; when built in 1923, the school bore his name.[27] For many years Claflin's presidents, including my father, laid wreaths at Dunton's grave annually.

Like many Black schools, Claflin at first depended on white northerners as teachers. In "missionary vanguard" schools these white educators taught the same curriculum that they had themselves learned in the North, including science, classical languages, and literature. Claflin also supported a normal school curriculum that produced teachers who received teaching certificates instead of college degrees. Some of its funders, such as beginning in 1883 the Slater Fund, favored industrial education, but trade-related courses were limited to portions of days.[28] Claflin was never "Hamptonized"; it was instead an early example of "modern education" for both white and Black colleges, "offering African Americans its vision of a modern education—part spiritual, part ideological, and part practical. This vision was a model that most denominational colleges, both black and white, embraced well into the next century."[29]

Until the 1896 split that produced SC State, Dunton presided over a triplex teaching staff, with three kinds of teachers: White northerners, Black Claflin graduates, and southern white men recruited to the agricultural and mechanical institute. This triplex was not to last. Dunton suspected that Black leaders such as legislator Thomas Miller were fomenting student discontent and actively trying to take control of Claflin away from him because he was white, a fear that was, in some ways, true.[30]

The 1896 splitting of the one school into two, Claflin and a separate agricultural college that was the forerunner of SC State, was due both to a particular dilemma and to a push for Black self-sufficiency. The church-state dilemma was clear: Claflin's agricultural institute was not separate enough to receive Morrill Act funds. The governor preferred a separate Black public college, but the primary instigators were Black legislators. One was indeed the man Dunton had suspected of undermining his job, Miller, who lobbied his legislative colleagues to create a public college for Black students. When Miller's proposed legislation passed, Claflin and its institute separated, leaving Claflin still with both Black and white faculty but without white southerners teaching agriculture.[31] Lewis's original vision of a mixed-race university had faltered.

The separate Colored, Normal, Industrial, Agricultural and Mechanical College of South Carolina, later South Carolina State College, arose as a testament to both Black power and Black powerlessness. In 1877 state government leaders had closed down USC to stop Reconstruction-era Black students from attending the university alongside of white students, reopening it as a white-only school in 1880. As Miller witnessed such moves against Reconstruction gains, he lobbied for a new college that could easily attract and safeguard the 1862 and 1890 Morrill Act funds. Only six Black state legislators, including Miller, remained in 1895 when the governor proposed to an ascendant majority-white legislature a new constitutional convention that would strengthen white power. Miller spoke out but failed to convince his white colleagues not to rewrite the constitution. He proposed a separate Black state college as compensation for loss of Blacks' ability to participate as voting citizens or elected representatives. The legislature enacted Miller's bill in 1896, mandating as he requested that only Black people could become state college administrators and faculty. Everyone understood that the school's board of trustees would be white. The first board quickly named Miller as president.[32]

Although the Black legislators won that battle, the new state college for "colored" people existed under the firm control of its white board of trustees. No Black people served as trustees from 1896 until 1966. For fifteen years as president, Miller struggled with his trustees to gain authority, but the trustees insisted on selecting all textbooks, and they chose new faculty members, favoring those not resistant to racial segregation. They loosened their grip somewhat with Miller's successor, Robert Shaw Wilkinson, a man of milder manner than

Miller. Unlike Miller, Wilkinson scrupulously avoided criticizing state political candidates or leaders, even when they issued racist statements, such as calling the Black college "a curse to Orangeburg and to the state of South Carolina."[33]

SC State was born, therefore, into a hostile environment, but both institutions struggled. Claflin was open for ten years before it produced in 1879 a graduate from the normal course, but it then graduated 82 men and 96 women from that program over the next seventeen years, and at least half of these went on to become teachers. It took thirteen years, until 1882, before Claflin awarded its first bachelor's degree. Between 1882 and 1916, Claflin produced only 111 college graduates, but 31 of these became teachers; 20, ministers; 14, physicians or dentists; and 10, government employees or lawyers. Claflin's elementary, high school, normal, and college classes gained thousands of attendees over the years but fewer graduates.[34]

In 1900 the total number of Black college or professional graduates in South Carolina, 12, was not far below the number of such graduates in other former slaveholding states.[35] SC State also found it necessary to educate at the elementary, high school, and college levels. In 1910 SC State had 646 students, but only 15 of them were in college. Between 1916 and 1921, the school produced only 20 college graduates, but 337 graduated from the normal program, thus contributing to the ranks of teachers. Total student enrollment per year varied from 592 students in 1911 to 607 in 1920, indicating that many attendees were in lower grades or did not complete college.

In contrast the state's white public universities concentrated mainly on college curriculum. By 1899 state government was funding four schools of higher education for white students: USC; Clemson University; the Citadel, a military college; and Winthrop, for female students. Appropriations for these four dwarfed by several times appropriations for SC State.[36]

Although both Claflin and SC State struggled, they constructed buildings, often with student labor; put students to work on farms that fed the campus or provided revenue; and created a small class of graduates who could serve society. Both schools kept liberal arts but included some form of industrial education to satisfy funders; in the case of SC State, trustees' instructions to focus on "practical education" were quite explicit. During the industrial education years, some of the courses offered—at Claflin in 1890–91 these included agriculture, architectural drawing, blacksmithing, carpentry and cabinetmaking, dressmaking, crocheting, lace-making, painting/graining/glazing, printing, mechanical engineering, and nurse training—were trade related but included higher-level skills. These complemented other courses that were "traditional classical and theological."[37] Such mixed programs offered graduates a degree of financial independence difficult for Black people in that era. By educating future teachers, ministers, physicians, or skilled tradespeople, these schools were constructing an alternative future, encouraging Black students to lead the race.

Coping Strategies

Personal experiences and stories can help us understand both the conditions facing Black students and the possibilities for a few to gain higher education. Fields's comments about Izzard's preschool showed the high quality of her early education. She was apparently able to distance herself from the objectionable qualities of her haughty white elementary school teachers, such as their insistence that the students learn "Rebel" songs and poems, treat the white teachers as racial superiors, and perform mind-numbing rote recitation. In an act of self-actualization, she escaped Charleston for Claflin's high school when she refused to attend Charleston's Avery Institute because she feared that light-skinned Black students there would disparage her dark skin color.[38] Charleston's Wesley Methodist Church, cofounded decades before by Lewis, provided community support, helping her attend Claflin through a full scholarship.

Revisiting Fields's normal-school training can help us see how one resource-poor Black college managed to raise service-oriented citizens. Claflin gave students, she says, an austere life filled with chores, long hours, and actual physical labor, but it evoked a sense of pride as well. She accepted training in crafts as a way to learn useful job skills. Rather than present these requirements as demeaning, she gives descriptions of millinery and dressmaking classes that are warmly appreciative and little short of lyrical. She notes that many of the female trade teachers were white New Englanders who brought innovative ideas to the classroom about turning inexpensive goods into serviceable outfits and household items. These skills served Fields well during her adulthood, since at times she fell back on dressmaking to earn a living. She gives detailed accounts of musical pieces that the college choir and quartets performed and of specific teachers, showing that she enjoyed the campus's cultural amenities and admired at least a few of her professors.

Her most important class at Claflin was in pedagogy, which included practice teaching as well as classroom work. There she admired the way that faculty and teacher-supervisors prepared their charges to go into an austere field.

Claflin faculty during her presence, 1905–8, urged teachers-in-training to be "a good influence on the children." This included making do even if they had to teach, single-handedly, 125 students in a one-room school. Faculty taught them how to set up daily schedules and manage when the school year might only last two months. They taught how to visit parents to encourage participation and student obedience and how to use the other students to help with disciplinary challenges. They taught how to manage with no textbooks and how to set up a rudimentary lunch program by asking students to bring soup in jars and then keeping the jars warm in a pan of hot water. They urged the future teachers to consider the students' conditions, such as long walks to school, and not to blame the child for failure. Notably, her faculty teachers emphasized service. "Many being missionaries, the white teachers had a strong sense of service, which the students took from them regardless of the particular subject. And although not missionaries, the black teachers gave the students the same desire to serve."[39]

As it turned out, her teaching required great creativity and fortitude. Here is a story from her work on Johns Island, where Gullah language and culture prevailed.[40] The story illustrates some of the practical effects of marginalized educational systems and inherent feelings of white superiority. As with the story of Fields's first two schools in Charleston, this one illustrates both constructive resilience and repressive white supremacy.

Mamie Garvin (later Fields) taught on Johns Island once she graduated from Claflin in 1908 with teaching credentials. This incident took place at Miller Hill School, where she was the only teacher. Several Black schools on that island struggled with one or two teachers who each taught dozens if not a hundred or more young charges of varying ages, in the crudest of wooden structures devoid of proper seats, desks, or blackboards. Garvin asked the supervising trustee several times if she could have an assistant, but she received no response.

Finally the white trustee, Mr. Wilson, decided to investigate her request in person; with no advance notice, he rode on horseback onto school grounds. The spectacle of a white man on a horse with dogs following him scared the children, who started to scream and run into the school. The man entered: "Now, here comes the trustee himself, clop-clop, with his boots and with his gun in his hand. I said, 'The dogs frighten the children, Mr. Wilson. Now, children, take your seats.' So, he whistled and sent the two dogs out the door. Meanwhile, not saying a word, he walked right up through the rows of children, puffing his pipe and taking his time. I can see him just as clear right now, in a red and black hunting shirt and that gun in his hand, and then those muddy boots, which made a racket. He looked at my pictures, my wall displays, my children's work. When he looked at the children, it frightened them—all the time he had that gun longwise in his hand. And when he passed between the children, they drew back as far as they could."

In this story the white administrator essentially put on a display of power. For her part the teacher recognized intimidation when she saw it: "I was still waiting by my desk to find out what it was all about, while White Authority tramped his dirty boots through my school. When he got through the inspection, our school trustee stood in the middle of the children, where all could hear him, and said 'Ga'vin, whar ya fin' all these niggers? I diddin know th' was s' minny damn niggers up here on this hill.' I was asking for an assistant teacher, I said, because I had over 100 children in Miller Hill School, and more wanted to learn. 'Yah got too minny t' han'l'? Jes' shut it daln, Ga'vin. Shut it daln!' Right there in the middle of all the children wanting to learn, he said that."[41]

Fields was in her nineties when she published her book recounting this incident, which evidently had a great effect on her. Notable in the story are the ways she tried to maintain dignity, through classroom preparation and pride in students' work, careful instruction to frightened children in the face of a threat, and her own astute observations. Eventually the trustee gave her an assistant, but he demonstrated that he had no respect either for the teacher or for her students. Walking among scared schoolchildren with a leveled gun sent an unmistakable message of disdain, and it reminds us that lurking beneath the surface of white supremacy was the threat of violence, here represented by a single gun.

Fields left the state for some years but later returned to Charleston and its nearby Sea Islands. She arrived at Society Corner, her James Island post, in 1926, but conditions had hardly improved since her first arrival at Johns Island. Many people were illiterate, and school facilities were rugged, with physical isolation even though James Island connected to the city of Charleston by drawbridge.

She waged daily battles to help her children struggle to learn. Even after she begged repeatedly, the school district said it was not necessary for Black children to have textbooks, certainly not new books; at best they received white students' worn hand-me-downs. Nevertheless she and her fellow teachers tried to transmit a sense of self-worth to the children, to use innovative teaching methods, to paint the schoolhouse in bright colors, to encourage dramatic presentations, to decorate for the holidays. Teachers served as de facto extension agents by demonstrating to parents how to plant gardens and can vegetables, and they helped families understand the importance of sending their children to school, even if they had to leave the fields and thus reduce the family's earnings.

Highlights were glorious: One year she marshaled her school community to march in Charleston's Emancipation Day parade. They created a splendid event float, decorated with art and bountiful James Island vegetables, and held a competition to select a James Island student to ride the float as queen for the day. Thus she and her fellow teachers stirred community pride and won the grudging admiration of Charleston's Black community, which looked down upon rural Sea Island folk.[42]

Fields's stories represent the efforts of Black teachers in rural areas, not unlike Walker's *Their Highest Potential,* an inspiring story of an excellent rural school in North Carolina, or other Black teachers in segregated schools,[43] although the Sea Islands were a special case because of their isolation and Gullah language. Civil rights icon Septima Clark also taught on Johns Island, and her experiences provide additional information about that particular teaching post. When she began teaching on Johns Island in 1916, Clark found comparable conditions to those Fields had contended with; Clark and another Black teacher had 135 students between them, and Clark earned a salary of thirty-five dollars a month. A white teacher with only three students earned eighty-five dollars a month.[44]

My own South Carolina family's history echoes many of the same themes. My father was born in 1918 in Cheraw, a small town located in rural Chesterfield County, just south of the border with North Carolina. His writing about his family's experiences offers insights into the life of one Black public high school graduate of the mid-1930s, when so few Black youths made it that far.

My paternal grandparents, Rev. Irvin "I. V." and Fannie Wilson Manning, came from different circumstances. I. V. Manning's father, John, was a sharecropper born during slavery who was never able to extricate his family from sharecropper status. According to census and family records, John fathered seven children by his first wife, Laura. At about age thirty-six, he married his second wife, Louvenia, my paternal great-grandmother; she was about fifteen years old at the time and went on to give birth to as many as fourteen children. As late as the 1900 census, when he was sixty years old, John Manning could read but not write, and neither could Louvenia. During that census count, several children still at home, including Grandpa I. V., thirteen years old, were not in school. One twelve-year-old son could neither read nor write.

In contrast two other great-grandparents, the Wilsons, were relatively prosperous. Great-grandpa William Wilson traveled throughout South Carolina and Georgia cutting "turpentine boxes" out of tree bark as part of the turpentine oil industry, supplementing income from his vegetable farm. He and his wife, Mary Rogers Wilson, owned their own home. They ensured that three daughters, including my grandmother Fannie, got a high school education, but this required a legendary family sacrifice. The Wilsons sent Fannie and her two sisters to live fifty miles away in Hartsville, since no Black public schools existed in Cheraw or Chesterfield County. Wilson himself had little education, but he

Unnamed church in Darlington or Florence County, South Carolina;
Rev. I. V. and Fannie Manning are standing on the first row, far right.
Reverend Manning built at least four brick churches as community
development projects for his congregations. Family album.

"believed in education" as well as in owning your own land, according to his
grandson, my father.[45]

My father's parents, Rev. I. V. and Fannie Manning, who married in December 1914, similarly valued education. Grandpa Manning tried to pursue
higher education at about the age of twenty-eight. In 1914 he accepted the offer
of one of his older brothers, a Methodist pastor in Morristown, Tennessee, to
travel there and attend college in preparation for the ministry. I have no record
of Grandpa receiving a high school or college degree, but I have the original
of his faded 1923 "teacher training certificate" from the Methodist Episcopal
Church. This was how Black people coped in those days, using the church as
an institution for faith-based community education, extending beyond what
we think of as "Sunday School." Grandpa Manning became an exceptionally
talented minister in the 1866 Conference, with a particular aptitude for helping
his congregations build community and construct new church sanctuaries.[46]
With her high school education, Grandma Fannie taught home economics in the

local public schools. Her education, earned at the cost of separation from her parents, rewarded her family in the end.

A few years after my father was born in 1918, his parents moved to Pickens, located near Greenville, at the foot of beautiful hills in the state's Piedmont district. They lived there for most of Dad's childhood as Grandpa Manning ministered to four churches in a Pickens "charge" (a set of circuit churches, with the minister visiting each one once a month). Dad wrote a brief account of his upbringing in an autobiographical document that honored his parents, grandparents, and teachers, and he mentioned the natural beauty of Pickens. He considered his parents to be professionals, even though their salaries were very low. They "took a personal interest in [his] well-being, physically, socially, intellectually, spiritually and psychologically."[47] For enrichment they took him to nearby Greenville to hear the great tenor Roland Hayes sing, and they also took him to concerts and plays at Greenville's Phillis Wheatley Center, a Black community center named after an enslaved eighteenth-century woman who became a renowned poetess.

As a mature man, Dad reflected upon his early education, offering short descriptions of his own grade-school teachers:

> In that small mountain school [Pickens], with little or no equipment, drab surroundings and very little else but an excitement about learning and a love for knowledge and students, there were ladies who worked with us, talked to us and helped us to know that we could make it if we tried. . . . One was my first grade teacher, Mrs. Amanda Rosemond, who lived long enough to see me become a college president. Two years before her death [when she was age ninety-three], Claflin College honored her as one of the great teachers of our times. Mrs. Dora Ferguson, who taught me in the fifth, sixth, and seventh grades, was a dedicated person, one who taught and gladly taught. Mrs. Elereta Bacoate, a scholar of no mean ability, proficient in the English language, one who was not only well versed in the classics but held her classes spellbound while knowledge was being imparted—all of us were inspired by this great lady.[48]

He also praised high school teachers who worked under major constraints. When Dad was fifteen years old, the Methodist Church reassigned Grandpa Manning from the Pickens charge to one in Timmonsville, located in the Florence district. This was two hundred miles southeast of where the family was living at the time. Reluctantly they pulled up stakes and moved to Timmonsville, where my father enrolled in Brockington High School along with his first cousin Gladys, who lived with them at that time. In the middle of their senior year, the school burned to the ground. Community leaders found temporary classrooms, and somehow my father finished high school in 1935. His comments: "Although the surroundings were drab and dull, the quality of instruction did not suffer. It seems as if the teachers worked harder than ever. It was at this time that my preacher, the Rev. Mr. D. J. Johnson, had included in the curriculum a course in Negro History . . . one of the few Black high schools in the state to offer a course in Negro history. The textbook we used was written by Carter G. Woodson."[49] This was a reflection of the growing popularity of Woodson's book on Black history, with effects even in Timmonsville, a very small town.[50]

Earlier educators thus equipped Dad as well as they could to continue his education. It took his parents' major sacrifices and Dad's own labor, however, for him to attend college at Claflin. Although there was no question that he would attend Claflin, he had to keep two jobs and drop out of college occasionally to earn money. Grandpa Manning served three or four churches at the same time, but many of his parishioners were dirt poor and able to pay only a portion of his salary, sometimes in the form of fresh vegetables and other farm goods. My grandmother had a very modest salary as schoolteacher. A pianist, she was the pastor's helpmate, and she played during services without charge as part of the bargain. Their parishioners mostly worked as day laborers or sharecroppers, occasionally as teachers. They all worked to feed their families and store up spiritual capital in anticipation of a reward after death.

Grandpa Manning was an extraordinary community leader. Generous of spirit, a happy extrovert unattached to material wealth for himself, and master orator in the best rural Black tradition, he galvanized his parishioners in rousing, praise-filled, foot-stomping worship services that literally vibrated the floors of the wooden churches in which he preached. His consistent message, in addition to standard country preacher fare—that he delivered with elegance, passion, and firm grounding in Black spirituals that he sang to great effect, moving his audience in ways that still ring in my memories and in my heart— was for his charges to educate their children. Claflin was always a part of his exhortation: parents should aim, he said, to send their children to Claflin for college. Several times Grandpa Manning put prospective students in the back of his old car, drove them to Claflin, and went to see its president. He always told the president that he had no money and neither did the students, but he hoped Claflin would take them.

A culture of support for sending youths to Claflin flourished among the state's Methodists (as it did for other denominations). My father was ten years old, and Grandpa Manning a seasoned minister, when in 1928 Claflin's president, Joseph B. Randolph, spoke at the annual meeting of the 1866 Conference ministers, urging them to support Claflin financially. Perhaps my grandfather attended; the speech took place in Cheraw, Dad's birthplace. Claflin was a magnet for the children of ministers; one survey found that 24 percent of the college's graduates were ministers' children, and 80 percent of the Claflin's graduates were Methodists.[51] My grandfather—famed champion of education, with no visible diploma but a full member of the 1866 Conference cofounded by Claflin's founders, living in a state where Black Methodist ministers supported Claflin with money and by sending their own children and parishioners there— urged my father, in certain terms, to attend Claflin.

Dad told me little about his education at Claflin, except to mention his own financial troubles and his miserably awkward social standing, about which he was very reticent. He mentioned the color line, noting that he was not light-skinned enough or rich enough to be popular. He did find at least one lifelong friend, James S. Thomas, a roommate, also of low income, who later became a Methodist bishop. Bishop Thomas came to visit us often, sometimes bringing his wife Ruth and four daughters and staying in our house or next door, as they traveled from out of state to visit Ruth's parents in the summer. Here is Dad's account of the roommates' college days, written for a later speech: "Whatever I am today, if anything at all, I owe to Claflin. It took me as I was in 1935, a green high school graduate—rough, crude, and broke—and honored me by permitting me to become a freshman. No one else would let me in, but Claflin took me and gave me a chance. I shall never forget those dedicated and devoted teachers who wrestled with me, inspired and motivated me, during those developmental and crucial years of my life. . . . James Samuel Thomas, my college roommate and an orphan boy, passed from parsonage to parsonage, hardly had changing clothes in college. He and I slept on the strand [sandy beach] at Myrtle Beach waiting for the season to open to get a job. Now he holds the distinction of [honor as a bishop]."[52]

Although Dad received his ministerial certification from the 1866 Conference immediately after graduating from Claflin in 1940 and could have become a minister with no further formal education, he also received teacher certification. He chose to teach and serve as principal in the Florence school district for two years; about that experience I never heard him speak, and no records give details. It is probably noteworthy, however, that Dad then decided to change directions and attend Gammon Theological Seminary in Atlanta, graduating from there in 1945. Stirred by John Steinbeck's novel *The Grapes of Wrath,* as well as by a recruiter who visited Gammon's campus, he signed up as a mission minister for migrant farmworkers, most of them from the British West Indies or

Native Americans. Dad traveled with these migrants in field conditions ranging from upstate New York to Homestead, Florida.

Dad sometimes held services for the migrant workers on the edge of a field, other times in a mess hall after meals. He found laborers with little job security and precarious finances. The children needed clothes and food, as did the elderly, who also needed healthcare. In an initiative that gave him broader contacts than he could have had in South Carolina, he worked with local committees to provide such help. These committees were often biracial. "On Long Island it was the town of Riverhead [that provided the committee], in New Jersey it was Camden on the banks of the Delaware River, in South Florida it was Miami, and Maryland it was Dover, Delaware." He particularly remembered the mixed-race committee on Long Island, which included "Mr. Thomas Talmadge, a wealthy farmer; Mrs. Carol who knew no prejudice but supported the program in many ways; Dr. Skeet, a black medical doctor."[53] These committees exposed him to one form of interracial cooperation.

The working and living conditions were "deplorable," although these improved over time, in part because of labor organizing, which Dad welcomed as a way to address desperate circumstances. "One of the high moments of my tenure with the migrant program was the time I met with Norman Thomas, the socialist who on several occasions ran for [US] President."[54] Dad kept excerpts of comments that Thomas made about civil and worker rights in his papers, in the same folder as his autobiographical statement. His brush with socialism seemed to heighten his social consciousness but did not shake his faith.

On one of his trips during Florida picking season, he met his future wife, Ethel Augusta Braynon. He walked into her classroom during a tour of Miami's Booker T. Washington High School and interrupted her mathematics class in mid-lecture. She told him curtly that she did not tolerate interruptions; he exited promptly but definitely noticed this attractive woman. (Mom was also evidently dazzling as a teacher; her students have told me that she was ambidextrous, writing equations on the board with two hands simultaneously.) She later consented to see him on friendlier terms.

Mom's family of immigrants had left Andros Island, Bahamas, after she was born and after the sponge fishing industry died, leaving Grandpa Braynon jobless. With eight children and day-labor skills, her parents struggled to feed the family in various Florida locales, finally settling in Miami. They sacrificed to send one child, Mom, to Florida A&M, an HBCU in Tallahassee; Mom later paid for the youngest of the eight, my Aunt Lenora, to attend the same college. At some point after college, Mom gained US citizenship.

By the time Dad saw her, she was a capable teacher and US citizen who had helped raise her parents out of poverty by living in their tiny home for eight or nine years. She had resigned herself to life as a single woman, but my parents married a few months after they met, in 1946. They stayed in Miami for a short while, but she wrote her beloved father-in-law, Rev. I. V. Manning, whom she addressed as "My Dear Father," that she and "Rev. Manning Jr." were "very lonely." This was true even though her St. Agnes Episcopal Church, sorority (Zeta Phi Beta), and fellow teachers had given them lovely wedding gifts, a shower, and a reception hosted at the high school. All this reflected her embedded place in Miami's Black community, a place sacrificed when she married a Methodist minister who intended to return to South Carolina.[55]

They headed to Boston University for graduate school, where they both obtained master's degrees in 1947, he in religious studies/ethics, she in education with a mathematics concentration. This was a major feat for two people who had grown up as did Dad, in small-town South Carolina, two generations removed from functional illiteracy, and Mom, who had grown up in an impoverished Miami neighborhood of immigrants.

I possess several written sources about my father's life. My mother's thesis concerns mathematics lesson plans, and she wrote no reflection that I can find about this era other than the above letter. Dad's very reflective thesis, however, says much. I did not see, look for, or find it until I had lived for almost seven decades. I found both theses online because universities now sometimes scan old documents.

A Thesis about South Carolina

Dad's Boston University thesis used standard sources, but he also commented from the perspective of someone who had once lived in a rural section of the state, in a family with constrained income. His experiences teaching in a Black public school and ministering to itinerant farmworkers may have sharpened his vision.

At the heart of this thesis is subdued outrage at the circumstances that white supremacy had created. Even though Black migration to the North had relieved conditions, and Blacks made up only 43% of the state's population in 1940, they made up 47% of people under the age of 20. Black South Carolinians still worked as underpaid agricultural laborers, and in 1940 almost 80 percent of Black people lived in rural areas. Their brand of farmwork meant long hours, deep poverty generating chronic hunger, and children as field workers, stunting their ability to attend school regularly.[56] Dad told of local police who during picking season rounded up Black victims and forced them to either pick cotton at low wages or work at the county farm (prison camp). He cited a 1944 escape of a Black person from a peonage farm where eleven others were still in peonage. One escapee said she could not get milk for her baby, but she watched as white plantation owners fed milk to their dogs. The dogs also had their own cook who served them lamb chops, while laborers "so skinny that our ribs stuck out" stood by and watched. Landowners entrapped Black workers with high prices for low-quality staple goods, and illiteracy blocked the workers from understanding contracts or their rights.[57]

Dad argued: "We can understand why this white system strives hard to keep this great mass of laborers in ignorance. They are the backbone of the system. When [the worker] is trained and given a sense of worth, guided to understand and experience the finer things of life, he is no longer fit to work year in and year out with no financial settlement except the slip of paper to the general store to buy a side of fat meat and a bucket of molasses."[58] He described an educational system designed to keep people "in ignorance." A former school principal who had left that placement, he noted that school boards told public schools to avoid teaching civics or social studies, so that Black students would not think about the privileges of citizenship or the nature of their lot.

Dad cited racial disparities in 1937 school expenditures, especially in rural counties. In Clarendon County, 100 percent rural, where Black inhabitants outnumbered white almost three to one, annual expenditure was $5.63 each for Black students but $57.20 each (8.3 times higher) for white students. In McCormick County, 100 percent rural according to the US Census Bureau, the average annual amount of public money spent for a white student was 11.6 times higher than for a Black student. In contrast Charleston County was half urban; its per pupil expenditure for white students was 3.4 times the average for Black students. In six urban counties that he selected, per pupil expenditure for white students was 4 times the per pupil expenditure for Black students. In six rural counties that he selected, per pupil expenditure for white students was 9 times higher. Black pupils suffered everywhere, but they suffered the worst in rural counties.[59]

My father cried out that these effects were devastating for Black children and families, putting children at severe disadvantage and keeping workers dependent on farm labor. The tenant farm system generated high turnover because of financial instability and exploitation. This, combined with short school "years" and compulsory farmwork, made children move often, receive disjointed schooling, and form weak bonds with neighbors. Obtaining a decent high school diploma was highly problematic in a state where in 1940–41 only

High schools in South Carolina, 1937. White dots represent white
high schools, and the much fewer black dots represent Black high schools.
Courtesy of the South Carolina Department of Education, from "A Survey of
School Buildings Grounds and Equipment in South Carolina," Division of
School House Planning, assisted by State Planning Board, 1937, 21.

two public high schools for Black students (neither of which was his own) met
national accreditation standards. Such racial inequality shamed a Christian society and left a Black person with a choice: "Sooner or later, one or two things
are prone to happen. Either he gives up and concludes that maybe the system is
right, that probably he does not deserve an equal opportunity, or he uses these
inequalities as lanes and comes forth, taking his place with other growing persons."[60]

Finding such "lanes" was very difficult, however. The system of white oppression was so pervasive that even within themselves Black people mimicked it,
adopting color prejudice based on skin color and socioeconomic status. "The
vicious caste system has emerged. The system is not confined to the whites of
South Carolina, but is also found within the Negro race. The educated snub

the uneducated. Those with straight hair refuse to associate with others with woolly hair. The mulattoes are against those with no white blood, and the blacks boast their purity. . . . This strange philosophy has given rise to many of the social ills of Negroes in South Carolina. It has [undermined] the very foundation of race pride and group solidarity." His next sentence, particularly heartrending, makes me suspect that my sensitive, dark-skinned father spoke of himself, or of people that he knew. "It [the racial plus color hierarchy] has created such feelings of despair that many Negroes wish they had never been born of black parents often times feeling that maybe the curse of the biblical character Ham does have some bearing on their destiny."[61]

Because I knew my father as well as any child could know a parent, I know the emotional background that led to such writing. As I knew him years afterwards, Dad was a talented administrator, skillfully combining his life's experiences with his divinity and master's degrees to run a Black college under challenging circumstances. Those who loved him best, however, knew that he wrestled internally with the scars of racism and colorism, as did many people, and that occasionally those scars ached.Like many people, Dad suffered in quiet frustration as he grew up and then lived in a place where race, skin tone, and income categorized everyone, with respect parceled out accordingly. Dad was personable, a self-assured leader, and an indefatigable worker, putting in long office hours with no visible diversions. He could stand before any audience and move people to rousing applause with his oration, learned at the feet of his father. I could go to him with any personal problem or concern, and he would offer the wisest, warmest advice possible, making all well again simply with his soothing words. Over time a compatible marriage worked its magic, income stabilized, and his life's work gave him an honored place in the world. Even so, except at home, he practically lived in suits, dress shirts, and ties for most of my childhood and youth. He warned us to dress well, silently commanding respect, whenever we went into the outside world. Gifted with conscientious and affectionate parents, caring childhood teachers, and a clear mission in life, he forgave and overcame the inevitable slights, but they also affected him in subtle ways I cannot describe.

His master's thesis did not mention the more graphic, physical violence against Black people of that era, a grievous situation that hung over all like a shroud. He addressed instead the challenges facing Christian ministers, socioeconomic conditions among the people they served, and difficulties educating Black children, but I know he hated lynching, the hidden threat that this implied, and the occasional appearance of organized white supremacists who terrorized Black families and communities.

South Carolina's last public lynching—that is, the last example of white mob "justice" delivered with no trial but a hanging rope and murder accompanied by torture and bodily mutilation, with all-white juries serving no justice against vigilantes—was of Willie Earle in Greenville, February 1947, when Dad was twenty-eight years old, finishing up his thesis. The murder of a white taxi driver had taken place in Pickens County, the same place where Dad had found admirable elementary-school teachers. It is quite possible that Earle was not the actual murderer, but the mob made it impossible to exonerate him. After they took him out of jail and lynched him, the judicial system acquitted thirty-one white men who had signed confessions, certain, perhaps, that their peers would not punish them for this despicable act.[62]

Claflin invited Mom and Dad to return there to teach when they finished their master's theses. Dad taught history and served as both assistant chaplain and assistant dean of men, filling several jobs at once. Dad also pastored part-time, driving 250 miles each week at one point; eventually, in 1951, he decided it was better to become a full-time minister.

I was born a year before that, when my parents were living in an old house that was itself symbolic of a smaller-scale and quieter struggle for equal education. This house, originally home to Claflin's third president, Dunton, had a name: Dunwalton, in honor of Dunton's long service to the school. After Dunton's death the college subdivided his house into three separate apartments for faculty families; my parents moved there along with two other families. Claflin eventually replaced the original house with the present one, still called Dunwalton.

Conclusion

This chapter begins to tell the story of how hard it was for Black people to receive an education, because of a purposeful strategy of repression. Formerly enslaved Black people eagerly sought education, but their gains soon faded. Reconstruction promised relief, but the end of that era ushered in another of increasing marginalization of Black education and political power. White supremacists sought to build up education for white students only, and philanthropists pressured schools to adopt a form of industrial education that promised to keep the Black race subject.

I also offered several stories about constructive resilience, as displayed by Fields in her classroom and by both Black and white supporters of education who founded schools intended for higher education for Black students. This started in 1869 with the state's oldest HBCU, Claflin, which in 1896 gave birth to SC State. Claflin weathered an unsteady beginning to offer substantive education to elementary, high school, and college students, as did SC State. Gradually both schools began to educate normal and college students.

At Claflin, Dunton and Randolph, the last white president and the first Black one, symbolize the complexity of one "missionary vanguard" school. Dunton exhibited strong support for industrial education to supplement the more liberal curriculum during his long tenure. Although this was due to financial concerns, this tactic was out of step with the general drift of the early 1900s, when Black educators fought against the Hampton-Tuskegee model. During his presidency Randolph turned the school more toward academics, and he steadily replaced all remaining white faculty members with Black ones. Randolph accomplished this feat with great pride, at one point ignoring Dunton's pleas to keep at least a few white faculty on staff.[63] He and the school honored Dunton before and after his life, but replacing the last white president and shedding remnants of industrial education were signs of independence for a fledgling Black college. The Dunwalton house therefore symbolized larger struggles, between white and Black college leadership, gratitude and resentment, paternalism and self-determination.

This chapter also offered basic information about the Manning family, highlighting its varied struggles to become educated and to display constructive resilience. My grandparents overcame major hurdles for themselves and became inspiring boosters for dignity and higher education in their impoverished communities even as they nurtured their son well. Hubert Manning's 1947 thesis helped us understand him as well as explore social conditions for Black people up until that time, but after that year conditions improved somewhat. Dad's thesis said that Black people could not vote in the state, but the US Supreme Court ruling in *Smith v. Allwright* (1944) prompted Judge J. Waties Waring, in *Ellmore v. Rice* (1948), to rule that South Carolina's white-only Democratic primary, the only primary that counted in a Democratic-controlled state, was illegal. Because of that ruling, many Black voters were able to register. Conditions had already improved for many Black public school teachers because Judge Waring's decision for *Duvall v. J. F. Seignous et al.* (1943) struck down two-race salary scales. In 1947 my parents returned to Claflin, Dad's alma mater, to begin the next phase of their adventure. They did so fully aware, because of Dad's life and his thesis, of the many educational challenges facing Black children and youth in South Carolina.

2

Struggling for Equal Education

The last chapter began to answer several key questions about the suppression of Black education as well as efforts to educate Black students in spite of such measures. In this chapter I shift more fully into the mode of memoir as I recount positive aspects of my own early education. This will show that for at least some Black people everyday life was protective and that Black teachers could educate Black students well under favorable conditions.

Unfavorable educational conditions persisted in mid-twentieth-century South Carolina, but there were organized resistance efforts to protect Black teachers. And at least two HBCUs strove mightily to provide ways for Black youths to move forward in essential ways.

Life under Largely Favorable Circumstances

Growing up, I had no idea that much of the landscape that surrounded me was the result of a century of a dramatic struggle between mighty forces in the South. This blissful unawareness was due in part to the fact that my immediate community had built a sheltered space for at least some of its children. Although we lived during a time when the forces of repression were firmly in place, it was possible to live with a fair degree of comfort and to receive a wonderful education.

In the 1950s Black children in Orangeburg could live without coming into frequent contact with Jim Crow restrictions and the swirling dangers surrounding us. The residential boundaries were firm but not fluid. If you lived in that town long enough, you knew where the white homes started and the Black ones stopped, even though the tracks were not a simple barrier, and so this was not a simple thing to know. Functions jumped sides, and a few Black businesses and households survived on the far edges of the white downtown. Yet no one was confused. Racial neighborhood change or turnover was rare, and the spatial boundaries between the two races did not change from year to year.

As a child I thought that our world was more interesting than the other one, although I could not know that for sure. Our world featured the two campuses, and each campus formed a miniature ecosystem governed by faculty relationships, student activities, building and food services, and sports events. Each hired not just college professors and academic staff but also janitors, cooks, security guards, librarians, maintenance workers, and secretaries, thus creating its own small economy.

The smaller of the two colleges, Claflin, was composed of a series of brick or wooden buildings arranged around a circular road that ran throughout campus and ended pretty much where it began, close to the T. Willard Lewis Chapel. Nestled within one southward curve of that circle lay a curious structure, an elevated bandstand that offered a perch for Dr. Martin Luther King Jr. to survey our campus during his visit to our town. Otherwise it served little purpose except as a stand for sports cheerleaders or the occasional step dance. At various times in the past, several fraternities and sororities had staked out their own space on campus grounds, building benches and circular sidewalks or walls painted in bright enamel colors and sporting Greek insignia. A few of the older buildings, including Tingley Memorial Hall, overlooked beautiful yards filled with interesting large trees, azalea bushes, and low, wide walls that invited you to walk upon them. Microcosm campus environments such as these dared you to engage in creative flights of fancy and play.

The campus of SC State was larger and linear rather than circular, but it too contained imposing buildings, outdoor spaces, and walkways. Several of these buildings held college departments that offered enrichment classes for area youth, and so we knew those walls held drafting studios for building construction majors and dance studios illumined by mirrored walls. We could bike from one end of SC State's campus to the other as a great adventure, an especially good one when the college students were afield, laughing and socializing and courting each other.

Even if the colleges had not existed, many other Black community institutions did, providing protection from the outside world that extended from birth to death. In this feature our town was like dozens or hundreds of others across the South, which varied only in their particulars. Although the hospital we were born in segregated its patients by the ever-present rules of race, in certain key cities or towns, such as ours, the doctor who brought you into the world was Black and a longtime friend of the family. This doctor shepherded you through the years of childhood check-ups and illnesses, and the family's Black dentist

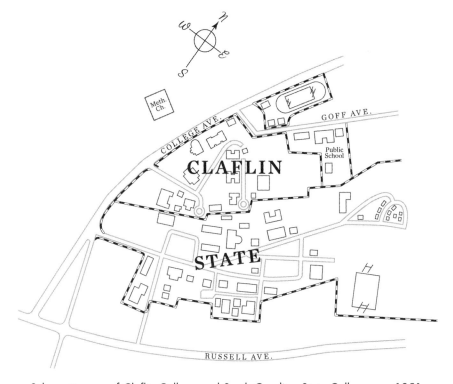

Schematic map of Claflin College and South Carolina State College, ca. 1951. Redrawn from Fred J. Kelly, *A Study of the Relationships between State A and M College and Claflin College* (Orangeburg, SC: State A and M College, 1951).

made sure your teeth got proper attention. Every girl's family had a neighbor who would "fix" hair in her living room/ bedroom/shop, and every father and brother could choose from barbershops or homes that served the same purpose. In Orangeburg the friendships formed within two barbershops located next to the railroad tracks lasted for an average person's lifetime.[1]

Other local businesses owned and operated by Black people included a very few small restaurants, a soda shop,[2] a well-stocked pharmacy, an electrical shop that also sold appliances, and a few candy/convenience shops built as modest extensions to small houses. For a few years, we even had a movie theater where you did not have to sit in the balcony, because it was intended just for Black audiences. At the end of your life, your family could choose from one or two Black-owned funeral homes, run by well-respected families who in turn treated their customers with respect. They buried you in cemeteries where you could be sure no one would object to your presence.

The churches varied widely in denomination, but with limited choices by race. For Black people our selections ranged from the small religious congregations led by charismatic but untrained ministers to very "proper" churches connected with well-known denominations. My own family's church, co-founded in 1866 by T. Willard Lewis and part of the 1866 Conference, was Trinity Methodist Episcopal Church. At first the congregation met in various places; then a building was designed by SC State professor William Wilkins and constructed over a sixteen-year period, from 1928 to 1944, by its own members who were carpenters, masons, and other craftsmen, as a tangible example of Black self-help.[3] This building boasted an imposing Gothic brick structure that was as appealing a church building as one could hope to find. It featured high front steps leading to heavy wooden doors and an attractive vestibule, which opened into a sanctuary filled with beautiful wooden pews, red carpeting, and stained-glass windows. Trinity had a basement of ample proportions that hosted community socials, a multistory attached structure that held Sunday school classes, and a small parsonage that comfortably housed the minister's family. If a Black person came to live in our small town and looked for a church to join, our Trinity was perhaps the most visibly grand, but it had subdued worship services. Other choices included the somewhat aristocratic Episcopalian or Catholic congregations and more energetic Baptist or AME venues. The charismatic Black churches were a little harder to find, but they were there too.

The schools, where we spent most of our days, provided the strongest sense of protection. Black families had two choices, public and "other." The "other" offered two options, a Catholic parochial school and Felton Training School. Felton's stated purpose was to provide close-at-hand "clinic" teaching for the college's education department and, unstated, to educate children of the two colleges' faculty and staff.[4] Since it sat on the campus of a public college, it was public, because the SC State board of trustees controlled it, but our parents paid fees, and its small size required selectivity; the maximum total was perhaps 120 students.

From outward appearances Felton was a throwback to ancient times. Later replaced with a modern facility, our brick building in the 1950s and early 1960s housed eight grades, starting with first, but it had only four large classrooms plus a vestibule and attached principal's office. Two grades shared one classroom and one teacher. Tucked in the middle of SC State's campus, Felton was not big enough for a school cafeteria, but SC State had built a modest one in Felton's backyard where we ate our hot lunches, prepared by friendly cooks, every day. Felton was an exceptionally good school, a testimony to the power

Felton Training School students, South Carolina State College, ca. 1963. Family album photo courtesy of Gwendolyn Hedgepath, author's Felton classmate.

of some Black teachers in these small, circumscribed, and segregated worlds to educate their pupils.

Each of my four teachers was dedicated to her job, as was the principal, Maxine Crawford, who commanded our little world with evident leadership skills. For the four teachers, handling two grades at once seemed natural; they simply alternated lessons and worked with us in turns. They were technically "clinic" faculty for the college's education department, with occasional access to student teachers and to other faculty for special classes in Spanish or industrial drafting, both of which were required. For drafting, similar to entry-level architectural drawing, we left our building to walk together to another SC State building equipped with drafting tables and a competent instructor. Except for such occasional forays, my class of fifteen students—eight girls and seven boys—stayed with the same teacher for two years, and we stayed with each other and in that school building from first or second grade through eighth grade. I entered Flossie Clinkscale's second-grade class when my family moved back to Claflin from Charleston. Felton's placement test assessed me as ahead of my age group, and so I skipped first grade; this was a testimony to the high quality of my Charleston nursery/kindergarten, located in some ancillary building of a church whose name I have forgotten.

Felton's teachers kept us busy, but they functioned as surrogate mothers as well as teachers. Their classrooms were never boring and always challenging. The doubled-up accommodations were quite handy for those of us who cared to learn the next grade's lessons at the same time that we learned our own. You could sit among your third-grade fellows, working on your math problems, and easily listen in as Lovely M. White explained more advanced math to the fourth graders who sat in the same room. This strategy worked extremely well until we were the fourth graders, but even then we could review last year's concepts simply by listening to the third graders' lessons. Felton team spirit was a real thing, with such a small student body. Every year we mounted a full-scale operetta, complete with costumes, plots, and roles for each student.

These teachers were wonderful role models. Mrs. White, our third- and fourth-grade teacher, was blunt, professional, and competent. I see her clearly even today, as she stood "commanding the troops" (us) with a firm but supportive hand. Our next teacher, Gwendolyn Edwards, mother of one of our classmates, Frances, was as cool as a cucumber, and seemed particularly skilled at handling the rowdiness that emerged as we fifth- and sixth-grade students began to enter puberty and "make eyes" at each other. She dedicated herself to us inside the classroom and out, leading the girls in Girl Scout activities and treating every one of us as her daughter's sister or brother. Alba Lewis, our seventh- and eighth-grade teacher, was elegant and confident, in striking contrast to our bumbling, pimply, gawking adolescence. Her cool demeanor and graceful bearing let us know that someday we could grow up to be cool and graceful. Her openness allowed us to come to her with great confidence that she could help us unwind the confusing knots of puberty and budding relationships. She was a demanding instructor, expecting the best performance and not being happy unless she got it, but she tempered demands with a wisdom and warmth that none of us would soon forget. As our last teacher in that four-room school, she was the one who prepared us for the inevitable separation, helping us plan and execute a formal graduation exercise complete with white dresses and white pumps with stockings for the girls, shirts and ties for the boys, and carefully memorized choral arrangements.

There it is, a short, rose-tinted description of the protective world that adults built for some of us during the 1950s and early 1960s. They worked hard to allow us this little island of peace and protection, this tangible evidence of constructive resilience. Although this account is by necessity short, it echoes themes of other work concerning the best examples of Black segregated schools. I find Walker's account of the Caswell County Training School in North

J. B. Felton (the tallest), County Superintendent Mr. Petterson, and Jackson Davis visiting Orangeburg, South Carolina, 1923. Felton administered the Rosenwald Program in South Carolina. Courtesy of Special Collections, University of Virginia Library, Jackson Davis photographer.

Carolina extremely affecting; the similarities are strong, right down to the caring teachers, extracurricular activities, and annual operettas.[5]

Various pieces of my deceptively tranquil picture of Orangeburg hid underlying problems. To describe these, I will focus on a few elements: the Rosenwald program for constructing Black school buildings; Black teachers' efforts in the 1910s and 1940s to earn jobs and decent salaries; and the long struggle to sustain two colleges. These elements illustrate early efforts to improve Black education using both resistance and resilience.

The Rosenwald Program

Physically, my own Felton was similar to thousands of schools built in the South by the Rosenwald School Program. Felton's simple four-room structure was the standard format for such schools, which could have one, two, three, or more classrooms plus other rooms used for some ancillary purpose. In South Carolina the leader of the program that oversaw the building of these Black schools was a tall white man named Joseph B. Felton, the namesake for Felton Training School.[6]

The Rosenwald School Program was yet another example of Northern philanthropists' efforts to educate Black students in the South during its most oppressive years. The Julius Rosenwald Fund worked in conjunction with several allied funds, such as the Jeanes Fund, the Slater Fund, and the GEB, funded by John D. Rockefeller Sr. and his family, but in South Carolina, up until the 1930s, the Julius Rosenwald Fund outspent them all in its support for Black education.[7] The Rosenwald Fund only paid a portion of the cost of building new schools; other money came from allied philanthropies, Black citizens, and school officials.[8]

Author Derrick Bell Jr. has suggested that historical gains for Black people in the United States have come largely when Black needs converged with white interests, leading to limited reforms. He calls this a process of "convergence."[9] Needs and motivations clearly converged during this period of support for building schools. Black people fled to the North for many reasons, but one was inadequate public education for their children. As W. E. B. Du Bois described in 1911, "many of the school authorities have shown by their acts and in a few cases expressed declaration that it was their policy to eliminate the Negro school as far as possible."[10] This southern strategy was a two-edged sword, however. High levels of Black migration reduced the plantation economy's labor force, motivating northerners to stem the tide arriving in cities and softening white southerners to the idea of providing limited schooling for Black children as a way to encourage their parents to stay put.

This situation birthed the Rosenwald school construction program. The original idea came from Clinton J. Calloway, an extension agent who worked under Booker T. Washington. Julius Rosenwald, the wealthy magnate of Sears, Roebuck, and Company, celebrated his fiftieth birthday in 1912 by donating twenty-five thousand dollars to Washington to support school programs that used the Hampton-Tuskegee model of industrial education. Washington distributed most of this money, but Calloway persuaded him to use twenty-one hundred dollars for schoolhouse construction programs for six Alabama communities. In 1914 Rosenwald enlarged the program to build one hundred schoolhouses, but with conditions. Black residents needed to raise enough money or in-kind contributions to match or exceed the grant amount. Furthermore local, county, or state school officials had to cooperate, and donors needed to deed all property to local public school systems. Tuskegee's extension department had to approve the school building chosen, with stock floor plans, and state agents needed to coordinate all.[11] In 1917 Rosenwald created the Julius Rosenwald Fund to expand and oversee this school construction program. As with the old

Old school building, Orangeburg "Colored School," 1923. Courtesy of Special Collections, University of Virginia Library, Jackson Davis photographer.

program, to get schools built, Black people had to deed their own money, land, and labor to local public school systems.

The Rosenwald program improved miserable public school facilities serving South Carolina's Black children. Beginning in 1917, GEB funded a white State Agent for Negro Schools to oversee the initiative. J. B. Felton, the second agent appointed, held this post from 1919 until 1947. He wrote in his first annual report: "The furnishings of the school buildings for the colored children in South Carolina could not be worse. The children are required to sit on benches without backs and their feet unable to reach the floor. A more uncomfortable position could hardly be imagined." In another report: "The negro school-houses are miserable beyond all description. They are usually without comfort, proper lighting, or sanitation. Nearly all the negroes of school age in the district are crowded into these miserable structures during the short term which the school runs."[12]

J. B. Felton was a passionate champion. He convinced white officials to provide at least some funds, but he also worked in cooperation with Black communities to get support for the match. He found Black people "eager and anxious to have better advantages for their children" and willing "to make whatever sacrifice is necessary, both in time and money to secure these advantages."[13] He

Carroll Colored Rosenwald School, York County, part of a regional program to build schools for Black pupils with a combination of philanthropy, government funds, and donations. Image courtesy of the South Carolina Department of Archives and History.

regularly attended meetings of the Black Palmetto State Teachers Association (PSTA). In 1925 this was the PSTA's glowing assessment: "Mr. J. B. Felton, the State Supervisor of Negro Schools, has broken down the barriers of misunderstanding and prejudice and has enlisted in our cause some of the leading white citizens of the State and Nation. He has the confidence, and the united support of every teacher in the State and Nation, and his Jeanes workers and Rosenwald teachers are among the most potent factors that are now making a people out of our people." By 1931, Felton reported, "Black residents raised nearly three times more money than whites for the building of [Rosenwald] schools."[14]

The Rosenwald Fund discontinued funding programs in 1932, but its schools had improved Black education. By 1928 20 percent of rural schools for Black southerners were Rosenwald schools. By the time the fund ended, it had helped build 4,977 new schools, 217 teachers' homes, and 163 shop buildings. US counties with a Rosenthal school saw significant gains in Black school attendance, years of schooling, literacy, and cognitive test scores. The educational quality of Black military recruits improved when they came from counties with such schools, and the racial gap in education narrowed in those counties as well. Ironically, given some of the motivations for white support, Black migration rates also increased as Black people moved to better labor markets.[15]

In South Carolina the breakdown of Rosenwald-sponsored structures built by 1937 was 481 school buildings, 8 teachers' homes, and 11 shops. Black South Carolinians contributed $508,000 to the state's program, more than the Rosenwald Fund's $435,600 and far more than individual white contributions of $224,800.[16] These schools served just over 56,000 Black children but left 170,000 in bad conditions. J. B. Felton by 1937 had helped establish six high schools for Black students, far short of his goal of one per county but an important accomplishment nonetheless. Still, Felton was disturbed: "When we compare conditions then and as they exist today, the gap as shown by different phases of comparison has not been materially lessened. While in some cases, it has been helped, generally where something has been done for Negro schools, *a correspondingly greater percent has been done for the white schools.*"[17]

In Orangeburg County the program helped build eighteen schoolhouses, one of which was "Training School State College (Felton)," 1924–25 construction, my own Felton Training School.[18] Although the funding structure for this campus school was different from that of rural public schools, the building blueprint was similar to other four-room schools. Like other SC State buildings constructed after the campus fires in 1916, Felton was made of red brick instead of the more usual wood (as on facing page, York County).

In spite of the program's accomplishments, the grants came at a price. In 1929 Black historian Gordon praised J. B. Felton's efforts but noted that "the plan usually results in the Negroes themselves investing most of the money. In the opinion of the writer the plan has been, on the whole, a blessing to the Negroes, but it is not without dangers, not the least of which is that it is in part used as an excuse for the Southern states to shift their rightful responsibility for the education of Negro youth to other shoulders."[19] Anderson, writing in 1988, agreed: "On the one hand, the process of double taxation and collective social action enabled [Black people] to improve tremendously the material conditions of their educational system; on the other, the same process was unjust and oppressive, and their accommodation to double taxation helped extend over them the power of their oppressors."[20]

The difficulties were obvious once the program ended. In 1935 several agencies sponsored a survey of the state's school buildings and facilities. Survey co-sponsors included the state's department of education, the South Carolina State Planning Board, and the US Federal Emergency Relief Administration. FERA employed 191 people to assess 4,000 public school buildings, serving 259,476 white student enrollees and slightly fewer, 229,246, "colored" enrollees.[21] They analyzed such physical criteria as square footage, water and sanitary facilities, and building structure. Their findings documented persistently unequal facilities for Black schools. For example no water supply was located on school grounds for 18 percent of white schools but 65 percent of Black schools. Inside toilets or approved alternatives (e.g., pit latrines) existed for 94 percent of white schools but only 23 percent of Black schools.[22]

The list goes on and on with such statistics for each county. One of the report's conclusions was that the large difference in property values between the richest and poorest school districts influenced the quality of facilities. The study ranked average valuation for all forty-six counties, each composed of several school districts. Charleston and Richland (home of Columbia) Counties ranked as the top two; each enjoyed more than $1,300 assessed property value per pupil. Horry County (home of Myrtle Beach) and Clarendon County (home of the future *Briggs v. Elliott* lawsuit) ranked last, forty-fifth and forty-sixth, with each county having less than $340 assessed property valuation per pupil.

Public schools for Orangeburg County suffered from similar problems, showing that the presence of two Black colleges meant little for Black children in the county's regular public school system. The county ranked thirty-sixth in assessed property value per pupil, $572, not much better than Horry and Clarendon Counties. Only one white public school in the county lacked a drinking water supply compared to fifty-nine school buildings for Black students lacking this basic amenity. The average classroom area's square feet per pupil was twenty-four for white students but only eleven for Black.[23]

The Black community effort necessary to build Rosenwald-funded schools was a magnificent example of constructive resilience, a banding together to act beyond the efforts of individuals and to create a better future under oppressive circumstances. The campaign required Black people to visualize that better future, consult with their neighbors, and devise ways to gather together enough money, property, and hard labor to raise up school buildings for at least a few grades. They thus confirmed their faith in education as a positive good and a path to that better future as well as their willingness to sacrifice to obtain that future, even though this required double taxation. For all of its benefits, however, the program barely budged the state's own inequitable system, enshrined in school finance.

Black Teachers Seek Jobs and Equal Wages

The Black community needed more than adequate school buildings; it also needed teachers who had the necessary training and education and compensation that allowed them to support their families. Many Black public-school teachers, however, handled large class sizes and flawed classroom buildings plus minuscule salaries compared to white counterparts. In the 1930s and 1940s, the majority of Black teachers in the South still taught in inadequate buildings during too-short school years that catered to crop schedules and enabled child labor. Because some salary relief came in the 1940s, Black professionals in cities like Orangeburg were on firmer footing than they would have been otherwise, but countervailing forces weakened these victories.

The battles for jobs and fair wages for South Carolina's Black teachers match in drama the story of constructive resilience personified by the Rosenwald program. That program did not require active "resistance," because paid representatives cajoled white support using the carrots of philanthropic funds and Black self-funding. Black South Carolinians even had a strong white ally, J. B. Felton, who met with white school boards to do the cajoling so that local Black people did not have to do this. In contrast the fights for Black teachers' jobs and salaries required carefully organized resistance.

South Carolina's Black community had some experience trying to protect Black teachers. The 1896 efforts by Black legislator Thomas Miller to create a college that hired only Black faculty and administrators was one way to gain assured jobs. Black Charlestonians also made a notable effort in the years leading up to 1920 to get public school jobs for Black teachers.

Charleston was one of the last Southern cities to hire only white teachers to teach Black children. The school board's rationale was the need to protect white teaching jobs, but this also reinforced white superiority. One legislator clearly stated this in 1914, noting the need to "teach the negroes from the very beginning that they are inferior to whites."[24] By 1900 Charleston's public school system employed only two Black teachers, even though the local Avery Institute competently trained many normal students every year.[25] A GEB observer visited Charleston in 1904 and attested to the effects of this situation, including abusive disciplinary practices at Black schools and teacher hostility: "These [white] teachers in many instances . . . do not even allow their pupils to speak to them on the street." Higher-income Black residents paid for private schools such as Avery, which offered elementary and high school for those who could pay tuition.[26]

Governor Coleman Blease, a man who openly endorsed lynching as "necessary and good,"[27] chafed at white teachers, especially women, working in Black public schools, but Charleston's school board resisted change. The legislature introduced bills prohibiting Charleston's arrangement in both 1890 and 1912, but the Charleston school board continued to defend its policy. Black Charlestonians' decades-long protests and petitions gained force when the NAACP established a Charleston chapter in 1917, with more than two hundred members by 1919, and it adopted jobs for Black teachers as a rallying cry. A 1919 delegation petitioned the state, calling for the civil code to require Black teachers for

Black schools. When Charleston's school board countered that only a few local mulattoes supported this request, darker-skinned Septima Clark took offense. She volunteered to seek petition signatures by canvassing Black Charlestonians; she and her students gathered thousands of signatures.[28]

Black people's desire for Black teachers and white political leaders' desires to get white teachers out of Black schools converged. Former SC State president Miller lobbied his former legislative colleagues for relief, evoking memories of his role in SC State's creation and playing to white segregationist instincts as he pushed for severance from multiracial Claflin. Pressured by the petitions and by ideology, the state government finally forced Charleston's school board to transfer white teachers and hire Black teachers for Black public schools, a partial victory, but in response the state created a salary scale for Black teachers pegged at two-thirds of white salaries—automatic discrimination.[29]

Nevertheless Black teachers gained jobs. The New Deal and World War II also created skilled jobs, and Charleston's gap in racial earnings narrowed. Black South Carolinians began to build up their incomes and their schools, with more highly trained teachers and with extracurricular activities that helped to retain students. In 1937 Burke High School—opened in 1911 as Charleston Colored Industrial School[30]—had only twelve of thirty-one teachers with bachelor's degrees, but thirty-seven out of forty-one had bachelor's degrees in 1941. These more educated teachers, taking control of the curriculum, moved away from industrial education and toward civics and social science lessons. Supporting them at the state level was the PSTA, dedicated to educational equality.[31]

Therefore when the NAACP initiated legal challenges to unequal pay scales in Maryland and Virginia, in 1939 and in 1940, many of South Carolina's Black teachers were ready to join these battles. Thurgood Marshall won initial court cases by arguing that salary differentials based on racial characteristics alone were unconstitutional violations of the Fourteenth Amendment. Teachers in other states began to file similar suits. South Carolina was similar in that way but different largely in state government's strategic response to such suits.[32]

At first the fight for salary equalization was slow to get off the ground in South Carolina. A 1934 campaign to raise the salaries failed because Black teachers feared repercussions and because the NAACP's state branch had fallen into inactivity because of white harassment.[33] Matters shifted nationwide when in the late 1930s Thurgood Marshall began to enlist teachers to help pay for salary-equalization lawsuits.

South Carolina's NAACP state secretary Modjeska Simpkins coordinated with the PSTA to organize and raise money for a case. She also set up a defense fund to assist teachers who lost their jobs because of their support for the case.

Simpkins used a combination of cajoling and shaming to get teachers to join efforts. For example, in April 1943 the PSTA issued a news release stating that it was backing down and would not file suit. Simpkins wrote individual teachers: "I know that you, along with every self-respecting Negro teacher in South Carolina, experienced a severe shock when you read last week's news release." She assured letter recipients that a suit would move forward but said that the NAACP branch needed more funds to do this. "Now, I shall make a suggestion which should be *a great insult to you:* if for any reason *you fear publicity or intimidation because of your contribution,* you may either send a check or a cash donation directly to me or you may leave your contribution at the Victory Savings Bank in a sealed envelope."[34]

Resulting litigation spurred salary equalization. Although the first case brought to the courts led Charleston's school board to fire the plaintiff, the second case brought by a young Burke High School teacher, Viola Duvall, in *Duvall v. J. F. Seignous et al.,* came before Judge Waring in February, 1944. Waring, in a fifteen-minute trial, established that the school board's attorney should have known about previous rulings favoring wage equalization in other states and then simply told the school board to rectify its dual salary system.[35] This was one of the first cases for social justice ruled on by this extraordinary man, who was born and bred as a white Charlestonian aristocrat and yet supported the cause of racial justice. Waring emerged at several points in the fight for South Carolinians' civil rights.

The state took advantage of the situation—lack of prohibition of anything other than racial standards by the court and an NAACP legal fight that focused mostly on outlawing race-specific criteria—by seeking other ways to justify unequal pay. Fully aware that standardized tests would disadvantage Black teachers—likely products of underfunded, vocationally oriented colleges, with no graduate education available to them—legislators worked with specialist Ben Woods to link salary levels with standardized test results. Woods was anxious to find customers for his National Teacher Examinations (NTE). NAACP litigation outlawing racial salary scales allowed Wood to expand use of the NTE, which provided "an ostensibly objective basis" for beliefs that Black teachers were inferior to white. Wood assured the state's legislators that at least some Black teachers would pass the test, making matters seem fair. The state board of education's sample tests showed that indeed 90 percent of white and 27 percent of Black teachers would get an A or B certification, allowing for higher salary, while 73 percent of Black teachers would get C or D certificates, meaning lower salaries. This confirmed perverse hopes; the state legislature put an NTE-based salary scale in place that Judge Waring then approved.[36]

This was, according to author R. Scott Baker, a new form of institutional racism. The state's new salary system rewarded those with master's degrees, but the state provided no graduate education for Black people, so this was a blocked pathway. The NTE exacerbated class divides, because Black teachers who could pass the test had attended relatively better-funded urban or private schools. Furthermore it was not clear that the NTE measured actual teaching ability in the classroom.[37] Nevertheless, after Judge Waring's ruling, other states followed South Carolina's lead. This was "the most significant response to the challenges posed by the NAACP salary litigation. South Carolina's adoption of the NTE . . . [became] a model that proponents of teacher testing used to expand use of the NTE in the South."[38]

The salary campaigns therefore marginalized the majority of Black teachers. If they were anything like luminaries such as Izzard, Fields, or Dad's first instructors, many of these underpaid Black teachers may have been very effective at shepherding their charges under constrained circumstances, exhibiting qualities that a standardized test could not measure.

Claflin and SC State Struggle

Black colleges literally gave birth to Black schoolteachers as well as to other professionals. Both Claflin and SC State struggled to survive and to protect their college enrollments, small compared to the state's Black population at large, in a series of constructive and resilient efforts.

Focusing on college presidents gives us a shorthand way to describe the colleges' efforts. In the mid-twentieth century, college presidents worked to navigate social, political, and legal changes during a tumultuous era. In favorable circumstances Black college presidents could exert great influence upon their students, faculty, and other HBCUs, as well as the wider worlds of the academy and public policy. Martin Jenkins, president of Morgan State College, was an inspiring example of the possibilities given the right circumstances and skills, as was Benjamin E. Mays at Morehouse.[39]

For most HBCU college presidents, however, the job was lonely and difficult.[40] Presidents coped not only with the loss of historic philanthropic sources but also with weak governmental support. Their colleges served an impoverished population, thus limiting tuition levels, and they necessarily offered remedial courses because of the sorry state of Black public education. Benjamin E. Mays, Morehouse College's president from 1940 until 1967, once said: "To be a president of a college and white is no bed of roses. To be president of a college and black is almost a bed of thorns." This was true, he said, because "money owned and controlled by whites flows more freely and more abundantly from white to white than it does from white to black. Moreover, the Negro president of the Negro college is almost daily confronted by stumbling blocks, hurdles, and personal embarrassments that rarely if ever clutter the path of his white counterparts."[41] This last sentence rings true; it sounds like Dad's experience as a college president.

Claflin experienced continued financial and enrollment problems from the 1930s until the early 1950s and beyond. In 1936, Dad's freshman year, Claflin had only 150 students in the college department, with another 150 in secondary school and 46 in elementary school. Competition for high school and elementary school Black students rose as the public school system erected, adjacent to the campus, Dunton Elementary School in 1922 and Wilkinson High School in 1937, both named after local college presidents. Claflin discontinued its high school in 1940 and began to disengage from its elementary school. Dad's 1940 graduating class contained 39 seniors, considered a success for that struggling division. World War II led to an implosion of male students, with a total enrollment dropping to 109 college students during 1941–42, and the physical plant continued to deteriorate.[42]

Claflin's second Black president, John J. Seabrook, instituted modest gains during his term, 1945–55. He made some academic improvements and enhanced the physical plant. He purchased a few surplus buildings from the federal government and created a building plan, with funds contributed by the 1866 Conference as well as the New England Conference. Still it was difficult to balance the financial books, leading to deficit spending starting in 1947. Borrowed money built a gymnasium, science building, a library, and several other buildings.

Even after veterans returned from the war, the lingering effects of the Great Depression continued. During 1946, 420 students registered, and by 1955 this total crept up to 498. There was good news in 1948 that the Association of American Colleges had approved membership for Claflin, but in 1953 the then-named Southern Association of Colleges and Schools put Claflin on probation because of the inadequate endowment. In March 1955 Seabrook indicated that the school could not pay faculty salaries coming due, a chronic difficulty he blamed on parents unable to pay tuition owed. At that point Claflin was providing financial aid for over half of its students. The Board of Higher Education (Methodist Church) advanced a loan against future allocations, but soon Seabrook accepted leadership of another college in Houston, leaving Claflin without a president for the 1955–56 school year.[43]

This is why my family moved back to Orangeburg. Dad had little inclination that he would become the next president. He never applied for the job or expressed interest in it. It was true that he was a Claflin alumnus and former faculty member. It was also true that he was an ordained 1866 Conference Methodist minister and that ministers or missionaries traditionally led the college, but other ministers were available, and many of these were alumni as well. He had received a northern master's degree, highly unusual at the time, but he was not preparing himself for college administration for Claflin or anywhere else. In 1951 he had left Claflin's faculty to accept the ministry of Charleston's Wesley Methodist Church, one of the churches co-founded by white missionary T. Willard Lewis, and Mom and my infant self went along with him. We settled into the comfortable parsonage, and Mom obtained a job at Haut Gap High School on Johns Island, continuing the tradition of teaching Gullah people on the Sea Islands adjoining Charleston and resuming her work of teaching high school mathematics. She taught students more comfortable with English than their parents, but raised in households with a strong, rich legacy of Gullah language and culture.

Dad had grown disenchanted with college teaching and wanted to concentrate on being a good minister; he and Mom both enjoyed serving Wesley and Haut Gap. He was surprised one day in May 1956, therefore, when his secretary told him that Claflin's board of trustees had called. They asked him to come immediately to Orangeburg to meet with them. Dad was mowing the lawn for Wesley's parsonage but dropped everything and drove up to Claflin, seventy-five miles away. When he walked into the meeting room, he was shocked to hear: Would you be willing to take on Claflin's presidency?[44]

Dad said yes but clearly did not know what he was getting into. Not only had Seabrook left the school leaderless; in February 1955, a few months before he left, a fire totally destroyed the Mary E. Dunton Dormitory, sparing the lives of its 165 young women and 9 faculty and staff but leaving the college with no women's dorm.[45] When Dad took over Claflin's presidency, the dorm site still lay in ashy ruins. Relatively young at thirty-eight, Dad needed youthful energy to take on this job, which involved many late evenings as he worked to rebuild the dormitory and other buildings and to gain accreditation. He worked late in the office, steps away in the Tingley Memorial Hall, making him seem not too distant.[46] This early presidency was one of the most difficult periods of his life. Upon his retirement he said:

> When I became Claflin's president, I realized I had inherited a nightmare. The school had been dropped from accreditation. Accreditation meant everything. Without it, graduates could not be admitted into grad schools, teachers could not be certified, nor would the University Senate of the Methodist Church provide funding. At that time the government was

not involved. But there was also the prestige of accreditation to consider. To the Black press, you were not a college if you were not accredited. We only had four Ph.D.s on the faculty at that time. And they were Chinese; the students had a hard time understanding them. Everything was most discouraging. . . . It was terrible that first year. I was like the lost children of Israel. But I was blessed with a Board of Trustees who kept encouraging me. And there was a nucleus of people on the faculty and staff who said— and it almost came to this—that if things get real tight, we'll wait on our check.[47]

The fight for accreditation required that Dad go to Atlanta to plead the case of the school. This is what he said about that trip, which must have taken place during his first year: "They [the Southern Association] gave us a last opportunity to come to Atlanta and make an appeal. Alfred Land, the late Dr. Shuler, and I went. Now I'm not a fundamentalist, but before we went down, the late Dr. Shuler, a layperson, asked a word of prayer for our mission. Well, it helped us psychologically if nothing else. We went in there fighting like three little tigers. They said, 'Since you have faith in Claflin, we feel you must be better than we think you are.' If real improvement could be shown, the committee would return to Claflin for reevaluation."[48]

Claflin was by 1958 approved, which was as much as was possible for a Black school at that time. Soon, however, the Southern Association abolished the dual system of approval for Black schools and accreditation for white schools. This placed more pressure on Claflin and other HBCUs to meet the same standards as white schools. It took effort, but finally Claflin did. Dad said about that process: "When we went back to the Southern Association we were striving for full accreditation, not just approval. We now had to meet the same criteria, the same number of doctorates, the same endowment as any college. We set out again. At the 1961 meeting in Miami, Claflin was admitted to full membership in the Southern Association. I must confess, I cried like a baby when I called my secretary from Miami to tell the news. I couldn't hold it back. That was more important to me than the first admission. It was a milestone."[49]

Dad was wrestling with giants, experiencing great stress to the point of tears, as he tried to save the college from oblivion. With apologies for the innocence of this part of the narrative, my worldview was much more limited. I was seeing through the eyes of a child and only dimly aware of the giant challenges he faced. I remember much more mundane things about that period, such as moving into our house, and the house itself. This I will describe, to offer insight into the lingering vestiges of industrial education and white philanthropy.

Newly installed president H. V. Manning at desk, Tingley
Memorial Hall, Claflin College, ca. 1956–57. Family album photo.
Courtesy Cecil Williams, photographer.

In the summer of 1956, our family moved into the president's home. This
house sat on a site that now holds the college's science center. The Women's
Home Missionary Society of the Methodist Episcopal Church, a group of white
Philadelphians, contributed funds to construct the house (starting in 1885) as
a "girl's industrial home" on Claflin's campus. Its first label, in honor of their
bishop, was "Matthew Simpson Memorial Home for Girls." When I was a teenager, groups of white northerners came once or twice to inspect the house and
pay for upgrades, such as central heating and window drapes, continuing their
philanthropic support for this structure and this college.

The home was originally designed to house twenty-two female students and
one matron who would offer classes in cooking, sewing, and domestic economy,
training young women to become, in keeping with the times, cultured maids,
wives, or housekeepers, although they took other classes as well.[50] This original
purpose explains the house's strange layout, which at the age of five or six I
encountered with great wonder. It had six second-floor bedrooms, five of which
were very large; a burnt-out attic, big enough for someone to have once lived

there, and therefore suitably forbidden, ghostly territory; and two formal living rooms, with one of these entered via glass-paned French doors. It also had a formal dining room with built-in cabinets stacked with china; a nearby kitchen and breakfast room with a pantry and its own second staircase to the second floor; and a family room leading to a study with built-in bookcases. All rooms were of capacious size. Add-ons over the years in the rear of the house increased its footprint, adding a second porch, a garage, a laundry room, attached gardening shed, chicken coop, and other mysterious rooms with no obvious purpose. Its side yard facing Tingley Hall hosted a huge chinaberry tree (which you could run around in circles), two fruit-bearing peach trees, and perennials that bloomed in sequence for most of the growing season, all surrounded by protective shrubs. Claflin demolished the whole glorious but aging, bulky confection, as well as its ancillary small guest house and beautifully designed gardens, in about 1971 to make room for the new science center.

After industrial education waned in popularity, making it less important to train Black women in domestic arts, Claflin turned this house into its president's residence and dropped "for Girls" from its original label. The Matthew Simpson Memorial Home also functioned as a reception venue for students and a guesthouse for visitors. Mom hosted such events, in addition to her faculty duties. This meant that she carried a normal course load, bringing home loads of papers that she graded with a red pencil, but she also managed a complex household. For many years she invited all freshmen to an opening reception, and all seniors attended their graduation reception in our home. We housed and fed many out-of-town dignitaries visiting Claflin, if they were Black, because they could not stay in white-only hotels. Other HBCU presidents or church officials stayed in our house as well or in the small guesthouse next door if they had families traveling along with them, as was sometimes the case with the charismatic Bishop Thomas, a family man to his core.

Mom, born in abject poverty on a rural Bahamian island and raised in a low-income Miami household with many siblings, bought an etiquette book. She used it as reference and rose to the standards expected for such hosting: glass punch bowls and candelabra for receptions; properly arranged silverware for meals, along with beautiful place settings surrounding garnished platters of food; guest beds with fresh sheets. She radiated nobility throughout all of this.

For Mom and Dad, I suspect that living in this lovely, overly large, and gracious home, a part-time hospitality venue, was tiny comfort for taking over leadership of a college that was on the verge of insolvency. I was innocent of this backstory and simply enjoyed the activities, visitors, and the mesmerizing house. Its big advantage for my education was that Dad kept stocked a

Ethel Manning greeting guests at the entrance of the Matthew Simpson Memorial Home, Claflin College, ca. 1957, with Mrs. Carmen Thomason. Family album photo.

wonderful library in the large study. It was here that I first encountered and read several theological books, such as C. S. Lewis's *Screwtape Letters,* and began to think of religion as a topic worthy of study. The advantage of all that hospitality was that I learned from Mom how to multitask, host multiple guests while remaining calm, arrange events, and set a proper place setting.

My parents put all of their hearts into Claflin, giving up all other diversions save for family and Trinity. They eventually helped educate thousands of Black youths, a scale of constructive effort that amazes and humbles me. Dad eventually transformed the campus, for example erecting nine new buildings and rehabilitating many others, and Mom herself educated legions. Others have judged their twenty-eight-year stewardship of Claflin successful in several other ways, not appropriate for me to list in more detail than this;[51] my sister says simply, considering what he found in 1956, that "Dad saved Claflin." Turning elsewhere, I will discuss SC State for now, returning in a later chapter to say more about Claflin and my parents.

Two broad types of HBCUs existed then. The public HBCUs were creatures of their state governments and often had land-grant status under the Morrill Act but suffered from unfair revenue distributions and white political pressure.[52]

Reception in our dining room, Matthew Simpson Memorial Home,
Claflin College. Woman on the far right is Mrs. Winbush or Mrs. Rose;
man is Claflin professor Mr. Wright; woman with no hat is Mrs. Delarge.
Staff or sorority event. Courtesy Cecil Williams, photographer.

The private HBCUs had more freedom from white power structures and support
from church sponsors, as did Claflin, but also suffered from lack of government
funding. This made the job of presidents of private HBCUs heavily dependent
on fundraising but less dependent on white politicians.[53]

Because of this divide, SC State faced similar but different challenges than
did Claflin. SC State had state government resources, but these were inadequate.
It answered to an all-white board of trustees that was sometimes controlling.
Annual reports, overseen if not written by SC State's president, and other
sources—particularly William C. Hine's history—show SC State's tenacious
efforts to survive against debilitating odds. As with Claflin, efforts of SC State's
presidents and faculty were essential.

SC State's second president, Robert Shaw Wilkinson, clearly demonstrated
constructive resilience. Wilkinson, who served from 1911 until 1932, ably helped
SC State transition from industrial education to a full-fledged college. He

began his presidency under Governor Blease, who was openly hostile to Black education and a malignant force, requiring constant reassurance that the college was of value. Such assurance was necessary even after Blease left office, since white legislators—beholden to no Black electorate, since Black voters were disenfranchised—were of the same mind. Indifferent to the offering of actual college teacher training, state political leaders relented only when the state board of education indicated in 1915 that it would no longer accept normal training as teacher qualification. This almost wiped out the entire company of incoming Black teachers, but Black college presidents successfully argued for accepting normal school training until at least the late 1920s, by which time they were able to increase the number of college students and graduates.[54]

Despite minuscule resources siphoned from land-grant funds and diverted to white schools instead of SC State, President Wilkinson offered able leadership for the state's rural Black population. Trained in physics and chemistry, he nevertheless became a prime promoter of agricultural programs. After SC State received a small legislative grant in 1913, Wilkinson scheduled and attended most of twenty-two conferences held across the state, attracting over nineteen thousand farmers.[55] He used such activities to boost an extension system and help farmers both white and Black. The patent inequality in land-grant financing meant that such funding often went to white Clemson, which refused to supervise Black extension agents, requiring SC State to supervise them without any financial compensation. Throughout such petty denigrations, Wilkinson continued to lead in a cool, calm manner. He continued writing reports asking for funding for better salaries and facilities, year after year, working tirelessly to raise money for the school and to bring the legislators' attention to the value of SC State. Not prideful, Wilkinson offered gifts to white officials to try to buy their largesse, such as freshly baked fruitcakes, custom-made shirts and suits, and other tokens of the students' industrial work, continuing even when recipients were ungracious, expecting such largesse as their due.

Through such efforts the school inched forward. By his 1929–30 annual report, Wilkinson noted that enrollments had increased to 823 students in college, 745 students in summer sessions, and 123 in Felton Training School. The philanthropic GEB had provided fellowships for six faculty members to take leaves and attend northern universities for further study. The Rosenwald Fund and the US Department of Agriculture had hosted a gathering for extension agents from Tennessee, Texas, and South Carolina that met during the summer at SC State. Even white SC land-grant schools' extension agents from Clemson and Winthrop attended the two-week 1930 sessions, focused on hands-on work with home improvement, rural sanitation projects, and marketing of farm products.

Wilkinson called the whole, interracial venture "one of the most remarkable achievements in the history of the institution."[56]

Calamities unfurled and stalled further progress after the great crash of 1929. Enrollment dropped for fall, 1930 to 649 college students. As the Great Depression deepened, faculty and staff took pay cut after pay cut. Wilkinson, widely regarded as a capable manager, died suddenly at the age of sixty-seven in March 1932.[57]

Commentators of the time pointed out that Wilkinson had worked relentlessly, day and night. He had served as an exemplary civic leader as well as college president. For six years he was president of the all-Black Palmetto State Teachers' Association; he was a member of several fraternities, including Omega Psi Phi and the Elks; he was secretary of the Voorhees College Board of Trustees; he and his wife were active Episcopalians; and he built several campus buildings, including Felton, all while improving the college's curriculum. His wife, Marion Birnie Wilkinson, had organized the Sunlight Club, a community service organization founded by Orangeburg's Black faculty and spouses. She was president of the South Carolina Federation of Colored Women's Clubs, supported women's suffrage, and made sure that women were among the visiting speakers at SC State. Most notably she started Fairhold Home for Delinquent Girls, a former farmhouse near Columbia purchased and established as refuge for women in a state that had refused to expend funds for Black females needing rehabilitation instead of jail.[58] In such ways this couple made constructive contributions to the Black community.

Wilkinson's successor, Miller F. Whittaker, SC State president from 1932 to 1949, inherited economic depression and World War II, plus the first glimmerings of the civil rights era. Whittaker was a SC State faculty member and dean of mechanical arts. The trustees named the thirty-nine-year-old interim and then permanent president upon Wilkinson's death. Unmarried his whole life, he lived with his mother and apparently dedicated all of his energies to his job, save for occasional architectural projects. He was one of the state's first practicing Black architects; as a registered architect of record, he officially oversaw unlicensed professor William Wilkins's design of Trinity Church, and he designed several SC State campus buildings as well.[59]

Keeping SC State alive and its agenda viable was a struggle. SC State's weak salary structure compared to other Black land-grant colleges led to the loss of several valuable faculty. The GEB and federal programs supported construction of a library but required a match; after some procrastination the state provided this through a college bond bill issued in 1937 but gave SC State only a fraction of the money given to white universities.[60] Although the student enrollment was larger than Claflin's, reaching 917 college enrollees by 1940–41, it could absorb only a small fraction of the state's Black students of college age. The white board of trustees continually steered SC State into agricultural and mechanical offerings, even though surveyed students wanted to become teachers.[61]

SC State did not admit many would-be students simply because of lack of dormitory space. In 1940–41 SC State rejected 100 students for this reason, and 131 students faced such rejection in 1943–44.[62] Nevertheless Whittaker noted that the faculty were consulting about the postwar future, and he envisioned a purposeful, "interracial" future. Public schools would need better teachers, and "the new world will demand justice and freedom through interracial coopera-tion." The college would help meet such challenges, he promised.[63]

Material needs dominated this era, but which needs to address first varied by observer. The ancient boiler system broke down frequently, and Whittaker pleaded several times for funds to replace it in order to heat campus buildings. In the 1944–45 annual report, his first priorities were heat for the campus and dormitory space for undergraduates. Not so for a special committee of ten legislators who visited in March 1945. The visitors were impressed with "the very apparent ability of the President" but also lauded the vestiges of industrial education. They praised training "in fundamental labor as a basis for life," such as in the shoemaking shop, where they repaired the campus's shoes; the tailoring department, where they made suits for the trustees and other public officials; and the mechanical training class, which repaired motor vehicles.[64] They praised the care with which SC State maintained of its buildings and grounds but be-moaned the campus farm's lack of farm buildings. Their first priority was to complete the heating plant, but the second priority, "scarcely less important, is the erection of at least a moderate amount of housing space for farm animals and equipment on the farm." Third on their list was a new laundry building, and only fourth did they list dormitory space. Whittaker in writing his conclud-ing narrative had surely seen this list, but he said, "the most pressing need is dor-mitory space."[65] These were starkly different priorities: housing farm animals versus housing college students.

The resolution of these differing perspectives came as the state decided to invest instead in defending racial segregation. By 1945 the whole system of racial separation in higher education was at risk. The US Supreme Court in 1938 ordered the University of Missouri law school to admit a Black applicant because the state provided no other facility for him. The Missouri legislature appropriated money to open a separate "Jim Crow" law school at Lincoln, an HBCU, much to the chagrin of civil rights proponents in that state, who argued that such a school could not match in quality the white one.[66] Legislators tried but failed to set up such a law school at SC State in 1939. Increasing pressure led to the mandate that SC State prioritize graduate education and a new law school over housing either undergraduates or farm animals.

The background for this? Teachers in schools such as Charleston's Burke High School and Avery Institute were training students to understand the US Constitution's Thirteenth, Fourteenth, and Fifteenth Amendments as a way to comprehend their citizenship rights. One student from Avery's NAACP youth chapter, military veteran John Wrighten, applied to the local all-white municipal college, the College of Charleston, in 1943. They refused him, but then thirty-two Black high school students from an Avery democracy class applied as a class assignment to the College of Charleston. College trustees considered turning the municipal school private to rebuff them but finally offered ten scholarships to Charleston's Black students with the stipulation that they attend SC State.[67]

When Wrighten and other students arrived at SC State, they found it severely under-resourced and overcrowded; enrollment doubled between 1941 and 1947. The college had no faculty with earned PhDs, and only one-third of its faculty held master's degrees. During the 1930s and 1940s, the number of Black high school graduates in the state had tripled, with no increase in SC State's capacity. Occasional concessions were not enough to relieve a college built to contain perhaps eight hundred students but trying to educate many more. Students who arrived found other kindred souls from other high schools from throughout the state who verbalized their resentment of the systematic oppression of their education.[68]

In 1938 a Black student applied to the USC Law School, but he was simply turned down.[69] With federal district court rulings such as in Missouri, white lawmakers realized that another strategy was necessary to defend segregation. SC State's trustees asked the USC dean of the graduate school, W. H. Calcott, to visit SC State to consider its ability "to give graduate work."[70] Calcott considered strategies that other southern states were using for Black students. He recommended setting up some graduate programs at SC State for fields where demand was sufficient, such as education, but providing out-of-state scholarships for professions such as medicine and law. He pointed out that the college lacked basic facilities; creating a new law school just for Black students would be difficult because of the limited number of potential students.[71]

John Wrighten applied for admission into the USC Law School first in 1946 and then in 1947. His applications prodded the state legislature to ignore Calcott's advice to outsource Black law education and instead mandate that

SC State establish graduate programs and a law school. Wrighten continued to pursue a lawsuit asking for admission to USC. Summarizing his court case, argued by Thurgood Marshall before Judge Waring, reveals the difficult situation in which President Whittaker found himself.

In *Wrighten v. Board of Trustees of the University of South Carolina, et al.,* Marshall charged that the state offered law education to white but not Black residents. The state responded that it would offer legal training to Black residents at a forthcoming law school at SC State. His employers expected Whittaker to testify on behalf of the state. He did, but he responded truthfully to Marshall's probes, stating that no legal education was available for Black students in the state, that SC State had received no funds for such a law school, and that the college had no law professors, no law library, and inadequate classroom space even for its existing programs. Whittaker did testify that law facilities were possible in the future. When Marshall asked whether such an effort would produce the qualitative equal of USC's law school, Whittaker replied that he did not think so.[72]

This response ironically pleased both parties; Marshall remarked in a subsequent letter that he had found Whittaker's remarks courageous, while the state's defense attorney appreciated Whittaker's expressed willingness to try to set up a law school.[73] Waring announced his decision in July 1947, at the same time that he rejected the state Democratic Party's all-white primary system in *Elmore v. Rice*. By far the *Elmore v. Rice* case overshadowed the *Wrighten* case, but the second case had profound implications for higher education. Waring gave the state until September 1947 to set up a law school for Black students; if this did not happen, either the USC Law School would have to admit Black applicants or the state would have to dismantle its only law school.

Whittaker valiantly strove to set up a law school in less than three months. His first step was to hire as dean Benner C. Turner, a law professor from the all-Black North Carolina College of Law, who had both an undergraduate and a law degree from Harvard University as well as years working as a lawyer. Whittaker and Turner hired two additional law professors, and they set aside one classroom and bookshelves within the college library. They acquired hundreds of law books and admitted nine students, who began taking law courses two months after Judge Waring's decision.

Whittaker offered a perhaps unconsciously honest assessment in the 1946–47 annual report: "Last year the legislature *imposed* graduate work on the institution. . . . The legislature has requested that we offer courses in law, beginning next year, and authorizing [*sic*] that funds from the appropriation for graduate work may be spent for this purpose. It will be necessary to outline a first year curriculum."[74] Whittaker then stated what appears to have been truer to his heart. He reported that 1,443 students had enrolled for the regular session but that "it is impossible to house and feed all of these students, and even classrooms and laboratory facilities are overcrowded. Approximately one-half of our students are now forced to live (room and board) in the city of Orangeburg." He continued: "The institution has outgrown most of its present facilities. We need more classroom space, more office space, more laboratory space, and more dormitory space, if the College is to meet the needs of the State. This can only be met by some appropriations for buildings."[75]

In 1948 the General Assembly appropriated $200,000 for a new building but specified that this was to house SC State's law school and graduate programs. This was an enormous sum in relative terms; the school's total budget request for 1946–47 had been for $250,000 for functions other than graduate work or a law school.[76] Although the decision to open up a "Jim Crow" law school placated Judge Waring, it infuriated the NAACP's Simkins, who decried the law school and predicted that it would only prop up segregation. Wrighten did not enroll the first year, but he did the next, earning a law degree and eventually passing the bar. He did this on his fourth try, after the state's bar association, when it was clear that SC State would produce law graduates, changed its previous system of automatically welcoming all graduates to the bar and required new graduates to pass a bar exam.[77]

Over its nineteen-year existence, the law school for Black students never exceeded twenty students. It diverted possible resources not only from SC State undergraduates but also from the USC Law School, which in 1948 had five full-time faculty and nine part-timers for 342 white students, while SC State had a dean and three faculty for eight law students. The American Bar Association never accredited the SC State Law School, but its graduates made a lasting impression on South Carolina's civil rights struggle as they filed desegregation suits and represented arrested civil rights activists.[78]

In 1949 President Whittaker died suddenly of heart failure, at age fifty-six. Hine theorized that Whittaker died relatively early because of the stress of the job, and he offers as partial evidence for that a family history of longevity and the pace at which he worked.[79] We should add to this list the fact that Whittaker had, two years before his death, found himself at the center of a major court case challenging the two-tiered system of higher education. Add also that this talented man and path-breaking architect created a law school in less than three months' time as a service to his white employers, whose main motivation was to protect racial segregation. Add the fact as well that he did this knowing that his undergraduates were ill-housed in inadequate dorms and ill-served in cramped classrooms and labs.

As evidence of the high regard with which both Black and white leaders held him in spite of (or because of) this, consider the attendees at his funeral. These included Governor Strom Thurmond, the mayor of Orangeburg, other prominent white politicians, and Claflin's President Seabrook, as well as thousands of others.[80] At the funeral Morehouse's Benjamin E. Mays called Whittaker "a very, very, very, very good man."[81]

The next SC State president beginning 1950 was Benner C. Turner, former law school dean, a surprise choice for many of the faculty but someone with whom the white trustees evidently felt comfortable. He, too, struggled to keep SC State functioning and called out needs that the state legislature sometimes listened to and sometimes not. Indirectly the Clarendon County lawsuit *Briggs v. Elliott* led the state to increase spending on Black education in the early 1950s, but most of those benefits went to K-12 education.

Wilkinson and Whittaker had asked for functional campus heat and sufficient dormitories. Turner's most consistent requests were for funds to replace the Felton's aging building and for a simpler institutional mandate. In the 1955–56 report, he asked to expand Felton through twelfth grade, and in the 1960–61 report, he noted "one of the major needs of this school is a new building for the laboratory training school. We have mentioned this on numerous occasions to our superior officers . . . and here we reiterate our hope that this, which is the *single most urgent need* at South Carolina State College, may receive some attention in the immediate future."[82] This he requested because "the greatest problem which [SC State] has to solve rises from the fact that it is a multipurpose institution. It carries seven programs (five undergraduate and two graduate or professional) any one of which has sufficient educational responsibility to be handled by an institution in itself."[83] The college had too many programs. An expanded Felton could have helped SC State focus on teacher education. With four tight, two-grade classrooms, Felton could hardly "train." As I remember, it did not have space for even four additional student teachers, and we seldom saw more than one or two at a time.

Turner was a controversial personality. In 1967 the governor asked him to step down after student unrest. He was the SC State president with the most direct interaction with my own life. He gained office the year I was born, and he served throughout my education at Felton, which was under his supervision. He was a common topic in my own household, because he and Dad were two local HBCU presidents serving at the same time during 1956 to 1967. Turner improved academic life at SC State, but he also fired faculty and expelled students for opposing the status quo or supporting civil rights. He spoke truth to power in his annual reports, however, telling the state what it needed to do to improve SC State's academic integrity and help it train capable teachers.[84]

Conclusion

It was sometimes possible for the Black community to protect and educate at least some of its children. My own life growing up in Orangeburg is an example of protected, favorable circumstances. Felton, SC State's training school, was an exceptionally good school, perhaps representative of other segregated Black schools during that era that provided engaged teachers, diverse curricula, and excellent instruction.[85]

Most schools were less favored. The 1920s and 1930s saw improvement in physical structures for Black schools but neglect by white governments that continued to divert public funds to white schools. Black citizens paid regular taxes for an inequitable public school system but received only a fraction of the benefit that white taxpayers received. On top of that, Black people used their own funds and resources to leverage Rosenwald grants that enabled wooden schools that they often had to build themselves. They did this willingly and even eagerly, in service to their children, demonstrating sacrificial and constructive resilience.

Black people fought as well for the dignity of their own schoolteachers. In Charleston this meant getting the school district to hire Black teachers for Black schools, an initiative that required considerable effort but concretized unequal pay scales. By the 1940s the state's Black teachers sued for salary scales not based on race. South Carolina responded by eliminating race-based salaries, but it then adopted salary scales based on standardized tests that favored white teachers, and it failed to provide the educational resources that Black teachers would have needed to succeed in this environment.

Throughout this period at least two of the state's HBCUs faced an uphill battle training Black teachers and other professionals. My father took on Claflin's presidency under such constrained circumstances. In their reports SC State's presidents also discussed the difficulties they faced. Black children and youth needed schoolteachers as well as functioning HBCUs that produced them, but the larger society set up multiple roadblocks by continually insisting on industrial education and by underfunding Black K-12 and higher education. Nevertheless SC State and Claflin presidents kept their schools resourced and relevant to the needs of Black students and citizens. SC State presidents

Wilkinson and Whittaker, in particular, demonstrated heroism and humility in the face of tremendous odds. As for my father, he managed to bring Claflin through a dangerous period of insolvency, recovery from fire, and lack of accreditation. A naturally quiet man from humble circumstances, he credited the school's survival to supportive trustees and faculty, but surely his own talents must have contributed as well. These two Black institutions struggled toward a constructive vision of a better future that included Black higher education and teacher training in spite of all that stood in their way.

3

A Neighboring County Arises

Despite the relentless battles of pivotal court cases in the 1940s, race relations in South Carolina during the next decade settled into a pattern similar to life in previous decades. People lived in two separate racial worlds. One was white, privileged, and surrounded by a network of institutions dedicated to protecting white supremacy at all costs. The other was Black and oppressed by the same network of institutions and yet made advances in important if small ways. Those ways included building Rosenwald schools, securing higher salaries for at least some Black teachers, and supporting organizations that could challenge the status quo. Those ways also involved maintaining Black colleges as constructive insurance policies for the future, enabling at least some Black people to gain higher education and thus assist their communities as teachers, lawyers, other professionals, homemakers, and purveyors of skilled crafts and trades.

At times these opposing racial worlds collided, such as when Black people refused to continue to submit to unreasonable subjugation, especially for their children, and white racists refused to give it up. The best example is the circumstances surrounding *Briggs v. Elliott,* one of the four cases that accompanied *Brown*. *Briggs* is not only a pivotal case in US history but also a remarkable example of two forces at work. These forces were constructive resistance on the part of the local Black community, determined to provide for the well-being of its children, and disturbing white supremacist repression on the part of white locals, equally determined to preserve white privilege. *Briggs* had major implications for public education for Black South Carolinians. The implications will become clear as the story unfolds, but here is a short synopsis: That case, formally argued in 1951, caused a positive change in the financing of South Carolina's public school education. This happened as white political leaders sought to maintain segregation by upgrading Black schools as part of their legal defense. Within a few short years, this case transformed public education in my home state in some ways but not in others.

This case gives further insight into the question of how Black South Carolinians were able to provide better public education for their children despite an ironclad system of institutional racism via underfunding of segregated Black schools. In part Black community progress emerged because of the power of community organization, illustrated in this story, but also because of good leadership. Pivotal as well was a friendly federal district court judge. This chapter relies on published histories but occasionally taps personal memories.

Situating Clarendon County

The case's main actors lived a very short car ride away from my own hometown and yet worlds away from Orangeburg's everyday life. The town of Summerton, the case's epicenter, is less than thirty miles as the crow flies from the town of Orangeburg. Clarendon County, containing Summerton, lies directly northeast of and adjacent to Orangeburg County. On county-line maps, Orangeburg County looks like a fat bent arm ending in a right-hand fist, and Clarendon County is the rag, cloth, or flame—depending on your perspective—that the fist is holding. On county-line maps that also show bodies of water, another large irregular object, Lake Marion, is located at the place where the fist meets the flame but within Clarendon County. That lake is so large that some refer to it as an inland sea.

Nowadays Lake Marion has a major bridge carrying traffic above it although at first, for several years, it did not. Artificially created in 1941 by flooding farms and homes as part of a New Deal project constructing the Santee Hydroelectric Dam, this lake displaced almost one thousand residents, mostly Black. As this project rearranged these residents spatially, it complicated accessibility and aggravated already overcrowded Black schools.

I have vivid memories as a child of riding over that lake, via the bridge built by the 1950s; as we traversed that long passage, I could see stripped, dark brown tree trunks sitting in the water like angry ghosts, watching us. The bridge seemed endless, threatening in some way. My father, as he drove, told us many times that this "manmade" lake brought much misery to the people who lived in that region and that those tree trunks and those waters sat where fields and forests, and people's homes, used to sit. He often said that one particular school was very important. He pointed to a school building as we drove that seemed like every other modern school I had seen in my life, and it looked unremarkable to my unknowing eyes. He said that this was a school, Scott's Branch, about which Black people had fought very hard.

White and Black high schools in Orangeburg and Clarendon Counties, South Carolina, 1937. White dots represent white high schools, and one black dot represents one Black high school. Courtesy of the South Carolina Department of Education, from "A Survey of School Buildings Grounds and Equipment in South Carolina," Division of School House Planning, assisted by State Planning Board, 1937, 21.

Much later in life I realized the importance of his words and chastised myself, once again, for giving him only partial attention when he tried to explain local history: this lake is a major origin point for battles against inferior, segregated schools in this country. The school was the epicenter of a minor revolution. South Carolina had many poor rural counties in the 1940s and 1950s. It also had many places where facilities for white schools exceeded facilities for Black schools. They did not have this lake; because of it Black parents in Clarendon County found the inferior public schools, such as the previous Scott's Branch school buildings, unbearable.

These parents' concerns, at first about lack of school bus transportation, led to a landmark court case overshadowed by the more famous *Brown*. Only by a quirk of fate is *Brown v. Board of Education of Topeka* the known name of the US Supreme Court's 1954 ruling; the *Briggs v. Elliott* case preceded *Brown* both alphabetically and in timing. Among the possible reasons that *Brown* and Topeka became famous, rather than *Briggs* and Clarendon County, is the deflective action of South Carolina's governor, James F. Byrnes. According to his biographer, Byrnes, who was intimately familiar with US Supreme Court procedures because he had once served as a justice on that court, managed to ensure that *Brown* appeared on the docket ahead of the case from South Carolina.[1]

Black parents in Clarendon County pursued several actions seeking justice, culminating in *Briggs*. First, in the mid-1940s, they petitioned for school bus transportation for Black children. In a subsequent lawsuit, they pressed for equal school facilities for Black students, and then again in a third suit they petitioned for full desegregation, arguing on the advice of the NAACP LDF that separate systems were fundamentally unequal.[2]

As the 1937 Department of Education survey carried out by Federal Emergency Relief Administration workers revealed, stark contrasts between Black and white schools were typical for South Carolina. Most counties required Black pupils to clean their own school buildings. Homemade benches or desks were rare in white school buildings, but Black pupils commonly used homemade benches and, to a lesser extent, homemade desks. Similarly the overwhelming majority of counties provided no lavatory facilities in Black public schools. The 6-0-1 funding system set up in 1924 used state monies for local school districts, but wealthier counties or districts could contribute more if they had the resources. As one of the state's poorest counties, Clarendon County's school districts were especially motivated to prioritize white school facilities. As elsewhere in the state, authorities left numerous Black schools to fend for themselves with uneven Rosenwald support, while that lasted, and self-help.[3]

Another statewide characteristic of those days was insufficient school bus transportation for Black children, but Clarendon County's system was a particular problem. The county provided thirty school buses for white students and none for Black students. The lake that the Santee Hydroelectrical Dam created posed an extreme hazard during flood season; the waters often cut off many of the Black students' walking routes. Some of them used dangerous rowboats to traverse the waters. Many of them walked miles each way to get to school, and sometimes buses passed them carrying white children who harassed them or threw objects at them.[4]

Their families had little ability to change these conditions. In the 1940s Black people made up 70 percent of the county population, but they worked as tenants, contractors, or sharecroppers on mostly white-owned land. Even Black landowners eked out a living with high debt loads and low or negative profit margins, and farm tenants labored hard in cotton or tobacco fields. Black people who did not work in agriculture did menial jobs such as domestic work or truck loading, and most had received no education past seventh grade; their children went to schools located in thirty separate school districts, in crudely constructed buildings with two, three, or four rooms. Segregated public schools had three times as many Black as white pupils in 1951, but per pupil expenditures for white students outnumbered expenditures for Black students by 300 percent. The financial value of school buildings for white students in 1945 was over four times the value of school buildings for Black students.[5]

The results were obvious disparities in school facilities. Judge Waring, a member of the three-judge panel that considered *Briggs*, later recalled that he had seen, while driving through Clarendon County, mean little wooden shacks with outdoor toilets, the schools for Black children, in sharp contrast to schools with running water and other amenities for white students.[6] In Summerton one school for Black students used wooden boards propped on top of fifty-five-gallon cans for seating. Another school required boys to maintain the building's heat and girls to keep school facilities clean; yet another, serving six hundred students, had only two toilets outdoors. Summerton's Scott's Branch School, which included elementary and high school grades, lacked a gymnasium and science lab, and it had no higher mathematics or non-basic English classes. The Black schools' shabby state was so obviously inferior that the school district's out-of-town defense attorney, Robert Figg, after arriving from Charleston to view Summerton's schools in preparation for his opening statement in the *Briggs* trial, dropped local school officials' absurd argument that Black and white school facilities were essentially equal. He instead pleaded before the court for time to equalize them.[7]

The arduous effort to change this situation is a heroic story of courage. Several books offer details, such as the narrative *Dawn of Desegregation* by Ophelia De Laine Gona, the main community leader's daughter. These books sometimes differ in details about this case.[8] I draw primarily on Gona's narrative, the latest and most heavily documented account, illumined by both interviews and firsthand experience, to illustrate two themes: constructive resistance and white supremacist repression. Black parents and their advocates lacked social, political, or economic influence, but they demonstrated vision and courage in the face of retaliation. Legal assistance and the presence of a capable local leader helped, but white locals opposed even modest requests to improve

Black education, as if inferior Black school facilities reflected the natural order of things. As Black residents broadened their unaddressed requests to improve conditions, white locals retaliated with oppressive and even violent tactics.

Resisting Oppression

The main Black community leader, Rev. Joseph Armstrong De Laine, belonged to the AME Church, an important source of independence because of the AME's complete separation from white Christian churches.[9] He was also relatively independent financially; he learned business and carpentry skills as well as teacher training at AME-sponsored Allen University. He earned his 1931 bachelor's degree at the age of thirty-three, and throughout the next few years increased his financial independence by buying property and working several jobs at a time, avoiding debt. By the late 1930s he was principal of a three-room, six-grade school in a small town near Summerton. De Laine helped found his county's NAACP branch in 1943, and he assisted in a statewide campaign to end the all-white Democratic primary system after Judge Waring ruled upon *Elmore v. Rice* in 1947. It took some years, however, for that legal victory to translate into political access, because of successful efforts to suppress the Black vote. Local, county, and state government continued for some time under the control of white segregationists.

When the AME Church assigned De Laine to Society Hill Church in 1940, the negative effects of dam construction were becoming obvious. The gradual multiyear flooding of adjacent land started before workers could completely clear out houses and trees, leaving these below the surface and making passage dangerous for rowboats, prone to capsizing, but this is how several schoolchildren and parishioners had to travel to schools and churches. This situation, combined with the already long walks Black schoolchildren had to take, led parents to plead for some form of relief. Two groups of parents, in 1943 or 1944, asked white local authorities for school bus transportation, but authorities said they did not have enough money to transport Black children. After the drowning of an AME Church member's grandson, who answered a playmate's dare by jumping from a rowboat into the murky water, never to resurface alive, Black parents grew increasingly concerned. Several parents came together and bought a decrepit and unreliable used bus formerly used as a chicken coop. When that inevitably broke down, they bought another heavily used formerly "white" bus, but that too broke down often. Parents formed a committee and went to the county superintendent, L. B. McCord, to ask for financial assistance to maintain the parent-owned bus; De Laine was lead spokesperson. McCord refused their entreaties, telling the parents they did not pay enough taxes to deserve a bus "for Nigra children."[10] At this point it was clear that appeals would not produce results. The struggle for racial equality in education had reached a new stage of urgency, necessitating legal strategies.

Turning to Legal Strategies

De Laine helped start the battle that at first aimed for school buses. By then principal of an elementary school in Silver, north of Summerton, he was taking a course at Allen University in the summer of 1947 when he attended a lecture by James Hinton, president of the state NAACP branch. Hinton detailed the obvious denial of educational opportunities for Black students in the state and challenged attendees to act on that injustice. He called for Black parents or teachers with "courage" enough to file the lawsuit needed to challenge unequal school facilities. Hinton's statement provided a potential answer for De Laine's frustrations with the school bus situation, and he promised Hinton that he would bring in a prospective plaintiff within the week.[11]

De Laine began to recruit plaintiffs. He met with his farmer neighbors, brothers Hammett and Levi Pearson, who were at first hesitant but then stepped forward and petitioned the school board for bus transportation for their children, even though they realized this action would put them in grave danger. They needed only financial backing, which De Laine promised to, and did, provide personally. The next week, De Laine and Levi Pearson met with Hinton, a PSTA officer, and Columbia's Black attorney Harold Boulware. With their help the virtually illiterate Pearson signed a two-page petition dated July 28, 1947, that asked his school district trustees for school bus transportation for his children. Hearing nothing, Pearson signed another letter, dated December 16, 1947, stating that he was referring the situation to Boulware. In February 1948 the local school board scheduled a hearing that brought no satisfaction.

In March 1948 Boulware filed the first case, *Levi Pearson v. Clarendon County and School District No. 26*. Although Thurgood Marshall traveled to the state to assist Boulware, in the end this first lawsuit was withdrawn. Several accounts describe why; one source says that the white defendants investigated and claimed that Pearson's property straddled two districts. Goya, however, suggests that the county surreptitiously gerrymandered Pearson's property after the filing to make it appear that he should have paid taxes to nearby School District 6 rather than School District 26, where he had sent taxes up until that time and where his immediate neighbor paid his taxes. Local school officials gleefully gloated that Pearson did not know what district he lived in.

Although that lawsuit died, Pearson's heroism drew both the great admiration of Black citizens and the ire of white citizens. He suffered in a way that made it clear that white locals would punish a Black parent who merely asked for bus transportation readily provided to white children. Every white-owned store and bank in the county cut off Pearson's line of credit. That year he had enough cash for seeds but not for fertilizer; he cut down trees to sell for fertilizer money, but the mill refused to pick his timber up when they learned who was selling it. Although Black locals collected enough money to buy his fertilizer, that fall he could find no white farmer who would let him borrow a harvester, which had not been a problem in the past, and he watched his wheat and oats and beans rot in the fields. White locals told him if he would just forget about the NAACP and school buses everything would go back to normal, but he refused to give up.[12]

In January 1949 De Laine, the Pearsons, and a few other attendees approached Boulware at a state NAACP meeting and raised again the bus inequity issue. In March 1949 Boulware invited De Laine to meet in Columbia and bring along people from Clarendon County. The meeting also included NAACP branch officers, the NAACP LDF's Marshall, and PSTA officers. Marshall surprised attendees by stating that his organization would no longer consider a Clarendon County lawsuit. Instead of focusing on bus equality, it would pursue a broader issue, school equalization, with cases in other parts of the country. When the alarmed parents pleaded, offering to do whatever was necessary to find justice for their children, Marshall at first did not relent, explaining his rationale as the need to attack the whole system of unequal schools. The group of rural folk refused to accept no for an answer. In desperation they pledged that they would file suit for equalization if necessary. Marshall finally relented but set conditions. He said having only one plaintiff would be too dangerous because of white reprisals; only with at least twenty Clarendon County families signing a petition would he ask the national office for permission to litigate. If they could find twenty families, the request would be for equal treatment for all school facilities, not just school buses.[13]

It is worthwhile to take a moment to consider the significance of this requirement. The Black community's main concern was lack of bus transportation, but Marshall was asking them to find twenty Black litigants who would request equal schools in racially oppressive Clarendon County. This seemed all but impossible to the small contingent of community leaders. De Laine himself had provided a considerable amount of his own funds and personal energy to fight the school bus issue, and now everything needed to begin all over again with a new lawsuit. He and his teammates, including fellow AME minister Reverend James Seals, held a series of meetings seeking people willing to sign such a petition. Because of the stark example of Levi Pearson's sufferings, it was hard to get petitioners. The parents most energized about school inequality lived in rural areas, but lawyers urged strategic focus upon one school district in the towns of either Manning or Summerton.

Summerton parents' support emerged because their teenagers arose in anger. Black students attending Scott's Branch School—located in the precursor to the school building that Dad had pointed out to me many times—ranged from first to twelfth grade. Students who graduated from twelfth grade in 1949 had suffered a number of indignities. A year before, the school board had fired their respected former high school principal because of his perceived support for the Pearson lawsuit. The newly installed principal was incapable of keeping disciplinary order. When students complained about not receiving the textbooks they had rented, this new principal told them that he could spend their money as he pleased. He also failed to show up to teach his own math classes most of the time. The students wrote up their grievances and sent them to several parties, including county superintendent McCord. With De Laine's support graduating seniors organized a protest meeting for June 8, 1949; about three hundred angry parents attended.

This was the opportunity that was needed; Summerton parents were angry and ready to act. In a masterfully orchestrated effort, a small team that included De Laine prepared for the evening, which unfolded as if it were the centerpiece of a well-thought-out play.

After hearing the students' grievances, parents discussed the need for someone willing to become their spokesperson. When no one arose to take on the charge, parents gradually realized that De Laine had the necessary skills and background to do this. De Laine at first declined, stating concern for his job and expressing a fear that people would not stick with him if he accepted leadership. They asked again; he declined again, but this was merely a tool to raise the level of enthusiastic commitment. He feigned, telling them that the inevitable harassment that would arise from white locals would make them fall by the wayside and blame him in the process. The passionate audience shouted their denials—they would support him, no matter the cost. Thus buoyed, he finally accepted service as chair of a parent action committee, to a chorus of acclamations. He then declared his own unwavering commitment, even if their case for equality brought hostile action and extended all the way to the US Supreme Court (which it did); he was not afraid. Two days later his school board fired him. School trustees also fired any sympathetic teachers and refused to dismiss the objectionable principal.

Despite pressures from powerful actors, the community refused to stop meeting regularly, appealing to officials and demanding justice. When matters did not calm down, the trustees finally called a hearing to hear grievances against the incompetent Scott's Branch principal. Several ministers tried to prepare the students and their parents for the hearing, because to speak out took enormous courage; they lived in a place where white supremacy permeated every aspect of life. The more confident speakers helped prepare humbler folk to testify in part by teaching them to recite the US Constitution's First Amendment as a way to stoke faith in their right to speak out. More than three hundred Black people showed up at the October 1, 1949, hearing, and several spoke about the need for a new principal, as well as other school reforms requested by the graduating seniors. Attorney Boulware drove from Columbia but turned over most of the presentation to De Laine. Black attendees then witnessed two Black men speaking for justice in a public hearing chaired by powerful white officials, a first in many of their lives.

In due time the school board forced the objectionable principal to resign and rehired two of the fired teachers, but it made no other improvements to the wretched conditions of the Scott's Branch School. The local school superintendent tried to get De Laine to stop the parents' outcries and offered him the carrot of the job of principal of the Scott's Branch School, but the minister recognized this as no solution if underfunding and racial oppression continued, and he considered this attempt to buy him off an insult to his honor as well.

By this time parents were determined to file a lawsuit, and it was easier to recruit plaintiffs. The lawyers sent required petition papers to De Laine, who picked them up at the local post office in full view of a hostile group of white residents on November 11, 1949. Rather than risk holding a big meeting in which people would sign the petition, since "handkerchief head" informants pervaded community meetings, the lawyers advised holding such a gathering in a private home.[14] Harry and Eliza Briggs, parents of 5 children, agreed to host the meeting, and they were the first to sign. The petition filed included 104 names, 29 adults and 75 children. It claimed that the deplorable conditions facing Black students attending public school in Clarendon County violated rights guaranteed by the Fourteenth Amendment of the US Constitution,[15] and it asked for school facilities for Black students equal to those for white. The district's board of trustees first stalled, then replied a few months later, after continued pressure from De Laine, that the county's facilities for Black students were not inferior to the white facilities. The petitioners filed a second lawsuit in response, but in November 1950 the federal circuit court's presiding judge, Waring, indicated to Marshall that winning a judgment for equal facilities would not solve the greater problem of segregation in public school education. Following his advice, Marshall withdrew this second case, *Briggs et al. v. Board et al.*

In order to file a third lawsuit targeting enforced school segregation itself—now named *Briggs et al. v. Elliott et al.*—De Laine and his team had to start all over again to recruit eligible plaintiffs who were willing to weather repression.

This was a pivotal moment in US history and in the history of the civil rights movement. A friendly Deep South judge had advised an NAACP attorney to abandon equalized expenditures as a strategy for Black education and to seek instead racial desegregation of public schools.

De Laine and his colleagues succeeded in finding plaintiffs for the new *Briggs*. The trial would take place not just in front of Judge Waring, and that was a setback. Instead a three-judge panel was required, because the suit challenged the state constitution. In their final judgment, two majority judges did not agree with the plaintiffs that school segregation was inherently unequal and instead accepted the argument that the school system and the state were working to equalize facilities for Black students. Judge Waring's brilliant written dissent provided a virtual roadmap for an appeal and therefore for future litigation challenging state laws requiring school segregation. Soon after this ruling, the ostracism and harassment that Judge Waring and his wife faced from fellow white Charlestonians escalated, compelling them to leave the state and move to New York.

White Retaliation Intensifies

Summerton's Black petitioners displayed great fortitude under duress. Harry Briggs immediately lost a job he had held for fourteen years. His wife, a housekeeper in a Summerton motel for six years, was told to leave if she didn't get her husband's name off the petition, which she refused to do, and so she lost that job. The couple stayed in the county for four years, trying to farm on rented land, but they could not get the credit necessary to operate. Unable to find a job in South Carolina, Briggs moved from place to place to support his family, living first in Miami and then New York, finally sending for his family to join him after many years apart.[16]

Of the twenty-nine families who signed the equalization petition, all refused to remove their names, and eighteen of them signed on again for the subsequent desegregation petition. Gona gives a detailed list of these "true American heroes."[17] They included a struggling single mother, tenant farmers, laborers, and war veterans who did not remove their names from the petition even in the face of threats and repercussions.

All of the petitioners suffered, losing jobs, having long-terms debts called in for repayment, and being unable to obtain supplies or equipment to carry out their trades or till their soil. One person from the plaintiff list died under murky circumstances, when a car mysteriously fell on him as he repaired it. Another petitioner stopped along a road as his family sat in the car; a passing, irate white man recognized him as a petitioner and beat him to death. This act, in keeping with the southern system of racial injustice, had no legal repercussions for the white murderer but terrorized the victim's family. Here is an account of the beating, by De Laine's niece: "Mrs. Richburg . . . told us about the Caldwell man that was kicked to death in the presence of his nieces and nephews because he went to the bathroom, got off his wagon and went into the woods. Came back and this white man in his little T-Model Ford got out and actually kicked him in his privates until he killed him in front of those children. Family never talked about it. . . . So the fear must be so deep that even now they don't discuss it."[18]

De Laine soon began to receive threats as well. Several white men gathered in a living room and plotted how to kill or at least severely injure the minister and get him blamed in the process; only because a coconspirator's wife secretly sent a warning about the plot to De Laine is the existence of this meeting known. This white wife, a school district employee, had once witnessed De Laine cite biblical scripture in a very affecting manner before a mundane meeting, and this incident apparently impressed her. Her husband's friends recruited as henchman a "Mr. Crawler" (pseudonym) who among Black locals was widely suspected of attending Black community meetings as an undercover agent. One reason for this distrust was that Crawler, "Black" according to social dictates but extremely fair-skinned and with a reputed quick temper, had several times disparaged all Black people while claiming that all of his friends were white. Consistent with the reported living room plot, Crawler, a large and hulking man, confronted De Laine on a public street in broad daylight and threatened to kill him on the spot. As planned, several white coconspirators stood waiting across the street, ready to support Crawler either physically or in court. Any jury would believe whatever the white men said about who was at fault, and these men planned to protect Crawler even if he killed De Laine. De Laine escaped because luckily he had a pocketknife in his pocket. He pointed it at the bully, using his coat as cover, and frightened Crawler into thinking he had a gun.

Several people approached De Laine to warn of other plots to take his life, and a mysterious fire burned down his Summerton parsonage as firefighters stood by. The school district's trustees persuaded the aggrieved and likely crooked dismissed principal of Scott's Branch School to sue De Laine for slander, as a form of revenge and a way to recoup the costs of the school desegregation battles. As was typical, only white men sat on the jury. Superintendent McCord knew the truth—he had heard extensive testimony from the parents and students themselves—but he testified that De Laine slandered the principal.

The jury awarded a judgment against De Laine leading to a fine of five thousand dollars, a considerable amount, says De Laine's daughter: "The total annual income of a Black family with two people working as teachers would probably have been considerably less."[19]

Because of this series of harassments, De Laine's supervising bishop persuaded him to move to Florence County's Lake City, a place that the bishop thought was a relatively safe haven. Lake City, however, had a history of Ku Klux Klan terrorism. There De Laine encountered irate white citizens. Stirring them up was Clarendon County's defense attorney, who traveled to Lake City to help form a white citizens' council and to alert white locals to De Laine's role in equalization and desegregation lawsuits. This made him a marked man in his new city and led to what he later called a "general terror campaign" against his family by "night-riding thugs."[20] Someone broke his windows and fired shots at his Lake City home; he received little assistance from the police.

Such incidents highlight the extent that white racial terrorism played in maintaining white supremacy during those years. They suggest a deeply engrained racist pathology that pushed white locals to do anything—harass, lie, cheat, punish—necessary to avoid granting Black students even modest facility improvements, such as a school bus or seating or a competent school principal. In Gona's account only a few white allies, notably Judge Waring and minor actors such as the living room plotter's wife, emerge in any way as having acted admirably. The social pressures facing the few courageous white people who dared to disagree with the harassment must have been strong since racist extremist views were "normal."[21]

Even though the petitioners were at first only objecting to poor school conditions, their actions threatened the existing social order. Several Black petitioners and leaders experienced arson, loss of jobs, and continued economic retaliation extending over several years. Wholesalers refused to sell to plaintiffs who were small business owners, and delivery people refused to deliver goods. Gona says: "They were refused service in stores, credit for farm essentials, loans from banks, and rental of farm equipment."[22] Such mean-spirited retributions had lasting effects for victims. Reverdy Wells, the student class president of the high school seniors who rallied parents to action and school valedictorian at graduation, was never able to attend college. Mysteriously, after his military service, he found out that his doctored high school records showed him as failing all classes. Not until 1991 did Wells receive a corrected transcript.

In several accounts De Laine emerges as a principled and constructive resistance leader who urged his charges to be loyal to one another and to a vision of improved education for their children. His knowledge of scripture was strong enough to impress the white woman who warned him of danger, and his sense of destiny helped give courage to his rural, undereducated companions. He continued his service as a minister and offered notable service to that statewide AME Church even during the heat of conflict.

Although in 2004 De Laine (posthumously), Levi Pearson, and Harry and Eliza Briggs received congressional gold medals as leaders in school desegregation,[23] De Laine suffered in exile for the rest of his life. Authorities charged him after he defended his house and his life on October 10, 1955, in Lake City. After a car with cruising white men fired two shots at his house, the minister fired back, aiming at the body of the car to visibly mark it (for later identification, as a police officer had advised him). In the moments thereafter, he realized the unlikelihood that he and his family could remain at their home. In that society self-defense was no excuse for a Black man to return fire from white men, even in self-defense. Heeding previous advice offered by many people to leave the state, he got into his car that same evening and drove to nearby Florence, where friends helped him fly to Washington, DC; his family later joined him. Lake City authorities immediately filed charges of assault the next day, making him a fugitive. He moved to New Jersey and then to New York, founding an AME church. Just before he died, in 1974, he moved to Charlotte, North Carolina, closer to and yet apart from South Carolina.[24]

Gains Painfully Won

Black South Carolinians throughout the state knew about the *Briggs* case, in part because of a Black alternative press. Throughout the various legal battles, John Henry McCray's pioneering newspaper, the *Lighthouse and Reformer*, gave sympathetic coverage to the ongoing drama. Until McCray suffered repercussions that forced him to shut down the paper in 1954—authorities charged him with slander as a way to repress his writings and put him in prison with hard labor for violating a punitive three-year parole—he championed the efforts of the Clarendon parents and their leaders.[25] Anyone associated with the Black teachers' association or the NAACP would also have known of this case, described along with other legal battles in statewide annual conferences. Such awareness further signaled to civil rights proponents that matters were changing. The striking down of the white Democratic primary in *Elmore v. Rice* was a potential door to political freedom to help select politicians and school boards. *Briggs* had narrower scope but was important in another way; it gave hope that justice for Black children would soon prevail.[26]

The effects among Black people were not long in coming. The 1951 *Briggs* hearing in Charleston provided a joyous spectacle. Black people turned out in large numbers to witness opening arguments presented before Judges Waring, George Bell Timmerman Sr., and John Parker, presiding. A caravan of battered cars and trucks left Clarendon County to attend the trial, seventy miles away in Charleston. Hundreds of Black people traveled there in jubilation, even though several had received threats of job loss if they did not show up to work that day. Along the route bystanders came out to watch the triumphant procession. At the Charleston courthouse, ropes were necessary to keep the crowds back; Black faces filled all courtroom seats to overflowing, and very few white faces were visible. The largely Black audience saw an amazing sight, indeed: an eminent Black attorney, Thurgood Marshall, who publicly cross-examined and rebuked white officials in a courtroom where traditions of white supremacy did not pre-determine the outcome. Afterward dozens of Black attendees left their seats and converged upon Marshall, trying to shake his hand in admiration.[27]

Although Figgs's acknowledgement that Clarendon County's school facilities were unequal undercut Marshall's planned legal arguments to some extent, he called expert witnesses that nevertheless had great effect. Kenneth and Mamie Clark, a married couple who were both psychologists, had been experimenting for some years with young Black children, showing that they unerringly preferred white dolls as "good" over Black dolls, "bad." This was evidence that they had absorbed, internally, the many signals the larger society sent that Black skin was inherently inferior. This research and testimony proved compelling, and later formed a part of the *Brown* lawyers' arguments before the US Supreme Court.

Although the Charleston trial signaled future victory, several years had passed since parents' first requests for buses and from the drowning until the 1949 filing of *Briggs*. Another wait was necessary until the 1951 Charleston trial, and yet again until appeal and various delays finally led to the US Supreme Court announcing the composite *Brown* decision in 1954, with clarification in 1955. In the interim some Black South Carolina schools' physical conditions improved because of the litigation. This was a positive development but also part of the state's efforts to block school desegregation.

Because the improvement in conditions came in defensive reaction to the *Briggs* filing, the Clarendon County parents and students were in effect sacrificial lambs for the sake of better educational facilities for both races. White state officials decided to heed the previously ignored separate but equal principle by finally stepping up to the "equal" part as a way to protect segregated schools. Led by Governor Byrnes, who in his 1951 governor's inaugural address called such a move both "right" and "wise" given pending litigation, the state legislature in 1951 authorized a 3-percent sales tax to help pay for bonds funding

$75 million, to start, for school facility upgrades. In April 1951 the legislature approved this plan a short one month before the *Briggs* hearing in Charleston. Defense lawyers for the state and the school system then relied upon these just-in-time improvement plans to defend school segregation by citing imminent plans to improve schools for Black students.[28]

Although not all of that money went to improve Black schools, because pressure arose to include construction projects for white schools, a considerable portion did benefit Black students. In 1954 the governor claimed that between 1951 and 1954 the state consolidated 1,200 school districts into 102 and eliminated 824 inferior rural school buildings, including 287 for white pupils and 537 for Black pupils. In those three years, the number of Black students transported by public school buses rose from 29,166 to 78,567, leading to substantial transportation equality for the two races, and facility-improvement expenditures averaged $106 for white pupils but $271 for Black pupils, flipping decades of lopsided allocations the other way.[29] Between 1951 and 1956, the state program spent $124 million on schools and buses, two-thirds going to Black schools. Black pupils in Clarendon County finally received a new Scott's Branch School, the building that Dad had pointed out to me many times. The state spent $894,000 for Black school construction and only $103,000 for white schools in Clarendon County's District 22, after years of inequity.[30] There and elsewhere in the state, appropriations led to many new, consolidated school facilities, effectively eliminating one-teacher rural schools.

The state's political leaders cited many justifications for their move from purposeful underfunding of Black public schools to massive investment in them. Governor Byrnes was the key spokesperson for the state's rationale. On the one hand, in his 1951 inaugural address, Byrnes presented a positive picture of the possibilities for improving the state overall and specifically education for public school students. He noted that "a primary responsibility of a State is the education of its children," and referring to the Clarendon County case, he urged action as a way to forestall litigation. "It must be our goal to provide for every child in this State, white or colored, at least a graded education" as well as to provide "for the races substantial equality in school facilities."[31]

Nevertheless, in this same speech he noted that seventeen states plus the District of Columbia provided separate schools as sanctioned over fifty years before by *Plessy v. Ferguson.* He opined that the Eisenhower administration, which was urging the US Supreme Court to declare segregation laws unconstitutional, would "thereby endanger the public school system in many States"; this would happen because the state of South Carolina and other states would "abandon the public school system" rather than see it racially integrated. In a 1954 speech, he declared that he and the people of his state were not "prejudiced against the Negro," and he cited as proof his funding of Black public schools as well as his support for SC State funds.[32] At the same time, he marginalized proponents for civil rights, indicating that he wanted interference from neither the violence-prone Ku Klux Klan nor the NAACP, as if they were equally objectionable. For Black people, he suggested, "negro preachers do not want their congregations to leave them and attend the churches of white people," and the majority did not want to "force their children into white schools." Thus, ignoring the example of parents in Clarendon County, he attributed school desegregation efforts to "professional agitators."[33]

Byrnes urged white citizens to support upgrading of Black (and white) schools as a civic duty and noted that "it must be the duty of humane white people of the State as individuals to see that innocent Negro children are not deprived of an education because of false leaders," hinting at noble motivations. At the same time, he verbalized fears of potential desegregation. He predicted that forcing white children to attend classes with large numbers of Black children would lead to "racial conflicts between children," and these would lead to "conflicts between parents. I fear that hatred and discord would supplant the peaceful relations now existing." "Peaceful relations," of course, meant continual subjugation of the Black population. Although he claimed a wish to act in humane ways, he also played the role of doomsayer, claiming in 1954: "Unless we find a legal way of preventing the mixing of races in the schools, it will mark the beginning of the end of civilization in the South as we have known it."[34] This was precisely true. Whereas Governor Byrnes saw this as a potential tragedy, others would have seen it as a necessary step toward justice.

Other white South Carolinians had varying degrees of Governor Byrnes's mix of gentility and prejudice. Clearly understanding the implications of *Briggs,* wary of the reliability of the federal government as a defender of their brand of segregation, and yet moving away from the visible violence personified by the Ku Klux Klan, in the early 1950s the state's white political and social leaders organized defensive action. They did this in the state legislature as well as in the press, and ordinary white citizens began to meet all over the state to consider next steps.

Educational problems for Black students remained deeply entrenched. The rate of Black adult total or functional illiteracy was high, above 60 percent compared to 18 percent of white adults in 1948. By the mid-1950s school buildings were newer, but Black students' drop-out rate was high. Instruction offered in Black schools was inferior and less varied than in white. Well into the 1960s, most of the state's enrollees in brick masonry classes studied in Black high schools, while the majority of enrollees in shorthand, Latin, advanced algebra, and mechanical drawing studied in white high schools. The state instructed all teachers to avoid "controversial" topics such as racial integration. The instructional guides that it issued, for topics such as social studies and history, glorified southern white culture, supported "states' rights"—a common cause for segregationists—and defended racially separate schools as part of South Carolinians' way of life.[35]

The 1950 census showed that many Black residents had already decided how to respond to oppressive conditions. The early to mid-century "Great Migration" that led to millions of Blacks leaving southern states for elsewhere in the US affected South Carolinians as well. According to the 1940 census, 168,571 Black former South Carolinians lived in non-southern states, with the largest number resident in New York, Pennsylvania, or New Jersey. This was of course just after the 1937 school survey revealed wretched public school facilities for Black children, but agricultural collapse played a role along with other factors. Many white residents left during that same period, particularly from farms, but they tended to go south and west rather than north and their exodus rate was not as pronounced. By the 1950 census, 259,727 Black former South Carolinians lived in non-southern states, again with the largest number living in New York, Pennsylvania, or New Jersey.[36] Overall, Black people made up only thirty-nine percent of South Carolina's population in the 1950 census, dropping from forty-three percent in 1940 and from forty-six percent in 1930. In 1950 Black residents were still a presence in the state, with 722,077 people, but over a third of that number were born in South Carolina but lived in other states, particularly in the north. The point had been not simply to leave, but to leave for the north.

Many stayed in South Carolina, at least for a while. Some of us studied in the new public school buildings built for Black students but did not realize the many sacrifices made by people in Clarendon County to bring them into being. Orangeburg County residents were beneficiaries as well as those in other counties and cities. A state agency report indicated that from 1951 to 1954, the number of school districts shrank from forty-three to seven in Orangeburg County, and that thirteen schools were built or substantially rehabilitated during that time for Black students, compared to seven for white. By the time my family moved to Orangeburg in 1956, these facilities were already in place. Wilkinson High School (for Black students), previously established next to Claflin's campus in a humble brick building that still stands on Goff Avenue, moved into a new building built in the elongated modern style so favored during that era of the state's school construction. Erected just to the north of SC State's campus and honoring that college's second president, the new Wilkinson High School opened in 1953.

By the time I attended Wilkinson High in 1963–64, the buildings still seemed new and the facilities more than adequate. We had a roomy gymnasium and a separate cafeteria; lettered corridors fed into a central "spine" corridor that was open to the elements; and rows of spacious classrooms sat on each branch corridor. This facility undoubtedly existed only because of those brave Clarendon County souls. When several of us transferred to the white Orangeburg High School after one year, its building was in much the same style and opened during the same era, in 1954; so as a result of the protracted Black struggle for equal education, white students in our hometown also benefited.[37]

Conclusion

The purpose of this chapter was to provide both essential civil rights history and graphic illustration of two themes, white supremacist suppression and Black resistance, related to the matter of school desegregation. White people viciously suppressed even mild requests for equal facilities, but at the same time, Black people displayed heroism as they arose with constructive resistance to fight against an overwhelmingly oppressive system.

Clarendon County provides essential civil rights history because, in the battle to shape the specifics of legal petitions that Black parents were filing, those petitioners, their local leaders, and NAACP lawyers shaped a legal strategy —influenced by Judge Waring's dissent but also by experiences throughout the country—that contributed to the US Supreme Court's composite *Brown* decision. As Black parents moved from asking for school buses to asking for the abolition of school segregation, they helped advance the cause of school desegregation nationally. The submersion of this case under the umbrella of the *Brown* case does not diminish its importance.

The length to which white people in Clarendon County and in Florence County's Lake City were willing to go to punish petitioners is symbolic of the willingness of the larger white society to use inertia, intimidation, punishment, fabrication, and even murder to support the existing social order. This story also serves as a tribute to true American heroes, those petitioners who weathered unconscionable repression to raise the standard of education for Black children. They were willing to sacrifice their livelihoods, their well-being, even their lives to stand up for the constructive vision of equal education for their children.

4

Defending White Schools

Thus far this book has focused on the "long civil rights movement," a period that reaches back to Reconstruction and extends to the present. What many call the classical phase of the civil rights movement is a shorter period, dating from the 1954 *Brown* decision to 1964 or possibly 1968, dates of two major civil rights acts.[1]

The classical civil rights era produced positive social change for Black Americans and for US society as a whole. When we focus only on accomplishments, however, we risk overlooking the era's conflict-ridden context. We need to understand how vigorously southern segregationists defended their beliefs. Looking at this civil rights era merely as a time of heroic action overlooks the tenacity of segregationists and leaves us unprepared to understand contemporary racism. The classical civil rights era was a contest of wills, a struggle between Governor Byrnes's "civilization in the South as we have known it" and Black people's centuries-old yearning for equal access to life's opportunities.[2] That contest of wills was not simply flat and plainly heroic, but rather multidimensional and hotly contested.

This chapter will explore southerners' pro-segregationist justifications at mid-twentieth century, but it will also reference the roots of their thinking. Southern politicians and journalists cited the need for states' rights or conformity with the US Constitution or peaceful race relations, but underneath such decoy arguments was a centuries-old train of thought. Such thought denied the common humanity of all people, upraised white supremacy, and denigrated Black people as inherently inferior.

This is a big topic. To narrow it down, I will focus on selected white reactions to the *Brown* cases. White supremacist leaders saw their own racism as part of the natural order of things. While they fought to prevent change, they mischaracterized Black life as degraded and Black people as content. I will begin to offer a counternarrative to that view: white people threatened by potential school desegregation organized to harass dissidents and weaken the NAACP, but at times Black people organized effective reprisals, as in my hometown. This chapter explains this history but also shows that a few voices and organizations, Black, white, or mixed, spoke in favor of equal rights. These tried to champion a constructive vision of the future.

White Justifications and Counternarratives

In 1958 the *Richmond (VA) News Leader*'s editor, James J. Kilpatrick, summarizing the reactions of white southerners to the 1954 *Brown* decision, called that decision "an earthquake: the ground still trembles, and the damage may be more or less severe than it seems." Southerners generated a torrent of state legislation in response, including 150 major laws in southern legislatures by 1958, as well as pamphlets, books, and magazine articles. By 1958 "not a single public school [was] racially integrated in Virginia, South Carolina, Georgia, Florida, Alabama, Mississippi, or Louisiana," in a massive show of refusal to change. Kilpatrick noted that in both Clarendon County, South Carolina, and Prince Edward County, Virginia, local officials would shut down all public schools rather than desegregate.[3] (This actually happened; officials in Prince Edward County closed all public schools from 1959 to 1964 rather than obey a court desegregation order). Charleston's pro-segregationist journalist William D. Workman Jr. saved Kilpatrick's article and filed it away in a folder. Workman was collecting sources for his own forthcoming book defending southerners and racial segregation.[4]

During this phase of the civil rights movement, attention focused on the practices and principles of white southerners, but the roots of racist thinking extended far back historically and far wider regionally. A few authors, such as Ibram X. Kendi, convincingly argue that the roots of such thinking extend to the early periods of European colonialism, ramping up as conquerors sought to justify the capture and enslavement of various people, including on this continent Native Americans and then, increasingly, captured sub-Saharan Africans.[5]

Justifications dating from as early as the fifteenth and sixteenth centuries emerged periodically, Kendi explains, with boosts given thereafter. The earliest arguments were that dark-skinned Africans were beasts, unintelligent, uncouth, fit only to serve white people because of such arguments as that the racial curse of Noah's son Ham doomed them to servitude. This supposedly justified forcing Africans into slavery. It also freed many white enslavers to impregnate enslaved women, increase property holdings by enslaving their resulting progeny, and thus create a people of mixed skin tone that we now call Black.

Ancillary arguments during and after slavery labeled Black people as sexually deviant, with no virtue among Black women and dangerous sexual aggressiveness among Black men, both myths that justified oppression. This thinking stamped itself into southern white society, which even today, in some corners, justifies slavery and the Confederacy, offering little sympathy for those who suffered from the heinous practice of enslaving fellow human beings. In the first half of the twentieth century, the white South worked to return Black people to economic and political subjugation, counting such subjugation as peaceful. The classical civil rights era forced racist beliefs into the open and threatened white dominance.

In the wake of *Brown*, the flow of white protests against desegregation and civil rights activities included at least three categories: reactions of politicians; responses of journalists such as Workman and his immediate boss, Thomas Waring, editor of Charleston's *News and Courier;*[6] and responses from the more general segregationist public. Here I will focus largely on the views of journalists, but first offer a few comments on politicians' role in this discussion.

Little incentive existed for politicians supported by a majority-white population steeped in a culture of white privilege to support changes to the status quo. The majority-race population denigrated the minority race as unworthy and inferior, and they supported only those politicians, of whatever political party, who continued to defend social separation from that race. Black citizens were slowly gaining access to the ballot in the 1950s, but they were far from politically powerful, not just because the Black proportion of the adult population was steadily shrinking as people left for other regions but also because of subtle or outright suppression of Black voters.

It is hard, therefore, to argue that politicians were leading their citizenry astray; they were in fact representing their constituency, white segregationists. Nevertheless, the enthusiasm some politicians showed in their arguments against the desegregation implications of *Brown* is notable. Strom Thurmond offers an interesting example of such a politician, because of his prominence, complexity, and tenacity. As described in Joseph Crespino's *Strom Thurmond's America*, Thurmond was not only a consummate southern white conservative but also a flexible politician who could reach beyond regional concerns to help shape modern conservatism for the nation, not just for the South. During his life he had several jobs and positions, but he is most widely known as a US senator, from 1954 to 2003, one of the longest Senate terms in history.[7]

As Thurmond ran for office for various positions within the state, part of his strategy was always to show that he was more committed to racial segregation than were his opponents, whose positions were never that different from his own. This was more than identification with any particular political party; racial segregation was at the essence of how the state's politicians defined themselves as human beings. Even those who were "liberal" in other ways, such as Thurmond in support for public education and for Franklin Delano Roosevelt's New Deal, opposed civil rights legislation for Black citizens or desegregation of any sort. The continued support and adulation of their white constituents only confirmed such inclinations.

After a short hiatus, Thurmond regained elected office the same year as the *Brown* decision, and he arose as a visible opponent. He had served as governor during early Clarendon County petitions, and he was good friends with both Workman and attorney Figg, who had defended Clarendon County against NAACP-supported plaintiffs. Senator Thurmond helped formulate arguments against the *Brown* decision, and he gave talks outlining these. In a 1955 talk to the "States Right League" in Sumter, he called *Brown* unconstitutional and blamed the NAACP for agitating Clarendon County's Black citizens and for sponsoring similar petitions elsewhere in the state. He told his audience: "We must resist integration by every legal means—and resist harder than the integrationists fought to end segregation."[8]

Joining with other Southern politicians, Thurmond helped draft a "Declaration of Constitutional Principles" known informally as the Southern Manifesto and signed in 1956 by nineteen members of the US Senate and seventy-seven members of the US House of Representatives. This declaration called the *Brown* decision a "clear abuse of judicial power." The *Brown* ruling had cited the Fourteenth Amendment's provision for equal rights for citizens, but the declaration noted that the same US Congress that adopted the Fourteenth Amendment in 1868 also provided segregated schools in its own District of Columbia. The declaration argued that the 1896 *Plessy v. Ferguson* decision validating separate public accommodations was legal precedent for their states' segregation laws and that the *Brown* decision destroyed "amicable relations between the white and negro races that have been created through 90 years of patient effort by the good people of both races." To blame for this, the statement claimed, were "outside agitators" and a US Supreme Court that did not respect the rights that the US Constitution granted to the states.[9]

South Carolina's state legislature fell immediately in line with protest. Three days after the declaration, the state's legislators passed a joint resolution "condemning and protesting the usurpation and encroachment on the reserved powers of the states by the Supreme Court of the United States."[10]

Governor Byrnes, in his talks about educational finance in the wake of *Briggs,* claimed that segregated schools forestalled violence between Black and white children and their parents. Senator Thurmond, in a 1955 talk before Virginia lawyers, claimed that racial mixing harmed those who were intellectually inferior, by which he apparently meant Black people. He railed against violation of the US Constitution and of the Fourteenth Amendment as he and *Plessy v. Ferguson* interpreted it. Then, citing the *Brown* ruling that segregation retarded Black children's development, he asked: Would not they suffer from being so close to superior white children, creating "an adverse effect . . . from the mixing of children of the same age level of lower intelligence with those of higher intelligence[?] Certainly, differences of inferiority and superiority would be emphasized greatly by close proximity."[11]

For plainer statements than these about the motivations driving segregationists, we can turn to others. Journalists had many opportunities to elaborate on their thinking. Two white segregationist journalists based largely in Charleston, Workman and Thomas Waring, offer particular insight.

Waring, quite different from his more famous uncle (Judge J. Waties Waring), charged that white northerners misjudged white southerners and did not understand the "difficulties" that Black southerners caused. He argued that racial segregation was necessary in order to maintain harmony between the races, especially in schools. He claimed that a "Paper Curtain" controlled the ability of white southerners to express their point of view.[12] By way of example, he described his own difficulties getting his pro-segregation work published in mainstream national publications. He sent one article to *Harper's* magazine several times only to face repeated rejection. A friend helped him moderate the language so that finally *Harper's* would publish it.

If Waring's published version is a moderated one, then the original must have been even more derogatory. Published in *Harper's* in 1956, this article laid out what he saw as the five major reasons that white southerners refused to associate with Black people on an equal basis. The first was health; according to him, venereal disease riddled the Black population, and their children were not clean. Other reasons Black people were objectionable included their home environment, which was culturally different and degraded; marital habits, which Waring called slack or nonexistent; and crime, more prevalent among Black people than white. Finally, he listed intellectual development: "Southern Negroes usually are below the intellectual level of their white counterparts. . . . Few Southern parents are willing to sacrifice their own offspring in order to level off intellectual differences" by means of school integration.[13]

Waring's staff reporter Workman took up the charge as well. In his 1959 book, *The Case for the South,* which the state's politicians heavily relied upon for speeches, Workman described the alleged injustices that white southerners suffered during the War between the States (as he called the Civil War) followed by a Reconstruction era oppressive for white citizens in its forced enfranchisement of formerly enslaved people. Echoing politicians, Workman raised constitutional issues, claiming that state laws supporting segregation were as legitimate as federal judicial rulings disparaging such laws. He chastised, as had politicians, the supposed perfidy of the NAACP in fomenting discontent. He disparaged northerners' lack of understanding of how dearly white southerners treasured memories of the Confederacy. Deeper into this book, in addition, he delved further into the psyche of the white southerner as he saw it.

While painful to read, Workman's words—more polished, more detailed, and more strongly written than Waring's *Harper's* article—provide essential background for this discussion. Workman made claims about the nature of Black people that need repeating here not because they were true but because he believed they were true, and because they reflected common post-*Brown* racist narratives. He claimed to describe the feelings of many white southerners, and we have no reason to disbelieve him about this. In his chapter "White Man— Black Man," he described Black people as "something of a white man's burden in the South" and claimed they were content to be such a burden. Although he acknowledged that some able members of the darker race had accomplished much, he asked, "What of the vast number of Negroes who have languished in that marginal land of economic indigence, intellectual inertia, and moral laxity? To ascribe their over-long continuance in that state of arrested development to the oppression of white Southerners is to condemn unjustly the white man and to overrate the black man. For even with all the obstacles of tradition and repression which faced them, energetic Negroes still found opportunity to improve their positions far beyond the limits at which most of their race stopped."[14]

Workman provided much detail about the shortcomings of those less than "energetic," but he ignored causative factors and lacked believable data. He claimed that the average Black man would be content with far less in his life than would the average white man, such as lower pay, easier work, and less accomplishment. He cited a pro-slavery scholar who called Black enslaved people, and by implication their descendants, "impulsive and inconstant, sociable and amorous, voluble, dilatory, and negligent, but robust, amiable, obedient and contented" in their proper work context, such as menial labor.[15] Workman described the social and economic conditions that afflicted Black people as if these reflected defects in character and nature rather than decades of systemic racial oppression. Echoing fellow journalist Waring, he listed these defects as high rates of out-of-wedlock births, venereal disease, and homicide, and he stated that these led to white people's deserved aversion to Black people. He claimed that Black people's unfortunate circumstances "go far toward explaining why white persons, as a category, are unwilling to accept social contact for themselves or educational contact for their children with Negro persons." Citing illegitimacy and venereal disease rates for one city, Washington, DC, he asked if it was "any wonder, in the light of such disclosures, the proposals for the forcible mingling of Negro and white children should draw such intense resistance from the mothers and fathers of the white children?"[16]

After this discussion Workman's subsequent chapter "Mixing the Races" was predictable. He decried as abhorrent racial mixture, which he called mongrelization, without mentioning that what mixture existed already was due largely to the actions of white slaveholders and their overseers who preyed upon enslaved Black women. Ignoring that historical precedent, he complained that excess freedom for Black soldiers during World War II, desegregation movements, and the objectionable examples of Black celebrities who chose white wives fueled contemporary interracial lust on the part of Black men. Some interracial liaisons took place voluntarily, he acknowledged, but this was no excuse for Black men to humor their (assumed) overwhelming desire for white women, or for Black and white people to mix in modern times, especially since many states had declared interracial marriage illegal. Workman declared, with some show of authority: "White Southerners' concern over race relations is in substantial measure a concern over sex relations." He found it "impossible to raise the prospect of integration without raising the specter of intermarriage, or of interracial sexual relations. Perhaps more than any other single factor, this apprehension has solidified white resistance to integration."[17]

He raised these points again in his chapter "The Academic Arena," although there he made the sensible observation that educated white people in the North also protected their children from Black children, by patronizing private schools or moving to white suburbs. While in the South, he claimed, white and Black people had established "a pattern of peaceable and practicable accommodation" with each other, "the non-Southern integrationists preach the brotherhood of man . . . yet in their day-to-day living they find it expedient and no doubt comforting to follow . . . 'the great white way' of life, for themselves and for their children."[18]

In such ways Workman mixed factual observations, some of them valid (such as his comments that white northerners exhibited prejudiced behavior), with declarations based on his own inclinations as a person embedded, with privilege, in a dominant culture rife with racial prejudice and oppression. It is tempting to dismiss his observations, but Workman was a respected journalist not just in South Carolina but in other parts of the South as well. He was part of the collection of writers who issued the monthly periodical *Southern School News*, gathering information about various actions related to school desegregation throughout the South in the decade following the *Brown* decision.

This periodical purported to be objective, but its journalists, such as Workman, were not neutral to matters concerning *Brown*. A moderator brought several of the paper's journalists together on September 30, 1957, for a panel aired on a major network, CBS. The moderator urged his four white male guests to be objective, but their comments leaned toward conservative southern white viewpoints. Workman feigned objectivity by presenting statements not as his own opinion but as those of others, as when he "quot[ed] from our political and educational leaders in South Carolina" that "they have estimated the coming time of integration as anywhere from a thousand years on." In this way he informed the audience that white South Carolinians would resist desegregation for a long time.[19]

Some white people fiercely admired Workman. He was so popular in his home state that, although he later lost his 1962 run for the US Senate, he could sign his columns with the initials WDW and everyone knew who that was. His performance on the 1957 broadcast earned Workman at least thirty pieces of fan mail that he preserved, along with the transcript and hate-filled brochures sent to him to stoke his pro-segregationist and anti-Black arguments.

He was, according to these letters, an articulate defender of southern white supremacy. Several mentioned with approval his labeling the Civil War as the "The War of Northern Aggression" or his statements that integration would not take place for a thousand years. A woman writing from Nashville reported listening to the CBS broadcast with "fiercest pride" because the only South Carolinian on the panel was the most "articulate spokesman" for the South. "Most of us fall into a state of sputtering incoherence when we are subjected to the scornful condescension of the de-segregationist. But you, God bless you, remain calm and cut their hearts."[20] One letter written on US Senate stationery, from South Carolina senator Ernest F. Hollings, was admiring as well: "Your performance last Sunday on TV was magnificent. There was no doubt but that the fellow members of the panel thought the same thing."[21]

Given such attitudes as the state's white politicians and journalists revealed, it is not surprising that they fought to hold back the tide of school desegregation. The headline for one of Workman's 1954 newspaper articles probably alarmed segregationists: "S.C. Negro Pupils Outnumber Whites in 24 Counties: Colored Children Have 2-to-1 Ratio in Nine Counties of South Carolina." Even though by 1950 white South Carolinians outnumbered Black in total population, making up 61.1 percent of South Carolinians because of Black out-migration, Blacks who remained had a younger demographic profile. The article included a map of 1952–53 public school enrollment figures for each race, showing that Lowcountry and coastal counties were especially prone to hosting larger numbers of Black school populations than white, an implied threat to white residents' majority status in any future mixed school system. His conclusion problematized the facts: "Thus, every county of South Carolina has a more acute racial problem, in terms of numbers, than any state outside the South."[22] In Orangeburg County Black students outnumbered white by two to one. In Clarendon County the ratio was three to one.

As I read these writings and transcripts, I reflected upon how vastly different they were from the reality of my own Black community during that time. I created, as a form of emotional defense, my own personal counternarrative.

In Orangeburg, a small town, we could find during that same time period accomplished Black musicians, visual artists, physicians, business owners, ministers, and funeral directors, as well as more humble cooks, janitors, housekeepers, drivers, and laborers. The campuses were a special world, with faculty and students who were striving to teach or to learn higher education and with chemists as well as historians, mathematicians, and architects, but other towns contained Black professionals as well, particularly public-school teachers, in spite of multiple imposed barriers to higher education.

When I visited rural folk at my grandfather's three or four churches, or on my grandparent's street in Darlington County's Hartsville, where he and many of his numerous siblings gave birth to a large extended family, I was aware that I walked among people varied in their occupations and income levels but noble in their demeanor. The simple but proud parishioners in my grandparent's church communities in Lake City, Pickens, Darlington, and the countryside formed social networks that rang with joy and a spirit of service. They served in choirs, taught Sunday school classes, raised children, tilled the fields, canned vegetables, worked their jobs. Even the women who worked in the fields put on their Sunday best and brought to the church grounds the finest products of their kitchens, using huge platters and bowls, when the circuit preacher came to town. My own Grandma Manning's humble house was spotless, her flower garden bountiful, and she sewed all of her own clothes on a manual sewing machine operated by foot power without electricity. From string she crocheted exquisite doilies that covered every appropriate surface. As a pianist she excelled on the shabbiest of untuned instruments. My great-aunt Elizabeth Lyde had even fewer resources, and yet she gardened, canned prizewinning produce, and fed multitudes from

Elizabeth Lyde in her yard, Timmonsville, 1963. Mrs. Lyde was the author's great-aunt. A self-reliant woman, she mastered skills that many rural Black women possessed during those days. She grew a large garden, beautifully canned its produce using only a wood-burning kitchen stove, and used that stove to cook for dozens of people at a time. Family album photo.

her wood-burning oven and stove. Were these people not clean and far removed from "moral laxity"?

I summoned vivid memories of Grandpa Manning, son of a sharecropper born enslaved. Grandpa died when I was eighteen, leaving me heartbroken, but I have met very few people in my lifetime, of any race, who come close to him in good character. Chronically low in income, able to own a modest house with a rentable upstairs apartment only when Dad grew up and bought it as a way to provide rental income for his parents, Grandpa's personality shone like burnished gold. His face radiated continual smiles and his joy was infectious. Generous with his few material goods, and to frugal Grandma Manning's chagrin, he gave freely to any needy person who arrived at his doorstep, providing food, clothes, money, and good cheer. He beamed pride in any accomplishment my parents, my sister, and I were able to manage, but he did the same for any of the children, youth, and adults in his congregations or his neighborhood. Constantly urging everyone within earshot to reach their highest potential no matter the obstacles, he voiced praise when parishioners were able to send a child to college or buy a house, and a splendid "outing" in his mind was driving around town showing us the various homes that Blacks were able to buy or build. He supported men and women alike; Grandma's pots were spotless because he scrubbed them as he washed the dishes every day. He must have had incalculable effect on his community and his circuit churches; his sermons drew enthusiastic and lively crowds, as his melodious voice intoned magnetically of nobility, spirituality, and redemption. Surely many other such spiritual leaders existed in their own communities, urging high character under oppressive circumstances.

I thought as well about the people throughout the early twentieth century in the South who had struggled mightily to construct schools for their Black children. They paid taxes and endured low wages and economic repression, and yet they somehow managed to scrap together the match necessary to leverage Rosenwald funds and build, sometimes with their own hands, inadequate but extant school buildings, even without help from white locals determined to finance adequate education only for white children. Were those Black people without ambition or intelligence, or were they instead extraordinary, demonstrating capacity and vision even if they were functionally illiterate?

Consider the people of nearby Clarendon County as well, with characteristics and acts of dignity well documented because of the *Briggs v. Elliott* case. There, status-poor parents worked up the courage to ask local white authorities to provide buses so that their children would not drown or fall to their feet with fatigue from walking several miles to school. Despite the dangers all around them, they organized themselves, bought and managed their own school bus, forced themselves to go to intimidating local school board meetings to register concerns, and withstood years-long harassment and economic repression for the sake of lawsuits that would better the lives of their children. Were these people shiftless, without ambition, as Workman would argue? Did they all arise to fight for social justice only because of outside agitators, as he and politicians had claimed?

Even if Waring's and Workman's assessments of social and economic problems among Black people were true, were these not due in great part to the systematic racial oppression embedded in white supremacy, dating back to slavery? This is the essence of the response to the *Harper's* article by two Black journalists writing in a Baltimore newspaper, the *Afro-American*. South Carolina journalist John McCray asked if Black people were so unclean, and so prone to venereal disease, why did so many white people employ Black servants to cook all their meals, clean, and even nurse white babies? He pointed out that the state of South Carolina contributed to lack of adequate health among its Black citizens by refusing to train "colored doctors or nurses in its 135-year-old

Medical College." He stated that the difference in apparent intellect was due to the difference in the quality of public schools. In the same newspaper issue, another editorial writer said that Waring's article "proves our case"; he refuted each of the five points, noting also that intellectual underachievement for Black people was a result of purposeful public policy. "For generations $70 per year was spent by Mr. Waring's South Carolina on the average white child's education while $6 was allotted for the average colored child's instruction."[23]

White Repression

During his four-year term, 1951–55, Governor Byrnes defended school segregation by creating a school building program; in court cases, talks, articles, and books, white apologists cited the state's recently ramped-up expenditures on Black public schools as part of their argument that schools were becoming "equal." Yet even as state government improved the physical quality of segregated schools for Black students, a self-serving initiative, it simultaneously devised rearguard tactics to protect white supremacy in schools as long as possible.

The main vehicle for this was a legislative committee headed by state senator L. Marion Gressette. This "Gressette Committee" was similar to other such committees set up in Georgia, Alabama, Mississippi, and Virginia.[24] Between 1951 and 1959, it proposed a number of initiatives to defend segregation. To dampen discontent the committee urged continued support for upgrading Black public school buildings and enabling salary increases for teachers. It encouraged the legislature to strengthen the authority of local boards of education; this buttressed their ability to resist undesirable change, such as forced racial integration. The committee also urged repealing the compulsory attendance law so that no one could force a child to attend school, an incredible initiative in any modern society, to free white children from having to attend school with Black. The legislature enacted this and other provisions, and further mandated that "state funds shall be withheld from any school from which or to which any pupil is transferred by or in consequence of a court order," another disincentive for desegregation.[25]

In 1956 the Gressette Committee urged passage of fourteen state laws that repressed civil rights activism and aimed to maintain segregation. The most significant was a statute that the Gressette Committee drafted, Act 741, making it unlawful for a member of the NAACP to work for any school district or governmental entity. When the legislature adopted this act, teachers had to submit an oath stating that they did not belong to the NAACP; this led to the dismissal of dozens of Black teachers who refused to do this. Those fired included Septima Clark, dismissed from the Charleston public schools in 1956. Clark tried to organize a protest among Black teachers across the state, but this was unsuccessful. She left to work with Highlander Folk School in Tennessee and then the SCLC. She founded grassroots schools that attacked illiteracy among Black people throughout the South, starting with Johns Island; these "freedom schools" specialized in training rural Black people to read well enough to vote, and so her firing produced positive results. Also failing to receive contract renewals were twenty-one teachers in Orangeburg County's town of Elloree who refused to deny NAACP membership. NAACP attorneys carried the Elloree teachers' case up to the US Supreme Court; before the court ruled, the legislature repealed the statute, replacing it with one that simply required teachers to list their organizational memberships. Such actions severely dampened NAACP membership, however; by 1958 statewide membership was 1,418, one-fourth of what it had been in 1954.[26]

George Bell Timmerman Jr., governor from 1955 to 1959, continued repressive policymaking. He forced Clemson University to reject a grant totaling $350,000 that would have required Clemson to accept people of various "creeds." Timmerman interpreted this as enabling possible support of communists, whom he equated with integrationists. He attacked Black faculty at Columbia's Allen University and Benedict College and at SC State that he considered too activist. At Allen he demanded the resignation of three faculty members, two of them white, that he considered pro-integrationist. When the private university's trustees refused to dismiss the three, Timmerman forced the state board of education to suspend Allen's certification for teacher training to insure their subsequent dismissal.[27]

At SC State, unlike the situation at Allen, the governor did not have to fight hard to impose his will. Timmerman had in place both his own white board of trustees and a college president, Benner C. Turner, willing to crack down on students or faculty too close to dissent. Even before Timmerman took office, Turner repressed critics of under-resourced Black education. In 1953 faculty member Lewis McMillan published *Negro Higher Education in the State of South Carolina,* offering a realistic picture of Black education in the state. Much of his book described K-12 conditions, but he also noted that Black colleges, including his employer, SC State—chronically underfunded for decades—had low academic standards compared to the state's white colleges. Turner, outraged, punished this revelation by refusing to renew McMillan's faculty contract for the 1953–54 school year. Although McMillan sought redress from various accreditation agencies, Turner had unchecked power over faculty hiring and retention. McMillan never taught full-time in college again.[28]

As noted previously, Black colleges under the control of white politicians tended to do their bidding, with greater or lesser buy-in. Compared to the three SC State presidents that preceded him, however, Turner appeared readier to repress dissent. A particular challenge for Turner was that, in physical appearance, he was white, as was his wife, although both were Black according to self-identity (and possibly state law). In a small town with its own challenges with colorism, his skin color combined with his actions posed a problem for Turner in later years when SC State students perceived him as too closely aligned, in word, deed, and appearance, with his white superiors.[29]

The most widespread forms of post-*Brown* resistance were the white citizens' councils. Although several white supremacist organizations emerged, including the Ku Klux Klan, white segregationists who did not relish night raids or lynching sprees gravitated toward more subtle means of intimidation. The citizens' councils filled that perceived need. Started in Mississippi, this movement blossomed in Orangeburg County, with high initial membership levels.[30] These organizations set the stage for both white segregationist response and defensive resistance among Black people.

The Orangeburg County organizations began in 1955, soon after fifty-seven Black Orangeburg parents petitioned our school board for public school desegregation. White Orangeburg residents immediately organized a citizens' council mass meeting, where more than 3,000 attendees listened to politicians denounce the *Brown* decision. In Elloree, twenty miles away, citizens' council membership grew from 225 to 800 members in just over a week. Membership spread throughout the state so that fifty-five councils existed by July 1, 1956. The loosely organized Association of Citizens' Councils of South Carolina joined with similar groups in other states to create a network of citizens' councils in the South. Orangeburg County was the most organized county in its state, with eight councils operating in various localities.[31]

Materials told local organizers how to administer these councils. One 1955 document advised: "Leaders must decide they need a local organization in order that their community can do its part in uniting with their State and their section of the country and destroying the monster integration that threatens our Nation." The document suggested logistics: "At the second meeting, a speaker can address the crowd, telling them of the erroneous doctrines behind the 'Black Monday' [*Brown*] decision of the Supreme Court." Concerning the NAACP: "There are only 250,000 members of the NAACP in the entire nation. There are 40 million white Southerners. We must have millions of patriotic law-abiding citizens as members of our organization."[32]

Thus, organized and stoked, white citizens' council members in my hometown aimed reprisals at the Black petitioners and their families. They fired those who worked for white employers, evicted those who rented from white landlords, and denied credit to those who used it. Mayor R. H. Jennings, who was the president of the Orangeburg Coca-Cola Bottling Company, a baking company, and an ice and fuel company, cut off supplies to three Black grocers and a gas station owner, James Sulton, who had signed the petition. The Coble Dairy stopped delivering milk to petition signers, and other white citizens followed such actions in turn. They refused to sell insurance policies to petitioners and threatened teachers with job loss at the end of the school year if they did not remove their names from the petition. Anonymous threats reached NAACP leaders. Within a few months, thirty Black residents had lost their jobs.[33]

The pressures began to take their toll. Some Black Orangeburg residents dropped their names from the petition. Soon only twenty-six of the original fifty-seven remained. In an October 1955 meeting, the NAACP urged the rest to hold firm. Calls went out for aid from national charities and for the state and national NAACP offices to help with families' financial losses. It was a difficult time for many people, but from such difficulties arose a homegrown civil rights movement.[34]

Black Resistance

The 1955 incidents described above took place when I was a small child, but many of us were familiar with the experience and with the people involved, and matters continued to unfurl throughout the 1960s. One of the leaders of the civil rights movement then was the same Sulton whose gas station the white citizens' council boycotted in the 1950s; he was a familiar presence to Black locals. Some accounts of the civil rights era in South Carolina ignore local NAACP leaders, but several Orangeburg leaders were ardent activists.[35] They were exceptional people, familiar to Black locals in part because this was (and is) a relatively small town, about fourteen thousand people in 1960. The town's racial bifurcation reduced by half the number of fellow community members that a person could get to know. Black residents knew local civil rights leaders because of their presence during an era of mass meetings, their organizing efforts, and their membership in our churches and clubs.

Therefore when I look at civil rights–era pictures decades later, I remember many of the people involved and their families. Orangeburg has an extensive pictorial record because Cecil Williams, a young Black man that Turner refused to register as an entering freshman at SC State, voiding the promised scholarship because Williams had photographed civil rights activities, ended up attending

Claflin. There my father, with full knowledge of Williams's SC State rejection at the hands of Turner, gave him a comparable scholarship and urged him to continue to take pictures of both local and campus activities. The local civil rights story was familiar to Orangeburg Black residents, and to many others, because Williams recorded key moments with his camera; he published many of his photographs and accompanying narratives in national publications and in beautiful, large-format books.[36] This pictorial record literally portrays courageous Black people in Orangeburg—and in other places in the state and nation—arising to defend themselves against repression.

Rev. Matthew Douglas McCollom, minister of Trinity from 1950 to 1962, served at the same time as president of the local branch of the NAACP. The branch at one point only had three active members, its officers, but it ballooned in importance after the *Brown* decision.[37] As soon as the branch began to respond to the decision, Reverend McCollom said, white locals targeted NAACP leadership as what he called the "enemy of all civilization."[38]

Reverend McCollom's role in the turmoil is evident in a single piece of paper located in his archived scrapbook. It is a petition followed by several signatures including his. Undated, this piece of paper must have been an early version of the petition, with many more names, that Black parents submitted in 1955: "We, the undersigned, are parents of children of school age entitled to attend and attending the public elementary and secondary high schools under your jurisdiction. As you undoubtedly know, the United States Supreme Court on May 17, 1954, ruled that the maintenance of racially segregated public schools is a violation of the Constitution of the United States and on May 31, 1955, reaffirmed that principle and requires 'good faith compliance at the earliest practicable date . . . .' As we interpret the decision you are duty bound to take immediate concrete steps leading to early elimination of segregation in the public schools." McCollom's is the last signature, and he lists our church's parsonage as his home address. Other signatories include my friend Patricia "Pat" Rose's father, Arthur Rose, a sculptor and art professor at Claflin, and eight others, including two of the Sulton brothers.[39] McCollom, the Sulton family, and Rose played major roles in Orangeburg's fight for social justice.

Of these first few signers, the strongest influencer on my life was Reverend McCollom. He was my minister throughout most of my childhood. He was one of those towering but underappreciated local Black heroes of this era who lived in various small places and who labored out of the limelight of national attention and just beyond the memory of historians. Not only did he lead the local NAACP for many years and eventually become state branch president for a time, but he also, according to his biographical statements, cofounded the

SCLC. Several short telegrams within his scrapbook confirm his direct interaction with Dr. Martin Luther King Jr.

McCollom offered up Trinity as a welcoming home for the Orangeburg Movement, the name eventually given to this epicenter of civil rights activism, acknowledged by the National Register of Historic Places when it declared the town of historic significance because of this movement. The National Register also recognized Trinity. Unlike other South Carolina towns, where (according to longtime NAACP secretary Modjeska Simkins)[40] the ministers were sometimes afraid to offer up their churches for civil rights protestors, but very much like Clarendon County ministers, McCollom turned Trinity into a veritable headquarters for movement activities.

Between the college students and the local NAACP, Black locals organized a sturdy counter-boycott to the white citizens' council. The state NAACP called an organizing meeting at Trinity, and James Sulton convinced SC State student leader Fred Moore to support it. Moore consulted Turner, who urged him not to get involved, but Moore quietly organized student support for the boycott without telling Turner. Black consumers stopped using targeted bread, ice cream, and dairy products distributed by local citizens' council members. They continued to patronize some stores but otherwise boycotted a list of local merchants, shopping instead in Columbia, forty miles away. The NAACP published lists of first six and then nineteen boycotted products, and they listed firms to avoid because of their citizens' council reprisals against neighbors. At SC State, which under Turner's direction continued to patronize boycotted white businesses, students organized a dramatic reaction by refusing to eat bread or drink milk supplied by objectionable local white businesses and then boycotting the dining hall altogether.[41] When they did this, local Black townspeople rose to the challenge and provided meals for them, thus rebuking Turner.

Eventually local white businesses buckled under the pressure. Realization soon dawned that white businesses were as dependent on Black patrons as Black patrons were dependent on them. White merchants began to suffer consequences and they began to worry as the boycott continued into several months. Pressure met pressure, and eventually matters abated.

Some suffered collateral damage in the process. It was about this time that the state legislature adopted several pro-segregation and anti-NAACP measures. One, proposed by Orangeburg's legislative representative, was to investigate NAACP activities at SC State. Governor Timmerman ordered state law officers to place the campus under surveillance. This prompted the student leader Moore to call for a walkout; 1,500 SC State undergraduates stopped going to class and held demonstrations against both Timmerman and Turner, hanging the latter in effigy. Encouraged by faculty members, student boycott supporters drew up a list of grievances that centered on Turner's leadership style and his repression of civil rights activities.

Six days after the walkout, students returned to class, but immediately Turner expelled Moore. At the end of the school year, he summarily dismissed five faculty members and expelled fourteen additional students, including a freshman girl, Alice Pyatt, whom seniors had asked to serve as secretary and who later said she did so only to obey them. Pyatt, who simply recorded names of students joining the NAACP, lost her four-year scholarship when Turner expelled her with no possibility of appeal. Because the cash-strapped NAACP failed to help her seek justice, she "lost faith in people." Several dismissed students suffered similar hardships and harbored decades-long resentment against Turner.[42] Some faculty quit in protest. Turner assured the legislature that no more civil rights activism was taking place on campus.[43]

White Allies

In spite of such hardships in the aftermath of *Brown*, cracks began to appear in the white public's resolve to organize councils that pressured Black petitioners. Citizens' council membership peaked at forty thousand in 1956, dropping over the next few years. Black counter-boycotts rattled white business owners, and the obvious fact that the state was not complying with federal desegregation rulings dampened white fears. By 1963 only one thousand members belonged to a citizens' council in South Carolina. Changing focus, many white South Carolinians switched political parties as a purposeful strategy.[44]

Not all white South Carolinians held negative attitudes about Black people and desegregation. Even before *Brown,* white individuals sometimes defected to the side of human rights, and small communities of interracial collaboration or support operated in less obvious ways.

The most prominent white defector in our state was Judge Waring. This judge, by his rulings, helped "liberate" Black South Carolinians from many of their fetters. He could only do this because civil rights lawyers and activists put together creditable lawsuits that they could bring to his district court for his just consideration, but for a while, until he left the state, both sides of that equation worked. A fair judge plus well-crafted lawsuits equaled pro–civil rights rulings. Those rulings not only adjusted discriminatory laws and practices, but they also changed the tone of public discourse.

One 1946 case had led to the moral awakening of Judge Waring, who had already ruled with just sensibilities for his 1944 *Duvall* teacher salary decision. The case involved a Black soldier, Sgt. Isaac Woodard, who got into an altercation with a Greyhound bus driver when he insisted on a bathroom break, February 12, 1946. Woodard was just ending three years of honorable US military service, returning to the US as did many Black veterans to outright white hostility. The driver contacted the local police who pulled the soldier off the bus. The Batesburg police chief, Lynwood Shull, took Woodard into custody but then beat him with a blackjack, purposefully blinding him in both eyes with the ends of his blackjack. Pressured by the NAACP and national publicity, the US Department of Justice filed charges again Shull but prosecutors displayed little competence or enthusiasm for the trial, refusing to call key witnesses. Judge Waring presided, but an all-white jury found Shull not guilty after consulting for only a few minutes. Judge Waring would later describe that trial and its obvious racial injustice as his own "baptism of fire," received at the age of 66.[45] His 1947 decisions requiring in-state law school access for Blacks (*Wrighten v Board of Trustees*) and striking down the all-white Democratic primary (*Elmore v Rice*) followed thereafter.

Judge Waring's 1951 dissenting opinion in *Briggs,* an opinion that laid the groundwork for plaintiffs' arguments in *Brown,* amounted to a stirring denunciation of both racial segregation and racial prejudice. He accepted the premise that race prejudice was wrong, and he referenced its effects on children, indirectly echoing the Clarks's research on Black and white dolls: "There is absolutely no reasonable explanation for racial prejudice. It is all caused by unreasoning emotional reactions, and these are gained in early childhood. Let the little child's mind be poisoned by prejudice of this kind and it is practically impossible to ever remove these impressions however many years he may have of teaching by philosophers, religious leaders or patriotic citizens. If segregation is wrong, then the place to stop it is in the first grade and not in graduate colleges." Noting that the federal courts had struck down discrimination in higher education, he carried this conclusion to its logical conclusion. "And if the courts of this land are to render justice under the laws without fear or favor, justice for all men and all kinds of men, the time to do it is now and the place is in the elementary schools where our future citizens learn their first lesson to respect the dignity of the individual in a democracy."[46]

His social life reflected his beliefs. He and his wife Elizabeth began a serious program of self-study and reflection about race relations after the 1946 Woodard trial. They also began to mix socially with Black Charlestonians. This was apparently one of their few social outlets, since white high society shunned them because he had divorced his first wife, a longtime Charlestonian, to marry New York–born Elizabeth in 1945, and Elizabeth had similarly divorced her former husband to marry the judge. The Warings, no longer bound by local elites' social rules, befriended educator Septima Clark; they even exchanged social visits with her in Charleston, a daring practice in those years.

Black civil rights activists recognized and appreciated their support. Clark, in her letters to Elizabeth Waring, referenced Black activists' high regard. In 1951 Clark told Elizabeth: "The teachers who came with me to see you . . . consider you a marvelous personage and the Judge superb." At an NAACP meeting in Atlanta, Clark continued, "those people talked about you both and told the Negroes what a wonderful leader they have in South Carolina saying that the Judge has stuck his neck out twice for us and we must appreciate him."[47] After her mother died, Clark told the Warings that she kept photos of each of them on her dining room table, where those who visited with condolences could see "how well I regard your friendship."[48] Clark wrote Judge Waring about Dr. King's praise in 1962, a decade after the couple had left the state: "I went with Dr. King all through South Carolina and he mentioned Judge Waring's rulings in every hamlet and town."[49] Clark corresponded with the couple for over fourteen years.

The Warings were not the only white people who refused to join their peers in exclusionary thought and practice. Workman found this out when in 1956 he wrote several white South Carolinians—selected, he said, as among those in the state long known to be "concerned with bi-racial amity"—offering them the chance to describe their pro-integrationist views.[50]

In response one former Batesburg minister said that a Christian should treat all the same regardless of race and that the *Brown* decision was justified. He blamed politicians for the racial tension that lingered. Another respondent, James M. Dabbs, a descendant of Confederate plantation owners but president for ten years of the antiracist Southern Regional Council, wrote back with a magnificent "Statement of My Position on the Race Issue." He told Workman that "I do not object to the segregation decision, nor was I surprised by it: for 18 years the court had been reversing, detail by detail, the famous *Plessy versus Ferguson* decision of 1896. Those who hope to set aside the segregation decision by interposition, nullification, or what have you, will find themselves more disappointed. Period. If we would quit thinking racially, and think as human beings for a little while, we should discover that our worst fears are baseless. What does the Negro want? Well what does any citizen of a democracy want?"[51]

Others stated similar opinions. Dabb's wife, president of United Church Women in South Carolina, wrote Governor Byrnes in 1954 claiming that her organization had always opposed forced segregation and that any other thinking contributed to the negativisms that communism promoted about America.[52] A school principal in Spartanburg County, T. E. Tindall, wrote a thoughtful, poetry-filled narrative, "Reflections of a White Elementary School Principal . . . ," that spoke of "the arduous task of the unification of the hearts and wills of the people" to "the point where the color of a man's skin is of no more importance than the color of his eyes."[53] Clark told the Warings in a 1952 letter that she attended a League of Women Voters' informational meeting about a referendum vote on repealing requirements for free public education, another state strategy aiming to thwart school desegregation. Clark found there "numbers of young white men and women who favor integration and spoke their convictions, but the majority in the State voted yes to repeal the amendment."[54]

It was dangerous for white people to speak out against the white majority. Leading up to the referendum, the League of Women Voters faced harassment even for their cautious statements in defense of public education, with detractors labeling them "race traitors and radicals."[55] Gressette gave a public speech accusing the league of colluding with the NAACP, and both radio stations and newspapers blocked the league's ads for informational meetings about public education, even as these media outlets hosted rabid denunciations of school desegregation. USC fired its dean of education, Chester Travelstead, only a month after he had received a contract and a large salary increase, because he gave a talk, after the US Supreme Court's decision, arguing for desegregation of public education.[56] Throughout the South white segregationists tried to silence white supporters of desegregation, in many cases charging them with sedition and association with the Communist Party. The Southern Conference Educational Fund and Highlander Folk School brought influential Black and white leaders together for conferences and publicized inclusive thinking through newsletters, but they fought powerful enemies. Anticommunist rhetoric and investigations succeeded in silencing many such initiatives.[57]

Only a few white organizations in South Carolina practiced the kind of prejudice-free approach to humanity that Judge Waring lauded. The Southern Regional Council started in 1944 with great hopes as a multistate initiative for white and Black cooperation. Over the years many of its most prominent white members left this council, especially in 1951 when it took a public stand against racial segregation, but the organization gave birth to several state-level councils on human relations.[58]

The South Carolina Council on Human Relations (SCCHR) and its predecessor, the Southern Regional Council state chapter, were two examples. A notable leader was Alice Buck Norwood Spearman Wright, executive director of SCCHR from 1954 to 1967. Wright, known as Spearman during her SCCHR leadership years, worked tirelessly to promote positive interaction between racial groups. One author has said: "With a statewide membership of about seven hundred, the SCCHR was 'the only organization strategically set-up for' coordinating activities within and between black and white groups. Partly because of Wright's tireless efforts, almost thirty groups—various chapters of the SCCHR, the YWCA (of Columbia, Greenville, Aiken, and Charleston), the United Church Women of South Carolina, and other religious organizations and social agencies—were working biracially."[59] SCCHR also began surveying the state of Black and white education, ranging from public schools to universities, and organizing student chapters composed of both races. SCCHR became a major actor in the mid-1960s effort to promote public school integration.[60]

One religious group, the Baha'i Faith, worked to build interracial harmony. Throughout the period discussed in this chapter, just before and after the *Brown* decision, most faith-based organizations took a backseat in such efforts, except to issue statements, as did some churchwomen, or to state pro-integration views, as did some ministers or priests. In practice congregations remained rigidly segregated by race. White churches did not challenge segregationist ideology and in many cases supported it. Black churches were too busy sustaining fledging civil rights initiatives or ministering to their charges to put much effort into interracial cooperation, especially in the face of white hostility. Mixed-race congregations did not exist, with very few exceptions, and churches of both races focused on ordinary religious activities rather than on social activism. One small religious group in the state, the Baha'is, had been working for interracial harmony for some time, in part by gathering regularly in integrated meetings, and it may have been the only one to carry this concept as far as it did.

One book tells the story of the state's Baha'is particularly well—Louis Venters's *No Jim Crow Church: The Origins of South Carolina's Baha'i Community*—but here I will offer a brief synopsis of the reasons this religious group stood out. Founded in 1844 in what was then Persia, this independent global religion relies upon its founders' sacred writings. These stated quite clearly that all humanity was fundamentally equal, with no essential difference between people of different races, nationalities, or ethnicities. That religion, furthermore, taught that human progress was dependent upon recognizing the essential unity of all humanity, and forbade expressions of prejudice of any kind for Baha'i adherents. These teachings gained special meaning for Americans when the head of the faith in the early twentieth century, 'Abdu'l-Baha, visited North America in 1912 and encouraged mixed-race audiences for his many talks as well as the establishment of mixed-race Baha'i communities in various cities and towns throughout the continent. He even went so far as to encourage the 1912 marriage of a Black Baha'i male and a white English Baha'i female, stating that interracial marriage was one way that interracial harmony would develop over time.

The Baha'i Faith gained members in the South very slowly, such as in 1912 in North Augusta, just on South Carolina's border with Georgia. In the 1920s and 1930s, exceptional individuals and then interracial teams visited several localities in the region and in South Carolina, offering lectures devoted to understanding the essential unity of all humanity. In 1935 Shoghi Effendi, then leader of the Baha'i Faith and a resident of Palestine, clarified that American Baha'is were required to hold interracial meetings whenever possible except when doing so would violate local law.[61] In late 1938 he wrote a book-length letter to North American Baha'is, *The Advent of Divine Justice,* urging them to establish the Baha'i Faith in all American states, with particular emphasis upon enrolling Black and Native American members. To make this possible, he stated, adherents needed to overcome personal prejudice and form harmonious interracial communities. He counseled white members to overcome inherent feelings of superiority and Black members to overcome historic suspicions and accept interracial friendship if offered genuinely.[62]

Such provisions made it difficult for Baha'is to gain a footing in South Carolina, where racial segregation and oppression were a way of life. Attracting white southerners proved particularly challenging. Small Baha'i communities arose and then waned in the 1920s and 1930s. By the 1940s, however, small nuclei existed in places such as North Augusta, Columbia, and Greenville, and these were indeed multiracial. These nuclei steadily grew during the 1950s and 1960s, serving as small outposts of interracial worship in a battlefield of interracial conflict. By the time I met my first Baha'i, as I stood battle-worn and weary on the grounds of Trinity on one propitious day in 1967, after attending yet another civil rights rally, the Baha'i community was still small but holding on, poised to expand rapidly over the next few years.

Conclusion

The voices of Strom Thurmond, Thomas Waring, and William D. Workman suggested that deeply entrenched racial prejudice drove white politicians, journalists, and, by implication, their constituents, especially on the topic of school desegregation. Echoing historic racist concepts, they characterized Black people as inherently inferior and happy to be so, but they often couched their guttural disdain in temperate words, writing and speaking about states' rights, the US Constitution, and peaceful relations.

Several prominent proponents of such thinking had national, not just regional, influence; they operated in Congress as well as in the US Supreme Court.

Southern conservatism joined with Sunbelt conservatism to develop a pro-business, antilabor, anti–civil rights ideology that influenced national decision making over several generations, leading up to and including the present day.

White citizens formed citizens' councils designed as homegrown but networked organizations responding to the threat of school desegregation and specializing in economic reprisal against dissenting Black people. Also, in response to *Brown,* the Gressette Committee constructed state laws designed to prevent school desegregation and to repress the NAACP. State government operated through SC State's president to repress dissent at the school in service to the status quo.

As demonstrated by rural and small-town Black South Carolinians, family members, Black journalists, and the Black resistance that arose in Orangeburg in the mid-1950s, however, Black residents exhibited many exemplary qualities, and they were not content with the prevailing order. The Southern Manifesto's arguments about "amicable relations" were false, and Black leaders gave notice that they would protest. Orangeburg's civil rights leaders courageously organized reprisals against citizens' council reprisals and thereby chastised discriminatory white businesses.

Further, white allies of civil rights ranged from Judge Waring to quieter dissenters polled by Workman to Wright, organizer of better "human relations." These, and at least one multiracial faith community, the Baha'is, bode well for the future.

5

Living There and Then

Race relations in South Carolina during the period 1954–1964 followed a pattern similar to previous decades. We lived in one of two separate racial societies, one that was white, privileged, and able to protect its racial status and the other that was Black and underprivileged but had made important advances in several important ways. Those ways included better quality schools serving Black students, increasing ability to vote, and the essential survival of the NAACP.

Nevertheless, life for Black people required some acquiescence to the order of things. This meant undergoing daily indignities that reinforced the racial hierarchy that prevailed. It might be useful to offer a short description of how that operated in our town. Life for Orangeburg's Black residents was relatively easy, compared to life in rural areas or small towns without HBCUs. Even so, during that time one could still encounter oppression. During and especially toward the end of that period, Black locals refused to submit to the most egregious aspects of such subjugation. Gifted Black leaders persevered and constructed an organized resistance movement.

Racial segregation forced our parents and their parents before them to try to protect their children from the most blatant humiliations. Their creation of institutions, businesses, and organizations designed to take care of our basic needs was a laudable testimony to these efforts. This fact, however, did not mean that we did not know what was going on. Given the situation, their protection could only be in some ways a sham, a stage set that created a shelter in which we could only stay for a while. Perhaps they hoped that we would gain strength and survive after we realized the truth. Despite their efforts, I suspect that most Black children and youth in the South at that time, as well as in other areas of the country, confronted racism on a regular basis. Those encounters must have made a big impression on all but the most naive of us.

Reviewing the nature of some of those encounters has two purposes. The first is to provide a fuller context for the social environment facing Black children. Our schools, churches, and other institutions were safe, but sometimes it was necessary to leave such zones and interact with larger white society. The second is to continue a counternarrative response to white segregationists, by highlighting the casual denigration that Black people, supposedly content with their lot, experienced for the sake of segregation. Black activism, furthermore, was not the product of "outside agitators."

Remembering Legalized White Supremacy

Those of us in the Black community shaped our lives around racial roadblocks as much as possible. For those living in rural areas, the options were few. There feudal relationships often prevailed, as described vividly in narratives about Clarendon County's "race relations" at the time of *Briggs*. In such backward areas, Black people needed to avoid challenging, interacting with, or even looking directly at white people or risk the dangerous label "uppity" or worse. Black people endured grinding poverty without alternatives, suffering from malnutrition and untreated disease but not daring to voice any outcry against the social order of things.[1] In Orangeburg in the 1950s, and in several other cities and towns that were more prosperous or less suppressed, many of us avoided these indignities yet confronted some variant of the above.

Examples of indignities that were more common to Orangeburg were tame by comparison, but they were part of the ever-present specter of white supremacy institutionalized by law and custom. For Black adults, even with access to the white Democratic primary, the practical benefits of casting ballots were not always clear. White locals made voting difficult and thereby controlled governance, and so, with few exceptions, all municipal officials and staff were white, as were all state officials. The dominant society was proudly white, with Confederate soldiers standing on pedestals and Confederate flags openly displayed. White people were the privileged class/race/caste; they both controlled and disdained Black people, rich and poor alike.

Orangeburg's local newspaper ignored its sizeable Black community except in the rare instance that a Black person perpetrated a notable crime or a college building burned down. This meant that, for many decades, Claflin and SC State—with their activities and sports events, their concerts and famed visitors and art shows—were almost invisible in the *Times and Democrat*. One exception occurred when the newspaper published names of the 1955 Black petitioners for school desegregation, but publishing those names and their petition was racial intimidation; the newspaper thereby enabled white locals to harass the petitioners, which they proceeded to do.[2] Black locals barely got coverage even when Dr. King came to visit in 1959, although a photograph did appear in print. The news, perhaps, was not that King came to town but rather that the local newspaper noticed this.

A child in the 1950s, I was unaware of the political dominance in our town of white residents over Black, of lack of local press coverage, or of the judicial system. Smaller examples of life during those times were truer to my existence. I share these humble examples not to inflate their importance—and with some reluctance, considering the much worse circumstances of those living in rural tenancy or urban poverty—but only to point out that it was not always possible, even for a Black child living in favorable circumstances, to escape psychological damage.

One example was the local white-owned movie theater. This might seem trivial because no one needs to go to the movies. When we did go, however, we encountered the racial social order in our town and began to understand that the larger society considered us inferior, and deeply so. This example might help transmit the tone of the era and the feelings it generated.

At first we had a Black-owned movie theater of our own, right across the street from SC State's campus. Once my mother took the extraordinary step of taking me out of second- or third-grade class to go to that theater to see *The Ten Commandments,* as part of my religious upbringing. Because of insufficient business, at some point this Black theater closed permanently. This left only Orangeburg's downtown theater, whose white owner strictly segregated the races. He directed patrons of color to the balcony via a separate entrance that had a "colored" sign, although, as with most such signs, that visual image escapes my memory.

I grew up during a time when "colored" and "white" signs demarcated the landscape, in a town whose white leaders embraced Jim Crow with gusto, but I remember few such signs. At some point I must have stopped noticing them, perhaps unconsciously denying their existence. What I do remember for the theater, rather than the sign, is the dark and damp entrance to the upstairs quarters. Walking in with a mixed-race crowd, everyone deemed colored turned to the right and crawled up a dark stairwell. Once we climbed those steps, we reached a balcony with several rows of seats facing the screen. The balcony seats and the floor were uncleaned and filthy, cluttered with paper, popcorn, and cups. We could then sit and watch the movie we had paid (equally) to see. It was hard to watch this movie, however, without being acutely aware of our situation. We were perched high above the favored people—those with blond or red or brown straight hair and pinkish skin, faintly glowing in the darkened theater—while everyone surrounding us in the balcony was Black. We could watch the movie, that is, or we could watch the real-life enactment of our own subjugation.

My parents had come up with a solution to this problem; once the Black theater closed, they simply did not go to see movies in our hometown, and they discouraged my going there with friends. We did go to the movies when we visited family elsewhere, particularly in relatively "free" territory such as Miami, Florida, racially segregated in its own way but with options including drive-in theaters. Otherwise, my parents had decided, it was not only possible but preferable to live a normal life without watching movies, since watching them in Orangeburg meant sitting in that balcony. They tried to guard me from humiliation, pointing out that we could see movies when we visited Miami, but that was a two-day drive away.

The same solution worked, most of the time, for food service. Although a few Black-owned restaurants existed in our town, we had mostly one hamburger stand and a soda shop. We knew that no white-owned eating establishment was open to us, whether in the downtown, on the main highways leading to town, or anywhere else nearby. As in other towns in the South, the main variety store downtown had a lunch counter, complete with red-covered, round counter stools, all of which were off-limits to people with any color in their skin. The gleaming soda fountains, milkshake blenders, and sizzling grill were in hindsight quite ordinary but at the time seemed exotic. We could not even sit on those stools, and perhaps because we could not, they seemed especially red and shiny, rimmed as they were with dazzling chrome. Likewise, the hamburger and sandwich shops lining the business highway seemed to have much brighter colors and snazzier menus than the one shop we could use. Years later I was surprised to see just how shabby those establishments were, but the act of official denial enhanced their stature and our own sense of inferiority.

The weight of this refusal to serve us was so unbearable for one of my best friends, fellow Felton student Jeanette, that one day she seized forbidden food in spite of Jim Crow rules. Although she was "Black," her skin was very light, with only the texture of her hair and the shape of her nose and lips marking her faint African links. One day Jeanette tied a scarf on her head and put on huge sunglasses. She then walked up to the counter at the window of an off-limits hamburger stand and ordered a take-out hamburger and beverage. Once served, Jeanette pulled off her scarf and sunglasses, yelled "Aha!" at the startled woman, and ran like crazy before the cops could come.

Such pranks were rare, however. My family could have pulled off no such tricks; my father's skin was quite dark, and my mother's was not light enough.

As their offspring I was a medium brown and unable to join Jeanette in such adventures. My family was obliged to abide by the rules of food service. When Mom and I shopped in the variety store downtown, she pulled me by the hand firmly and made no comment as we walked past the lunch counter. My parents did not even acknowledge that we could not eat in almost all local restaurants. We simply ate at home, in the campus cafeteria, or in the few off-campus places owned and controlled by Black proprietors.

Other situations were not so easy to handle. Health care offered a particularly challenging problem. Although many towns were large enough to support at least one Black general practitioner, it was difficult to support a wide range of medical specialists. Hospital care was also problematic, with white and "colored" wards and with limited privileges for Black physicians. Our community was fortunate to have a very competent Black dentist and at least one general practitioner, but we had no ophthalmologist. If something was wrong with our eyes, to get them treated locally we had to go to a white doctor. Like most white physicians, the eye doctors maintained strictly separate waiting rooms for their Black and white patients.

Some of my earliest memories are of my mother and me sitting in the eye doctor's colored waiting room. My eyes were nearsighted, and I suffered from other symptoms aggravated by family history (strabismus). Our eye doctor's colored waiting room was particularly dingy. The walls were an ugly light-green color, with glossy brown trim, and the dark vinyl that covered all the furniture cushions was torn and frayed. We could not see fully into the white waiting room, which had a separate entrance, but I saw glimpses occasionally and then imagination took over and sketched out the invisible specifics of that forbidden place. In my imaginary (or realistic?) version, the white waiting room had amenities that ours did not, including bright sunlight, beautiful colors, floral arrangements, and new magazines. The fact that we waited a long time every time we went there only led to even more comparisons, imaginary or realistic. While we waited, we could hear the white nurse calling on patients from the other waiting room: "Please come in and see the doctor, and isn't it a nice day?" or something like that. Our turn came eventually, but were we served last?

In hindsight part of the horror of this situation was not the fact of the separate waiting rooms so much as the fear that a physician who did not value your human dignity would certainly not value your eyes. He had already sent the signal, that is, that we were second-class citizens. Given this framework, it is not surprising that the "forbidden" side seemed more attractive, whether or not this was true. Something else lingers over that memory as well, which was my mother's almost imperceptible embarrassment. I remember her making sure that I headed directly to the door leading to the colored waiting room and that I did not ask too many questions. The faint odor of anxiety, of course, made the situation even more memorable. She was struggling not to alarm me and to project normalcy.

I pause here to consider the possible effects of such situations on white people, particularly on white youths, those that we were hoping would become future classmates. Just as eventually I took as a matter of course the signs, the prohibitions, and the alternate facilities, they must have as well. In court cases of that era, starting with *Briggs,* psychologists engaged by the NAACP speculated on the effects of such social restrictions and educational segregation on Black children.[3]

One of the effects for white children must surely have been a sense that segregation offered protection, that it insulated them from something dangerous or contaminating. They lived in racially insulated schools, churches, informal sports teams, neighborhoods. Orangeburg's schools could have seemed parallel, particularly since, by the mid-1950s, the state had upgraded the exteriors of Black public schools. To innocent eyes this could have seemed like "equal" separation. A situation like the theater or restaurants was not so simple; such settings buttressed the sense that the separation had something to do with fundamental, deserved inequality.

We all went together into the movie theater, but some of us were required to turn to the right and some of us were not. If we could not mix even in such an innocuous place, why not? There must have been something dirty, contaminating, shameful about the people shunted upstairs. Restaurants were a similar case; white patrons apparently accepted and even welcomed complete absence of service for us at places like lunch counters. Here was a matter not just of the need to separate but also the need to separate when people ate food. The vast majority of white people lived by a southern taboo that Black and white people should not sit and eat at the same table; white southerners rigidly enforced this rule in private homes as even long-term, "like family" household help ate in the kitchen and not at the family dining table.

All of this distancing extended into hospitals and doctors' offices, where as a matter of expected service the medical professions kept Black patients out of sight of their white counterparts. But was this a matter of the health professional disregarding us as second-class citizens or of a busy professional acceding to the expectations of white patients? What would have happened if the ophthalmologist had set up one waiting room? I do believe that the white locals would have ostracized him; a similar fate happened to white teachers who taught at Claflin. One such faculty member, Dr. Germanotta, could find no housing for his family in white neighborhoods because he worked at Claflin; my parents bought a rental house in a Black area so that his family could rent it. The wall of racial privilege was therefore quite strong; white patients and their children accepted their special waiting rooms as legitimate given their sense that white superiority was natural, even if this was not an innate sense but rather one carefully nourished by their own society.

I cannot end this section without describing travel. Although many Black people avoided problems with segregated public accommodations when we stayed close to home, by simply not going to restaurants or movies or the doctor and by using our own toilet facilities before we walked out the door, no such protection existed on the road. When traveling by car, it was necessary to get gasoline, to use the restroom, and to eat. It was also necessary to sleep somewhere en route for long journeys. This is why the worst stories many Black people tell about that era center around travel, because jazz musicians, baseball players, and ordinary families going to see family members all had to leave the security of home when they traveled. On the road they could not count on being able to eat, sleep, or go to the restroom at any commercial establishments, except for those that were Black owned.[4]

Travel was very much a part of our household. My father was Rev. I. V. and Fannie Manning's only living child, and they depended on him to help them keep up with their affairs. We often went to visit them two hours away in Hartsville. My mother's parents and seven siblings lived farther away, in Miami; we regularly drove there as well. A ten- or twelve-hour driving day was the most my father, our main driver, could handle. Before the turnpike and interstate highway system were finished, the one-way trip to Miami took two full driving days. Our family also drove frequently to Atlantic Beach, a small municipality located north of Myrtle Beach. The only strip of Myrtle Beach's Grand Strand beachfront that Black people could live on or visit during that era, Atlantic Beach is only three blocks wide and two blocks long. In 1958–59, in this small, Black-governed hamlet, my parents built the only house they owned (besides Dr. Germanotta's rental) as a planned future retirement home, since our campus house came with Dad's job. Occasionally visiting this house also required a drive, three hours one way.

This era of racially segregated travel facilities presented two main challenges for Black travelers: access to food and access to toilet facilities. The trip to Miami also required us to seek overnight accommodations. For each difficulty my resourceful parents had developed practical and resilient solutions to the problem of casual oppression.

Rev. I. V. Manning, Mrs. Fannie Manning, baby Michelle Manning,
Mrs. Ethel Manning, June Manning, Pres. H. V. Manning; presenter is
president of student government association. "This is Your Life" ceremony
honoring H. V. Manning, ca. 1960. Family album photo.
Courtesy Cecil Williams, photographer.

Mom's solution to the food problem was simple: like mountaineers we carried our food with us. Our typical cargo for a three-hour trip included an ice
chest with several choices of beverage nestled in ice cubes; a picnic basket with
fruit, boiled eggs, crackers, peanuts, cold fried chicken. and other such portable
fare; paper towels or napkins; and trash bags to contain it all. The longer the
trip, the more food. Mom's selections were certainly better than much of the
fare we could have bought along the way, if we could have bought it, but this
was a forced picnic. Since the long trip to Miami made it difficult to carry
everything we needed, we watched anxiously for the border between Georgia
and Florida. Georgia's rules were very similar to South Carolina's, so we could
not stop to eat unless we identified Black-owned places. Once we hit Florida, we
could eat in takeout restaurants that served people of all races, such as Burger
King, savior for hungry Black travelers able to reach Florida. We walked into

their restaurants and ordered Whoppers. These hot, innovative burgers were truly welcome, but the real treat was being able to order food in a modern eating establishment.

As for restrooms, we had no practical way to carry toilet bowls. Gas station owners played their part in upholding the Jim Crow rules of separation. They marked restroom doors with signs that customers had to read and obey. The choices varied, but they were at heart the same. "White women," "white men," and "colored" were the most typical trilogy, with the assumption that "colored" women and men could use the same dirty and neglected facility. You could also find establishments that provided only two doors, one for white women and one for white men, with no provisions for anyone else. At best you might find an enlightened gas station owner who provided four choices, for white women, white men, "colored" or "Negro" women, and "colored" men. The only exception to this general rule was Sunoco, a gasoline company that despite common practice steadfastly insisted on offering only two doors, one for women and one for men, or at least did so along our accustomed route. That company consequently resides in my own hall of fame along with Burger King.

Sunoco gas stations, however, were not as popular as their high social equity standards warranted, and they were sometimes hard to find. With this dilemma my father's ingenuity met its greatest travel challenge: how to let us take care of our necessary bodily functions without losing our dignity. Here too we were mountaineers, and he was the scout. Dad made mental notes about where the acceptable or almost acceptable toilet facilities were located and remembered these from trip to trip. He seemed to have a mental map for each of our regular trips, built through trial and error, and that map included not only which highways or roads to take—as supplemented by Mom's excellent paper map reading—but also which gas stations and restrooms to use.

We stopped at the rest stops on the Florida turnpike once this road system began to open in the late 1950s. We visited these rest stops regularly, whether we had to go or not. As for South Carolina and Georgia, here was the hierarchy: first choices were gas stations with two doors, open to all races; then four doors, which at least recognized gender differences between us; then three doors in an emergency. When we could not find even three doors, for many years my parents expected us to hold it until Dad could find some place, which was difficult for me and for my younger sister. Then my parents heard the story of a Black minister's young daughter in our state who had developed kidney problems. They too traveled a lot, and the parents expected that child to hold it when no bathroom was available. Word of her kidney problems spread throughout the

Black ministerial community, forcing families to decide whether to change their "hold it" policy.

My parents reconsidered and determined it was better for us to go by the side of the road than to die of kidney problems. From that day on, if one of us two girls had to go with no other options visible, my father would choose a relatively isolated spot and pull along the side of the road. My mother would open both the front and the back doors as shelter and direct us to squat between them to urinate. This humiliating solution obviously offered a strong incentive for my sister and me to put off this option as long as possible.

As for the overnight accommodations needed on the long trip to Miami, we had two choices, which was more than most Black families had. The first was a limited selection of perhaps two Black-owned motels, extremely modest, located in southern Georgia and northern Florida. For the second choice, infrequently we stayed overnight in one of several guest rooms at Bethune-Cookman College, an HBCU in Daytona Beach. Once we reached Miami, we stayed with Aunt Lenora, safe for a while from the hazards of southern travel.

From the white side, awareness must have been dim of the humiliating inconveniences that Black travelers suffered, and empathy even dimmer. White travelers enjoyed the same rules of separation that governed food service and public accommodations. They had service station bathrooms that were separate from bathrooms set aside for the supposed lesser race. Their children rode in the backseat perhaps without enforced coolers and without convoluted efforts to find restrooms for them. It must have all seemed like the natural order of things.

While the modest examples above focus on a child/teenager's viewpoint, the level of inequality and subjugation was much deeper than that. The deepest subjugation took place in law enforcement, governance, and the economy. I have already mentioned the first two, but the economic subjugation existed as well even in towns such as Charleston or Orangeburg, where many Black residents depended on menial jobs in local processing plants, commercial or institutional facilities, or households.[5] That subjugation was even deeper in rural areas with large proportions of the Black population tethered to the remnants of the plantation system. There tenant farming prevailed, and even Black people who managed to own their own farms or businesses were dependent on the larger white community for services such as occasional loans, retail credit, food processing, or distribution. The web was a strong one, encircling us all.

Given this web of casual subjugation, it was a miraculous accomplishment when civil rights proponents won several significant court battles that centered on public schools, K-12. Such schools were the most sensitive places of all, the places where the larger white society nurtured its progeny, aiming to "protect" its youngest charges from inferior facilities and from contact with Black children. White schools were the places where the Confederacy lived as a glorious era, where the Civil War was something else entirely, and where slavery was a blessing for African savages and the best solution for all. Their schools were the birthplace of future white leaders, schooled in supremacy. Launching the first successful challenge of this situation were Black parents in what might seem an unlikely place, rural Clarendon County. That *Briggs* arose in a rural area, rather than in places with more opportunities such as Orangeburg, was perhaps inevitable.

Black Leadership Leads Resistance

By the late 1950s, it was clear that local people devoted to racial justice needed to arise and carry forth the battle that those in next-door Clarendon County had started and then others had continued with the 1955 boycott against citizens' council milk and bread. We had such people: students in temporary residence at Claflin and SC State and adult veterans of the 1955 boycotts. The college students had come to Orangeburg because they had few other choices; no public state university was open to them except SC State. Some had come because Methodist ministers had urged their charges to go to Claflin, as did Grandpa Manning. These students needed only a match to ignite the flame of action and a well-built bed of aged wood that could keep those fires going once lit.

The aged-wood fuel in this analogy is the capacity that the NAACP had built up in the state and in the city over many years of trials and tribulations. The state's NAACP branch, after many successes during the Judge Waring era, had struggled to move forward in the face of legislative campaigns to wipe out its membership. It had persevered in part because of the extraordinary durability of its leaders.

The state NAACP branch was important not only for supporting Clarendon County's Black residents but also for accessing competent national assistance for other legal cases. Key personalities provided the oxygen necessary to support these and other battles. Hinton's role, as long-term president of the state branch, helped rejuvenate a faltering state branch in the 1940s and inspired Reverend De Laine and others to file pivotal lawsuits. A plumber named Levi Byrd who lived in the town of Cheraw had a rudimentary education but an indomitable spirit; he led the rejuvenation of the state's branch, recruited Hinton, and served for many years as state treasurer.[6] Since others have told their stories well, here I will describe briefly only two statewide NAACP officers: Modjeska Simkins and Rev. I. DeQuincey Newman.

Simkins was the state branch's executive secretary for sixteen years, 1941 to 1957, and she stayed active in the state's civil rights and other progressive activities for much of her long life, extending from 1899 to 1992. Her crucial role during the long, hard years in the 1940s and 1950s was to build innate organizational strength. Although her gender placed her in the executive secretarial role rather than the presidency, for many years she was quite visible as the one who corresponded on behalf of the state's branch. She sent letters to the state's Black teachers when they faltered in the salary battles, corresponded with numerous Black organizations to drum up support for various initiatives, and wrote brave missives directly challenging white supremacist leaders as they fought to keep Black citizens from voting.[7] She also offered economic support to the resistance effort, having founded Columbia's Victory Savings Bank in 1921; because of this Black-owned bank, northern benefactors were able to send money and relief supplies during difficult years, including the 1955–56 Orangeburg boycott, and Black customers had a safe place for deposits, financing, and donations.

Simkins also helped in many ways behind the scenes. Given the white-only hotel situation, she provided her home for visiting NAACP lawyers on numerous occasions. "Thurgood Marshall always stayed in my home, as did the others, as far as my home could accommodate. . . . Some lawyers stayed across the street from me, . . . but they would have their meals and jam sessions around the table in my home."[8] She provided trial assistance as well. Because of her fieldwork with her former employer, the state's Tuberculosis Association, Simkins had traveled throughout the state, becoming familiar with local conditions. Marshall would therefore ask her to sit behind him in federal district court. "He'd say, 'You sit right up at the rail, because there might be something we'll have to ask, something about somebody. We might need you right here.'"[9] She helped with even the minutiae of various campaigns, drawing up the lists of boycotted goods, mimeographing these lists on her own machine, and then helping to place these on the windshields of cars attending SC State games during the 1955–56 boycott against white citizens' council businesses.[10]

Simkins received a lot of pushback from other NAACP leaders because of her assertive role in that boycott and in another Orangeburg County crisis, the mass firing of Black teachers in Elloree. Ever fearless, she once publicized the fate of Orangeburg's Black farmers, workers, teachers, and others suffering from the repression of the white locals by simply sharing the story with a visiting reporter from *Jet* magazine. This story generated mass mailings from people thus informed of the oppressive tactics that change-resistant white locals were using to punish local Black residents. Written messages of support from all over the country expressed outrage. From Chicago, accompanying a money order for $16.40, came one such letter: "After reading of South Carolina's plot to starve Negroes in October 20th [1955] issue of Jet Magazine, a group of fellow-workers, in the Main Post Office in Chicago, decided to take up a collection to help you fight your battle. You are not fighting alone—we are with you." One Philadelphia woman wrote leading newspapers in her city asking them to publicize the plight of desegregation petitioners and urging them to ask readers to send money and supplies to Simkins.[11]

Such reactions and pleas brought donations of food, clothing, and money but also pushback from national NAACP executive Roy Wilkins, who once telephoned Simkins and told her to return monetary donations because the NAACP "was not a relief organization." This was true, but Simkins had immediately found willing recipients for the goods and money sent for Black people who had been economically harassed. Although she had not asked for such donations and she was surprised that the *Jet* article generated such a response, she reminded Wilkins that Black South Carolinians were suffering grievously because of the actions that the NAACP had advised them to take. As she recalled later, she raised "much hell" on that call with Wilkins. She told him: "These people are under pressure. You all asked us to get those petitions signed, and that's what we're doing. We have an obligation to these people." After sharing a few more colorful words that referred to what she called Wilkin's access to "big sirloin steaks" and to his comfortable distance from the struggle, she ignored his request to send relief money back to donors and instead created a one-woman relief program that helped many Black people survive.[12]

State branch president Hinton managed to block Simkins's reelection to a statewide officer position, a rebuff eased by unproved accusations that she was a communist. This was a common way to shut down civil rights activists during this era; white political leaders along with the *Charleston News and Courier* led that charge against her. In 1957, for the first time, no NAACP member nominated her to serve as the state branch's secretary, a situation that Hinton called voluntary but that Simkins denied, in a letter she wrote to the officers of local NAACP branches. Her letters show how hurtful she found the unproven allegations that came from both foes and former friends. Once he ousted Simkins, however, Hinton continued what had already become obvious: a decline in executive functioning. He failed to call meetings or to attend them, and he lagged in pursuing university desegregation efforts. Simkins readily pointed out these problems. In addition statewide NAACP membership numbers continued to plummet to alarmingly low levels because of white repression, and Hinton did not seem able to address this issue. Such circumstances, noticed by many others and eventually investigated by Wilkins and other regional and national officers, led to pressure for Hinton to step down in the fall of 1958, after eighteen years of sometimes very effective leadership.[13]

Emerging from this wreckage was another statewide leader. Rev. I. De-Quincey Newman, who served the statewide NAACP during the crucial years of 1958 to 1970, displayed a different leadership style than had either Hinton or Simkins; his mode of operation was steady, understated hard work dedicated to rebuilding the state's branch and pursuing protest action.[14] Of these three leaders, Rev. Newman was the only one I knew personally, because of his visits to Orangeburg and his relationship with Dad. I remember him as a genial, radiant, modest person.

Newman was one of the people who floated in and out of our lives as part of my Dad's friendship circle in some way. He called my father "Cuz," claiming that they were related, but Dad never could figure out how; speculation about the exact connection fueled endless conversations in our household. Dad's family had many extensions dating back to John Manning's (Dad's paternal grandfather's) two successive wives and what I have now determined to be at least twenty-one children—thanks to modern genealogy software, not available then—not to speak the family of Fannie Wilson Manning, Dad's mother, and no one had kept up with them all. Once Newman passed away in 1985, his widow later affirmed the "cousin" connection to Dad, but again with no specifics.

Cousin or not, Newman seemed to me, during the 1960s, to be little more than a kindly uncle. In terms of the civil rights movement in South Carolina, this was a serious underestimation; he was a civil rights warrior. Throughout his long career, culminating in his 1983 election as South Carolina's first Black state senator since 1888, Newman demonstrated extraordinary drive, courage, and dedication to human rights. His stature is well established; his personal papers were among the first that USC archivists sought as they began to collect documents concerning the history of Black participants in South Carolina's civil rights movement.[15]

When this movement blossomed once again in Orangeburg in 1960, similar in passion and commitment to the 1955 movement, Newman was in a strong position to support it through his full-time work with the state's NAACP branch. He brought structure and focus to that organization through simple hard work, well documented and easy to trace in his monthly and annual typed reports; these date to his acceptance of the role of full-time field secretary from 1960 to 1969. Newman moved in the same orbit as my dad, although Newman was seven years older. A graduate of Claflin's high school, he had served in the 1940s as pastor for Orangeburg's Trinity. From 1956 until 1958, he took over the ministry, replacing my father, at Wesley Methodist Church in Charleston.[16] When

Newman took over Wesley in 1956, my father introduced their new minister to the congregation as a man who had already distinguished himself by tackling "social and community problems."[17] Indeed he had; Newman had served as the NAACP state branch's vice-president since 1948. His organizational talents, and the branch's Hinton-led collapse, led to his 1960 hiring as full-time paid staff.[18]

Newman's service as field secretary was a tour de force, with accomplishments summarized in Sadye L. M. Logan's *The Spirit of an Activist.* His own written reports mostly list the number of miles traveled, letters received and sent, and other objective accomplishments, but others who worked with him cite his singular role in other ways. He was a personable and effective moral leader, holding fast to the creed of nonviolence and high moral principles but not backing down from direct action strategies. He not only led the state branch as it pushed for equal facility, voting, and educational rights, but he also helped to organize the essential student movement. One of his first actions in 1960 was to hire a Claflin graduate to organize the state's students during that summer; her work pushed the organization far toward a proposed goal of one thousand youth members.

Once the lunch counter sit-ins took place in Greensboro, North Carolina, starting February 1, 1960, student demonstrations emerged in many places. Newman and local NAACP branch presidents, including at that point Orangeburg's Matthew McCollom, strongly supported student efforts and sponsored student-led demonstrations throughout the early 1960s. Newman bailed students out of jail, encouraged them to march even if this would lead to their arrest, and went to jail with them, perhaps a dozen times, in a show of solidarity. In one account US Congressman James Clyburn tells of an incident when he and a fellow SC State student dressed well before they attended a 1961 rally at the state capitol, intending to avoid jail. Seeing their conspicuous attire, Newman thrust them into a leadership position with marching high school students from their alma mater, Mather Academy, and this positioning led to their arrest. The two students were not physically comfortable in the jail, but they expected Newman to bail them out, until they discovered that the good reverend was sitting in jail with them.[19]

Although statewide leaders were important, my own church's Reverend McCollom, a consummate communicator, most directly helped me envision a better world. McCollom was still active during this phase, as he had been in 1955. This time around, in the early 1960s, I was old enough to hear and understand what he had to say. My most vivid memory of him is as the tall, thin prophet of righteousness standing in the pulpit and speaking with as much ease on Sunday as he did for Trinity's civil rights rallies on other days of the week.

In this mental picture, I am sitting in my family's customary pew, looking up at him with admiration and awe, and he is holding forth with vigor, wisdom, and righteous indignation.

Although little of what McCollom said or wrote remains, one can get a sense of the power of his presentation by reading his remarks for an oral interview. His words bring back memories of the articulate and compelling thunder of his oration, the commonsense rationality of his indignation, the deep passion with which he spoke. Consider his rolling, unscripted, almost breathless description of racial oppression, as spoken during that interview:

> From the time that Reconstruction ended there was a deliberate effort to turn back the clock to as near slavery conditions as possible. The separate-but-equal doctrine and that sort of thing. The Black codes, so far as voting was concerned. To be sure, what we experienced in the political arena was also true in the area of religion. How people could pronounce such things as are pronounced in our Declaration of Independence and the Constitution and Preamble and that sort of thing—how they could stand up and say those things and then live daily the absolute contradiction of them is more than most of us can understand. There is no way of rationalizing it except to say that while we say all of these things, at the same time we are really selfish human beings, self-serving, self-seeking, and we build up myth, and we resort to clichés and stereotypes in order to get our own way, in order to create advantage for ourselves. It is this kind of pride and arrogance and self-seeking and self-serving that permit us to live such contradictions.[20]

By contradictions, he said, he meant "Jim Crow Christianity," the facts that Black worshipers could not attend white churches, that white churches' signs saying "Everybody welcome" meant everyone except Black people. He meant that such ministers could preach Christian love and yet disparage all Black people fighting for fair treatment. Contradictions meant requiring that Black people approach white houses only from the back door, that "Blacks have no rights that whites have to respect," not even the right to equal public education. He spoke of the past but suggested that injustices continued: "All we want are equal schools. How are you going to have equal schools if the white people are in charge of all the decisions, all the money, all the school lines, the textbook commission, the tax commission, which assesses all the taxes"[21]

McCollom and Trinity provided a necessary emotional component, helping us frame our daily battles for self-respect—challenging under Jim Crow rule—within the spiritual principle of human nobility. It was almost impossible to gain equality in public goods, but we needed to understand our right to such public goods. He explained this concept: "Because you are born in the image of God, you have inalienable rights. Not because our Constitution or Declaration of Independence would say that you have these rights, but unalienable rights, *God given,* because you are made in his image. This is where the church stands. So often when I hear the young person say the church does not mean anything to him, I have to remind him that from the beginning in America, the church is the only agency that has been saying to you and about you, 'You are a child of God. You are not a *thing.* You are not a thing. You are not something to be used and abused and taken advantage of and proscribed and disenfranchised. You are a child of God.'"[22]

Nurtured by such rhetoric, very much typical of the many sermons he preached in our church, I gradually became aware of a movement that had already been underway for several years. I did not have to go to the movement; it came to my church and ricocheted back and forth to both campuses. Trinity hosted not only protesters but also civil rights dignitaries, including Thurgood Marshall, Roy Wilkins, and Dr. Martin Luther King Jr. Of these the visitor who most impressed me was Dr. King, who came in 1959, speaking from the pulpit of Trinity Church and visiting as well Claflin's campus. My memory of his visit to Claflin is somewhat faded but reinforced over the years by a fuzzy image taken by photographer Williams of Dad talking to King and standing on a bandstand. About nine years old, I am off to the side in pigtails and a plaid skirt, standing a short distance away. The photograph is severely out of focus, but Williams gave it to us anyway, as a memento. Stronger is my memory of King's talk at Trinity. I remember the power of his delivery, the fevered pitch of his crescendos, and most impressively the ecstasy with which the packed audience shouted in enthusiastic assent. I remember where I was sitting, toward the back and near the south end of the church, hardly able to see over the waving arms, enthusiastic nodding heads, and then standing bodies as energy levels rose. And I remember the singing, song after song, civil rights melodies based on old-time spirituals, filling our capacious church with rhythm, movement, passion, heat, and fervor in a way unlike our usually more staid Methodist services or even our spirited NAACP rallies.

Grounded by experience and leadership such as that of Simkins, Newman, and McCollom, with occasional visits by civil rights dignitaries, students and seasoned adults relit the logs with the kindling of activism. In 1960 sit-ins, picketing, and other protests emerged all over the state. Newman's annual reports referred to such activities, such as two Claflin students' attempting to attend

Orangeburg's white Methodist church for Sunday services on November 5, 1961. The mayor turned the students away at the church's door and had them arrested; the *Times and Democrat* published a photograph of the three standing, in opposition, at the church's front door. (This incident and photograph I remember vividly; it was devastating proof of the spiritual decay, in my mind, of local white Christians, as well as of the law's collusion with racial injustice.) Newman's reports listed other incidents as well: youthful college marchers converging on the state capitol and students picketing downtown Orangeburg's stores in waves of protests extending over several years.

Newman had organized "strategy committees" in both Orangeburg and Columbia to oversee such efforts. The strategy committee for Orangeburg included three students at large from the NAACP youth chapter and three students each from Claflin and SC State for a total of nine, plus perhaps five adult advisers.[23] Newman continued to organize NAACP youth chapters, support at least four campus chapters, and simultaneously pursue both direct (pickets, marches) and legal action. Local activists entered an intense period that extended from 1960 to 1964 at its peak, leading to numerous jail sentences.

I have no memory of Newman speaking at rallies, but his speaking style was understated and slow-paced whether he was speaking or engaged in ordinary conversation.[24] Documents show that he was always involved, even if only to guide local strategy, support student and youth chapters, raise bail, and lead the more visible marches. Many different people were present at these rallies, but McCollom was always among them, along with other local NAACP leaders such as a courageous woman named Gloria Rackley (later Blackwell), mother of two of my Felton schoolmates, Jamelle and Lurma. She was a striking figure, an enviable "Mom," a role model for young Black girls. At some point she also became one of the vice-presidents of the state NAACP branch.

Rackley more than lived up to her informal designation as lead civil rights woman of our town. A public-school teacher, she undertook several heroic acts as branch officer and as ordinary citizen. The most notable: when the local branch was waiting on an opportunity to litigate against the unequal, unsanitary facilities at the local hospital, she took advantage of the occasion of her daughter Jamelle's painful dislocated finger to take her to that hospital. She sat with Jamelle in the emergency room but then refused a nurse's instruction to move to a nondescript area in the hallway reserved for "colored" people, where the only seats were actually wooden crates stood on end next to vending machines. Rackley instead took Jamelle and sat in the white people's waiting room—which was beautifully decorated, with comfortable chairs—and refused

Rev. I. DeQuincey Newman, Gloria Rackley, and Claflin student MacArthur
Goodwin at a mass meeting in the basement of Trinity Methodist Church.
Newman was the state field secretary NAACP, and Rackley was a local
NAACP leader fired from her public school teaching position because of
civil rights activities. Courtesy Cecil Williams, photographer.

to leave. Two white policemen, apparently embarrassed to carry out this dastardly deed, arrested Rackley, a physically handsome woman who was extremely
articulate.[25] The local branch posted her bail and went to court over the resulting charge.

When the public school system fired her because of this and other civil
rights activities, all Black public high school students went out on strike. As
normal I went to the all-Black Wilkinson High School on strike day, October
8, 1963, but the classrooms were almost empty.[26] One teacher said that she was
surprised to see me because she thought my parents supported the civil rights
movement. I was deeply ashamed to be present but pretended to be unbowed;
my parents did not want me to miss even a day of school, I said defensively, and

so they had sent me in spite of the strike. My true thinking: the boycott was in honor of *Gloria Rackley*, a local heroine, my friends' *mom*, for Pete's sake! This humiliating incident, combined with my parents' refusal to let me participate in picket lines, which they deemed dangerous and indeed often led to jail (in my thinking part of their glory), caused profound disappointment for me. It seemed—from the perspective of an impatient ninth grader—that attending rallies would be the limit of my civil rights career. I was afraid I would not have a role in a historic campaign for racial justice.

As for my parents' role in this energetic, burgeoning civil rights movement, their importance was not at all apparent to me at the time. From my perspective my parents were watered-down reflections of the colorful leaders described above, such as Newman, McCollom, and Rackley, but I had severely underestimated them.

Conclusion

Even in protected environments, Black children were likely to encounter Jim Crow racism in a damaging way. Parents tried to protect us and to raise us well under the circumstances. In families such as ours, this meant giving us the best schools possible, providing a strong religious upbringing assisted by ministers stressing human dignity, and accommodating endemic denigration without alarm. Such parents held a constructive vision for their children's growth and development but lived lives of cautious resiliency, avoiding objectionable situations, urging accommodation with equanimity, and packing lunches for car trips. A few exceptions existed such as Rackley, but parents like mine did not comment or complain, did not challenge or confront, but rather carried themselves with grace and studied indifference if their livelihoods allowed this or with quiet submission if trapped in more desperate circumstances such as sharecropping or day labor.

Unlike the claims of white political and journalistic leaders, however, such carefully balanced adjustments did not signal racial harmony but rather racial oppression. Apparent accommodations were temporary concessions. Black people soon arose to counter the prevailing social order, requiring no outside agitators because we had our own indigenous leaders. Black leaders took courage from agitation elsewhere, but they themselves initiated courageous local initiatives. Firing of a teacher, which would have drawn little notice before, generated a citywide boycott; the state NAACP, headed by homegrown South Carolinians such as Simkins and Newman, organized resistance; local leaders such as McCollom and Rackley inspired us all. As my ruminations suggest, from the vantage point of most white people, the old order was probably a normal, comfortable way to live alongside an objectionable subject race; the growing civil rights movement showed that this old-world order was doomed to fall, at least partially. It would fall even in protected white public schools, bastions of privilege and of the Confederacy.

6

Struggling to Learn

In the early 1960s, my juvenile definition of civil rights leadership was a willingness to march in picket lines and go to jail, give speeches at rallies, and, in Dr. King's case, write stirring books, but this was an oversimplification. Many other activities were necessary. Rev. I. DeQuincey Newman and his collaborators organized new local NAACP branches; filed court cases arguing against discrimination in public facilities; encouraged victims to register complaints about police harassment; increased Black voter registration to neutralize the white political machine; and pressed for public school desegregation. Such herculean efforts required not only protesters and speakers but also community organizers, lawyers, ordinary people willing to complain about police action or to knock on doors and register potential voters, and parents willing to send their children to integrate all-white schools. This last category was crucial. In 1962 our state's NAACP branch was still trying to get Black students accepted into public schools and universities. Such initiative required willing students or parents who would apply to such schools and litigation that challenged denials in court.

Reverend Newman's reports chronicled initial successes for school desegregation. During 1961 and 1962, he focused on Black admission into USC, Clemson, and public schools in two cities. The national press praised state government for engineering Harvey Gantt's relatively incident-free entry into Clemson in January 1963; white political leaders had purposefully avoided the white violence experienced in Alabama and Mississippi. Gantt's arrival, however, provoked a reactionary student press, harassment, and a torrent of hateful letters sent to the Governor.[1] In 1963 a US district court ordered USC to admit Henri Monteith and two other Black students, and Charleston's School District 20 admitted several Black students, including Millicent Brown, daughter of the

NAACP state branch president, Rev. J. Arthur Brown. The teenager experienced quiet racial harassment and apparently deep trauma.[2]

This chapter describes this process in Orangeburg District 5's white high school, which thirteen Black students desegregated in the fall of 1964. Up until the mid-1960s, the drive for school desegregation was widely supported within the state's Black community. As Black families found out throughout the southern region, however, school desegregation came at a price. In Orangeburg, echoing experiences in other places, my parents and others had different motivations for sending their children to be the first wave of Black students to integrate schools. And in our town as elsewhere, Black enthusiasm for school desegregation waned as harsh racial realities set in.

My Parents Step Forward

My parents were not visible leaders in the civil rights movement, but they provided constructive support for Black education. Their lives centered on Claflin, and events there and at affiliated Trinity helped cement their marriage. They lived in two worlds; one appeared to be their own relationship, supplemented by family members, and the other was the world of Claflin and Trinity. Their dinner conversations reviewed what happened in their classrooms or on campus, and these conversations extended well into the evening. Although they had friends, and they belonged to a sorority and a fraternity, these were tangential relationships associated with our larger extended family, Claflin, or Trinity.

This somewhat circumscribed world provided a complex life of dedication and service. Claflin had its own social networks of faculty, staff, and students and its own calendar of events. Dad worked hard to build buildings, recruit and retain faculty, inspire the students, and steady the college's finances, all while elevating the curriculum.[3] Mom worked hard to teach her classes, manage our household, raise a late-in-life baby born in 1959 (my sister), and serve as the school's first lady. Within this world they were respected, and others assisted them to carry out daunting tasks, such as keeping Claflin's accreditation and hosting receptions. The off-campus white world, more difficult, required careful conformity with oppressive racial norms, but it was necessary to engage in that world to carry out Claflin's banking, oversee construction, and order or purchase supplies. My parents had little time to do anything else but navigate these worlds, our household and Claflin, on the one hand, and sometimes-hostile surroundings, on the other.

Mom's role in this constructive project was mostly apparent as I watched her navigate her complex professional and home life while maintaining a calm, professional demeanor. Dad's role is apparent in a modest collection of other papers. He sometimes typed out his own talks; existing fragments show a side of him that was less visible at home but apparent there as well. He was, in some ways, a quiet revolutionary, not accepting of the status quo.

Dad's speaking style was to charge his audience with a vision of constructive resilience grounded in Christianity and the Bible. Consider one of his campus chapel talks. After quoting 1 Kings, several verses in chapter 19,[4] he explained that the prophet Elijah took refuge under a tree because a queen named Jezebel wanted to kill him. God spoke to Elijah and told him to get up, according to Dad's paraphrase of the story: "In other words, [God said to] Elijah, there are seven thousand in Israel working for the Kingdom. They are busy going about their tasks. . . . and here you are sitting under the Juniper tree licking your wounds when there is work to be done. . . . In the academic community—students, teachers, staff, administrators—my challenge to you this morning is to get out from under the Juniper tree. Lock arms and join hands with the seven thousand positive thinkers who have not bent their knees to Balal and together we will march facing the rising sun . . . with courage."[5]

He then said that some at Claflin were acting like Elijah, and others like the seven thousand, but they all needed to engage, unafraid of "Jezebel," whom he characterized as the worst aspects of the 1960s. These aspects were loss of faith in God and in the power of education. In contrast he offered a vision of educational progress and racial unity: "We [Claflin] will continue to hang out our shingle of quality education, character and knowledge saying whosoever will, be he Black man, white man, brown or yellow man, let him come if he is concerned with education. If he is in pursuit of knowledge, be he student, faculty or administrator, if he is desirous of joining a community of learners, we bid him come. If he has other motives, then for God's sake pass us by and return to the Juniper tree and sleep."

Here is another excerpt from his talks, one that states explicitly the charge for Claflin as an institution striving to uplift Black students and shows his intellectual links as well with Trinity's Reverend McCollom. "The uniqueness of Claflin is . . . its role of helping young people discover their identity to be proud of themselves; helping them to know the truth about themselves and their fellowman; prevailing with them to understand that they are children of God, that the color of a man's skin and the texture of his hair have nothing to do with his character and his soul. . . . In every man is a spark of divinity, and he is eligible for communion with God. And in the words of the text, 'If they do the will of God, they have kinship with the eternal.'"[6]

In addition to this constructive project of racial uplift at Claflin, Dad played a key supportive part in the local Orangeburg movement. It took me some years to understand this. He provided an important anchor for Claflin students who participated in marches and picket lines. His stable leadership of a church-supported college gave him a certain amount of independence, and his largely Black board of trustees free of segregationist politicians released him from the oppressive fetters that SC State faced. His and Mom's active participation in the life of Trinity exposed them to civil rights activities, and Dad's friendships with fellow 1866 Conference ministers McCollom and Newman must have cultivated sympathy for that movement. If Dad had forbidden Claflin's students to participate in protests or expelled them for doing so, as did Turner at SC State, matters could have turned out very differently.

In some ways the presence of Turner as an anti-activist HBCU college president highlighted the importance of my father as the other local HBCU college president, the one who was supportive of the NAACP and its efforts. Turner strongly discouraged NAACP membership.[7] Hence, not surprisingly, various state-level NAACP program or meeting notes mention only my parents (not the Turners) as honored guests or as sponsors during the crucial period of 1959 to 1962. Notations indicate NAACP-sponsored programs held at Claflin but not at SC State.[8]

I have two vivid memories of the effects on Claflin of the protest marches. First, at some point during the boycott years, Dad simply transferred Claflin's cash accounts from one objectionable local bank to another. This was his quiet way of registering protest against—boycotting—an offensive institution. The second memory is of the consternation caused in our household when the police jailed marching college students. For a family dedicated to uplifting Claflin's students, many of them native South Carolinians from low-income families and all of them Black, their incarceration in a hostile white world was very distressing. After my father died in 1996, I discovered a memento from that era while going through his papers: a canceled check, drawn from my parents' personal bank account, made out to the NAACP for four hundred dollars and dated May 28, 1962, with the notation "refund of bond posted for students." The surprise was not that my parents wrote the check but that they had kept it for over thirty years. Finding the check brought back memories of Dad's going to the jailhouse after one set of arrests, circling the building in frustration, trying to find out if arrested Claflin students were okay, and returning home unsatisfied. The canceled check reminded me of late-night murmurings, as my parents tried to make sense of a chaotic situation. My sister remembers our parents telling her that during that era Dad set up weekly "Chat and Chew" meetings with Claflin students, to talk to them and let them air their fears and concerns.

Orangeburg student civil rights demonstrators, from Claflin and SC State, arrested and placed in a stockade next to the Orangeburg County jailhouse behind a chain-link fence, ca. 1962–63. Officers are firefighters, ready to use hoses on the students. Courtesy Cecil Williams, photographer.

One march of several hundred people, largely college students, took place on March 1, 1960, in spite of Turner's warning that SC State demonstrators could face disciplinary action. After another larger rally on March 15, 1960, 388 people went to jail "in the largest single mass arrest up to that time in the civil rights movement. Those taken into custody were among approximately 1,000 people who marched peacefully to protest segregated lunch counters in Orangeburg."[9] On that cold day, with temperatures hovering in the forties, police turned firehoses and tear gas on the students. A photograph of the harassed students rounded up in a fenced outdoor yard next to the jail appeared the next day, in the *New York Times;* Williams's photography books show several similar photographs. Local Black businesses and branch leaders organized food collections, dry clothing, and bond money in response, at one point throwing goods and supplies over the yard's chain-link fence. When police released Claflin students from jail after some of the arrests, the students regrouped in Claflin's gymnasium, a shelter from the outside world that Dad must have approved.[10]

Orangeburg's NAACP branch published a newsletter for 1963–64, the *Torch,* that meticulously chronicled the marches, the associated economic boycott of downtown businesses called for and supported by local Black citizens, and the names of hundreds of marching protestors arrested, many of them jailed multiple times.[11] The *Torch* published those arrested as members of an "honor roll." Some of those jailed were students my age or only a bit older, students whose parents were more "liberal" than mine in that way, such as Leona Ferguson and Theodore Adams, who would later form part of the first wave of desegregating students, and my Felton classmate Frances Edwards, daughter of my fifth- and sixth-grade teacher. Frances during that era went to jail seven times, an honorable accomplishment during that movement.[12]

On the ground this produced a lively set of activities, even for those of us not allowed (by our parents) to march downtown with placards. In our church basement, starting in about 1960 and continuing for several years, Trinity's status as Orangeburg movement "headquarters" meant offering practical accommodations. Long tables in that basement served as both ways of serving food, their original intention, and flat surfaces upon which to make protest signs. In came the raw materials, poster paper, markers, and string (for hanging posters around necks), and out went those materials transformed in the hands of dozens and then hundreds of marchers carrying those homemade signs. The atmosphere was convivial and courageous but informed by careful attention to exhorting all to nonviolent action.[13] Everything unfolded as if protesters were carrying out a sacred Great Crusade pursued with the enthusiasm of sports fans at a playoff. Periodic rallies offered opportunities to sing freedom songs, gather up courage, and pray for divine assistance. The sense was palpable that we all were in the right, saving America from itself, and gaining self-respect and justice for our subject forebears.

Dad's former college roommate, James Thomas, recalled the dilemma facing HBCU presidents during those days. Before he became a bishop, Thomas worked from 1953 until 1964 as associate director of the national Methodist Church's board of education helping twelve Black Methodist colleges remain viable. This was one of the reasons he sometimes visited Claflin, staying in our home or its guesthouse. Many of the colleges under his charge had students jailed during 1960s. During one of his trips, Thomas accompanied Dad to the police to determine the welfare of arrested Claflin students. As he recalled in an interview: "I was told that the chief of police, who didn't like colored men, called the kids 'agitators.' I told the president [Dad], 'Let's go to see the chief together.' I got my courage up and looked the chief in the eye and said, 'Chief, I was born here and this president does not stand alone. He belongs to a family of colleges.' I just looked him in the eye. If you're not a southerner, Black or white, you won't understand [the courage this took]."[14] Such assistance was surely helpful, but Thomas lived out of state and tended eleven other

HBCU Methodist colleges. Left to navigate the Orangeburg situation were those on site.

Although Dad was not an identifiable NAACP leader, he gave at least one prominent keynote address supporting the protests. In 1961, a year after the police fire-hosed students, Dad spoke at a minister's conference associated with the NAACP Southeastern Regional Convention. During that talk he defended "church action in civil rights" as part of the church's role as "an instrument of God's purpose for man." He cited scriptural references in support of the equality of human beings as well as a Methodist creed upholding "civil liberties and civil rights": "'We stand for the recognition and maintenance of the rights and responsibilities of free speech, free assembly and a free press and for the encouragement of free communications of ideas essential to the discovery of truth.' [Underlined in typed text:] *This latter paragraph is most significant:* 'We stand for the rights of all individuals and groups to advocate any peaceful and constitutional method for the solution of problems that may confront society.'" Finally Dad called for "a dynamic program of social action" led by "an intelligent and dynamic ministry."[15]

The NAACP's national church secretary, Edward J. Odom, wrote a week later asking for a copy of Dad's speech and praising his "support of the creative student protests. . . . Your perceptive, balanced, and articulate presentation was inspiring as was evidenced by the response of the group." Odom even gave Dad a label, thanking him for his "constructive leadership": "You have shown the way of constructive leadership for church related colleges during this period of change and transition in the relation between the races."[16] Somehow mimeographed copies of this speech appeared, with unclear circulation; several copies rest in Dad's archives. Two weeks after his talk, police arrested a peaceful group of high school and college students (including Claflin students) demonstrating at the state capitol building. Their legal defense led to a 1963 US Supreme Court ruling that affirmed the rights of peaceful civil rights marchers.[17]

My parents proved their mettle by stepping forward to join a school desegregation lawsuit. In 1964 and for some years thereafter, even for independent professionals, it took considerable courage to sign a petition asking for transfer of one's Black child to an all-white school in South Carolina. The experiences of Clarendon County had shown how lethal such action could be, as had the 1955 Orangeburg desegregation petitions. Not until 1963 did the first Black plaintiffs successfully enter petitioned schools in our state. These were mostly relatives of NAACP leaders, as were Monteith and Brown. In Orangeburg several of our local NAACP leaders had placed themselves on lists of petitioners for public school desegregation in 1955, including McCollom, but such leaders only had

Pres. Maceo Nance; Benjamin Hooks, national NAACP executive director;
Pres. H. V. Manning, 1967. Hooks visited Claflin for its 1967 Founders' Day
celebration. Family album photo. Courtesy Cecil Williams, photographer.

so many children, and these gradually aged out. By the early 1960s, it was necessary to recruit other parents and their children as well.

It is my understanding that, for the first cohort, NAACP leaders in our town approached local families whose children were best prepared academically, including several Felton students' families. We were, in that sense, "chosen." Rachel Devlin notes in *A Girl Stands at the Door* that civil rights leaders tended to select girls for several reasons, partially because our gendered upbringing had given us the temperament needed to conform to social norms and act with decorum. (With Mom's attention to etiquette and calm demeanor, this certainly characterized my upbringing.) Again, our town echoed this strategy; most of our chosen students were girls.

As Devlin also notes, "first" children's families had a wide range of motivations for accepting such a call to action. Several factors probably motivated my parents to join the first wave of petitioners in our school district. Influential must have been Dad's quiet revolutionary spirit, close association with Newman and McCollom, tangible support for Claflin's student protestors, immersion in NAACP culture, and belief in civil liberties; possibly Mom would have been a little less enthusiastic about these things, but she supported Dad in all things. Of more concern for her may have been school quality. In spite of Turner's pleas, the state had not expanded Felton to include a high school that could offer an alternative to the school district's Black public high school. The carefully nurtured education that my classmates and I had received at Felton ended after eighth grade. Throughout I had done well in school and very well on national standardized tests. When I entered the all-Black Wilkinson High School in 1963–64, Wilkinson had wonderful teachers but easier classes compared to Felton. My parents saw that this left me plenty of free time with little homework, and this may have concerned them.

In addition I must have expressed my desire to do something for the Orangeburg movement. This is in keeping with Devlin's finding that some "first" girls petitioned their own parents to let them step up to this movement task. I do not remember doing this, or their asking my opinion, but I would have been a willing participant if they did; they knew of my disappointment in not being able to picket for freedom. Perhaps I did petition them. This lawsuit was a chance for me to play my part in a great crusade.

Getting Ready to Integrate

They joined the lawsuit filed during school year 1963–64, destined to become my only year attending Wilkinson High School. At Wilkinson I was happy to find a new universe of friends to complement my close-knit Felton schoolmates. This automatically broadened my perspective, since Felton had mostly middle-class students, whereas Wilkinson included more working-class students who would have to struggle to make a way for themselves in life. I joined the choir, a wonderful group of youths who sang beautifully under our competent director's tutelage, and I became publicity manager for the yearbook staff, unusual for a freshman but part of their strategy for nurturing potential future editors. Some of the teachers, such as Mrs. J. Roland in English and Ms. E. Samuels in French, which was the only foreign language offered, provided great positive feedback and inspiration. Watching team sports and attending chaperone-studded school dances were good diversions, as were the National Honor Society, the French Club, and the Student Council, all of which I joined. Along the way I picked up two "boyfriends," which meant boys that I talked to in the hallway between classes. My yearbook pictures show an obviously happy and active thirteen-year-old girl with a broad smile.[18] The only marring incident, previously mentioned, was the fact that I had to go to school in spite of a boycott set to protest the school board's firing of Mrs. Rackley.

Orangeburg itself had exploded with civil rights activity that the local police and politicians suppressed in frightening ways. Their reactions justified my parents' caution, especially their decision to forbid me from marching.

One instigating event for an elevation in activism in the summer of 1963 may have been requests from the Orangeburg NAACP for the mayor to establish a biracial committee. A June 27, 1963, handwritten memo indicates that the mayor had not responded to several such requests, and so the "steering committee in meeting 6/25/63 voted to recommend program of harassment," including sit-ins, at certain local businesses. The memo also mentioned arrangements for the possible need to raise bond money in case of arrests. Two weeks later a letter to the mayor typed on my dentist's stationery proposed fifteen names for such a committee, including Pres. H. V. Manning; all other names were prominent local Black citizens.[19] Another incident: earlier that summer my friend Pat's father, Arthur Rose, asked an attorney how to get Arthur "Artie" Rose Jr. enrolled in a nearby white elementary school; Artie eventually entered that school, and Pat entered the junior high, but not until a year later, under court order.[20]

Although it is not clear if the mayor ever responded to the committee request, pickets increased by August 1963. The first issue of the *Torch*, published on August 28, 1963, reported that the steering committee for the Orangeburg movement had presented a list of ten objectives to the mayor and city council. These objectives included removing segregation signs from public buildings; upgrading city government employment for Black citizens; opening all training, playground, and recreational facilities to all persons regardless of race; and influencing all school districts to begin to comply with the 1954 *Brown* decision. That list evidently generated little response. Picketing of downtown stores ramped up, leading to arrests of thirty-one "freedom fighters" in August, with eight young men sent to chain gangs, harsh punishment for college students. This happened after seven of them, in solidarity with the eighth one (sentenced to thirty days on a chain gang), refused to pay the one-hundred-dollar fine.

The September 5, 1963, issue of the *Torch* reported that police surrounded picketers but that incidents of heckling, rock throwing, and physical intimidation by white locals went unchecked by the police. Numbers of those arrested exploded by October; for several weeks lists of jailed picketers took up entire pages of the newsletter. In one incident sixty high school students marched peacefully, but the police arrested and held fifty of them in jail overnight, with no food. Some children, from eleven to seventeen years old, sat in jail for two days and two nights without bail, in dark and smelly cells, with feces-encrusted toilets and the cold floor for beds, all for the crime of marching peacefully.[21]

The newsletter also reported significant victories, however. White locals received notice that the old days were over. National NAACP leader Roy Wilkins came to speak for a November branch event held at Trinity one Wednesday evening.[22] Downtown merchants lost business and applied pressure to resolve the issues. Black residents stepped forward to supply food and refreshments for picketers who, at some points, maintained picket lines every day. Significantly, picketers maintained their dignity throughout all, following the newsletter's admonition to "be the most excellent citizen possible under all circumstances."[23] The protestors' excellent demeanor and training in nonviolence, which Reverend Newman's statewide leadership doubtless enabled, were on full display.

All this was, of course, local reflection of a national civil rights movement, with its own complement of pickets, boycotts, and police repression. The movement leaders in our town identified largely with the NAACP, but other groups were more active in other states. In 1963 several membership-based civil rights organizations, including the NAACP, the Brotherhood of Sleeping Car Porters, CORE, SNCC, SCLC, and the Urban League, came together to dialogue with Pres. John F. Kennedy about support for his proposed civil rights legislation. Those leaders planned what became the March on Washington on August 28, 1963. There Dr. King, the last speaker, gave his "I Have a Dream" speech to two hundred thousand people plus posterity.[24] White resisters at the local level were not impressed; harassment and suppression escalated, and on September 15, 1963, white supremacists bombed Birmingham, Alabama's Sixteenth Street Baptist Church, killing four Black girls gathered there for Sunday school.

Soon after that dastardly church bombing, Orangeburg movement leaders organized a local protest march and demonstration ending in the downtown square that contained a statute of a Confederate soldier. Williams took photographs of the dignified demonstration. Marchers surrounded the square and knelt in prayer. One protester, writing in the *Torch*, captured the outrage but also the optimism of those days:

> As I stood at Confederate Square last Sunday . . . my eyes wandered over the crowd of nearly 800 standing with me—and I felt a sweet tremor deep inside. For this crowd swelled with the hopeful, the fervent, the dedicated, the undaunted adults in our community who are united, specifically, in the building of a better Orangeburg. And there were the energetic, youthful, disciplined, informed, commanding students bearing beautifully the heritage of the past and the challenge of the present. And there were the children. They were alert and unafraid. They were emulating their parents and teachers around them. Well versed in the magnificent history of

our race and loyal to the American dream, they stood, quietly ordained, tomorrow's leaders. . . . The silent crowd knelt as one and prayed. The eloquently silent crowd was ONE. . . . Suddenly, my sad heart was joyful.[25]

In Orangeburg, throughout that year of constant pickets, burgeoning arrest lists, downtown businesses' crises, shopping boycotts, and inspirational rallies, the topic of school desegregation was never far below the surface. School desegregation was part of the original list of ten objectives/demands given to local government leaders. It was also part of the list of twenty actions that the *Torch* asked all readers to undertake: registering to vote, joining boycotts, helping to plan mass meetings, participating in sit-ins and picket lines, writing letters to editors, learning about "Negro history," and helping "integrate schools and colleges—yours and others," to name a few. By the November 8 issue, parents of fourteen Black students had requested transfer to the all-white Orangeburg schools. The district's school superintendent held private meetings with several of these parents, according to the February 13 issue. By March 16, 1964, parents of twenty-three Black children, including me, had filed suit.

Probably during that spring or summer of 1964, Williams photographed a celebration for those who would integrate the local white schools. I have only faint memories of that evening, but photographs clearly show many of the nineteen who integrated schools that fall. The NAACP sponsored this event; we were standing in the pews at Trinity as we received recognition. Almost all of us were girls, as Rachel Devlin would have predicted. In one of the images, my father and sister are standing as well, several rows behind us, so families and parents must have received recognition. At the time it seemed to me this was just another, inevitable stage in the civil rights movement. We might even find new friends at the white school, as soon as they realized that we were just normal human beings.

Court papers for *Adams et al. v. School District No. 5 Orangeburg et al.* are dated March 20, 1964. Listed is the name of each Black student plus one parent; my mother signed on my behalf. Also listed are a few students who did not end up joining us in desegregating local schools that fall, such as Rackley's younger daughter Lurma, who had gone to jail regularly but experienced selective harassment because of her last name, so perhaps she had already done her penance.[26]

The language of the petition filed with the US district court, Orangeburg division, is standard legal fare, but two sentences stand out. The first: "The operation of a compulsory biracial school system in Orangeburg County violates rights of the plaintiffs and members of their class which are secured to them

"First" students planning to desegregate formerly all-white public schools, Orangeburg District 5, under court order. The NAACP honored this first wave possibly in the spring of 1964. Person in striped dress with glasses is June Manning, standing between Leona Ferguson (taller) and Patricia Rose (shorter). The male student with a striped sweater is Tyrone Dash. The parent and young child standing to the rear are Pres. H. V. Manning and Michelle Manning. Courtesy Cecil Williams, photographer.

by the due process and equal protection clauses of the 14th Amendment to the Federal Constitution." The Fourteenth amendment had come in handy once again. The other sentence: "The injury which plaintiffs and members of their class suffer as a result of the operation of a compulsory biracial school system in Orangeburg County is irreparable and shall continue to irreparably injure plaintiffs and their class."[27] And so we were irreparably injured, a claim that seems obvious in hindsight. A copy of our lawsuit papers sits in Workman's archives, so that segregationist journalist considered our *Adams* case significant.

The lawyers told our parents that if pending civil rights legislation passed, our lawsuit would be moot since it challenged the state constitution's required racial segregation in schools. President Kennedy's support for such legislation had gone nowhere in Congress, but his tragic assassination as well as other pivotal civil rights events that embarrassed the country's leaders on the international stage finally led to Pres. Lyndon Johnson pressing for, and receiving, congressional support for the 1964 Civil Rights Act.[28]

My parents knew that this was a significant landmark. The four of us were in the car, and I was sitting in the back seat behind the driver, Dad. We were driving back from one of our periodic treks to visit Miami relatives. Here are some notes I wrote many years later, relaying the tone of enthusiastic anticipation I felt at that moment in 1964.

As we were driving back from Florida, my parents were listening to the radio; an important announcement came over the air. It was July, possibly July 3rd; President Lyndon B. Johnson had on the evening of July 2nd signed the Civil Rights Act of 1964, which was now the law of the land. One moment this was a typical family car trip, my parents in the front seat and my sister and I in the rear, all of us wrapped no doubt in happy memories of our Miami sojourn. The next moment everything had changed. With no celebration, little emotion, using her normally even-toned voice, my mother turned around in her seat and said: "Well, June, this means you'll be going to a new high school in the fall."

I had just turned fourteen years old two weeks before. I knew this was coming . . . but for some reason the reality of changing schools did not hit me until that moment. Tenth grade would be such an adventure! Everyone in our community knew that "separate but equal" was a farce, a pretense of equality for Black children's educational experience, and so I would be going to a better school! The civil rights movement was always in the news, and I had felt my part in this great mission was too small, but now I would be in the forefront! I said very little, but in my mind and heart excitement began to grow.

Actually, more was required than the signing; a district court order was issued mandating approval of the request that the school district allow nineteen of us to transfer to formerly all-white public schools. We were all excited and eager to prepare for our new schools. Somehow local sponsors quickly put together a tutoring program for those of us who would be making the transition.[29] The sessions took place in a Quonset hut owned by Trinity and located adjacent to its parking lot.

I remember the tutors well. Most of them were young white college students who had driven down from the Northeast expressly to help us prepare for our transition. Some freedom schools in the South that summer focused on Black history and political education, but our 1964 program offered mostly academic tutoring sessions on various topics depending on our grade level, operating under the assumption that our Black schools had not prepared us well for our new venture. The tutors' efforts centered, for me, on English and chemistry, which I would be taking in tenth grade at Orangeburg High School. Since time was limited, for chemistry the major task set out for me was to memorize the periodic table of elements, leading to a tangible accomplishment that gave me some confidence.

What was memorable about that summer program was not the quality of the tutoring in terms of academics, however. Instead I remember the kindness and genuine interest that the visiting white students seemed to show us. Many of them came from Ivy League schools and saw their tutoring service as a contribution to the civil rights movement. This was probably, for most of us Black students, our first encounter with friendly white people in close quarters.

Not only were they friendly; they actually took an interest in us personally, almost as if they were trying to inoculate us against the hatred we might face. One tutor gave me a book, Edwin A. Abbott's *Flatland,* introducing me to geometry. Another tutor, a product of a northern family that had moved to nearby Columbia, was particularly kind. Larry, also a high schooler, promptly won my heart, with feelings reciprocated, and memories of this remarkable young man who seemed to have no fear of walking me home, in broad daylight, served as a comforting talisman during the hardest days. My father's disapproving face, evident when Larry came to call on me at our house, evocative perhaps of both present dangers and ancient memories of illicit interracial sexual liaisons, put an abrupt end to wherever that interracial friendship might have led. As I weathered the hostile storm of high school over the next three years, I thought back many times to the kindness of those white youths, as a way to remind me that not all white people were hateful toward Black people. These students had prepared us in different ways than they anticipated.

A Rude Awakening

At the beginning of the school year, the school superintendent asked the thirteen Black high school students—the other six of the nineteen went to elementary or junior high schools—to stay home the first day or two while he convened a meeting in the gymnasium.[30] The purpose of that meeting was to explain the situation to the white students and to ask for a peaceful transition. We Black students came on the second or third day. Most of us came by bus, but I lived too close for that; I arrived in the back of a police car, which dropped me off next to a corridor purposefully emptied of white students. Because of this, we faced no heckling or angry crowds upon our arrival. We went to the office to find out locations for our various classes.

The rude awakening was realizing that the students, and some of the faculty, had already figured out a way to resist what they saw as an unfairly imposed integration process. They did this by using an age-old process, ostracism, coupled with a steady program of harassment. This I had not expected. My fledgling hopes for friendship or at least tolerance immediately died.

Because others have written about some of the hardships that the first students to integrate white public school systems faced, I do not wish to dwell upon this unduly. However, I will share several additional short remembrances that I wrote much later in life, maybe twenty or thirty years after high school, as a form of self-reflection and healing. When I wrote them, it was still possible to remember many events and impressions with fresh urgency, and writing them down was helpful, because it allowed me to forget them. I did forget many of the details, but I had saved these pieces of writing, set off below in italics, and I have other memories as well. Here is a reflection concerning the very beginning of that year, describing everyday harassment but trying to explain it to myself.

We [a few of the students] had arrived at school on the first day in the back of police cars, summoned by the school superintendent as a way to avoid possible trouble. Our new white classmates had never attended school with a black student or teacher—with the possible exception of a few whites who had moved from elsewhere in the country and did not eagerly publicize this fact—and neither had their families. . . . The students' response to our presence seemed to be an organized effort to resist by harassing us in whatever way was possible, using such means as catcalls, mocking and twisted faces, racial epithets, spitballs, and other creative mechanisms. It was common for an innocent action such as accidentally bumping into or brushing against a fellow student to cause major reaction, among the most active resisters: he or she used the occasion to jump backwards and feign contamination. Trying to make eye contact opened the door to getting a hushed but vicious whisper—"What you lookin' at?"—accompanied by baleful glares or sneers. Some more reticent white students were prepared to tolerate their peers' gross behavior, as a show of passive acceptance, or else they embraced simple ostracism and shunning, all in reaction to "forced" racial integration. During class I'd see no smiles directed my way, and experience no sharing of notes or ideas or even simple pleasantries about the weather. The sense of isolation, therefore, was carefully constructed, by means both vigorous and less so.

Before long it became clear that this was my new reality, a high school population determined to broadcast their antipathy and hatred toward intrusive Black people. This came after years of living in the same community with these people but living in a way that was profoundly isolated. The careful shelter that my parents and Black adults had built no longer worked. My parents made sure that at least I arrived safely.

> A young man usually drove me to school because my parents were very much afraid for my safety. Although Orangeburg High School was just over a mile from my house, and I could have easily walked there, this would have required me to walk through white neighborhoods. People were angry enough; my parents did not want me to have to walk through all of that anger. They both worked, Mom in her classroom or taking care of my sister and Dad in his office, and so they hired a Claflin male student to drive me to school. This made sure that I arrived without having to walk through hostile neighborhoods, but it also offered an initial bit of protection, because the white students could see that a young black man dropped me off and made sure that I made it out of the car and into the first building safely. Only once or twice did someone actually throw an egg at the car, or spit on it; mostly they let me enter that building without incident.

This was more than the other Black students had, but once we all arrived in the morning, such protection ended. My reflections chronicle my steady deterioration in self-confidence and joy. I found out later in life that the kinds of emotions expressed in the next passage, particularly stomach tension upon awakening, were possible signs of juvenile depression or anxiety, but I had no way of knowing this. This was not a self-generated depression, born of genetics and ordinary circumstances viewed through a clouded lens; this was the result of a systematic policy of racial harassment at a public school. Here is a series of passage describing my own emotional and physical response to awakening on school mornings.

> I awoke suddenly. For a long moment, I lay in bed, trying to get oriented. The birds were chirping, the sounds of morning drifted through the window, a few cars passed by. Everything should have seemed normal, but did not. I struggled to remember what was wrong, to snatch some meaning from the faint but familiar sense of dread that hung over my bed in spite of the dawning light. When I remembered, a slow tight knot began to form in

my stomach, and gradually spread throughout my body. The problem was simply that it was time to go to school.

Until that year, so memorable for many reasons, I had always adored school. Almost all of my best childhood memories were tied up with school, with the excitement of going to nursery school and then kindergarten, with the flush that came from the exhilarating experience of learning something new and learning it well. Now it seemed as if my favorite pursuit had become my greatest torture. Every school day required me to live in a state of persistent and generalized anxiety. The weight of my people and their progress was upon my shoulders, and my duty was to get up and go to school every morning in spite of the weight on those shoulders and the knot in my stomach. It was getting harder and harder to pretend my life was normal.

One way of coping seemed to be to refuse to wake up. Every week day morning I resisted, finally awakening as if snatched from the world of sleep by an impatient vixen. Every morning I lay in bed as long as was possible, savoring the safety of cool white sheets, yearning for a day off, a week off, the year off. And every morning that I was not truly sick, I somehow managed to overcome inertia, and to get up from my womb-like bed.

With determination I straightened the bed coverings, dressed, combed my hair, greeted my parents and my sister, ate breakfast, collected my books. On those mornings before a quiz or test I reviewed the assignments that I'd spent all afternoon and evening studying. On Friday morning, this meant reviewing assigned vocabulary words. One advantage of this new school, I thought: I was learning a lot of new vocabulary words. The short ride to the school provided just enough time to review each of them in my mind—loquacious, voracious, vivacious. Over and over I repeated the words and their definitions, tucking them into appropriate sentences, imagining ways to use them in everyday conversation. These new words would not make me more acceptable to my classmates, it was clear, but they were certainly expanding my capacities. I could now read sophisticated books and articles without having to look up words in the dictionary every few pages, and my writing was getting better.

By the time the young man who drove me to school dropped me off, I was almost ready for the day. He parked the car next to the drop-off point, wished me a pleasant goodbye, and waited while I collected my things and got out. Pulling my jacket around me, I dove into the moving stream of students, a brown spot among the white, all of us going to our first class of the morning.

Once we had arrived, the fate of the day depended on the whims of the white students we passed in the hallway and on the particular class. Some teachers made it clear our presence was unwelcome, as these passages describe, but even then, I strove to learn.

My first stop during a school day at Orangeburg High School, after leaving the drop-off point, was my assigned storage locker to pick up or leave materials and books. Then the next destination after homeroom was my first class for the morning, which was English during my sophomore year. Before entering this high school filled with hostile white people, English was a well-loved class, evoking great confidence and feelings of security, for I had always loved books, reading, and writing. Books were, in fact, a chief means of travel and escape during my childhood and adolescence. I had long ago mastered the technique of using a flashlight under the bed's sheets to continue reading after my parents thought the lights were out; my white cloth sheets formed a very effective tent that kept me sheltered and warm during these flights of fantasy. I spent much of my modest allowance buying Scholastic Book Club books via mail order. As a voracious reader, commonly running through two or three adolescent novels in a weekend, English had never required a lot of study, thought, or anxiety, and instead evoked joy and confidence.

This English class was very different from the previous year's English class, however. For starters, as with every class in this high school, I could count on no comrades or friends among the students. We all filed into the doorway and sat in silence, but in spite of my desire for social contact it was quite certain that I would not to be included in any friendly chatter on the way in or out.

Bullying and ostracism are a rampant disease of the young, and social exclusion is one of the reasons people dislike high school. For that age group, any excuse will do to cluster in groupings and to bifurcate between the popular and the unpopular—perceived looks, sports acumen or lack thereof, socio-economic class, physical disability, intelligence, even unfamiliarity due to a recent move into the school district. And of course race, ethnicity, or religion. But what we experienced during the first years of public school integration in my home town was different somehow. The very few Black students knew the history of our context; the NAACP had convinced our parents, in spite of their fears, to file suit in order to get us into that school. The confrontation of "difference" was new, for everyone involved, and challenged decades-old lines of firm separation, ensconced in law, faith, and political ideology.

The extent of the racial harassment during active class periods depended somewhat on the teacher's philosophy concerning the need to check unruly behavior. In sophomore English, for example, visible harassment did not commonly take place, because the teacher ran a well-organized operation with no room for frivolity, but neither was it possible to count on good will or respect. The typical mode was to ignore a black student's existence altogether, and in this the teacher was little better than the students. This made it awkward to raise one's hand, since she might ignore it, or to share writings and ideas, since these were widely scorned as soon as their author's identity became obvious. It was, indeed, a very lonely class-room. . . .

This first English teacher, to her credit, seemed to have everything plotted out for the class period, and actually offered instruction that was in many ways useful to anyone who cared to learn. I settled into my seat, near the door and wall facing the hallway—giving me at least the illusion of being able to escape in case of emergency—and struggled to rise above the hostile environment and learn something. I'd watch as she created complex constructions on the blackboard, sentence diagrams, which were new concepts to me. We started out by placing a subject and predicate on one line, separated by a vertical bar, and then progressed by adding and extending diagonal modifying lines this way and that. By the end of the year most of us could create one of the many-layered concoctions for ourselves, and we were able to diagram just about any sentence we encountered. This useful set of skills would in the future steer me through many a convoluted sentence, paragraph, and paper.

The literature we read, however, seemed designed to punish us for our transgressions, real and imagined. The teacher was especially fond of Charles Dickens and William Shakespeare, although her teaching style for

Shakespeare was far short of inspiring, and the Dickens novel she selected, *Great Expectations*, was as I discovered later in life among his works that I found least interesting. The novel did address social mobility, and some aspects of poverty and wealth, but it pretty much ignored the more pressing issues of social justice that arose vigorously during England's grimy industrial era, so fraught with working-class hardship, child labor, and economic oppression. . . .

As we plodded through verse after verse and page after page, I remembered with fondness our much lighter reading and writing assignments at Wilkinson High School. Mrs. Roland, my English teacher there, favored informal essays, and she had once asked us to write about the man we most admired in the world. I wrote about my Uncle Leroy, extolling his wonderful qualities and dedication to his wife, my Aunt Lenora; both lived in Miami. . . . I remember that essay in particular because over two decades later Mrs. Roland sent it to me in the mail. She was clearing out her keepsakes and had kept it all of that time. In striking contrast, my tenth-grade English teacher didn't seem to care if I lived or died. It was hard to write about anything I felt strongly about in that classroom of sentence diagrams and *Great Expectations*, a classroom where even an innocent smile provoked hostile glares.

It was however in that English class that I most pointedly experienced Orangeburg High School's superior academic preparation compared to the all-Black Wilkinson High School. This was due largely to vocabulary tests, designed to introduce us to ten words, weekly, that we were to memorize and begin to use in our writing and speech. We practiced enunciating these words as well as spelling and defining them, although I struggled to fit into an environment where I could barely understand everyone's "Southern accent," which characterized speech in the white community but not the Black. Once it became clear that "ah-peen-nyeen" was actually "opinion" and "rahgt" was actually "right," it didn't take long to learn to make the translation. For those school years and for the rest of my life, I stubbornly continued to pronounce things the way we did at Felton, very close to the way the national television newscasters did, rather than to use the contorted "Southern drawl" that does not characterize all Southern speech, composed of multiple dialects depending on state and locality within a state.

Part of the culture of that high school was to cling to all things related to the "Old South," including the drawl associated with whites in central South Carolina. The vocabulary words, fortunately, were immune to dialect, and some of them I've actually remembered over the years.

On one of the first days of school in that English teacher's classroom, I made a tactical error that I would soon regret. For some reason the teacher called on a series of students, expecting a "Yes" or "No." In the white Southern tradition, however, each of the other students, all white, answered "Yes, Ma'am" or "No, Ma'am." Having been raised with more of a generic American verbal tradition than a Southern one, in a Black community that did not use "Ma'am" regularly, I didn't know what to say. It was a sore point in our community that few whites addressed Blacks as "Ma'am," even if they were their elders; their tendency was to call Blacks of all ages by their first name, as a sign of disrespect. The only Blacks I knew of who said "Ma'am" to whites were maids, groundskeepers, or sharecroppers address-ing their white employers, and the use of that term among my friends was almost taboo. I decided at that moment to say what I was used to saying when speaking to teachers, "Yes." As she fastened her steely eyes upon me, this teacher who was not to smile upon me for the whole year proceeded to tell me, and the class, that she would not tolerate impudence and lack of respect. Anyone who was raised correctly knew enough to respond "Yes, Ma'am" to an adult, she noted, and under no circumstances was I to ad-dress her in any other way. As my fellow students smirked, I apologized and obeyed, tightly holding onto my safe seat by the door. Of course it was best to try to fit in.

The above account recalls happier days at the Black high school, implicitly ques-tioning the wisdom of this desegregation process under such circumstances, but it also acknowledges the stronger academic standards at my new school. The price for stronger standards was high, however. The English teacher described was one of the teachers who seemed most annoyed by desegregation, but others existed as well. Two of us—Evelyn Dash and myself—had tried to sign up for choir, remembering happy times in the Wilkinson High School choir, but the choir director refused to accept us. His excuse was something like we would not fit into the looks of the choir, especially for its annual operetta. In this case it was possible to go to the principal and raise a complaint, because the exclusion was so blatant. Grudgingly he tolerated us signing up for his precious choir, and our voices enriched his alto section in ways he might have found surprising. Other teachers showed their resistance largely by ignoring us as much possible or by simply tolerating in-classroom racial harassment.

In some classes it was possible to progress anyway, either because the teachers kept order in the classroom or turned out to be relatively supportive, a few examples of which I remember, or because the subject was so captivating that the teacher's attitude did not matter very much. In the category of supportive teachers, I can remember three. For eleventh-grade English, Celeste Daniel was a wise, judicious soul who once read aloud my short essay as an example for the class to emulate; the essay concerned compassion for an impoverished playmate in Charleston. My twelfth-grade physics teacher, Doc Moore, a polio survivor with an impaired gait who was happy to be alive, favored any student interested in his topic, which I found fascinating. Mrs. Higginbotham, who taught, of all things, Latin, was genuinely friendly, and I even joined her Latin Club; I missed her when she left after one year. Here is a comment that recounts how I ended up in her class and again echoes the theme of my personal loss after leaving friendlier Black teachers.

In striking contrast [to my new English teacher], another language teacher, Mrs. Higginbotham, was notably warm and friendly even in this context, and she did not allow racial harassment in the classroom. I will not soon forget her kindnesses. She taught Latin, a "dead" language I would never have thought to take except for my mother, who suggested this path as a way to build up my vocabulary in preparation for one of several possible careers. Switching to Latin would also help me recover from the grievous loss of my former French teacher, Miss Samuels, who had dressed like a Parisian model, introduced us to lovely French novels, and entertained us with stories of her travels to France. I did not continue French because my new high school's French teacher, wife of one of the most rabid of local white segregationists and a popular radio commentator, told me that I could not enter her second-year class without taking the first-year students' final exam within the next few days. If I did not want to take the test, she intoned, I should take first-year French again, which my already-wounded pride would not allow. I believed that the dark-skinned, elegant Miss Samuels had taught us first-year French quite well at the Black high school, and I did not trust this white teacher, whose husband publicly railed against the evils of "forced" integration.

In the category of classes where it didn't matter much what the white teacher thought, I would place all of my mathematics courses, including algebra, geometry, and calculus. Mathematics, for me, seemed captivating, doubtless because of my mother's influence. Here is a post-experience narrative with another tone, one of joyful survival:

> I enrolled in several mathematics classes, including Geometry. This class built upon and confirmed a lifelong love of equations, logic, and mathematical relations, a love that was true even though, in the end, it did not determine my career choice. Although I enjoyed math classes, the same social rules of racial hostility applied there as in all my other classes. Except in those rare classes with one or two other Black students, these rules were simple: except for the teacher, no one spoke to me or looked at me unless this was to stare and taunt. If I spoke to the students, either they did not answer or they answered with obscenities. This steady, day-to-day ostracism occurred because the local white community was not ready to accept Blacks in their schools and they wanted to make sure we knew this.
>
> Beyond such regular rejection, however, I don't remember actual experiences in my several math classes. I believe that the reason for this strange gap is that I put myself fully into the material, and paid little attention to anyone else in math class, including the teacher. I was much too focused to notice what was going on around me.
>
> I do remember a book I read just before transferring to that high school. *Flatland: A Romance of Many Dimensions*, made a strong and lasting impression upon me. Although published in the late 1800s, this book must remain popular with the hardy few, since many web pages refer to it or reproduce it, and several editions are available for sale even today. A young white college student from up North recommended it to me [during the 1964 summer tutoring sessions].
>
> *Flatland* was a "geometry fiction," in contrast to a "science fiction," and told of a world where everyone lived in two dimensions. The narrator was a square, and he was as flat as a mat. Everyone else in his world was also flat, since each person was a line, triangle, square, circle, pentagon, or some other such polygon. Most of these flat beings had no clue that it was possible to have three dimensions, as human bodies and other ordinary

objects do, and they could not imagine that other types of creatures existed. They looked like paper cutouts, moving sideways on the surface that formed their world, but they were perfectly comfortable with themselves, their society, and its rules of conduct. Unaware of their limitations, they even adapted to not being able to see how many sides their fellow beings had. Each one judged the shape of another by feeling for the sharpness of angles, or by looking for other subtle clues.

Flatland was fun to read, and it challenged my perceptions of space and time. This challenge was excellent preparation for the abstract worlds of algebra, geometry, calculus, and physics, and later for my chosen field of urban planning. The book was a pleasant diversion from the reality of life, and yet at the same time, in hindsight, it was an allegory for my life. In those three high school years I was trapped in a Flatland, surrounded by creatures bounded by their own narrow-mindedness and inability to perceive a different reality. My white classmates were happy enough with their limited vision, even though they missed seeing the complexities of life. They had trouble envisioning a three-dimensional existence, which would surely have included opening the doors of the human heart to all fellow human beings, no matter the color, race, or ethnicity. Instead, their parents and their community had raised them to be flat, intolerant of difference, isolated from diversity, lulled by a self-righteous society that was sure of its own one-dimensional view of the world.

Such fantasies as *Flatland*—and my continual reading of both juvenile and adult novels as well as other such pastimes—helped keep me alive during difficult times. Mathematics was a way out, good stuff for both idle and serious diversions. Once I entered the door of whatever math class I was taking, my focus for that moment became whatever we were working on for that particular unit of study. I was determined to engage fully in each new math lesson, and I was determined to master each skill and knowledge set. This determination had something to do with love for the subject, and something to do with my need to help prove the racists wrong. We needed to support our civil rights argument that blacks were not stupid. We had to show unassailable evidence of intelligence. One sure way to demonstrate intelligence was to excel in doing something, and math and science suited this purpose very well.

I had several coping mechanisms. Reading had always served as a means of escape, and it did during that time as well. I also continued piano/organ lessons and youth activities at Trinity. In addition school itself helped; the ramping up of academic standards was welcome challenge for me. Some of my friends found comfortable niches in their studies or in some other sphere of influence. Evelyn's brother Tyrone began to play basketball, and eventually he experienced a certain amount of acceptance from his teammates, at least to the point that they would defend him when other white teams confronted him. Evelyn sang very well, much better than I did, and the choir was a primary sphere of influence for her. Mine was taking difficult classes whenever possible. I determined that it was necessary for me to prove that Black students could be intelligent, *more* intelligent. This became a calling.

We Black pioneers also coped by huddling together when possible. For the first year, the thirteen of us were in different grades and homerooms, making it likely that we were the only Black students in our classes, but we would gather at any other opportunity, such as lunchtime, to provide an ounce of friendly chatter. By the time I reached twelfth grade, with dozens more Black students attending, these gatherings provided welcome ways of sharing battle stories. During that first year, one incident stands out in my mind as a minor rebellion on our part.

The white students refused to sit at any lunch table with a Black person, but the lunchroom was always crowded because of cramped quarters. We soon realized that we Black students would always have a seat; all we had to do was send one of us to sit at an empty seat. All the white students promptly stood up, holding their trays aloft—instant seats for the Black students. Inspiration hit: let's have a sit-in! One day we spread out, several of us each sitting one per table. All of the white students sitting at those tables stood up. The room was pandemonium, with white students standing arrayed against the wall, holding their trays, unsure what to do. This happened for maybe two or three days. The principal called us into his office. He scolded us, but after a few somber moments we delinquents could not stop laughing. We reduced the scope of disruption after that meeting, disrupting only one or two tables at a time. As the years wore on, white students were less likely to stand up so quickly, and I had at least one funny story about that school to tell my future classroom students.

Perhaps the strongest coping mechanism was belief in the civil rights movement as a spiritual mission. Being one of the "first" was indeed a weight, but it was an honorable weight. The civil rights movement had a messianic quality honed by its association with people of great character and vision. Although our local leaders had not written much, Dr. King's writings inspired us all, as did his speeches. Rallies—national, state, and local—reinforced the vision: we were steadily moving toward "freedom." We were undertaking a venture that would change American society for the better. We were forcing the issue on desegregation, and we felt our efforts would not be in vain. We had absolute faith in progress and something approaching pity for what we saw as the moral backwardness of our local white community and its children.

My parents, however, were very concerned with the turn of events, heroic or not. They had not expected to see me undergo such hardship. They watched their happy ninth grader, involved in multiple school activities, potential yearbook editor, turn into a girl who did not want to get out of bed in the mornings and could barely speak about what she had experienced during the school day.

Only once did I experience a bodily attack other than spitballs. One day a hostile white classmate, mumbling some epithet, shoved me into the lockers so hard as he passed by that my leg starting bleeding. I went to the bathroom to clean myself up and later told Pat Rose about this, but I did not tell Mom when I got home. When in the evening Pat came by to see how I was doing, Mom knew nothing about the incident; she was not pleased that she heard about this from Pat instead of me. She did not realize that I did not tell her and Dad even a fraction of what was happening to us, to protect them. I loved my parents too much to reveal to them to the fullness of the awful truth, especially my steady decline in self-esteem and well-being.

They knew anyway. At some point during my first or second year, my parents said that I should leave and attend the Black boarding school in Camden, Mather Academy. I thought about this for only a moment and then begged not to go. First, I did not want to leave my family, but second and most important, I had a charge, and I was determined to finish it. Many of the other Black students' families could not afford boarding school; it would have been a loss of face for me to leave that situation with them left behind. A few Black students did leave, but I stayed until bitter end, graduation.

I have described only one person's experience. Each of the Black students who entered such schools in the first years of desegregation had a different experience. From 2008 to 2013, Millicent Brown videotaped several oral histories of "first" integrating students from South Carolina and other states. She recorded some of these in Claflin's studio. Charleston's Avery Research Center has processed a portion of these tapes and posted some of them online.

Artie Rose's oral interview, shared with me by archivists, shows that he had a very different experience when he entered his white elementary school. There he had but one teacher all day; she largely accepted his presence and, gradually, so did at least a few of his classmates. Such a soft landing helped when he entered junior high school with the same classmates. As he noted, his big sister Pat, the only Black student to integrate that junior high school in 1964, weathered systematic harassment, particularly in the hallways, where she had no protection from the taunts.[31] Pat had a fighting spirit (like her dad), and she did not take insults lightly, sometimes returning them in kind. In that sense, she was an anomaly compared to the rest of us local "first" girls, socialized to absorb harassment without rebuttal. She would regale me with accounts of her tart replies to hecklers, but she often went home after school with chewing gum stuck in her hair. I stayed in contact with Pat for many years during adulthood; in my opinion this wonderful, articulate woman never relinquished her anger, never recovered from her desegregation experiences. She faced other challenges in life as well, including death of a child, but she seemed to hold the trauma of our shared history within herself much more than I did. Sometimes she reminded me of events I had long before suppressed as a coping strategy, such as the bleeding leg incident. Her health faltered with stress-related diseases in her fifties, placing her in a nursing home; she later died there at age sixty-three.

Tyrone Dash, who entered tenth grade along with me, came from a family that had signed the desegregation petition in the 1950s, causing the father to lose his job and need to work in Northern cities to support the family. The Dash family contributed three children to the 1964 lawsuit, Tyrone, Evelyn (my fellow choir member), and Jacqueline. Tyrone, a fervent supporter of the Orangeburg Movement, walking many picket lines and going to jail several times at the age of thirteen, called the 1964 signing of the US Civil Rights Act "one of the happiest days of my life," because of its promise of future racial progress. When we entered high school, however, "hell on earth started in my life." He recalled that local civil rights leaders tried to prepare us with anticipated scenarios, but they could not "prepare us for the brutal and horrific experience we encountered." At times he walked down the hall with people throwing rocks at him; no one spoke to him except to call him a n----r; in physical education three white guys blocked the entrance and started beating him so badly that he suffered scars that he still carries. He started playing basketball his second year and helped win games and grudging, partial acceptance, but letters came regularly from white schools saying they had never had a n----r play in their gym before, and "if I came they would hang me on an oak tree behind the gym." He traveled to those games anyway, because he had a purpose, "to make life in our society better for everyone."[32]

As I write this, the only archival tape available of a Black student who attended Orangeburg High School at the same time I did is one for Theodore "Teddy" Adams, from the Adams family listed first in our joint lawsuit. Teddy entered as a ninth grader. He had graduated with Bs from eighth grade at Christ the King Catholic School, the local Felton alternative that Black parents respected as a good school. His experience with desegregation was humbling. He took Algebra 1 at Christ the King, and as a boost a white northern tutor helped him review the material during the summer of 1964. If he had attended Wilkinson, he would have automatically entered Algebra 2. Orangeburg High School required him to take Algebra 1 over again. He made only Ds in that class, and he worked hard to get those Ds. He had similar problems with several other classes, including English; even after-school help from Wilkinson's English teachers did not raise his grades above Cs and Ds. This confirmed for him the inherent weakness of our Black educational system.[33]

Teddy remembered Black boys getting into physical fights as they tried to protect less assertive Black girls. This I did not remember, but what did resonate was his memory that we lost friends at Wilkinson when we disappeared from our old classmates' daily lives. His Black friends said that he thought he was better than they were because he was attending the white high school; mine seemed to drift away simply because of infrequent contact and my self-imposed study schedule. He recounted one alarming incident that I probably blanked out in my mind, as a defense mechanism: at some point during our first year, a white man broke out of the local jail and threatened to kill all thirteen Black students attending our new high school. Police found the fugitive in the woods behind the school on the second day of his escape; they converged in several police cars and arrested him before he could carry out this dastardly deed.

When Teddy and his Black classmates finally graduated in 1968, the local chapter of the NAACP took them out to dinner and gave each of them certificates. His grades were subpar, but both Claflin and SC State told him not to worry about grades and to apply; he chose Claflin.

Conclusion

This chapter is in large part a testimony to my parents and their role in a greater movement for constructive resilience in the Black community, with a focus on education. As an HBCU president, my father played a less-than-visible role in educating college students and in supporting civil rights activities in the early 1960s, but his was an essential role nonetheless.

The chapter also provides a glimpse into why Black people began to the cool to the idea of school desegregation as a cure-all for inferior Black education. Our experiences at Orangeburg High were eerily similar to those of other first students in other states in the southern, midwestern, and border regions. In some places, as Rachel Devlin describes, the experiences were much worse than ours, with daily physical beatings and white teachers' outright encouragement of harassment. Inhumane responses to desegregation were not isolated experiences in our small town; the tactics were too similar from place to place. This fact reveals either an organically emerging response of white people schooled in racial superiority devising their own forms of harassment or a set of calculated strategies carried out by networks of white resisters such as citizens' councils. Devlin suggests the latter.

Hence the harassment we suffered was not dissimilar to that in other towns, complete with racial epithets, ostracism, refusal to sit at the same lunchroom tables, the ever-present spitballs, frigid or hostile teachers, and just plain meanness. Not many places could tell of an escaped prisoner who threatened to kill all of the desegregating Black students as could we, but death threats, warnings, shouting mobs, and other such strategies unfolded for several years. Devlin describes the trauma the firsts experienced and their attempts at bravery, including protecting their own parents from detailed knowledge of daily events, as had I. Those parents and their communities must have known the truth. Enthusiasm among Black people for school desegregation began to wane—Black children were suffering, and other problems arose as well. Nevertheless the Black community sent more and more students into battle, in part to protect the few who were already there.

7

Struggling to Desegregate

After harrowing experiences for first Black students, we slowly started to recover from trauma. My own recovery was good, blessed by good fortune. Before describing that recovery, it is important to explain other efforts to improve education for Black children and youths in our state during those years. The relevant question is who, in the 1960s, supported school desegregation as a strategy for making such improvement and whether their goals triumphed. Desegregation goals soon faltered in several ways, but small successes made life easier for desegregation pioneers.

During this era the major promoter of desegregation and civil rights in our state was the NAACP, but it worked with CORE, SCLC, and SNCC on specific areas of concern. Because of the state NAACP branch's many agenda items, allied organizations worked on specific issues. The Black Palmetto Education Association (PEA, the new name of the PSTA), for example, continued representing Black teachers and working to improve education for Black students. For school desegregation white allies led two other organizations with supportive roles: the SCCHR and the state's American Friends Service Committee (AFSC).

Within the context of the efforts of these organizations, my own high school story involved several wonderful events leading up to and just after graduation, events that allowed me to move on with life.

Wright Champions Human Relations

Behind the scenes, unknown to many of us, a few people were working to try to build a multiracial society in our state. They faced enormous obstacles, as did SCCHR, one of the first white-led organizations to encourage interracial dialogue about the need for racial integration in all social spheres.

Mentioned briefly in an earlier chapter, Alice Spearman Wright, SCCHR's executive director, was "one of the few white women in her state deeply committed to advancing civil rights for African-Americans."[1] Wright herself had trained in interracial work while a college student, serving on Converse College's student YWCA interracial committee. With the support of the Southern Regional Council, she worked to find like-minded white people and to set up interracial state and local councils for South Carolina. Before her tenure SCCHR hosted interracial dialogues, but often their gatherings retained hallmarks of white supremacy; white and Black state council members did not eat at the same table, for example, in keeping with southern mores. In 1954 she ordered lunch for all of her state council's members so that Black members did not have to make a difficult hunt for food service in the middle of the daylong meetings. In this way she set up the expectation that Black and white members would eat together.[2] As a well-educated white woman, she was able to address powerful white people as an equal, but she also built strong, respectful relationships with Black people. Earl Middleton, a Black business owner from Orangeburg who worked with SCCHR for many years, noted this quality: "She never tried to act superior around us because she was white, as some others I had been around did, and I could relax during my conversations with her. She believed that Blacks and whites are equal. That inspired me to continue to do what I could to promote racial harmony. . . . Mrs. Spearman [Wright] was a daughter of privilege. She was educated and 'married well.' If she had so chosen, she could have lived a life of ease and spent her time entertaining, shopping, and traveling. Instead she chose to make a difference. She was hated by a lot of whites, but she was fearless. She knew she was doing the right thing, and their opinions did not matter to her. She knew who she was. Those in the white power structure . . . despised this fine lady."[3]

One of the intentions for SCCHR was to engage white South Carolinians who realized it was time to give up strict racial segregation, but this was a difficult task. The SCCHR collected essays and articles that chronicled the voices of such white people but also described the repercussions some of them faced for speaking out about their beliefs. This collection includes papers or talks written about white educators who called for compliance with the *Brown* decision but who soon lost their jobs because of their opinions.[4] Because such vocal white people were relatively few, Wright struggled to find others willing to serve even on mildly courageous local councils. At one point in the mid-1950s, she told two members of her statewide council, NAACP's president Hinton and secretary Simkins, that she could find no white people willing to help form interracial councils in the cities of Greenville, Spartanburg, and Rock Hill. As she later recalled in an oral interview, "I could not find one, not one person."[5] During the years of legislative oppression following the *Brown* decision, as the state legislature passed laws designed to discourage school desegregation and the NAACP, white moderates fell away from SCCHR, and between 1955 and 1957, its membership dropped from five hundred to one hundred.[6]

Wright instead chose to work with Black activists, sometimes as cheerleader: "Modjeska [Simkins] would call me sometimes and say the people in Summerton [Clarendon County] were getting so low and scared and the Reverend De Laine wants us to come down there and get them pepped up. And we'd go down there and speak and try to get their morale boosted again, you see. So really what I turned into more than anything else was pretty much full-time service to the Blacks." That service included making an exhaustive study of Black grassroots organizations in the state in order to invite them to a five-day 1959 SCLC meeting in Columbia, where Dr. King spoke; ghostwriting the invitation letters; and then sending them out by mail through her own office. She did this because the SCLC had a weak presence in the state and no ability to market such a conference.

The task gave her extraordinary insight into the complex network of the state's Black organizations, making her "a complete walking encyclopedia of any organization" in the Black population. She also participated in civil rights activities; CORE invited her to speak at a 1960 demonstration against segregated waiting rooms in Greenville's airport. Her state council's chairperson asked her not to speak, to avoid negative publicity (among white people), but Wright defiantly showed up as a participant anyway, one of only two white people to march with 250 Black people. She marched again with the NAACP, at Newman's invitation, in front of the state capitol to demand civil rights.[7] Yet Middleton says she was not a political activist: "Rather she advised Black people on what they could do about voting, organizing, and distributing information on basics such as cleanliness, running water, and education. . . . As I think back, she reminds me of the late Mother Teresa."[8]

For some years SCCHR supported the school improvement agenda indirectly. It analyzed public education expenditures, showing continued underfunding for Black students in the separate systems, and it monitored illiteracy rates, showing the continual lag for Black people.[9] Beginning about 1964, it played a stronger role. In 1964 SCCHR jointly sponsored, with the Georgia Council on Human Relations, a two-day conference on desegregating public schools. Wright invited, among many others, the coordinator of Greenville's summer tutoring program that had helped prepare fifty Black children to attend white schools in fall 1964. SCCHR cosponsored another conference on tutoring in

1965, offered a summer of tutoring in Columbia, and advised local human relations councils to visit families and meet with student leaders in desegregated schools as a way to cultivate cooperation.[10]

During the mid-1960s SCCHR participated in a statewide coalition of organizations committed to school desegregation, providing the coalition with at least a few white partners. Wright, the NAACP's Newman, and the Penn Community Center's director signed the invitation letter for a 1965 conference on desegregation held in Frogmore; other signers were state leaders of SCLC, the PEA, CORE, the Voter Education Project, the National Sharecroppers Fund, and the Parent Teachers Association. These were largely Black organizations, and all but the last were devoted to advancing civil rights. The conference's purpose was to "discuss ways to achieve substantial school desegregation for the school year 1965–66," which required Black parents to apply for transfer to white schools. As another example, in 1966 the PEA asked Wright to find white teachers willing to attend a conference on faculty desegregation, showing that they were active in this role as well; she delivered a list of such names.

SCCHR aimed to do even more on the ground. In 1966 Wright successfully applied for federal Office of Economic Opportunity funds to launch SPEED-UP, a program that offered tutoring and citizenship training to Black students in several towns, including Orangeburg. SPEED-UP hired tutors from an array of colleges and universities, including historically white in-state schools such as USC, Clemson, Coker College, Winthrop College, Limestone College, and Wofford College as well has HBCUs Claflin, SC State, and Benedict. Although SPEED-UP lasted only one year because of lack of funds, it engaged Black and white college students in educating younger Black public school students.[11]

Soon after SPEED-UP ended in 1967, Wright resigned from the SCCHR directorship, citing exhaustion after many years of effort: "I was just burned out; I absolutely was just shattered—I was nearly going to say tormented."[12] She had weathered isolation and various forms of harassment from white people, including physical attacks and sequential office eviction. When asked to name white supporters, she could name very few, but said that her Black associates gave her emotional sustenance. When she left SCCHR, it had 1,335 members, a sign of some success. Wright's successor, Paul Matthias, served as executive director until 1974, but he steered the organization toward racial inequities in welfare reform and in criminal justice. By the time SCCHR collapsed in 1975, membership was only 500.[13]

Wright's experiences showed how reluctant white South Carolinians were to support interracial dialogue, much less Black fights for equal civil rights. The tendency instead was to ostracize white allies such as Wright and several others who showed any support for Black civil rights. Her efforts to establish inter-racial councils faced fitful success but unearthed at least a few white citizens willing to join multiracial coalitions that supported school desegregation efforts through such means as recruiting and tutoring Black students. Her engagement in the civil rights resistance struggle encouraged Black people who otherwise had little visible local white support.

The school desegregation coalitions that she joined provided a shadow world of supporters not always visible but existing nonetheless. Their confer-ences offered one of the few places we could share experiences; my own par-ticipation seemed to have been in the coalition's 1965 desegregation conference, chaired by Rev. Newman, at Frogmore's Penn. Evidently I served with several other students on a panel titled "Emotional and Psychological Factors in School Desegregation." My name is on the program, located in SCCHR archives, but I have no memory of that panel; it took place during my first year at Orangeburg High, a time of personal trauma.[14]

Wright had more success building working relationships between Black and white youths than adults, and those young people went on to offer important service. The South Carolina Student Council on Human Relations, founded in 1961, included during its pilot year 280 students from thirteen white and seven Black institutions of higher education, providing a venue for Black and white students to get to know each other. For several years these students held conferences, participated in civil rights activities, and formed friendships. One of the white student members that Wright mentored through this council was M. Hayes Mizell, a USC graduate student who eventually led AFSC's state office.[15]

Mizell's American Friends

As I searched for people involved in the state's initial efforts to desegregate schools, a USC archivist told me that I should be sure to meet Mizell. Mizell worked with the AFSC for almost twenty years beginning in the mid-1960s. He met me for lunch one day in October 2017. He told me that he had kept detailed written records during those years and that I should refer to his archives for ac-counts of his opinions and experiences. He had kept written records, indeed. Mizell donated one of the largest collections ever received by the USC libraries; the collection now extends to 208 linear feet, an extraordinary trove. It includes several organizational records and numerous personal papers. When I asked him why he had kept such meticulous records, he said that when his father died he left almost no record of his life, leaving his son in the dark. Mizell, who had worked briefly in an archival library and was a history graduate student (eventually leaving that pursuit for the sake of activism), was determined to avoid doing the same.

Mizell's articles, reports, talks, letters, and memos to coworkers give important insight into the web of activity designed to support school desegregation during the 1960s and 1970s, as well as recording how difficult were the tasks. A staunch proponent of school desegregation as a pathway to improved education for Black people, Mizell fought hard to advance that process. One of his major contributions was to document how the process evolved in South Carolina.

Mizell's early life helps explain how a young southern white man of comfortable circumstances turned into a champion of school improvement for Black students. Mizell's family lived in several southern states during his childhood but settled in South Carolina. While at Wofford College, Mizell traveled to Washington, DC, where he and his fellow students, representatives of colleges from around the country, heard speakers such as Eleanor Roosevelt and US senator Hubert Humphrey. Enrolling as a graduate student at USC in 1960, from 1960 to 1963 he participated not only in Wright's student council but also in the parental SCCHR itself, helping to plan conferences and programs. In 1961 he joined seventy-five Black students from HBCU Benedict College in staging a sit-in at a segregated Woolworth's lunch counter in Columbia. In 1966 he started working for AFSC, supposedly for only seven months. His tenure actually included another eighteen years with AFSC, an independent Quaker-sponsored organization, and a long career of dedication to educational desegregation and then public school reform.[16]

AFSC did such work in nine states in the 1960s, promoting school desegregation in collaboration with the NAACP. AFSC had a presence in South Carolina even before it hired Mizell as its only full-time staff person in that state. In the mid-1950s AFSC assisted civil rights activists by sending food and clothing during the most difficult days of Orangeburg's boycott of white citizens' council businesses, and by arranging financial support for Black farmers harassed because they had signed school desegregation petitions.[17] In 1964 two AFSC workers, one of them a former Furman faculty member, visited Greenville and helped initiate a large tutorial program for Black students undertaking desegregation. They worked with local citizens and both faculty and students from Furman, which was itself newly desegregated. That initiative evolved into a tutoring program for Black public school students that extended for at least three years.[18]

AFSC did other work as well. In 1965 it participated in the desegregation coalition's conference held at Penn Community Center, sending one person to talk about tutorial programs.[19] That year it also issued guidance for "friendly visitors," "local citizens" urged to visit homes and talk to Black parents, encouraging them to help advance school desegregation. The mimeographed instructions told "friendly visitors," after introducing themselves, to describe the local school board's desegregation plans and to encourage parents to send their children to white or formerly white public schools. It instructed visitors to persuade Black parents by pointing out that "white and Negro citizens need to learn to get along together to build a community for all" and that it was important for more families to send Black children to desegregated schools because "there is more safety in numbers."[20] Without AFSC staff in the state, however, AFSC's role in helping such efforts on the ground was limited.

New AFSC staffer Mizell's 1966 hiring came at an opportune time. The Civil Rights Act of 1964, several successful pro–school integration court cases, initial school desegregation, and the visible presence of federal oversight (by the US Department of Health, Education and Welfare and by federal courts) had boosted momentum. This limited success could have led to less activism. Federal oversight proved fitful, however, and progress slow; the state's public school districts often operated under "freedom of choice," which placed the burden for applying to formerly white schools upon Black parents. AFSC played an important role as a nongovernmental watchdog and supporter for a process unpopular with white people and sometimes with Black people, as well, once the challenges became clear. Mizell brought to AFSC youthful passion, and he energetically launched assertive strategies. Relatively free to speak out because AFSC paid his salary, he took difficult positions for a white person. He regularly wrote letters to newspaper editors and authored opinion columns. He published his own newsletter for people seeking information about desegregation, and he spoke in numerous community meetings and church gatherings, responding to whomever asked him to speak.[21]

Mizell's first major report on the desegregation process in South Carolina, issued December 1966, was a detailed, passionate critique composed of twenty-two pages of single-spaced text. This report summarized federal guidelines and analyzed how school officials misunderstood or purposefully ignored those guidelines. It documented inadequate efforts to inform local citizens about their rights if they wanted to support desegregation, and it assessed published statements by the state's political leaders—including the governor, state legislators, and US congressional representatives—opposing federal oversight of school desegregation and continuing to berate the very idea of racial integration. Mizell summarized a litany of editorial attacks on school desegregation and cited several instances of school districts refusing legal efforts by Black families to transfer their children to all-white schools. Mizell's report captured issues related to both students and to faculty. He noted cases of harassment of Black students in desegregated schools for 1966–67, in a narrative that brings a strange sense of comfort, confirming that we in Orangeburg were not the only ones suffering:

> In Dorchester District #1 a child threw a baseball at a Negro student, a Negro girl was hit by a white girl in the restroom, and white students threw rocks and other missiles at the Negro students. Students are segregated in the classrooms and on the school buses. Students report that white teachers ignore the Negro students in class and make no effort to involve them in class discussions. . . . In McCormick County Negro students attending the desegregated high school were called names, hit with paper and pennies, and did not feel that the academic environment was such that they could study properly. In Beaufort County a Negro girl was hit with a piece of glass and had to have five stitches taken in her face. . . . In Colleton County there were reports that Negro children were forced to sit in the rear of the school buses and that they were harassed on the school buses. In Lee County one Negro student in a desegregated school had his house shot into.[22]

In his report Mizell also highlighted difficulties integrating faculty. Few full-time teachers taught in schools of the opposite race, and Black teachers in formerly all-white schools received assignments to teach agriculture, band, or physical education rather than academic subjects. "School officials feared faculty desegregation even more than student desegregation," he noted, because they did not trust Black teachers' competence, even though they had traditionally argued that segregated school systems were "equal."[23]

In August 1967 Mizell and an NAACP colleague gave testimony before a US Senate subcommittee regarding the Elementary and Secondary Education Act (ESEA). Mizell charged that the ESEA was perpetuating racial segregation by shoring up all-Black public schools with grants; integration was exceedingly slow, with only 7 percent of Black public school students in the state attending desegregated schools, and Black students were experiencing continued harassment. In his opinion matters were regressing: "For the past year and a half I have watched the erosion of federal implementation and the withering of local compliance. As a result, the landscape of our national commitment to equality of educational opportunity is scarred and unproductive."[24]

Mizell wrote a few articles before 1970, and many more afterward, but his unpublished memos from the 1960s have rawer form and offer more insight into the opinions of participants than his published articles.[25] In two 1967 memos, Mizell outlined ongoing challenges. One memo reported on a school desegregation seminar held at Claflin, convened by Leonard Buxton, head of Claflin's federally funded Title IV Institute. Mizell, a southerner even if liberal, described Buxton as "a Yankee white professor at Claflin."[26] The keynote speaker was Cyril Busbee, state superintendent of education, and respondents included panelists William J. Clark, superintendent of my own Orangeburg District 5; Mizell, AFSC; a local white civic leader; and Charles Thomas, SC State professor of education and head of the South Carolina Voter Education Project. Thomas, the father of my Orangeburg High schoolmate Anne Marie, a "first," was the only Black person on the panel, although the audience was almost all Black.

Using his usual detailed style, Mizell summarized the meeting in four single-spaced pages. By Mizell's account Busbee said that schools had to obey the law and that "we have to get on with the business of school desegregation even though we may not like it." Clark claimed that Orangeburg's school board was making progress in school desegregation but looked forward to building a "new Negro school" that would be just as good as the white schools; he saw no contradiction in planning a separate school for Black students while under court order to desegregate. He complained that "he had to spend half his time dealing with matters related to school desegregation when he should be spending such time trying to improve the educational quality of the school system." In his own panel response, Mizell lamented the slow progress in school desegregation, expressed concern about the future for Black teachers, called on Black and white teachers to upgrade their skills and leadership activities, and declared school desegregation an essential "part of civil rights." Thomas said many of the same things as Mizell and read aloud passages from the Southern Regional Council's report on slow progress with school desegregation. The discussion among panelists somehow grew heated. Busbee accused Thomas and Mizell of "emotionalizing matters," quickly grew "extremely defensive" about the state's progress, and praised "freedom of choice" because it would allow Black parents to decide if "it will be psychologically damaging to send their child to a desegregated school."[27]

This memo's synopsis demonstrates that school officials had a long way to go in adjusting to reality and accepting the value of school desegregation, even for a Black audience. The state's top K-12 education officer, apparently, recognized the psychological damage desegregation was causing for Black students yet considered it Black parents' responsibility to prevent it by not taking the initiative to transfer their children. This neatly removed responsibility for any resulting problems from white administrators, teachers, and students. Who was trying to change white actors' objectionable behavior?

Mizell also pointed out the subtle cultural miscues that took place in this meeting, a reflection of years of casual white dominance. Busbee's surprising (to Mizell) turn to extreme defensiveness seemed to center somewhat on Thomas's remarks about compensatory education; being challenged, even moderately, by a Black professor could have been a new experience for Busbee in a state where all Black college faculty worked only at Black colleges.

Language also showed the challenges. One of the persistent problems that Black people faced during that era was casual disrespect, such as white speakers' mispronunciation *nigra*, which sounds similar to an epithet, rather than *Negro*, emphasis on the long vowel sound of *o*, the only pronunciation acceptable to Black people at that time. Few white people had the extensive interaction with Black people that Mizell had experienced in his work with human relations councils. As Busbee began to talk, Mizell was astute enough to note, "he said 'nigra' several times. Since most of the people in the audience were Negro, there was considerable cutting of eyes and shifting around when he said this." Panelist Mizell, in an attempt to rectify the wrong pronunciation mishap, then told the audience a story about a mixed-race meeting. In his story Black people, after leaving the meeting, complained to one another that the white attendees said "nigra" and white attendees complained that Black speakers made grammatical errors. Mizell's story did not help his fellow white panelists: "I thought that this illustration would get the point across to Busbee but during the ensuing discussion both he and Clark said 'nigra' often. A couple of times there were audible murmurs rippling throughout the audience, but apparently neither Busbee nor Clark caught onto what was happening."[28]

That same year, in February 1967, the US Commission on Civil Rights invited Mizell to join its SC State Advisory Committee. Mizell did and then participated in a series of four frustrating advisory committee hearings, all duly summarized in his memos, that the committee called to listen to concerns about school desegregation. White attendees were usually school officials who lauded their own progress in meeting federal guidelines but with stoicism rather than enthusiasm. In some of the meetings, the officials left the meeting early, sometimes all of them getting up and leaving at once. Black attendees, sometimes angry and sometimes simply discouraged, stood up to testify "that there was no meaningful faculty desegregation, the school buses are segregated, and there is overcrowding in the Negro schools." Black participants also testified that "freedom of choice" was just "another form of segregation." Some hearings descended into chaos while others unfolded peacefully, but all ended with little resolution.[29] After a year he left the advisory committee, disappointed with its limited scope, timidity, and tendency to operate only by pressuring federal agencies to do a better job.

Mizell wrestled with much larger questions; in February 1967 he asked colleagues if AFSC should convene an interorganizational seminar to discuss the future of school desegregation in the South. He suggested ten sets of questions. The first set was broad: "Is school desegregation desirable? Is there merit in the 'Black Power' view on school desegregation? What is the future of the Negro school?" The second set of questions reached for specifics: "What is the future of school desegregation, and civil rights and human relations efforts in this area? Now that we have tokenism, is our job finished? When is a school in the South desegregated or integrated (numbers, percentages)?" The fifth set of questions honed in on a specific problem: "What is the future of the public school in the South? Will the private school movement drain off the better students from the public schools? Are there legal methods of stifling the private school movement? How serious is the private school movement? Is the threat worth fighting?"[30]

All of his questions were thought-provoking, harbingers of future problems, but his fifth set, concerning "the private school movement," was particularly timely. By 1967 white parents disaffected by desegregation had formed a growing network of white-only private schools. Discussion about private schools had emerged around the time of the *Brown* case. In 1959 the Southern Regional Council published a study arguing that it would be financially prohibitive to close all public schools and place all white students in private schools, as some southern states threatened to do. That report also suggested that "freedom of choice" would be a better alternative, since only a small number of Black parents would send their children to previously all-white schools.[31] Then years passed as inertia led to no action to desegregate. By the early 1960s, however, it had become clearer than the federal government would enforce the law and push for racial integration of public schools, for a while at least.

In South Carolina twenty-five private white K-12 schools formed between 1961 and 1964, adding to the three that existed before. These schools formed the South Carolina Independent School Association. Student membership rose from 1,600 in 1963 to 4,500 in 1964; Orangeburg's Wade Hampton Academy, "the most advanced school" of this genre, alone had 439 students in 1964–65 with more expected the following year.[32] Wade Hampton, opened in a private home and Baptist church just before Orangeburg public schools desegregated, soon moved onto a well-appointed campus financed by donors and a key local leader, T. Elliott Wannamaker, headmaster and former owner of a local chemical plan. Classrooms apparently contained Confederate flags as a complement

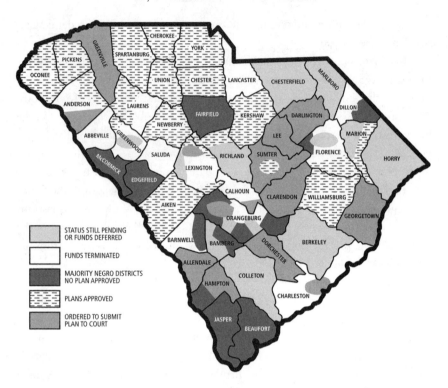

School desegregation progress for various districts, 1969. This shows that the
school districts in South Carolina were having varied success in following
federal and court orders to desegregate. "Desegregation Progress Varies over
State," *Columbia Record,* May 18, 1969. Clipping in M. Hayes Mizell
Collection, box 142, "Education-Desegregation 1968–9." Courtesy of
South Caroliniana Library, University of South Carolina.

to the school's namesake, Confederate general Wade Hampton III. Wannamaker commented that Black people had not come out to "do anything" to
damage the school or its buildings but that "colored people built this school"
with their physical labor.[33]

Senator Thurmond praised private white schools in a 1967 newsletter he
sent to constituents. He called such schools a response to "the crisis for local
control of public education" and boasted that "South Carolina has become one
of the leaders in the independent schools movement."[34]

My Recovery

Reviewing the papers of the SCCHR and Mizell's AFSC helped me better understand the context of the school desegregation years. In that sense my recent

review of those archives, carried out as I wrote this book, has contributed greatly to my own recovery, since on the topic of my own high school experience I displayed post-traumatic symptoms most of my adult life. The story of SCCHR's Wright confirmed for me belief in the goodness of human nature and helped me add another heroine to my own personal civil rights pantheon for South Carolina, which already included Rev. I. DeQuincy Newman, Rev. Matthew McCollom, Modjeska Simkins, Septima Clark, Judge J. Waties Waring, my own parents, and several others. Wright's personal and SCCHR history clarified for me the very real dangers that faced white allies who promoted equality in Black education and urged other white people to do the same. Those SCCHR records also demonstrated the positive power of interracial cooperation, particularly through Wright's youth council and her networking with myriad Black organizations that cohosted conferences aiming to improve Black education. Those records gave me greater empathy for the few white people who tried to treat Black people as fellow human beings rather than inferior nothings.

The value of Mizell's AFSC is similarly great, but with a broader set of contributions. On one level Mizell's value is that he served as an informal historian for a crucial period of civil rights history in our state, at the same time that he offered a courageous white person's public support for the unpopular cause of school desegregation during a contentious period. Although several scholars, circuit courts, and federal agencies assessed progress toward school desegregation in the mid-1960s and early 1970s, these usually looked at such issues for the southern region as a whole or for specific school districts and did not home in on the overall challenges facing South Carolina. Furthermore federal agents or courts assessed progress in a fitful manner, dipping into data periodically to assess compliance. Mizell, in contrast, stayed in the state and in a progressive campaign long enough to see school desegregation's evolution. He wrote articles about public school desegregation and similar issues for decades and, in later years, looked at such matters as discriminatory actions against Black students.

Almost unconsciously Mizell also reported on the cultural difficulties that the school desegregation process entailed and thus offered insights not available elsewhere. His discussion of the panel that included my public school superintendent and the state superintendent of education, as well as his descriptions of uncomfortable school officials who attended US Commission on Civil Rights advisory committee meetings, drove home the reluctance those officials must have felt and helped clarify for me the awkwardness that characterized their handling of desegregation. While some of us interacted with teachers and noticed their discomfort, higher administration officials were something of an enigma.

Mizell peeled back the curtain, revealing how conflicted such officials must have felt, unused to the tasks associated with leading their districts in a direction so counter to the white supremacist culture in which they had grown up. His memos offered firsthand observations of white discomfort.

The broader questions that Mizell posed in his February 1967 memo, particularly about the future of federally enforced school desegregation, show that even white allies had serious doubts about the goals of such activity. In his formal papers and testimony, Mizell displayed no such doubt. In his memos, however, he showed that he was beginning to understand the dilemma. He knew that his own white society was extraordinarily resistant; that it would not yield completely to racial integration, especially in public schools; and that the broader question was not how fast schools could be desegregated but whether school desegregation was desirable, particularly given early signs that it would place Black teachers and students at a decided disadvantage.

The papers of both SCCHR and AFSC also helped demystify the tutorial programs of that era and explain both why more Black students began to come to Orangeburg High School and why matters became more tolerable for me in year three as opposed to year one. A coalition of organizations actively recruited Black parents to apply to send their students to formerly all-white schools. The AFSC provided the "friendly visitors" material, but the lead recruiters must have surely been Black, probably associated with the NAACP and coalition partners. Records indicate that more Black parents and students applied for transfers than were accepted, and so the recruiters were even more successful than those of us on the ground could perceive. Thus, as I think back to my senior year of high school, I remember welcoming the comfortable presence of more Black students. Simultaneously, however, the number of resistant white students must have decreased, if those students could afford to leave. They had simply paid private tuition and gone to the new Wade Hampton Academy. This was a happy result for us pioneers: many diehard white opponents, faculty and students, simply got out of the way at the same time that more Black people joined our ranks.

My obsession with diligent study as a strategy for survival and as a way to force resistant white people to respect Black people's intelligence soon paid off. Of course I had it all wrong, conceptually, in my thinking that we could prove our worth. White people could tolerate a few accomplished Black people but not the overall population of Black students, hampered by generations of purposefully flawed schooling. Nevertheless it felt good to get good high school grades as a part of my own personal campaign. Teachers came to expect good results from my efforts, as did, to their audible chagrin, fellow white students. Although I remained anxious and repressed throughout those three years and had no social interaction on those school grounds except with other Black students, similarly harassed, an important reprieve came for me in the summer after eleventh grade, in 1966.

Sometime that spring a school administrator recommended me for a special summer program for "gifted high school juniors" at Furman University in Greenville. Only two people could have made such a recommendation: either O. K. Cook, principal at that time, or Clark, the district's superintendent. I remember early interactions with Clark dating back to 1964, and he participated in several activities at Claflin several years later (after the raw feelings associated with desegregation had worn off), so I suspect it was him. Given Mizell's notes mentioning Clark's discomfort with having to spend time on desegregation matters, it is possible that he was looking for an opportunity to champion at least a few Black students, but this is pure speculation on my part. Either he or Cook nominated me, I was accepted, and that summer my parents drove me to Furman's beautifully landscaped campus, complete with all new buildings situated next to a lake, and located about two hours' drive from Orangeburg.

Furman was affiliated with the all-white South Carolina Baptist Convention at that time, but its faculty had participated in tutoring programs for local Black students, and the university had admitted its first Black student, Joseph "Joe" Vaughn, in January 1965. The high school juniors' program was entirely separate from the university's regular school year, and so I did not meet Joe until later. The summer program was composed of perhaps twenty students from all over South Carolina, but I was the only Black one. We took classes in English and history from the two faculty members who staffed the program, John Henry Crabtree Jr. and William E. Leverette Jr.[35] It was frightening, at first—here I was again, a Black student among all white classmates and teachers; what was I thinking?—but then delightfully surprising. Led by two girls who befriended me first, Mary Beth Hare and Susanne Pincham, those students and teachers appeared to accept me as an equal.[36] Although some portion of me held back a little, compared to my previous two years this was a wonderful, full student experience. We actually had conversations, a first for me with white fellow students, and we talked about our lives. I participated in class discussions and exchanged ideas out of the classroom as well. We lived in the same dorm, ate our meals together, walked to class together. Somehow a critical number of these students had decided to forget racial barriers, at least for the summer.

At the end of that too-short session, Dr. Crabtree asked if I'd like to skip twelfth grade and simply enter Furman's freshman class that very fall. This was tempting, indeed, but I had just turned sixteen that summer. I did not feel ready to leave my family and especially my younger sister, and entering as a sixteen-year-old freshman did not seem appealing. I decided I could tolerate another year of high school, but later when the time came to apply for colleges, I only applied to Furman, sure that I wanted to go back there in the fall of 1967. This was a decision I later regretted, but it was a reflection of my true admiration for Furman. That summer experience was an enormous stabilizer for me emotionally and a booster intellectually as well. It helped me tolerate my high school classmates' boorish behavior, which continued during twelfth grade. It expanded my engagement in the world of ideas and offered some compensating preparation for my future adult life, which would include many white friends and coworkers.

Several reasons might help explain why that summer experience was so different from experiences in Orangeburg up until that time. The northwest Piedmont district of the state had its own history of racism, since Jim Crow segregation ruled the state and all parts of it contained a violent history of racial oppression, including by the Ku Klux Klan, but South Carolina had as well cultural variation partially caused by varied economic histories. The southeast and central portions of the state had depended on the plantation economy, while the Piedmont district had firmer grounding in industries related to forestry and cotton mills.

Greenville, while still southern and resistant to racial integration, and home to flagrantly white-only Bob Jones University, had a very different history in the mid-1960s than did Orangeburg, birthplace of white citizens' councils and of a leading white private academy. Greenville had its own shortcomings; every step forward for the civil rights movement required activism, including sit-ins in the early 1960s to demand desegregation of airport facilities, public libraries, lunch counters, and parks. Lawsuits forced these practices to go before the courts, where defenders of segregation eventually lost. It also had progressive leadership. A local industrial leader, Charles Daniel, former US senator and member of the State Development Board, gave a talk in 1961 saying that the state's economic future depended on it changing segregationist practices; his talk took place a few months after Vice President Lyndon Johnson warned that future federal contracts would require a nondiscrimination clause. In 1962 several white industrialists and community leaders formed a biracial committee—homegrown but similar in spirit to Wright's local human relations councils—to ease transition into desegregation. The Greenville Education Committee's 1964 tutorial program had plenty of white buy-in, especially by Furman faculty and students.[37]

Furman itself, despite its ties with conservative white Baptists, had a history of relative progressivism compared to other white universities in our state. As far back as 1955, one of Furman's student editors, Joan Lipscomb, had written an article for a student publication supporting the *Brown* decision. Furman's administration refused to allow distribution of 1,500 copies of the issue of the literary journal that Lipscomb edited, the *Echo*, because of this article and other pro-integration content. Fellow students rallied in her support, however, and since that time Furman faculty and students had periodically expressed support for racial desegregation. For this and other reasons, many white people in the state considered Furman "liberal." Somehow my father must have known something of its history; Dad admired Furman's president Gordon Blackwell for some reason that was at the time unclear to me. This school legacy might help explain the friendly acceptance I felt during the 1966 summer program.

Some compensation came from returning to Orangeburg High for twelfth grade in 1966–67. The lists of National Achievement and National Merit Scholarship finalists came out, based in part on results of the Preliminary Scholastic Aptitude Test (PSAT). Three people in my high school were finalists for the National Merit Scholarship, including myself. It was important confirmation to see the article in our local newspaper, the *Times and Democrat,* accompanied by a photograph of me standing on a school corridor with the two other finalists. Another photograph appeared in the yearbook's "Hall of Fame," and so I had more presence in that yearbook than just the senior individual photographs and the group Latin Club and choir pictures. Of course Evelyn and I had fought to get into that choir in spite of the director's prejudice, and the Latin Club was only a way to hover in Mrs. Higginbotham's presence. Other extracurricular activities had been impossible because of racism, but that photograph of the three National Merit finalists, in the yearbook for all to see, accomplished one goal.

Several important things happened in the summer of 1967, just before I entered Furman University as a freshman. I met a young SC State student, Steve Moore, who introduced me to two things: Black activist literature, particularly the writings of Malcolm X, and his own Baha'i Faith, which I a few years later adopted as my own. This may seem a strange mixture, particularly since Malcolm X was a Black separatist during his affiliation with the Nation of Islam, while the teachings of the Baha'is stress the unity of humanity and the need to live lives free of racial prejudice or exclusion. Actually, however, blending the two made a lot of sense at the time. You would have to have known Steve to understand fully how this was possible, but also the atmosphere of the mid-to-late 1960s supported many forms of Black student activism; the civil rights movement and Black urban rebellions were taking place at the same time. Some Black student activists used "Black radical" language but realized that the overall goal was to build a future society where race did not matter so much, a truth that both Dr. King and, late in his life, Malcolm X taught. Although the Baha'i Faith supported only peaceful reform activities and counseled multiracial gatherings at all levels, it also urged its members to be at the forefront of progressive movements.

My introduction to the Baha'i Faith came as I stood outside of my church, Trinity, after yet another day of civil rights activity of some sort. Those rallies continued into 1967 and 1968, because several private businesses still refused to serve Black customers. After the event I started talking to Steve and happened to mention during the conversation that I was one of the students that had integrated our local high school. I asked Steve something like this: Why do you think white people in this city are so oppressive? Why is it that white teachers and students at my high school who call themselves Christian can treat us with such hate and refuse to talk to us or even to touch us? Steve responded that I should investigate the Baha'i Faith. I'd never heard of it before. He told me that the Baha'i Faith taught that all human beings were equal and that Baha'is did not allow segregated meetings of their members. Instead, he said, they followed guidance that both races needed to work toward unity and that white people would have to learn to give up their unconscious sense of superiority. Guidance to give up prejudice of any kind dated back to the origins of the faith in the nineteenth century, but a 1939 book by the Baha'i leader at that time, Shoghi Effendi, confirmed implications for US race relations. Steve's words were extremely affecting; I had been worried about religion for some time, wondering how my white Christian schoolmates could ever forsake their un-Christian behavior and gain redemption.

Another culminating event during summer 1967 was my family's trip to Washington, DC. Some administrator, probably Superintendent Clark, submitted my name to the state Board of Education for nomination to the US Presidential Scholar program. This federal program, only four years old at that time, recognized a few academically capable high school seniors from around the country. The national selection office picked only two student nominees from each state to receive the award. The letter informing me of my selection was a happy, thoroughly unexpected surprise. The letter invited my family to travel with me to Washington for a program that would include a visit with President Johnson; during the visit Johnson presented each awardee with a heavy medallion, a smile, and a handshake. Perhaps our trip, made by rail, was sweet justice for my parents as some small compensation for family sacrifices. For as long as Dad was alive, he saved both the professional photograph of me shaking hands with the president and the photograph's transmission note sent on White House

Dr. Milton Shuler and Carl Kennedy, president of the NAACP Orangeburg branch, presenting an award to high school graduate June Manning for selection as 1967 US Presidential Scholar, on behalf of the local chapter, Phi Beta Sigma fraternity. Pictured with June are Michelle Manning, Ethel Manning, H. V. Manning. Family album photo. Courtesy Cecil Williams, photographer.

stationery. Dad affixed the large, glossy photograph to a bulletin board at home, securing it with cellophane tape and ordinary thumbtacks so that he could see it every day, and he kept the note as well.

Meeting President Johnson, signer of the 1964 Civil Rights Act, was a decided honor, as were the several days of activities planned for the approximately one hundred US Presidential Scholars of 1967, days that included trips to the US Supreme Court, where a serving justice spoke to our group, and the US Congress. We stayed in dorm rooms with bunk beds, chattering into the night, while our parents stayed in hotels. The photograph taken during the award showed me beaming and wearing white gloves; the moment was short but unforgettable.

One special incident stood out during that trip. Tradition held that each state's two US Presidential Scholars had lunch with their state's congressional

Pres. Lyndon B. Johnson presents US Presidential Scholar award to June Manning, late spring or summer 1967, Washington, DC. Transmitted by the White House with note dated July 28, 1967. Family album photo.

representatives. Almost all of the scholars were white, and I doubt that my sena-tor expected to see a Black student included in that group. I, in turn, had not expected to have lunch with Senator Thurmond, famed defender of segregation, 1948 segregationist US presidential candidate, staunch opponent of the 1957 and 1964 Civil Rights Acts, and champion of white private academies.

We sat at a large, round table in the US Senate dining room, and we ate their famous bean soup as a starter; I still have my souvenir copy of that menu, bear-ing his signature. Also sitting at that table were the other Presidential Scholar from my state, three South Carolina members of the US House (who also au-tographed my menu), and Thurmond's young administrative assistant Nancy Moore, a former Miss South Carolina. I know that even sitting at the same table with me went against southern social mores intact for most of Thurmond's life. For whatever reason he seemed nervous. Thankfully his attention focused not on me but on his assistant. He hardly looked at me, except at one point to stand up and dump his own french-fried potatoes on my plate, saying he was full, but he spent plenty of time looking at Nancy, who clearly was not much older than me. Watching this flirtation in full view tamped down my own nervousness. Thurmond autographed my menu with a statement that, in hindsight, seems to offer a wink from the past, a faint acknowledgement of future trends: "Best wishes to an *intelligent* SC Presidential Scholar. [Signed,] Strom Thurmond, U S. Senator—S.C." (emphasis added).

A year later Thurmond, a widower, married that young assistant; he was sixty-six at the time, and she was twenty-two years old. They gave birth to four children, and Thurmond served as senator until 2003, when he was one hundred years old.

Sen. Thurmond was a complex man, on many levels. He fathered five children, one of them when he was a very young man, with his household's young Black domestic servant; this was a well-kept secret for many years but widely suspected among Orangeburg's Black community well before that. He provided some funds for that daughter to attend SC State, where he sometimes visited her. She, in turn, sporadically visited him at his Senate office. At least one author, Joseph Crespino, has suggested that this bifurcated life—staunch defender of racial segregation and anti-miscegenation but also father of a Black child that he did not acknowledge publicly but met with occasionally and whose expenses he supported—helps explain the extremity of some of his political positions.[38] It would have potentially harmed his reputation among whites if this friendly liaison had been widely known; championing racial segregation and opposing civil rights, according to Crespino, may have provided him with a form of professional cover. After Black South Carolinians gained more voting power in the 1970s and 1980s, Thurmond moderated his public racial stance, trying to serve both Black and white constituents. I met him before that moderation phase, during the year that he wrote his constituents praising private white academies, and three years after he had opposed the US Civil Rights Act of 1964. I met him the year before he published a book lambasting the *Brown* decision.[39]

Conclusion

The efforts of coalitions that worked together to support school desegregation, and the most prominent white members of those coalitions, SCCHR's Wright and AFSC's Mizell, help explain how desegregation expanded to include more Black transfers but also how early problems appeared, as noted by Black parents attending hearings and by Mizell. White private academies provided, in some ways, relief for Black desegregation pioneers as die-hard segregationists fled.

Not mentioned but surely obvious by now is that it would have been better if white people did not feel it necessary to form private academies. It would have been better if they had accepted integration as the natural course of events, a reprieve from the burden of upholding the myth of white supremacy. It would have been better if white South Carolinians had accepted Black students and teachers as equal in spirit and possibly gifted in different ways than the majority because of their deep faith, resilient community institutions, and courage. Then it might have been possible to steer the course of society differently, to start to become antiracist, multiracial. This was not to be.

Against this backdrop Furman's summer program gave me contact with a larger world, and academic achievement softened the blows of racial harassment. These, and a series of extraordinary events and connections, prepared me for the next chapter of life.

8

Struggling to Survive

Gaining access to South Carolina's all-white public and private universities had always been a primary NAACP goal. Having only one underfunded public university available for Black students was a clear indication of educational inequality. Limited access to professional programs such as law school, and no access at all to in-state schools for several other professional fields, deepened that inequality. For such reasons some of the first civil rights cases filed concerned access to institutions of higher education.

South Carolina was one of the last states to open its all-white colleges and universities to Black students. Between January 1961 and February 1963, the number of desegregated colleges and universities increased by 30 percent in seventeen southern and border states, as eighty-nine institutions desegregated. These included twelve in Florida and twenty-six in North Carolina but only two in South Carolina: Clemson and Our Lady of Mercy Junior College in Charleston. By the end of the 1964–65 first semester, at least twenty-five Black students had enrolled in formerly all-white colleges and universities in the state, including Clemson, USC, Winthrop, Wofford, and Lander. SCCHR helped fourteen of those twenty-five students by recruiting them or offering counseling.[1]

Experiences varied widely for the first Black students integrating those schools. Harvey Gantt entered Clemson in 1963 without physical violence, but Gantt suffered subtler harassment from his fellow students.[2] James Redfern, who entered USC in 1967 when perhaps seventy Black students attended, assessed his experience as nightmarish, with opaque teaching methods and hostile white faculty and students; he transferred to SC State, where I met him as one of the local Black activists in summer 1968.[3] In contrast Joe Vaughn, entering Furman as its first Black undergraduate, became very popular with fellow white students and faculty.

Joseph Vaughn, the first Black undergraduate to attend Furman University, Greenville, South Carolina. Color Guard photo, ROTC. Photograph taken from the 1966 yearbook, *Bonhomie*, 323. Image courtesy of Special Collections and Archives, James B. Duke Library, Furman University.

The Furman case illustrates the pressures that led a private university to desegregate and the importance of racial climate. School desegregation of universities succeeded in part because pressures to integrate at that level were difficult to circumvent. The climate for incoming Black students, although not perfect, was relatively favorable compared to K-12 schools, suggesting that university desegregation could work. This turned out to be true long-term but with some short-term challenges, as historical sources about Furman's desegregation and my own memories illustrate.

In 1968, however, SC State students had a standoff against the last vestiges of legalized segregation in Orangeburg. Administrative reforms at SC State brought positive changes, but the surrounding city had not given up its culture of exclusion. As students protested a segregated bowling alley, the state amassed armed troops. When unarmed students gathered around a bonfire one evening, those officers opened fire. Their barrage killed three students and injured twenty-eight others as another indication of white oppression, this time with police force wielding excessive violence. The "Orangeburg Massacre" was a severe setback for human rights.

Furman's Evolution

In the last chapter, I described Furman's relative liberalism, but Furman had pro-slavery roots. Established in 1826 by the South Carolina Baptist Convention (SCBC), Furman took its name from Richard Furman, an evangelical minister and prominent apologist for slavery.[4] Furman began as an academy for men and an institute for ministers in training. By the 1920s it had morphed into an academic institution still controlled by the white SCBC but more open intellectually.[5] "Progressive" thought began to flourish as some students and faculty went as far as such thought could in the 1920s; for example, they criticized slavery and Jim Crow laws as repressing Black civil liberties but accepted racial segregation.

Leadership loosened thought. In 1933 Furman's trustees selected as president a prominent local industrialist, Bennette Geer, who oversaw the school's 1938 merger with Greenville Woman's College. Geer launched an audacious social experiment very much in keeping with the era of Progressivism. He applied for a General Education Board grant to encourage both students and faculty to "exchange the ivory tower for a social laboratory."[6] This grant, received in 1936, allowed Furman to set up the Greenville County Council for Community Development (GCCCD), focused on leadership training and community education; it established a series of service courses offered in Greenville County for both white and, separately, Black citizens. The courses helped adults learn to identify community problems, study their extent along with possible remedies, and undertake appropriate action, all leading to volunteer activities ranging from studying traffic conditions to administering standardized tests in local schools. One of the most active faculty members involved was Gordon Blackwell, a sociology professor and future Furman president; he considered the most successful GCCCD program to be the pedagogical outreach program for high school teachers, which transformed for the better local high school education, making it more interactive. GCCCD also set up a Committee on Interracial Cooperation composed of both white and Black members. Together they created interracial initiatives such as connecting Furman faculty and students with Black high school teachers and with community betterment projects in Black neighborhoods.[7]

Such actions, and ill-timed efforts to reform local politics, spurred conservative reactions. The Greenville City Council pushed back against proposals for community development and disparaged the GCCCD. At the site of a GCCCD-sponsored Black college in the town of Fountain Inn, the Ku Klux Klan launched a pogrom, destroying Black businesses and beating up Black residents, and they did much the same in a neighboring town. Conservative Furman students complained about progressive faculty and speakers, and both the SCBC and Furman's trustees began to criticize Geer's liberalism. Particularly controversial was his support for Herbert Gezork, a free-thinking religion professor who taught that Christians had a moral duty to treat all human beings, including Black ones, with love and respect. Gezork also regularly allowed his Black gardener to ride in his car's front passenger seat, a breach of white mores. The trustees fired Gezork. Facing collapsed trustee support, Geer resigned in 1938.[8]

The trustees hired one of their own members, Judge John Plyler, as the next president. As a trustee Plyler had led the charge against Gezork. As president he reversed many of Geer's reforms, let the five-year grant for the GCCCD lapse, and fired several faculty members who had supported Gezork. Furman settled back into conservatism. Plyler presided over the 1955 censorship of the *Echo*, the student literary journal that supported the *Brown* decision. He began to analyze US Supreme Court decisions related to race, assessing whether or not Furman was in "danger" of forced desegregation. He determined that Furman was "safe" as long as federal funders did not threaten repercussions against nonpublic universities.[9] It was Plyler who was at the helm when pressures to desegregate Furman arose in the early 1960s.

By then much had changed, including the attitude of faculty and students. A 1957 survey asked students their opinions of fraternities and sororities, dancing, and desegregation, all suspect in SCBC thought. Over a third of the students polled thought that Furman should desegregate, with some commenting that this was a Christian obligation. In 1961 a majority of members of the state Baptist Student Union Convention voted to open membership to students of all races. Alarmed, the SCBC ordered Furman to abolish Greek organizations and voted against desegregation. A few weeks later, several Furman students polled their fellow students and faculty; the faculty voted 68 to 12 in favor of admitting "all properly qualified applicants regardless of race or color," while the students approved the same statement 512 to 432.[10] One of many bitter signed letters in response said: "I was badly disappointed that our College would show up as the soft underbelly of resistance to the communist inspired mongrelization program being presently pushed in America."[11]

A Furman faculty member created a committee that drafted a resolution calling on Furman to desegregate. The faculty overwhelmingly approved the resolution. Realizing that Furman was losing federal and corporate funding because of its segregationist policy, the trustees voted in September 1963 to admit all qualified student candidates.[12] In response the SCBC asked for time to reconsider, but at a contentious fall 1964 convention, SCBC attendees voted to maintain segregation in all SCBC colleges and to protest Furman's decision to desegregate. By that time Furman's trustees were desperate to desegregate. They disobeyed the SCBC and reaffirmed their previous decision to open admissions.[13]

Furman Desegregates

The trustees acted against the SCBC's vote for a number of reasons. Not only had they hired as president Gordon Blackwell, who made desegregation a condition of his employment, but they had also begun to feel the displeasure of the faculty through resolutions and polls. In addition external sanctions were a threat. Similar sanctions influenced many white colleges and universities during that era.

Trustee J. Wilbert Wood, board chair, explained the threats in a letter to the SCBC's president. Failure to desegregate, Wood wrote, jeopardized accreditation by the Southern Association of Colleges and Schools, which would lead to severe loss of good faculty members and students as well as diminished morale. Without a policy change, Wood continued, the university would continue to lose financial support from the federal government, foundations, businesses, and individuals, and this would set back Furman's essential building program, graduate programs, and planned summer institutes for high school teachers and students.[14] Former president Plyler, originally hired as a conservative stabilizer, also advised desegregation. He said that the negative publicity alone had done "inestimable damage" to Furman: "We have already lost ground academically, financially, and spiritually because of the actions of our Convention. To make the wrong decision now could set us back ten to twenty years and we would probably never recover the lost ground."[15]

When Furman's board of trustees reaffirmed its prointegration admission policy, Furman's vice president, Francis Bonner, had already asked a Greenville civic leader to find a Black high school student with leadership ability, academic success, and "personality that could handle the pressures" of desegregation.[16] The scout identified Joe Vaughn. Furman administrators sent Joe to an HBCU to start his first year while they awaited decisions during fall 1964. He arrived at Furman uneventfully in January 1965; after a short period, he started connecting with teachers and students, joining as many organizations as would have him. That turned out to be quite a few. By the time I arrived as a first-year undergraduate in the fall of 1967, Joe, then a senior, seemed to have been involved in everything. This included Pershing Rifles, the Baptist Student Union, Collegiate Educational Service Core, and the Color Guard, plus he acted in several plays and joined the cheerleading squad. He cofounded the Furman chapter of the Southern Student Organizing Committee (SSOC) and convinced me to sign up as well. Yearbook pictures show him smiling broadly in several extracurricular photographs. He graduated cum laude in 1968.

Furman now regards Joe as a beloved Furman "first," and it celebrates him with all the attention and accolades that he deserves, years after his premature death.[17] He was important as the first Black student, but he was important as well for Furman's survival and success. Arguably, without Joe, Furman would have lost financial support, federal grants, foundation support, accreditation, and respect in the academic community at large. As Plyler explained, exclusion was also hurting Furman spiritually, as it became increasingly difficult for a Christian university to justify blanket exclusion of Black students even as it accepted international students and other non-white enrollees. That Joe was able to flourish is to his personal credit, but he was also of tangible value to his university.

Furman lucked out. Its own scouting process brought much of the luck, but no one would have been able to predict how Joe would adjust as the first and only Black undergraduate on campus for well over a year. No one could have predicted that he would become popular, in a limited but genuine sense.

Describing Joe's personality might help explain his impact. Student leaders from that era remembered him well; one called him "a delightful person," while another said people "couldn't help but love the guy" and that "Furman fell in love with him."[18] In outward appearance he was happy, extroverted, and gifted with boundless enthusiasm. He would literally bounce into a room, radiating a huge smile and establishing an immediate presence. He was friendly to the point of alarming some of us shyer people, and it took me a while to get used to his assertive, in-your-face cheerfulness—he looked me in the eye when I first met him and said in a loud voice, "Why, aren't you cute as a button!"—but he was utterly charming. When I first saw him in his cheerleader role during a football game, it all made sense. He loved revving up a crowd, performing energetic maneuvers, leading rallies for school spirit. His joy and exuberance were infectious, on the field and off.

Joe also had a quieter and more somber side. Occasionally a few of us could sense how heavy the load had been. Underneath all the laughter and good spirits was an undertone of profound sadness, the quiet gravity of a survivor. He obviously felt a need for social time with those of us who understood. He had withstood the pressures because he actually felt honored to be a Furman student, but breaking open this pathway was a lot to ask of any one person.

Joe was a brave soul. This was obvious not only in his ability to survive as a first in such a spectacular way but also in other acts of bravery. One of the strongest was his public announcement of his conversion to the Baha'i Faith. He did this in, of all places, the weekly student newspaper. The article appeared February 10, 1967, two years after his arrival on campus and a few months before my undergraduate year began. Although he probably did not choose the sensationalist title for the article—"Why I Am a Baha'i, Not a Christian"—it was an accurate summary.

In the article Joe recounted having studied the Baha'i Faith for two years and then detailed why he converted to this new global religion. Unlike the title, the article's text strove to build bridges between different religions, arguing that Hinduism, Buddhism, Zoroastrianism, Judaism, Christianity, and Islam all stemmed from one God and that overemphasizing differences only led to conflict. As he noted, "The Baha'i view reconciles basic concepts of these [varied] faiths without requiring repudiation of belief in the divinity of their founders. . . . Baha'is regard all major faiths as part of one evolving religion, restated and reinvigorated periodically by a new prophet." He then described the crux of Baha'i belief, the essential unity of all human beings: "Baha'u'llah urged elimination of prejudice and superstition, particularly racial. Prejudice is dealt with more specifically and emphatically than in past religions, and is regarded as spiritual responsibility, not merely [a] humanitarian or educational problem."[19] The text was unsurprising to anyone familiar with the Baha'i Faith but surely stood out as a remarkable deviation from the typical dialogue characterizing that student newspaper. No evidence suggests that this bold declaration led to any repercussions for Joe, who thereafter joined the cheerleading squad.

Furman's new president helped provide friendly, fresh leadership for Joe's presence; Blackwell's inauguration took place the same term that Joe entered. Blackwell retained the social consciousness tradition of the progressive President Geer, under whom he had worked. When hired in 1964, Blackwell was president of Florida State University, where he had overseen desegregation, so he had relevant experience. At Furman he created a climate of openness, and he markedly ramped up Furman's pursuit of academic excellence. His inaugural speech set the tone for his tenure, and his attitude toward student unrest showed that he viewed liberal arts universities as necessarily tolerant of student diversity and activism and not bound by doctrinaire thinking. Accounts by Furman student activists during the 1960s confirm the strong support they felt from

Blackwell. Blackwell brought diverse speakers to campus, such as Morehouse's president Benjamin Mays. The Danforth Foundation supported such visiting lecturers as a way to strengthen liberal education on campus.[20]

Attending Furman

For myself, choosing to attend Furman held the promise of great adventure and racial relief. In hindsight it might have been wise to consider a distant HBCU or northern university. At the time, however, Furman seemed best. My summer there had shown me that it was possible to stay in the state and thrive in an integrated racial environment. Some of the faculty and program classmates from the previous summer would be at Furman. The cause of school integration in the state still needed much traction in 1967, and attending Furman offered me a way to continue to assist this cause.

Furthermore I really did not want to leave South Carolina. My younger sister was only seven years old during college application season; I did not want to leave her. It made no sense to stay in Orangeburg for one of the two HBCUs. I'd lived on Claflin's small campus almost all of my life, and enrolling as a student would have made an independent college experience impossible given Dad's and Mom's jobs. SC State was a sometime rival for Claflin, and attending there was not an option. Overtures sent from various universities in the form of brochures evidently mailed to National Merit and National Achievement finalists meant little; they touted strange places that none of us knew anything about. Radcliffe College in Massachusetts offered early admission even without application, but this was worrisome: What would a medium-brown South Carolina girl with a history of experiencing racial abuse do at Harvard's sister institution? Would I be sophisticated enough? Furman seemed just far enough away to offer relative independence; it was relatively familiar, plus they offered me a full tuition scholarship. I did not realize that Furman's voluntary 1965 admission of Joe, my acceptance into their 1966 summer program, and their 1967 scholarship offer were part of the school's necessary fight to excel despite SCBC conservatism.

In my own experience, most of Furman's white students were not hostile; they just were not particularly friendly, and very few reached out. Black students were so few, and the campus culture so white, that it was easy to feel lost. Lillian Brock Fleming, Sarah Reece, and I, Furman's first three Black female undergraduates, roomed together and interacted largely with the seven or eight Black men on campus in 1967–68. We played Scrabble and card games in our own corner of the student center almost daily. This was the university version of the behavior the first Black students exhibited at Orangeburg High: huddling together when possible as a survival mechanism. It was during those sessions that Joe sometimes showed up and opened up, but he had more extracurricular activities than we did.[21]

Consider the circumstances: in 1967 most public school districts in the state were still desegregating. Quite a few were under court order to do so or had lost funds because they had not; similar situations existed in a few other Deep South states. White students who came to Furman had possibly never attended school with Black students or had not formed friendships with them. Baptists who had grown up in the SCBC's white churches came from families that had possibly cast votes against university desegregation during the fall 1964 SCBC gathering. Out-of-state students from other regions attended Furman because of its relatively low tuition rates compared to US universities of comparable quality, but quite a few students were southern.

First Black students who did not fade into the woodwork had to barge confidently past all hesitation, as did Joe. Joe initiated social connections, looked into your face until you melted in his personality's sunshine, and put himself on energetic display in campus plays and on the cheerleading squad; not all of us had the personality or courage to be so aggressively assertive. Actually this was a tough situation even for Joe. When asked twenty years later, he bemoaned not having a social life on campus, in spite of all the activity; "I felt cheated," he said.[22] Noteworthy, however, is that as early as 1985 Furman hosted a commemoration of his pathbreaking arrival, another sign of his positive impact on campus.

White Furman students in the 1960s split in half along the continuum of liberal to conservative, with the faculty more liberal than were the students, and a few students did oppose desegregation.[23] During those days the boundaries between white conservatives and liberals were not rigid, but hallmarks of conservatism as oppositional to Black civil rights did exist. For example during my first semester some students formed a chapter of the Young Americans for Freedom (YAF), and the student senate unanimously approved its creation. The YAF was the nation's largest conservative youth group, with a national board that included a supportive Senator Thurmond as well as Ronald Reagan and Barry Goldwater, all national political leaders who had either opposed civil rights legislation or supported states' rights at a time when that meant opposing racial desegregation.[24]

The Vietnam War was growing increasingly unpopular, but Furman had a strong military program, requiring all undergraduate males to sign up for two years of ROTC. School characteristics aligned with social conservatism had positive effects; mandatory chapel attendance, strict curfew hours for women, restrictions on dancing, male ROTC membership, and a ban on Greek organizations brought a level of sobriety and protection for women from sexual predation. However, the school also attracted conservative white students who opposed the civil rights movement and antiwar activism. This meant that attending Furman as a Black student during those years was not nearly as traumatizing as desegregating lower-grade schools but was still immersive within an atmosphere of only partial acceptance of desegregation.

One campus student organization showed that some white students were searching for a new, more open identity. The new SSOC chapter was composed largely of such white students, and Joe was vice president; somehow, perhaps at his urging, the initial group chose me as its first secretary. The SSOC was the closest thing on campus to a leftist student organization, substituting for other youthful groups from that era, such as SNCC or Students for a Democratic Society (SDS). In the 1968 yearbook, my photograph appears with a small group of fellow SSOC students, ironically on the same yearbook page as YAF members. Joe and I are the two Black students, with Joe standing alongside Jack Sullivan and seven other SSOC students.

Jack, tall and amiable, helped create a campus SSOC chapter as a way to find an organizational home, and he served as our first president. In summer 1967 he began the search for such an organization for liberal students, looking at six movements that he described in six articles published in the student newspaper that fall. He found some of these movements palatable for liberal Furman students, but others, such as SDS and SNCC, were not.[25]

Jack recommended that Furman students consider SSOC, "a distinctly Southern organization" that could "relate to the needs and background of Furman students better than any other New Left organization." By November 1967 the new campus SSOC chapter included twenty-five student and faculty members. For one of its first efforts, a "teach-in," the SSOC invited a pacifist concerned about Vietnam to speak.[26] Other causes for that school year included opposing mandatory chapel, for which it organized a student petition that gained more than two hundred signatures, and inviting "radical" speakers, which led to trustees and a dean imposing a moratorium on SSOC speakers. Nevertheless over the next few years SSOC membership rose, and some of these initiatives brought policy changes.[27]

From my perspective the SSOC's greatest value was its forthright labeling of itself as a liberal enclave and its embrace of at least a few Black students. That embrace seemed genuine within the wider campus context of benevolent but silent tolerance. The 2004 oral history of one contemporary, John Duggan, detailed his own relationship with Joe as well as his memories of me, thirty-six years later, as a testament to this connectedness. Susanne and Marybeth were SSOC members as well, extending personal linkages from our 1966 summer program experience into our first undergraduate year. Later in this chapter I recount how SSOC students stepped forward at two points of personal crisis during that school year, showing courage and true friendship.

Two other primary paths shaped my social connections. Steve, the SC State student who had simultaneously introduced me to the Baha'i Faith and to Black radical literature, continued to visit me as his "girlfriend"; he was a native of Greenville and could drop by Furman occasionally. At that time Greenville was one of the few cities in South Carolina with an active Baha'i youth community. This was in part because of the efforts of Ricky Abercrombie, a Black high school student with a reputation for juvenile "trouble"; notorious Ricky's embrace of the Baha'i Faith shocked his large family and eventually led them all, from grandparent down to his many siblings, to embrace it as well. As recounted in Ricky's book, *Crossing the Line,* that family gradually rejuvenated the small Greenville Baha'i community. Ricky's active promotion of the Baha'i Faith at the same Sterling High that Joe attended was undoubtedly responsible for Joe's and Steve's affiliation. Steve took me to a few local Baha'i events and introduced me to this network, including the elder Mr. Abercrombie. At these events I witnessed for only the second time in my life—the first being Furman's summer school—apparently genuine biracial friendships. This seemed even more amazing because it involved middle-aged and older white people, not just summer school youth, supposedly more flexible. I watched as diverse members of this faith community met, hugged, prayed, and laughed together, acting as if they were all equal, not bound at all by traditional restrictions based on skin color.

That Joe had joined this religious community—and boldly announced this in Furman's student newsletter—was impressive, as was the happy socializing that I witnessed. As for myself, however, I was for a long time skeptical about this religion, new in the world compared to other major religions, founded in the mid-nineteenth century by a man raised in Islam, which was itself foreign to me. The first concern was whether the apparent was actually true—did these people really forget their own racial prejudices and form friendships across racial boundaries? The second concern was whether, after helping to integrate two schools, it was wise to risk involvement in yet another pathbreaking initiative, this time by joining a religious organization that promoted multiracialism. How could I, daughter and granddaughter of Methodist ministers, adopt a faith other than, though accepting of, Christianity? As a spiritual and biological descendant of 1866 Conference ministers, as well as someone nourished at both Claflin and Trinity, how could I leave a safe and secure Black church home for something else? It would take me a few years to resolve these dilemmas.

My second off-campus social network also gave me pause. The Black student movement was increasingly influential in my life. Here too Steve was the link. He had introduced me not only to new books but also to Orangeburg's Black activists. The literature they studied offered me a way to process intellectually my own experiences in life. The problem, according to such sources, was with the wider society rather than with Black people in general or with me specifically. *The Autobiography of Malcolm X,* paired with other more international books read by that clique, such as Frantz Fanon's anti-colonialist *The Wretched of the Earth,* gave me a new perspective on a worldwide struggle against racial injustice. The local activists were well-read and educated in a different way, not through courses but through books such as these, with firm grounding in Black history. Cities were burning in other parts of the country, with people in the streets provoking violent confrontations, and the Black Panthers had arisen as a visible presence, but these local "Black radicals" lived nonviolent lives and read books. Their epicenter was SC State, where students were increasing their own political consciousness, stoked during the civil rights movement and never actually set aside.

Particularly interesting were a couple, Cleveland "Cleve" Sellers Jr. and his wife, Sandy.[28] They had rented a house just across the street from Claflin; Steve and I visited them during the 1967–68 school year on my trips home. Sellers and Black Power advocate Stokely Carmichael attended Howard University together and became friends as well as SNCC coworkers. Although the white public associated the term *Black Power* with violent confrontation, Carmichael and Hamilton's 1967 book argued that the main purpose of that movement was "to establish a viable psychological, political and social base upon which the Black community can function to meet its needs."[29] Many young Black people understood the term as associated more with economic and political power rather than violence, although a few radical SNCC workers, such as H. Rap Brown, did support armed resistance. Sellers's work in Alabama and Mississippi, however, had been in collaboration with SCLC and the Mississippi Freedom Democratic Party, designed to end voter disenfranchisement that shut Black people out of government, not to foment violent rebellion.

Sellers, who was not an SC State student but who had ambitions of finishing the college work he started at Howard, was the driving intellectual force behind the emerging dialogue in Orangeburg. He was widely read as well as articulate, but my conversations were largely with the quieter Sandy. She wore a soft Afro hairdo and was the first person to talk to me about the beauty of natural Black hair as opposed to hair straightened with chemicals or hot combs. At my comment that curly hair seemed best, by which I referred to my wooly hair chemically straightened and then set on rollers, a laborious and sometimes painful process, she responded that her hair was curly, too, just with very small curls. From her perspective my adoption of other races' hair texture and suppression of my own was a form of self-hatred that ran counter to the Black liberation movement.

Sandy and Cleve Sellers's words, and the times we lived in, had impact. At some point I made an outward gesture toward Black political consciousness by adopting a short, natural Afro, which freed me from chemically straightened hair. At about the same time, I considered my future at Furman with some concern. What would be my major? Mathematics and physics were no longer fascinating, divorced as they were from social movements unfolding around me. My beloved religion classes at Furman (Old Testament for fall and New Testament for spring) held no obvious future, since professors did not address the racism engrained within their churches and all ministers seemed to be male in those days anyway. Political science, history, or sociology could have worked, but Furman's Black students were few, and its all-white faculty were new to racial integration, reducing prospects for relevant classroom discussions. No courses existed in Black history, civil rights, or African studies. Enticingly broader views beckoned to me from two directions, the Baha'i Faith and Black activism.

The thought occurred to me that it was time to transfer to a university that offered more curricular choices than Furman. At some point I resigned as SSOC secretary in favor of my admittedly nonexistent Black activism. (My "Black activism" entailed reading, occasional socializing with Orangeburg activists, and huddling in Furman's student center with the other Black students.) I found out many years later that SSOC's Jack held onto my resignation letter for years.[30] It was sad to hear this, since I did not mean to sadden him. Two events however, in Orangeburg and in Memphis, confirmed it was time to move on, regretfully, from Furman.

Rejuvenation and Massacre

During 1967–68 Dr. King and SCLC were reshaping their agenda, making forays into northern cities, labor unions, and the antiwar pacifist community. In cities the tone of Black activism changed drastically as civil disturbances provoked by police action and social inequities led to violent reactions, sometimes including burning and looting. While at first SNCC appeared to be at the forefront of the Black Power movement, soon the even more radical Black Panthers arose as armed guardians of some Black communities. The antiwar movement grew as people arose in protest against the Vietnam War. In South Carolina the civil rights movement remained resolutely nonviolent under the influence of the NAACP's Reverend Newman.

In Orangeburg college students continued to protest public or semipublic facilities that remained racially segregated even after the US Civil Rights Act of 1964. Rallies continued at Trinity, always accompanied by singing of such songs as "We Shall Overcome." Much action came from SC State students with support from Claflin students and the NAACP, but much of it was internal to SC State's campus, as students turned against the college's President Turner.

HBCUs faced many challenges during that period. They had educated Black students at a time when southern white institutions would not accept them. As court decisions and legislation forced white institutions to open their doors, the better-funded ones began to attract talented Black student scholars and athletes. SC State had survived as the only in-state public institution available to South Carolina's Black students, but it no longer held that status. As some Black students trickled into formerly white institutions, others chose to attend SC State or other HBCUs. These, however, still lagged behind in terms of resources; SC State could never catch up with the state's legacy of public investment in more established, historically white universities, and now it faced a talent drain as well.

In addition SC State's power structure was all wrong for this era, in terms of both optics and structure. The governor appointed an all-white SC State Board of Trustees up until 1966. The 1950 trustees had chosen Turner, presumably trusting him to support their segregationist policies, but his repressive actions so alienated many attending SC State that years later former students disparaged him in graphic terms during oral interviews.[31] No system existed for student disciplinary appeals, and no faculty tenure or governance system with any power existed. No check on Turner's power existed except for the often-absent trustees. He was not an empathetic or flexible leader, but according to some contemporary observers, Turner was an efficient administrator driven by his desire to improve SC State's academics and protect it from the wrath of white society. Often mistaken as white by local establishments, he and his wife held firm to their own racial identity and did not try to "pass."[32]

Many SC State students and faculty chafed under Turner's administrative style and similarly viewed their trustees as symbolic of institutional white supremacy. In the wake of the Civil Rights Act of 1964, the legislature expanded the number of trustees to include two Black members but made them minorities by simply adding them to the six white trustees.[33] SC State also hired its first non-Black faculty members, but in spring 1967 Turner refused to renew yearly contracts for two of the first three white faculty. He had already told the third, who left on her own, that she was "unwelcome" at SC State. William C. Hine, a white historian who first came to SC State during that era but survived as a faculty member for forty years, described his predecessor white professors as "young, easygoing, and generally popular among students" but "amazed and appalled at the rigid and stultifying academic atmosphere that pervaded the campus." Turner used various rationales for not renewing contracts for the two white males, such as that they were too informal or did not "fit into the program."[34]

In response, partially in defense of the white professors, SC State students launched an initiative nicknamed "The Cause." They held irate gatherings and launched student boycotts in March 1967; at one point 60 or 70 percent of students stayed out of class. Turner suspended three student leaders in retaliation. Students continued to stage protests and boycotts against these actions and the repressive rules that governed their lives, such as compulsory classroom attendance, no slacks for women, and required participation in vespers services, all vestiges of historic attempts to keep HBCU students under tight reins. Students asked for more involvement in campus government, nationwide hiring of qualified faculty, enhanced state funding for SC State, and reinstatement of the three students.

Gov. Ron McNair supported Turner and the trustees in their inflexible response and sent twenty state highway patrol officers to Orangeburg during that school year. (This was an unfortunate harbinger of the following year.) At first McNair refused to meet with students, but after the threat of a massive march, he invited the four class presidents to come to his Columbia office. McNair listened to their arguments for educational reform, amnesty for suspended students, and the firing of Turner. With his assurances that he would act, the representatives left his office, the boycott ended, and students returned to class. McNair informed the judge overseeing the NAACP's lawsuit seeking redress for the three students that the state would not appeal if the court reinstated them, which it did. Sobered by the widespread dissatisfaction with Turner, McNair ordered him to retire early.

These events took place during 1966–67, my twelfth-grade year. They helped to embolden SC State students, who had managed to get SC State's unpopular president fired through boycotts, demonstrations, and negotiation. In addition these events brought Claflin and SC State closer, as the two schools then entered

Presidents H. V. Manning and Maceo Nance at the new gate inserted as a symbol of increased openness between Claflin and SC State, fall 1967. Student on the left is Miss Claflin College; student on the right is Miss South Carolina State College. Courtesy Cecil Williams, photographer.

into a cooperative program allowing their enrolled students to take classes at the neighboring college, thus expanding course offerings for each. Dad and SC State's new leader, interim (and later permanent) president M. Maceo Nance Jr., signed the agreement putting this arrangement in place on August 17, 1967.[35] Later Dad happily reported to the Claflin community that Nance, in another sign of openness, had created a new gate in the fence that separated the two campuses. At home Dad told our family that Turner had strengthened that fence years before to emphasize separation. Nance, an extrovert, began to walk the campus seeking conversations and to build a SC State administration more open in tone and flexibility.

At first 1967–68 seemed to start out peacefully at SC State. Faculty started designing an empowered faculty senate to enhance voice in governance. The South Carolina Commission on Higher Education charged a twelve-member committee with investigating the situation at SC State. Headed by Furman's president, the "Blackwell Committee" had five members from other universities and six from SC State, and so Furman played a part in supporting reform.

The committee did not address the still-inequitable funding structure for SC State, but it supported faculty efforts to create a meaningful senate and recommended other initiatives. The committee's advice included improved policies for academic affairs, promotion and tenure procedures, and student appeals of disciplinary action. As these reforms took hold, students could pay less attention to injustices on campus and refocus on those in the surrounding city.[36]

Those injustices were many. In 1968 separate waiting rooms still existed for Black and white patients in local white physicians' offices, and the local hospital still had separate waiting rooms. Black patrons could not use the two drive-in movie theaters, open only to cars with white patrons in them, and the local movie theater maintained its "colored" balcony in spite of law. Housing discrimination was blatant, and a laundromat still displayed a white-only sign. The All-Star Bowling Lanes refused to admit Black people.[37]

Freed of Turner's oversight, students organized a collegiate chapter of the NAACP and chose Prof. Charles Thomas as faculty adviser and a ROTC student as president, signs of moderation. When Sellers came to town, he began to advise informally a group of SC State students who formed the Black Awareness Coordinating Committee (BACC), which leaned to the left of the NAACP but had at most twenty students, including my friend Steve. Their primary agenda was educational; they formed reading groups around Black history and activist thought.[38]

Sellers grew up in nearby Denmark. When Carmichael chose not to run as SNCC chairman in May 1967, his friend Sellers chose not to serve again as SNCC program secretary rather than work with the new chair, H. Rap Brown. According to his book, Sellers moved to Orangeburg in October 1967, well after the "Cause" student movement and months after student leaders met with Governor McNair. Not long after Sellers and a few colleagues arrived in town, however, they realized that they were "being watched." A local newspaper article referred to "a group of long-haired Black militants" traveling about the state trying to cause "trouble."[39] Cleve Sellers did sport a long Afro hairstyle, the male version of Sandy's, but he saw himself as a community organizer helping local people realize their rights and their potential.

The events that unfolded during the week of February 5, 1968, have been the subject of much examination but never an officially released investigation. Among the accounts were Bass and Nelson's *The Orangeburg Massacre* (1970) and Dubose and Williams's reflective *Orangeburg 1968* (2008), with detailed oral histories and photographs.[40] Published more recently is Shuler's 2012 *Blood and Bone*, based on interviews with white and Black locals decades later. The massacre informed portions of Sellers's 1973 *The River of No Return*, Gore's

1994 *On a Hilltop High,* the 2008 edited *Toward the Meeting of the Waters,* and Hines's 2018 *South Carolina State University,* as well as other books already cited.

Over the years I bought each of the above books in sequence, as I tried to make sense out of a senseless tragedy. Each book provided some piece of the "truth." It is difficult to summarize the bare facts: sources conflict, and some details in the mainstream 1970 book are misleading. Furthermore resulting judicial trials did not bring justice for shooting victims and led to one wrongful imprisonment, of Sellers (leading to less than a year in jail and eventually, decades later, to a pardon) but no sentences for the officers who opened fire on unarmed college students. Some media accounts and government leaders of that era distorted basic facts. Nevertheless, in spite of these challenges, here is a short synopsis.

Segregation of the local bowling alley was galling. There were more than two thousand students studying at SC State and more than eight hundred at Claflin, and yet their only off-campus recreational possibilities were a soda shop and the balcony at the movie theater.[41] During the summer of 1967, SC State administrator Oscar Butler and three other Black leaders tried to persuade bowling alley co-owner Harry Floyd to admit all paying customers. Floyd said that civil rights law bypassed him because the bowling alley was a private club. On Monday, February 5, 1968, a SC State student who loved bowling, BACC member John Stroman, teamed up with one of the few white SC State students, John Bloecher, to force the issue. Bloecher entered and began bowling without incident, and then his fellow Black students entered, sat, and ordered food at the lunch counter. Staff not only refused to serve the Black students but also threw away anything that they touched, including silverware and saltshakers. The students continued to touch objects, pointing out the different treatment for Bloecher, who was a member of no club but whiteness.[42]

Butler arrived and assessed the situation, as did local police; when Floyd turned off the lights, the students left. Orangeburg's police chief asked Stroman to stop by his office and spoke to him at some length, discouraging the young man in his plans and warning of arrest, but Stroman said he welcomed arrest since a legal charge would enable a civil rights court defense. Stroman, not SNCC-associated Sellers, originated the sit-in. It was a planned civil rights strategy to force a facility to desegregate, not a spontaneous action by restless students agitated by "outsiders." Stroman remained "angry," forty years later, that Sellers got all the attention in the bowling alley strategy, going to jail because of it.[43]

The police were aware of BACC as well as the presence of SNCC members in town, and they conflated the two, thinking that BACC was the same as SNCC, which was not the case. Rumors spread among white people about an outsider Black militant who was stirring up the students; this echoed the national conservative political environment that agitated for "law and order" amid Black unrest. Sellers knew that white locals' rumors referred to himself, even though neither he nor BACC supported Stroman's sit-in, preferring instead to work on community development and voting rights.[44] The local and state police, however, knowing of Sellers's background, consistently and inaccurately blamed him for being an "outside agitator" and ringleader.

It is possible that if local police had been the only forces on hand, matters would have abated, but local police notified the state. When Stroman and additional students returned to the bowling alley the next day, they found it filled with police officers and state troopers, including Chief J. P. Strom of the State Law Enforcement Department (SLED), a special division of troopers that worked directly under the governor. Local police arrested Stroman and several others for trespassing and started walking toward the jailhouse, but by then hundreds of students, upset at news of arrests, began to pour into the bowling alley parking lot. The police released Stroman to Butler's custody and walked him back from the jailhouse as a deliberate strategy to assure the students that he was okay and to encourage them to go home, which they started to do, but then a blaring fire truck pulled into the parking lot. Since no visible fire existed, the truck evoked memories of fire hoses turned on civil rights demonstrators a few short years before, and this caused pandemonium.

Some students who had begun to walk peacefully back to campus turned back around when they saw the fire truck. With the crowd of several hundred surging and shouting, someone broke a plate-glass window at the bowling alley. A state trooper went to a parked car, opened the trunk, and started handing out three-foot-long batons to other troopers. They moved in with the batons and began swinging, beating men and women alike. This melee sent eight students and one trooper to the hospital with wounds.

As enraged students ran away in fear and anger, some of them bleeding from their wounds, they smashed a few business windows and damaged cars on the way back to campus (a sure sign that Reverend Newman was not directing from the wings). While this disorder did not involve looting, such property damage, not typical for Orangeburg demonstrations, may have evoked in white minds images of the previous summer's riots in other US cities. Hine concluded this: "Most white residents were convinced that the town was on the verge of a racial catastrophe brought on by vicious Black militants led by Cleveland Sellers. The destruction of property the previous evening was the first step in a Black uprising that—if not crushed—would leave Orangeburg in ashes." In turn, "people in the Black community were outraged that the city police officers and state highway patrol officers had beaten young Black men and women."[45]

Dialogue and some accommodation could have possibly defused the situation at this point, but Governor McNair chose to send in more troops and make public statements about Black militants causing trouble. Fifty highway patrol officers were already present in Orangeburg, and he sent in 50 more. He also called up 250 members of the South Carolina National Guard. All of these officers were white except for one National Guardsman, George Dean, who had suffered persistent racial harassment from fellow officers. During that week, Dean claimed years later, he heard Chief Strom say as he grabbed ammunition: "I'm tired of playing with these n----rs now."[46] In the meantime Butler went downtown and asked for a parade permit, which was denied. Instead the city manager and mayor asked to meet with students in the SC State auditorium. This meeting was a disaster. The two white men, unprepared for the hostility they faced, persistently used the mispronunciation *nigra* instead of *Negro,* and they could not answer questions about race relations. Students then prepared a list of grievances, asking for bowling alley desegregation but expanding to ask for an end to police brutality, a biracial human relations committee, elimination of health care discrimination especially in doctor's offices, and a fair employment commission.[47] The mayor gave no indication that he would act on these requests.

Armed troops rimmed the edge of both campuses, which were under curfew. That evening three Claflin students attempted to leave campus; a nearby white neighbor shot at and wounded all three young men. The shooter claimed trespassing (which the students denied) and faced no repercussions. Two white men drove onto the SC State campus and fired shots; as they retreated from a dead-end street, students hit their car with bricks and rocks. Campus security police chased and caught those men, who did face charges. All of this happened on a Wednesday, February 7.

On Thursday, February 8, acting president Nance circulated a memo asking students to avoid violent acts and to stay away from the fringes of campus. SLED's chief J. P. Strom arrayed highway patrol officers near the front of campus, and they were there when students built a bonfire and began to taunt the officers. Strom decided to extinguish the bonfire and called the fire department, and several patrol officers advanced closer, onto campus grounds, to protect the fire department.

What happened next has several different narratives, but this seems clear: someone hit one of the patrol officers with a wooden porch railing, drawing blood. By this time between one hundred and two hundred students, woefully overmatched, were yelling at the patrol officers to get off their campus and tossing debris as well. Confronting them were sixty-six highway patrol officers armed with live ammunition, backed by forty-five members of the South Carolina National Guard, whose rifles had not been loaded. Also present were twenty-five SLED agents, city police, and FBI agents. At least five minutes after the officer was hit with the rail, one of the other officers fired a shot or sounded a whistle (accounts vary), but then more patrol officers opened fire, in a barrage that lasted eight to ten seconds. When this ended, they had wounded thirty-one students; three of these died within the next few hours. The dead: Samuel Hammond Jr., SC State student and son of an SC State alumnus, shot once; Delano H. Middleton, a Wilkinson High School student mingling with the crowd after a game of table tennis, shot seven times; Henry E. Smith, a SC State student dedicated to civil rights, shot five times.[48]

Patrol officers shot most of the students in the back or the bottom of their feet, silently disputing their later claim that they fired in self-defense. Wounded SC State students who could move crawled away, screaming, some dragging their peers, toward their college infirmary, which was soon overflowing. The campus nurse began to assess and then coordinate transport for students to the local hospital, but the situation was one of general mayhem. A young pregnant woman who was helping to rush students to the emergency room was, on her third trip, "stopped, beaten, and sprayed by three Orangeburg police officers." At the hospital she somehow fell off a table; she miscarried a week later.[49]

Over the next few days, law enforcement officers could not find any weapon in the area where the students stood, or anywhere, in contradiction to media reports of students firing at the officers. The officers had not tried any mitigating strategies for crowd control, such as warnings with bullhorns or tear gas; they simply started firing live ammunition into the crowd, continuing even as students ran away. Black state leaders later argued that such action at USC would have been unthinkable, because troopers would not have fired on white students. (This was well before the Kent State shootings, when officers did indeed fire on white students protesting the Vietnam War).

Six of the wounded were Claflin students. On that dark night, they somehow made their way back to Claflin's infirmary. Campus vehicles took them to the local hospital, but Claflin's nurse could not get them admitted. She returned them to campus where two local Black physicians, Spencer Disher and Monroe Crawford, treated them and then recommended driving them to hospitals in

SC State infirmary to which students fled after the Orangeburg Massacre, February 8, 1968. Courtesy Cecil Williams, photographer.

Columbia, Florence, and Sumter. Drs. Disher and Crawford were family as well as campus physicians, and so we all knew them well. SC State students in Orangeburg's hospital, aware of its reputation, struggled to trust the fifteen local white physicians who treated their wounds that night.[50]

Sellers was wounded in his upper arm, spared more injury because he had found a trash can to hide behind during the volley. Sellers helped several other students back to the infirmary. He was on campus because he was afraid to stay in his house, feeling targeted because a National Guard tank sat next to Claflin with its barrel aimed at his house. He slept earlier in the evening in a vacant dormitory room, but he came outside and saw the crowd already formed around the bonfire. He approached the crowd, intending to urge them to disperse after seeing the armed forces and realizing that the situation was unsafe, but then the patrol officers opened fire. At the infirmary he at first resisted going to the hospital, feeling sure "that I would be blamed for whatever action or incident that occurred," but he reluctantly consented. There, indeed, an officer recognized him; officers asked doctors to treat Sellers immediately and then placed him under arrest. Officers charged him that night with a series of major felonies, only one of which they "proved" in later trials. They drove him at high speed to Columbia, where, in a show of force, they placed him on death row of a high security prison.[51]

In Claflin's president's house, the former Matthew Simpson Memorial Home for Girls, located one small guest house away from Tingley Memorial Hall, which sat next to the T. Willard Lewis Chapel, almost a century after initial white philanthropy and steps from the street where troops had amassed, my mother heard the commotion as well as the shots. My sister Michelle was eight years old. Mom put her on the bedroom floor and surrounded her with pillows for protection, covering her ears to block her hearing. I was not home for this defensive action; that week I was safe in my Furman dormitory, living out my first college year. Michelle remembers that Dad was out of the country at the time, traveling with other HBCU presidents, and so she and Mom were alone in that big house. It was all very close, too close, right down the street, across from Trinity. If any of us had been standing on the front steps of our family church, we would have seen the backs of the officers arrayed directly across the tracks as they fired into the night. If we had been standing on the steps of our beloved Trinity, we would have seen the mighty force of armed white power and smelled the stench of overkill.

Aftermath

In the immediate aftermath, Governor McNair praised the actions of the highway patrol officers. He blamed Black Power advocates for the incident and claimed that protesting students had charged off campus and attacked armed forces after taking guns from the ROTC arsenal, all falsehoods. The mainstream media picked up some of these erroneous facts, dampening any sympathetic coverage that might have emerged, but Black media all over the country recognized injustice and protested, decrying this throwback to the era of mass slayings of ordinary Black citizens and violent attacks on civil rights activists.

Both campus communities suffered trauma; the colleges suspended classes for a week. As people tried to heal from physical and emotional wounds, their anger and bitterness increased, particularly with McNair's public statements that Black militants had caused all the trouble. As one columnist in the SC State student newspaper noted: "We cannot be convinced that SNCC, Black Power, Carmichael, Cleveland Sellers, etc. are responsible for what took place in Orangeburg, for not one of them set up a segregated bowling alley in our city, nor did they put up 'white' and colored signs at the doctor's offices." Another student asked: "Did the state have to 'murder' three of our students? Must blood flow? . . . Is this the only way to get the ear of the white power structure?"[52]

The SC State student body president and seven other students met with McNair in early March. They asked for several things, including approval of President Nance's previously requested and spurned $8.8 million appropriation for the next school year, an increase in professors' salaries, and withdrawal of the charges against Sellers. McNair refused to support these things or to withdraw his previous praise for law enforcement. On March 7 between two hundred and three hundred students traveled to Columbia in protest. They entered the statehouse carrying signs and demanding in vain to meet with McNair. Police arrested six students including my friend Steve, although charges were later dropped. One week later one thousand students gathered at the state capitol. Most were SC State students, but others came from USC, Benedict, Allen, and Voorhees. They met with various parties, including Lt. Gov. John C. West, and again presented demands. One was to honor the slain young men with an engraved memorial. They also launched a barrage of letters mailed to McNair and to West, and some of these entreaties had influence; it was hard to explain why the students were so passionate about their cause if the only reason for the violence was the intervention of Black militants. Among the concessions won by these students were the governor's support for the $8.8 million appropriation and reaffirmed support for a bond to build two dormitories and expand the student center. Students likewise pressured the trustees to name the new physical education complex in honor of the three slain students, which they did.

I do not remember how I responded to first news of the massacre. At that point it had no name; it simply was "the incident," an awful shooting in my hometown. Two people that I knew had been shot, Sellers and another young man from Greenville that I had gotten to know only slightly. That young man also did not trust Orangeburg's hospital and went home to Greenville for hospitalization; I visited him there, and he did recover, although some of the wounded never did and remained paralyzed or in physical pain for the rest of their lives. Some of the pain was indirect; for all of my life, while speaking about the massacre, my voice would tremble or tears might well up, a similar response to how I felt when I talked about high school desegregation. At the time it was hard to be in Greenville when so much was happening in Orangeburg. The beauty of Furman's campus, with its uniform brick buildings and tranquil lake, began to fade as I considered SC State's cramped, violated campus. I remember being very sad and disheartened.

We Furman students were too far away to do much, but a few of us decided to stage a protest march in Greenville. Our own brave Joe was probably the initiator of this idea, but the student newspaper said that "Joe Vaughn, Tyrone Haynes, and June Manning, all Furman students," organized the event.[53] We determined that the street in front of the federal building was an appropriate place to protest. Naively we thought that the federal government would somehow intervene to demand justice, which the US Department of Justice did initiate by charging nine of the patrol officers, who were promptly acquitted by an overwhelmingly white jury. Even before the SC State students marched on Columbia, we demonstrated in Greenville, in mid-February. We gathered maybe fifteen or twenty of us, too few for a "march," but we walked in a circle in front of that building with placards asking for justice.

My SSOC friends arose to the occasion. They made sure that the little circle of protesters had more white participants than Black. One of the white protesters was John Duggan, who later recalled that cars drove by with angry white people in them and that some called out racial epithets particularly against the white protesters, whom they called "n- -lovers." I remember none of that name-calling. Racial epithets were what I had experienced in high school, sometimes on a daily basis, and this would not have seemed remarkable to me. Instead I remember feeling relief at being able to show some small bit of solidarity with Orangeburg's Black students and gratitude for the white SSOC students who chose to march with us.

SSOC came to my rescue one more time. During that awful spring, another traumatic event took place on April 4. This was the Memphis assassination of Dr. King, two months after the Orangeburg Massacre. When I heard about that event, I was sitting in my dormitory room, studying, all alone because Sarah and Lillian were out of the dormitory for some reason. My white suite mate knocked on our adjoining door and asked if she could come in. She asked if I had heard the news. Very gently she said, I thought you should know that Dr. King has been assassinated. I stared at her in disbelief. How could this be? She asked if I wanted her to stay with me. I appreciated the gesture but said no, I wanted to be alone. I turned on the radio to confirm this incredible news and to listen to what was happening nationwide. In this way I found out that American cities were burning, as Black people acted out their grief and rage over the oppression that had shaped our lives. I turned off the lights, sat in the dark, and cried.

I did not know where to go with those feelings. Orangeburg was still grief-stricken from the massacre; no need to go home for solace. Greenville is only a two-hour drive from Atlanta, but it would never have occurred to me to drive there for Dr. King's services, and I had no car. Then my fellow SSOC students contacted me and said several of them were going by car to King's funeral; did I want to go? Why, yes, of course. This must have been long after I had resigned as SSOC secretary, spouting off some words about the need to organize Black students, empty words that never went anywhere.

The students, including Jack, picked me up early one morning. Five or six of us traveled. We drove as close as we could to the historic Ebenezer Baptist Church in Atlanta, site of King's funeral. In those days a bluff loomed directly in front of the church, and it was possible to walk up to an overlook. We got there early enough to get on the edge of the bluff and stay situated as the crowds grew and surged around and below us. We had a front-row seat for the procession as the hearse and other funeral cars arrived, and as people came to pay respects to this noble man, including ambassadors, federal officials, and others we could barely see who were of obvious importance. We stayed up on that bluff looking down upon the scene of crowds and mourners for several hours. When the dignitaries had left, ordinary spectators stood in line and passed by King's open casket. There we were, a small band of Furman students, filing with great solemnity past that noble leader's remains. The moment was heartbreaking but enabled by the kindness of those SSOC students.

It was all too much. I had already been thinking about transferring, but the Orangeburg Massacre sealed my decision. I developed a burning desire to get out of the Deep South. The decision to leave Furman was partially driven by my desire to major in something that I cared about, but I told my parents that I would rather drop out of college than stay in the South. Other northern universities would take me as a transfer student, and I wanted to leave a region that had caused so much pain. My plea: Please let me go; I will work hard to help support myself to repay you as compensation for my giving up a scholarship, and I will travel home for summers and holidays. Most of this narrative was true, but the claim that I would drop out of school was grossly untrue, I now admit. I was desperate enough to exaggerate.

To their credit, my wonderful, kind, incredibly frugal parents yielded to my pleas. They must have remembered the bright promise of ninth grade at Wilkinson High. They must have remembered my three years of ostracism and decided this was a time to show lenient love. They must have remembered their short respites from Jim Crow at Boston University. They let me transfer to Michigan State University, up North. In that way I joined the flood of Black people that had left the state in the previous few decades, fleeing repression and seeking opportunity in the illusive "promised land." Over the next few years, I never earned enough money as a college student to pay for more than airplane tickets home and spending money, but I always kept a student job of some kind, menial or not.

Conclusion

Crafting this chapter summoned happy times and people I deeply admired, but also reminded me of the worst of those times, and of the personal uncertainty and sadness that descended after choosing one path in life and then realizing I could no longer follow that path. It forced the retelling of a violent story that still haunts my hometown and my home state. Even so, perhaps, the reader may find something of value in the chapter, and in its summary. The story of Furman was, in some ways, an antidote to the story of Orangeburg High School. We described an instance of university desegregation that took place under relatively favorable circumstances during the mid-1960s. Furman not only had a history of comparatively progressive thought, but it also experienced both internal requests and external pressures for racial desegregation. Administrators' identification of Joe Vaughn as Furman's first Black undergraduate succeeded in many ways; his radiant, over-the-top personality fit the pathbreaking situation, and he provided tangible benefits to a university that feared segregation more than integration. Even so Joe and other first Black students experienced feelings of isolation within a context of split ideologies and fresh experience with integration. My own Furman experience provides more detail about that but also explains the importance of several factors that supported desegregation then and are important as well today. These include an expressed desire for racial integration by faculty and students, a friendly university president and administration, the presence of other Black students, and the support of at least one set of white students, here represented by SSOC. Adding the presence of Black faculty and more diverse classroom offerings and programming would in the future make desegregated universities more tenable for Black students and more broadening for whites.

Administrative changes at SC State and warming relationships between the campuses of SC State and Claflin brought a new era for Black higher education in Orangeburg. The events of February 1968, however, were examples of continued white resistance to desegregation in public accommodations as well as excessive use of force against student demonstrators. The Orangeburg Massacre was just another stage of an ongoing struggle to provide equitable education for Black college students in an environment of respectful treatment and equal rights. It was a direct attack on our safe haven, safe no more.

The spring of 1968 was, in hindsight, a very difficult few months for South Carolina but also for the nation. Not only did we lose King, a galvanizing civil rights proponent and a ringing voice for social justice. We also experienced, in the Orangeburg Massacre, an indication that large-scale police violence could unfold without justice, in that case in service to the last vestiges of segregation in a small town. On the international front, news of the Tet offensive against South Vietnamese cities may have turned media attention away from the Orangeburg Massacre. North Vietnam dealt a setback to the US when its Tet offensive, begun in late January, proved that the US and its allies were not handily winning that war. The snowball effects of that offensive and of the Vietnam War itself changed the US political landscape in many ways. Years later, I realized that yet another pivotal event happened during that spring. I had been too distracted to notice when it happened. In March of 1968, the Kerner Commission released its *Report of the National Advisory Commission on Civil Disorders.*

Johnson had appointed this commission to investigate the root causes of the civil disorders that had torn apart cities such as Newark, Detroit, and Cincinnati. The Commission's voluminous report, printed and distributed widely, pinpointed the pervasive role of racial prejudice and racial segregation that led to urban discontent, citing in particular massive Black migration from the rural South into inner-city enclaves that provided inadequate housing, employment, and public services, and calling out the pernicious effects of ongoing police brutality. This volume and its implications proved very important for the work I did as an adult, teaching future urban planners and writing about the nature of racial injustice and inequities in cities. As a blueprint for national social action, however, the report was not successful.

9

Keeping up a Struggle

Thus far this book has covered events dating from the 1860s until the late 1960s but with a focus on the classical civil rights era, 1954 to 1968. This chapter briefly summarizes relevant topics related to public education in South Carolina during and after 1968. That topic is much bigger than this short chapter can tackle, but we can at least explore a few pivotal issues related to the events covered thus far.

Challenges continued during subsequent decades as described by a few observers at both the national and state levels. Some of the worrisome signs apparent in the 1960s turned out to be harbingers of dilemmas that continued for some time. Efforts continued to improve educational equity in public education, but with decidedly mixed results.

State NAACP and School Desegregation

A good place to start is with how the NAACP's role in the state's school desegregation battles changed in the late 1960s. The 1968 Orangeburg Massacre proved pivotal. Days after that event, the Orangeburg NAACP branch issued a list of its concerns in a detailed declaration supported by the national NAACP. It listed police brutality and the need for a community relations task force and a better county penal system, but it also discussed lack of economic stability for Black families within the city and the county. Only eighth in its list of nine concerns was public school education. The need was to eliminate the dual school system, accept compulsory school attendance, and change the status of SC State "from the state-supported institution of higher learning designed to educate Negro youth to a regular branch of the University System, serving the whole community."[1] This implied that the racial fragmentation of the state's university system needed to end.

The local branch's list of priorities was understandable. By that time school desegregation was well underway. NAACP agendas for local and state branches remained multifaceted because of continuing problems confronting the Black community. The big push to desegregate the first few and then additional public schools was over; most school districts contained at least a few Black students attending formerly white schools, and resistant school districts were in the hands of the federal government. The state NAACP branch retained lawyers to handle continued lawsuits as these emerged. Other issues began to come to the fore as priorities.

Reverend Newman, spiritual as well secular leader of the state's civil rights movement, began to turn to other pursuits. In the summer of 1969, one year after the massacre, he announced a "Conference of the Indigent Needy in South Carolina." More than three hundred low-income people registered, and their summation report highlighted basic needs such as food, welfare, housing, jobs, legal services, and political involvement. They mentioned education only to call for vocational training as a way to help the "indigent needy" advance in life.[2] This was a legitimate response to pressing concerns; many of them suffered grievously because of lack of schooling, constrained employment opportunities, and a rural economy based on racial oppression.

Newman stepped down as NAACP field secretary in 1969 and began to work more closely with housing and economic programs for low-income people. A much younger man, 1967 SC State graduate Isaac Williams, picked up the job of state field secretary.[3] One of Williams's first annual reports, in 1971, listed Reverend McCollom as state president, Newman as head of the NAACP's housing efforts, and Newman's younger brother Omega as head of educational initiatives. The agenda for education included placing Black officials in policymaking positions for agencies and school boards, promoting Black heritage series on television, replacing racist textbooks, and offering job protection for misplaced Black teachers, as well as reviewing disciplinary codes unfairly applied to Black students.[4] Such initiatives were essential but ambitious for an executive committee that also claimed agendas for housing, labor, legislation, political action, welfare rights, veterans, and other topics, all using voluntary agenda leaders and one paid field secretary, Williams. Williams, who led the state branch until 1983, continued to keep education in his portfolio, but he also addressed other pressing issues. He eventually ran successful political campaigns that helped to elect Black state legislators such as Newman for State Senate and James Clyburn for US Congress.[5]

In 1970 legal scholar and desegregation lawyer Derrick Bell Jr. began to raise important questions about the NAACP's embrace of school desegregation as the principal strategy for improving Black education. At the local and state levels, it seemed the issue was being handled; at the national level, Bell was seeing worrisome signs. His credentials for making observations were impressive; he had worked for two years with the Civil Rights Division of the US Department of Justice (DOJ), six years with the NAACP LDF, and two years with the Civil Rights Office of the US Department of Health, Education and Welfare (HEW). In addition Bell undertook meticulous legal research tracing related court decisions at all levels. Having argued more than three hundred desegregation cases, many of them for school desegregation, he could see that this national strategy was limited. An article he published in 1970 argued that those wanting to improve the quality of education for Black students needed to diversify their approach. The article, both sobering and alarming, contained the seeds of his future work.[6]

Bell noted that progress had been excruciatingly slow not only in the 1950s but also in the 1960s, because the 1954 *Brown* decision and its subsequent 1955 clarification urged desegregation with deliberate speed but without enforcement. Built into these decisions was plenty of room for noncompliance. The success of *Brown* depended on the cooperation of lower courts and the DOJ as well as local school officials. Assisted by district courts hostile to change, local officials ignored the call for school desegregation as long as possible. As of 1970, in spite of a substantive body of school litigation, the quality of education for Black students was still markedly inferior to that of their white counterparts, and only a small percentage of Black pupils in the Deep South attended a desegregated school. He also described school segregation problems in the North, with little clarity about whether or not school boards were required to correct segregation if it was not due to deliberate school board action.[7]

Bell argued that the legal process that was the prominent strategy of that day was too slow and expensive to improve the quality of Black education. He suggested that advocates make support for Black education beneficial to white people's self-interest, such as by suing local school officials for legal fees or pressuring state and local agencies to improve Black education or face lawsuits for damages. Crucial to his argument: the supreme goal was not desegregation per se but rather improving education for Black children, whether or not that entailed school integration. He charged that too much focus on integration had left Black parents helpless to pursue other means toward that goal. NAACP LDF lawyers, furthermore, were diverting local protests against poor educational conditions toward the more expensive but in some ways easier (for attorneys) route of desegregation lawsuits.

Black people, especially in the South, were becoming reluctant to press for "one-way integration"; the pattern was for Black students to go white schools but not for white students to go to Black schools. Black teachers were losing their jobs, as were principals, in part because white parents did not want Black people teaching their children. This placed the burden of desegregation on the shoulders of Black children and families without yielding commensurate benefits.

Bell was calling out the regional and, to some extent, national trends already appearing in places like Orangeburg. The mighty movement for desegregation was not yielding a solution for the problem of under-resourced and underprivileged Black public education. It was indeed placing the burdens for desegregation upon vulnerable children who entered white schools as soldiers sent into war, without winning the battle for the rest of their peers.

"Structural Desegregation" Is "Over"

In South Carolina, Mizell and the AFSC continued to monitor and observe the school desegregation process, a regional strategy for the AFSC in several states. As part of that effort, Mizell began suggesting that the burden for reform should fall upon white, not just Black, people.

Two weeks after the local NAACP branch responded to the Orangeburg Massacre, on February 25, 1968, Mizell gave a talk titled "The Crisis of the White Folks" at the Columbia Unitarian Fellowship, in which he discussed the implications of the massacre. He decried the moral status of white people who perpetrated such an incident and then, as did Governor McNair, justified its draconian measures. He pointed out that McNair insisted on defending the state patrol in spite of no evidence that they had acted in self-defense and that the governor seemed ready to find a scapegoat rather than investigate underlying conditions. Mizell charged that a new biracial committee in Orangeburg, an initiative under way, was several years too late, and he asked why white people were so afraid of Black Power when the violence came from white racists and law enforcement officers. He called for change among white people: "We must know that not only do we have the power to effectuate change but that the real challenge before us is to use this power unaccompanied by the traditional white arrogance and pride which has brought us to this point in history. Only when we divest ourselves of such arrogance and pride can we even begin to successfully confront the challenge of using this power to speak to the genuine despair and frustration that we have created in the Black community." He asked near the end of the talk whether white folks could accept equality, given that they would "no longer be treated with the deference and undeserved respect which has so long been the Black man's technique of self-protection. For many white folks this will be hard to live with."[8]

The next day, February 26, Mizell sent a letter summarizing educational problems in South Carolina, listing ten items of concern. School districts throughout the state had resisted desegregation, he charged, and school officials and administrators focused on the negatives the Black students brought rather than their assets. Resegregation had already begun in some schools, and "because of the lack of meaningful progress in school desegregation, particularly in the majority Negro school districts, some Negro citizens have become disillusioned and are now beginning to focus their efforts on improving the all-Black segregated school rather than on pressing for more desegregation."[9] This was, of course, an observation made by Derrick Bell.

In remarks to a national teachers' conference held at about the same time, Mizell noted that matters were going badly for Black parents who previously hoped that desegregation would provide better resources for their children; instead they watched their children attend segregated schools and graduate from high school with education only at the eighth- or ninth-grade level.[10] As for "freedom of choice," he noted particular barriers to this concept of forcing Black people to initiate school desegregation after their history of internalized racial subjugation. "There can be no freedom of choice when such 'freedom' is dependent upon the courage, inclination and determination of the Negro citizen to throw off the psychological and social restraints placed upon him by generations of slavery, legally enforced segregation and prejudice. The fear of white power and the threats, either real or imagined, to the Negro's economic and physical security still chain many Negro citizens to those institutions born of servitude and segregation."[11] These passages made me admire my parents' court action even more; even with their positions of relative economic security within the Black community, they were not immune to the "psychological and social restraints" that Mizell spoke about in this talk.

In 1968 the US Supreme Court declared most freedom-of-choice plans illegal, but district courts generally allowed for gradualism. In early 1970 the Fourth Circuit Court ordered immediate dissolution of the Darlington and Greenville County dual school system. Governor McNair appointed an advisory committee to help these districts create a unitary school system, but Senator Thurmond and US Congressman Albert Watson demanded that the state defy the court order. President Nixon sent attorneys and marshals to monitor the situation, but white picketing, bomb threats, and armed guards followed.[12] In Darlington County three thousand white students boycotted desegregated schools during the transition. Two buses carrying Black students to a newly desegregated Lamar, Darlington County, school faced a white mob that attacked with bricks, ax handles, and chains. They overturned one of the buses, shattering glass and injuring six Black children. Fifty years later an occupant of the bus that did not turn over, who was fifteen years old at the time, said, "All of my life, I never forgot that day. I talk about that day with my children and everybody who I came in contact with. I traveled the country. I'm still astonished. It's heartbreaking that you can have hatred like that for children, and why were they after us as children."[13]

By the end of 1971, the pressure was off, and HEW was not aggressively enforcing the law. In 1969 the AFSC had directed its state offices to assess school desegregation and to note noncompliance as well as to monitor the response of HEW and DOJ to noncompliance.[14] Even as Mizell's staff began to grow, however, the tasks far outweighed available resources. The AFSC received some financial help, such as with the Washington Research Project, headed by Marian W. Edelman, but that required additional work with the Children's Defense Fund on top of other tasks.

Nevertheless South Carolina's AFSC office continued to support both desegregation and improvement of education for Black children. They created a public information newsletter; distributed booklets about Title I of the Elementary and Secondary Education Act of 1965, designed to assist schooling for low-income children; and advised parent advisory councils monitoring Title I progress. They also disseminated material on student rights concerning suspensions and expulsions in public schools, supported several Black student organizations, examined school finance reform, followed up on cases of in-school discrimination, and in other ways supported higher-quality education for Black students. By September 1974 the AFSC staff for such tasks included Mizell as director, four additional full-time people, five half-time people, and an attorney on retainer.[15]

Mizell spoke of continuing concerns in 1974 in a talk given for a symposium on desegregation. By then he had been working on educational improvement issues for eight years. He stated once again that "freedom of choice" desegregation plans required Black parents and children "to bear the brunt of dismantling the dual system of segregated schools by individually applying to attend formerly all-white schools." This meant that "all the forces of a hostile majority society could work on the Black parents' alleged freedom to choose."[16]

At the time of Mizell's 1974 talk, fifty-seven school districts were operating under voluntary plans and thirty-six were under federal court order; but many court-ordered district plans were obsolete, and litigation was dormant. School districts were not updating their desegregation plans, and plaintiffs were not seeking new motions. DOJ civil rights review of compliance had lapsed, and matters of employment discrimination, forwarded to the Equal Employment Opportunities Commission, languished in piles of backed-up cases. Mizell concluded: "The movement for what I call the 'structural desegregation' of the schools in this state is over." He called for a refocus on the primary goal: achieving quality education. "While we have substantially eliminated the system of dual schools in the state we have not devoted the same energy to eliminating the barriers which still block the road to a quality education for Black and poor children."[17]

Among the barriers he listed were practices such as grouping children by ability or standardized test scores, without compensatory assistance; problems with school financing, with uneven funding for educating low-income and non-white people; and expulsion and suspension of Black students for minor matters, in far greater proportions than actions against white students. Finally he described the disempowerment of Black education professionals, particularly at the principal level. In South Carolina nearly half of the state's forty-six counties had totally displaced Black principals.[18] Around the state continued white opposition to desegregation morphed into less violent means described by Mizell, such as tracking, expulsions, suspensions, and consolidation, but only with the demotion or firing of Black principals and teachers.[19] Schools became technically desegregated but racially oppressive.

Superintendent Clark displayed positive leadership in Orangeburg School District 5 by treating Wilkinson High School's Black principal, Robert Howard, with respect, offering him the job of assistant superintendent upon 1971 high school consolidation and giving him substantive responsibilities instead of just an empty title. This was not typical.[20]

Large and small changes indicated that desegregation was going to be very different than we thought when we set out on our glorious mission in 1964. By the time my younger sister entered high school in 1973, the two high schools in our district had merged into one, Orangeburg-Wilkinson High School (O-W). The new school had simply become majority Black, with only a few white teachers, administrators, and students; other white students had disappeared into private white academies or surrounding suburban areas and small cities. In my sister's 1974 O-W yearbook, I can see three white teachers that I recognize who remained. One was Doc Moore, still teaching physics. The yearbook lists teachers' degrees; Black O-W faculty included quite a few SC State or Claflin graduates, cementing the HBCUs' connections with O-W.

Bell continued to write about desegregation and to urge necessary revision in civil rights lawyers' national strategy. In 1975 he warned again that the *Brown* decision could neither integrate schools nor assure that minority children received a good education. He spoke in particular of a pivotal desegregation case based not in the Deep South but rather in metropolitan Detroit. Argued in 1974, the *Milliken v. Bradley* case was a failed attempt by civil rights lawyers to push for desegregation plans in northern metropolitan areas. This case concerned busing across district lines, but its implications were deeper than that; it was another indication that civil rights lawyers overemphasized desegregation as the major strategy for Black educational gains. Because of geographic spread due to suburbanization, however, Black northerners were less enthusiastic about putting their children on school buses for long-distance trips and relying for all of their school improvement needs on metropolitan school desegregation.

Bell echoed Mizell in his concerns about the high costs that came with the single-minded school desegregation strategy, costs paid by Black teachers and Black students. Both the NAACP and the NAACP LDF, which handled the bulk of civil rights litigation for school desegregation, were pushing for balanced racial proportions within schools, assuming that thoroughly mixed schools were better for Black students than majority-Black schools. Bell called this a "foolish rigidity," because racial segregation was not the real problem; that was "the maintenance of white superiority." Black schools were sometimes inferior, but often they were "quite good. On the other hand, desegregated schools have never provided a racism-free atmosphere for Black children." He noted that studies about the benefits of school desegregation for Black children were disappointing; some Black students improved, others did not, and still others stayed about the same as measured by "available testing."[21]

Moving to School Finance

Many challenges remained after formal dissolution of the dual system of public education in South Carolina. These included demotions or firings of Black teachers and administrators, aggravated suspensions or expulsions for Black students, tracking into low-achievement classes, poor school performance especially for low-income Black children, and underfunded school districts in minority or impoverished areas. These challenges also included, as Newman's "indigent poor" report noted, inadequate vocational training that could lead to meaningful careers with or without four-year college degrees.

Of all these challenges, each myriad in its implications, K-12 school financing is a particularly difficult problem, because the whole nation rests upon school systems financed with inequity. Municipal fragmentation in metropolitan areas, home rule legislation allowing for easy incorporation but difficult consolidation of local governments, and reliance on property taxes mean that it is quite common for some public school districts to provide privileges unattainable for others, and this is true in many states.[22] In some states, however, the stark contrast between richer and poorer districts led some to believe that judicial relief could reduce extremes in school district wealth and poverty that meant unequal access to education. Proponents of good quality education for Black children tried over several decades to address that concern in South Carolina. One state historian credits progressive governors with undertaking the first few initiatives,[23] but as with most such social change, these initiatives required vocal, active proponents. Their campaigns brought about limited improvements but did not resolve many problems of structural inequality.

Efforts to create more equalized school financing emerged nationwide in the early 1970s because of a California case supporting school finance reform, but in 1973 the US Supreme Court struck down a Texas lawsuit arguing for equitable school funding. Nevertheless, in response to that litigation, many states passed school finance reform by the late 1970s. Gov. John West campaigned in 1970 on promises to improve South Carolina's public schools, and in 1972 he asked the legislature to appoint a special committee to study the state's high K-12 dropout rates, low per-pupil expenditures compared to the nation as a whole, and teacher salaries that were 25 percent under the national average. In 1972 the AFSC investigated and found that school districts with the greatest need received the least funding from state government and contained markedly low market values compared to the wealthiest school districts. Their study also found that the state's flat-grant system for distributing state funds rewarded wealthiest school districts. This led poorer districts, composed in large part of low-income and Black families, to increase tax rates in a desperate but unsuccessful effort to fund their schools at acceptable levels.[24]

Representatives of civil rights and citizenship organizations in the state picked up the charge by speaking at numerous organizations, working to educate the population, and lobbying state legislators for support. The coalition included the NAACP, the AFSC, and the League of Women Voters, all participants in past educational desegregation campaigns, as well as the ACLU. Their efforts, and the cooperation of Governor West, led to the legislature's passing the state's Education Finance Act (EFA) of 1977. This reformed, to some extent, the state's formula for fund dispersal.[25] While this provided relief for the poorest school districts, a legislative study in 1984 found that poorer districts did not receive enough funds under the EFA to compensate for massive differences in district wealth. The Education Improvement Act of 1984 (EIA) created a dedicated one-cent increase in the state sales tax, with additional plans for educational reform, but it tended to counteract the EFA's distributional attributes by favoring schools aiming for higher school achievement, which were located in wealthier districts. Over the next few years, the state stopped funding 100 percent of the costs of pupil transportation and fringe benefits for employees, a blow to finance equity. Again the poorest school districts found themselves lacking.[26]

Inadequate school finances had real consequences for the poorest districts. Lack of money meant that they could not upgrade physical school facilities, many of which suffered from age and long-deferred maintenance. Lack of funding reduced not only the ability to transport students regularly but also extracurricular activities, since some districts could not afford to bus students after school and yet again in the late afternoon. Without such extracurricular functions, it became harder to attract and retain at-risk students. Well-funded schools were able to buy extras such as computers, books, and audiovisual equipment not available to the poorly funded schools. Significantly, depressed salaries in financially struggling districts meant that capable teachers sought to move to school districts that paid better living wages, leaving behind those teachers who were either not mobile or not marketable.

Educational proponents entered a long period of frustrating litigation. In 1987 several residents of Richland County filed suit against the governor and legislature charging that the EFA and EIA led to gross inequalities among school districts. The circuit court dismissed the lawsuit, a decision that the state supreme court affirmed, finding in *Richland County v. Campbell* (1988) that the EIA and EFA were constitutional ways to handle school financing in spite of the inequities. In 1993 forty school districts, mostly arrayed along I-95 in a string of low-income counties—including districts in Orangeburg and Clarendon Counties and counties ranging from Beaufort and Jasper in the state's far south to Marlboro, Dillon, and my grandparents' Darlington County in the northeast—filed what became a legal battle extending over twenty-five years. This was *Abbeville County School District v. South Carolina.*[27]

The first phase, known as *Abbeville I*, argued that the state's funding formula was unconstitutional and grossly inequitable because of extremely varied local conditions and poverty levels, leading to lack of an adequate education for children in many districts. It took from 1993 until 2003 for an initial ruling, various legal counterpunches, and a return to circuit court. During that time span, the plaintiff's attorney reduced the number of districts filing suit to eight of the most grievous cases. In 2005 the circuit court ruled in plaintiff's favor, but this was a limited victory; the court ruled that state government did indeed provide students with "a minimally adequate education," as the state constitution required. The only failure, according to the judge, was in early childhood programs. Of the districts for which attorneys had presented evidence in 2003, 88 percent of pupils were non-white, compared to 48 percent for the state, but the court had not allowed consideration of racial data, only recognizing information on poverty. Similarly the circuit court judge resisted obvious comparisons with *Brown* and *Briggs*.[28]

Realizing the flaws with this ruling's determination that only early childhood programming was inadequate, which in effect upheld skewed funding for higher levels than that, plaintiffs asked for permission to appeal, initiating *Abbeville II*. First argued in 2008, this case led to a favorable ruling for plaintiff districts from the state supreme court, but no order to disperse additional funds, which was the whole point of the litigation. Instead in 2014, six years after initial arguments, and many years after the first lawsuit, the court simply ordered the plaintiff districts and the defendant state to work together to develop a plan and submit this in 2016. At that point the court did not set a timeline for implementation but retained jurisdiction for further work on the plan. Finally in 2018 the case ended without any substantive revision in overall funding for rural, low-income school districts. The results of all of that effort: a school system that was "still segregated, still unequal, and still inadequate." In Clarendon County's Summerton district, 26 percent of the population, of which 97 percent was Black, lived in poverty, and public school students were majority Black. Scott's Branch High School in 2017–18 had a non-white population of 96 percent, and the white private school Clarendon Hall a Black population of 3 percent.[29] However, although Scott's Branch High School had only 201 students in 2018–19, and students scored only from 40 to 49 percent in math proficiency compared to a state average of 45 percent, reading scores were higher, from 60 to 79 percent proficiency compared to the state's average of 45 percent proficient. This suggested some level of accomplishment for a majority-Black high school where gross inequities led to *Briggs* so many years ago, but the school had lost hundreds of students, declining from over 600 in 1995 to 201 in 2018. All of its students qualified for subsidized free lunches, a sign of low income levels.[30]

One Orangeburg County school district, number 3, was among *Abbeville II's* eight trial districts. This was the small town of Holly Hill, located thirty miles southeast of Orangeburg city and just below the massive Lake Marion. As in other trial districts, underperformance shadowed this district. In 2017 it contained 2,800 students studying in six schools, with 88.4 percent of the students coming from impoverished households. The South Carolina Department of Education rated student performance as "unsatisfactory" during the 2002–3 school year, but this pulled up to "average" performance for 2011–12 and 2013–14, making it slightly better than some other of the eight trial districts. However by 2018 the average student passage rate on statewide proficiency tests was only

33 percent in this Holly Hill school district, falling from 59 percent in 2015.[31] In 2018 the 450 Holly Hill Elementary students, 88 percent minority, scored only 28 percent math proficiency, compared to a 45 percent state average, and 27 percent reading proficiency, less than the 45 percent state average. This suggests that the *Abbeville II* plaintiff districts were right; they were under-resourced and yet hosting students severely challenged by their circumstances.[32]

Two researchers in the years leading up to 2020 interviewed a number of plaintiff superintendents from the high-minority, low-income school districts that had joined this marathon litigation. Some had long since died, but a few remained. While few interviewees expressed regret for engaging in such lengthy litigation, noting that it was necessary to fight against injustice, the results after so many years of legal effort were deeply disappointing. As one plaintiff's superintendent noted, his former district still suffered from lack of resources, in spite of a few more preschool programs. "The state threw out a few dollars here and there, a year or two, but they never involved themselves in a sustained effort to try to improve the conditions in the district based on what the court ordered. . . . The state never had the political will to try to mitigate the situation in these rural districts."[33]

Assessing Results

The history and data narrated in this chapter do not form a pretty picture. The period from 1968 until 1974, a time period that was supposed to move the state into a unitary school system and provide equal education for Black children, instead provided a rocky journey to what ended up being yet another iteration of a dual school system. Among the many challenges that this generated, I chose to highlight flawed public school financing and its implications for a specific set of school districts. The marathon court case that ended up leading to nowhere, except the same disadvantages, does not generate a hopeful narrative.

A 2004 documentary telling the story of *Abbeville II* trial plaintiffs labeled the I-95 corridor of plaintiff districts' counties the "Corridor of Shame." The documentary summarized evidence presented for the eight trial school districts and revealed the challenges that faced rural schools in this state and, by implication, other states. A visit to one of these districts by then-presidential candidate Barack Obama in 2007 highlighted the shameful specifics. The Corridor of Shame nickname stuck, but it struck some of the plaintiff superintendents as piling yet more denigration upon their trouble-beset school districts.

Sometime around 2014–15 producers at the BBC decided to feature one high school in the Deep South that had become resegregated many years after efforts to desegregate and to improve public education for Black students. They determined that they would follow students at that school for one year, creating six broadcasts that aired not just on BBC but also on PBS in the United States. This series aired in the fall of 2016. The high school they chose, 98 percent non-white, was the consolidated O-W High School, my two old high schools rolled into one. The series offered considerable insight into several issues: why racial segregation had prevailed at that school; how students felt about their chances in life; and why a few white students chose to attend an almost all-Black school. The series was startling: my two good high schools had rolled into one with significant challenges for its students.

For 2018 O-W High School served 1,060 students, down from 2,000 in 1988. It was 97 percent non-white, with 92 percent Black students. Math proficiency was 33 percent, far below the 45 percent average for state schools. Reading proficiency was 54 percent, slightly above the state average of 45 percent. As an indication of poverty, an amazing 100 percent of the students were eligible for free lunch, compared to 62 percent for the whole state. Competing with this high school were not only overwhelmingly white Wade Hampton Academy but also one vocational school and one charter school designed for future health professionals.[34]

When compared to other states, South Carolina's public schools were not as low-ranked in 2020 as they were in previous decades, so in some ways the EIA, which aimed to encourage higher school achievement, had worked. The state's dropout rate was 13 percent, similar to the nation's 12 percent rate. A full 88 percent of South Carolinians had graduated from high school or higher, the same percentage as in the nation as a whole. The percentage with a bachelor's degree or higher was slightly lower for South Carolina, 28 percent compared to the national 32 percent, but not far off from Georgia and North Carolina. The percentage of public school students attending public as opposed to private schools was 86 percent in South Carolina, only slightly higher than in the United States as a whole, 84 percent.

As with most such statistics, however, racial disparities lingered within the numbers. Among the state's white population, 33 percent had obtained a bachelor's degree or higher, compared to only 16 percent of Black South Carolinians. Only 10 percent of white citizens had less than a high school degree, compared to 18 percent of Black. Surprisingly, however, the same number, 31 percent, for Black and for white, had obtained some college coursework or associate's degree. Let us for a moment assume that these statistics are not due entirely to in-migration of an educated population. If that assumption is true, HBCU colleges were apparently making successful efforts in some way to educate Black students, as were the state's non-HBCU colleges and universities; 47 percent of

Black South Carolinians had either a bachelor's degree or some level of college coursework, less than the comparable 64 percent for white residents, to be sure, but not inconsequential.[35]

This reminds us that HBCUs continued to be important in the larger scheme of higher education. SC State within the last decade, at one point, lost thousands of enrollments. It regained energy with new leadership, brought by Pres. James Clark in 2016, who immediately moved to raise enrollments and improve financial stability. According to the 2021 issue of *U. S. News and World Report*, SC State retained affordable in-state tuition for undergraduates, $11,000; maintained small classes, with the student to faculty ratio at 15:1; and established a pathway for those earning associate's degrees from three "technical" institutions, thus allowing their graduates to gain a baccalaureate degree from SC State. The institution, in such ways, continued to serve as an important provider of Black higher education. In-state tuition for USC was also affordable at $12,688, but with 17:1 student to faculty ratio and an undergraduate population of 27,502. USC was considerably more diverse than in previous decades, with different races and ethnicities of faculty, staff, and students.

According to the same report, Claflin's tuition was higher for undergraduates, at $17,192, but its student to faculty ratio was 13:1, and it ranked ninth in the country among HBCUs for overall academic excellence. It ranked ninth in the South as a Regional College South, for both HBCUs and non-HBCUs.

Dad led Claflin up to the year 1984, when he retired in a flurry of accolades and expressions of appreciation. Subsequent administrations built upon previous efforts. Pres. Henry Tisdale served ably from 1994–2019, making many tangible improvements to academic programs, research, and physical facilities. Following him was Pres. Dwaun Warmack, a native of Detroit, who brought many innovations and a youthful spirit to the job. The campus now has not only new buildings, new facades on older buildings, and a reconfigured road system but also a bustling, predominately Black student body of almost two thousand, an unimaginable number in years past, almost as many as attend SC State. Claflin's faculty, staff, and students hail from many countries and territories; about that T. Willard Lewis and L. M. Dunton, as well as alumna Mamie Garvin Fields, would be pleased. An online magazine available at Claflin's institutional webpage ably sums up the college's assets as well as accomplishments of each presidential administration leading up to the present day.[36] One welcome news item came in late 2020; philanthropist MacKenzie Scott (formerly Mrs. Jeff Bezos), looking for 374 mission-driven institutions to which she could donate part of her considerable fortune, chose Claflin for a substantial gift. As is usual with this philanthropic source, this gift was a surprise; Claflin's development staff had not actively sought money from her. This was confirmation of the school's promise and its future.

Two buildings located on Claflin's campus honor two college roommates who once slept on the beach while they sought summer jobs as waiters. These two became ordained Methodist ministers and lifelong friends; as adults, one often visited the other in Orangeburg, staying for those visits in the Matthew Simpson Memorial Home or in the small guesthouse next door. In the 1960s the two visited the hostile local sheriff to ask if Claflin students, jailed in civil rights marches, were safe. One of the two buildings is the Hubert V. Manning Library; this contains Claflin's library holdings, audiovisual equipment, and study spaces. The other, constructed on land that once held the Matthew Simpson Memorial Home and its guesthouse and gardens, is the James S. Thomas Science Center, one of the campus's major centers for STEM classes and for a wider scientific Claflin community hailing from many nations and peoples. Appropriately the two named buildings stand next to each other, in silent testimony to constructive resilience.

Conclusion

Moving to the Future

In some ways this book has been a contradictory saga. On the one hand, it tells a story of dashed hopes. It recounts the shining dreams of those who thought that decades of educational suppression for Black students ended with a 1954 Supreme Court decision or with desegregation efforts in the 1960s, but it notes that reality dissipated those dreams. It reveals the sacrifices made to get a few Black children into all-white schools that were sheltered by privilege and supremacy but then suggests that those sacrifices may have been, in some ways, moot. It points out that efforts to provide Black access to high-quality public education before, during, and after the classical civil rights era were limited in many ways. It provides only a fraction of available information about such limitations, but that fraction is largely disheartening.

The contradiction is that this is also a story of hope, of constructive resilience, of the fighting spirit of an oppressed people to ensure a better life for themselves and their children. It is a story of more than 155 years of post-slavery efforts to better educational prospects for a population that the dominant society felt should not be educated, should receive only an inferior education, or should be satisfied with limited gains even though the results were subpar. It is in some ways an awful story of human beings' inhumanity to other human beings, but it is in other ways an uplifting account of struggle and of triumph. How should we judge these contradictory storylines, both destructive and constructive forces?

Destructive Forces

One of the initial questions for this book: What was the nature of white suppression of Black education in South Carolina, particularly leading up to the civil rights movement? As we have shown, suppression dated from the slavery era but gained force with the 1877 end of Reconstruction and then the 1895 state constitution that mandated racial separation in public education and disenfranchised Black voters. Lack of political power left Black adults helpless to challenge unequal treatment as the next stage of repression unfolded with minimal funding for Black public education. Black parents tried to educate their schoolchildren regardless, even if only for a few weeks or months during the school year, but their efforts left them at a considerable disadvantage compared to white people, favored on several levels. Philanthropic sources helped but at times supported a model of industrial education for Black students that taught them social, economic, and political inferiority.

Clarendon County provided a major case study of the dual forces of constructive effort to uplift Black education and white supremacist suppression. Although the 1937 state survey showed that this county was not unique in its denigration of school facilities for Black children, the geographic situation there was so dangerous that Black parents arose first to fight for bus transportation, then equal educational facilities, and finally public school desegregation in South Carolina and, upon appeal, the nation. White reaction to the local Black community's pleas and petitions was punitive in the extreme, displaying white locals' willingness to do anything—lie, harass, terrorize, eliminate any means of livelihood, kill—to stop Black people from gaining equal education. Black residents of Clarendon County endured nonetheless, becoming sacrificial lambs for the hard-won goal of improved school facilities for South Carolina's Black children, with ancillary benefits for white children as well.

State government carried out a number of repressive tactics. It complied with Judge Waring's 1944 judicial decision mandating equal pay scales for Black and white public school teachers' salaries by designing other ways to justify higher salaries for white teachers. To protect segregated graduate and professional education, in 1947 the state government imposed upon an under-resourced SC State a new law school incapable of gaining accreditation and graduate programs that the school reluctantly accepted. The state ignored the college's requests for adequate resources for undergraduate education and for an ability to focus its efforts on training schoolteachers. State government made some amends in the early 1950s as it defensively tried to deflect *Briggs* by temporarily rectifying its historic underfunding of Black public education, but it also defended dual education. In a burst of mid-1950s actions, the legislature suppressed NAACP membership, decentralized school decisions to local boards controlled by defensive white officials, designed sanctions against schools that desegregated, and declared the *Brown* decision illegitimate and unconstitutional, among other tactics. The state's leaders in the US Congress led the way with their own rhetoric of challenge. During the classic civil rights era and beyond, the state continued to underfund SC State and suppress dissent. It made some improvements in school finance, but not enough to assure Black children of a well-financed public school system.

Another question posed in the introduction: Why did school desegregation generate hostile reactions from white people, and how did they subvert it? This was an ambitious question, assuming that it is possible to explain racial hatred. Others have written whole books on this subject. The best I could do was to describe the narrative that leading white South Carolina politicians and journalists used to defend their hostility toward school desegregation just before and after *Brown* and then to describe resulting behaviors. Segregationist journalists highlighted the supposed inferiority of Black people without acknowledging white society's efforts to make them inferior in status and opportunity, dating back hundreds of years. Politicians cited such excuses as constitutional purity and states' rights or the need to keep white children safe and both races from fighting. I suggested that the underpinning of the politicians' claims was a widespread culture of repressive white supremacy, bolstered by tradition, privilege in situations both small and large (e.g., restrooms, rural farm tenancy), and institutional racism within schools and elsewhere.

White pro-segregation journalists hypocritically opined about the need for sexual purity and protection of white people from disease and moral decay, crying out against miscegenation in a region where Black people varied in skin tone only because of historic white rape of Black enslaved women and their daughters who were servants. Such journalists led major newspapers and appeared on national television broadcasts, to great acclaim. US senators and congressional representatives spouted much the same verbiage within the halls of Congress as they did in talks given before lawyers, in books detailing their views, and in political addresses offered to ordinary citizens in the state, region, and nation. A system of justification for white oppression by means of legally enforced racial segregation emerged that was breathtaking in its glorification of social, political, and economic power for one race over another.

Such justification drove white efforts to subvert school desegregation. In addition to the ways already mentioned, such as simply resisting the *Brown* decision and undermining teacher salary reforms, white citizens' councils emerged, and white students and teachers led resistance to the presence of Black students in public schools, represented here by Orangeburg High School. Such petty, daily harassment characterized the first years of desegregation throughout the Deep South and border states. Other tactics arose besides simple harassment and ostracism—deeply damaging in and of themselves—including banning Black students from extracurricular activities, desegregating by forcing Black students to choose to attend formerly white schools ("freedom of choice"), placing Black students in low-achievement tracks, demoting or firing or trivializing Black faculty and administrators, and stepping up racially inequitable suspensions and expulsions.

Although this kind of overt hostility abated eventually, this was true in part because many white parents abandoned the public school system, as they did in the North and in other regions, by setting up private schools or fleeing municipal boundaries.[1] They often set up parallel school systems blessed with strong revenues and low poverty levels, leaving poorer school districts to fend for themselves after limited school finance reforms failed to resolve fundamental problems. Oppressive conditions that should have abated by the end of the twentieth century continued via alternative means, bolstered by simple inertia, municipal balkanization, and lack of social commitment to equal education. Federal district courts that once dismantled dual public school systems retreated into years-long, slothful inaction when confronted by evidence of severely under-resourced—but "desegregated"—public school districts located in high-poverty, high-minority areas. Mechanisms that protected white and middle-class Black privilege in other parts of the country did the same in the South.

A 1968 incident that does not fit neatly into any of the above categories of destruction was the Orangeburg Massacre, and yet this event was symbolic of violent white suppression of dissent, manifest in previous eras with lynching parties, Ku Klux Klan raids, shootings, and fire hoses. The Orangeburg Massacre revealed state government for what it was at that time: determined to protect white privilege, even in the form of a segregated bowling alley. The state's governor assumed that the proper response to protesting Black college students was armed repression, and he defended state troopers who fired upon unarmed demonstrators. As a result South Carolina lost its ill-deserved reputation for peaceful transition, earned because of its uneventful desegregation of Clemson University. For their part SC State students responded with brave protests, successfully demanding from the governor and the legislature some form of financial compensation for their violated campus.

Constructive Forces

How did Black parents educate their children and youth in spite of such negative forces? In some cities in the late nineteenth or early twentieth century, they set up their own schools, sometimes with the help of white philanthropy. During the 1920s and 1930s, the Rosenwald Program offered Black people a way to undertake constructive action by building schoolhouses and teachers' homes even if the state and local school districts would not. They did this even though this program required an economically oppressed people to finance their own public education facilities, imposing a dual system of taxation on top of a dual system of economic opportunity. Their efforts yielded fruit nevertheless. First was the immediate gain of sturdy school buildings for their children. Then subsequent studies of US counties with Rosenwald schools showed that this program provided at least some improvement in life chances for Black children and youth.

Ironically the Rosenwald program actually furthered Black migration, and it was not enough to stop Black people from seeking higher opportunity in the North, because of continued lack of economic opportunity and changing agricultural patterns.[2] Black South Carolinians made up 49 percent of state population in 1920 but fell to 43 percent by 1940 and 30 percent by 1970. The white population continued to grow larger even as the Black population fell or grew more slowly. In 2019 Black residents made up an estimated 27 percent of the state's population. Black exodus during the early and mid-twentieth century was a form of constructive action in partial response to conditions I have described throughout this book.

Support for Black education for those who remained in the state came sometimes in the form of direct action and protest but also in less visible ways. I used the concepts of constructive resistance and constructive resilience to describe this duality. Concerning constructive resistance, the Black community initiated many forms of direct action, enabled by the NAACP. Courageous Black South Carolinians challenged the suppression of Black education even at the risk of their own lives and livelihoods in Clarendon County, Elloree, Charleston, Orangeburg, and elsewhere. Activists engaged in such endeavors included Septima Clark, Modjeska Simpkins, Rev. Joseph De Laine, Rev. Matthew Douglas McCollom, Gloria Rackley, and the Black students who first applied to the College of Charleston and the USC Law School. They also included junior high, high school, and HBCU student protesters during the activist years of the civil rights era, along with many other parents, teachers, and ordinary citizens. The NAACP, particularly through such state leaders as Simpkins and Rev. I. DeQuincey Newman, led the way through the most difficult years.

I described a few of these people only briefly but in the process turned the spotlight on local and state-level civil rights resistance leaders not always recognized in narratives about this era. These activists worked in extremely perilous circumstances and yet exemplified brave tenacity. They did not simply arise and lead the civil rights movement as if it were some sort of regular job; they did so at considerable risk to themselves. De Laine, for example, faced numerous threats on his life, including a man who went up to him in broad daylight and threatened to kill him on the spot, feeling sure that the white men standing across the street would back him in this plot. De Laine's family was so grievously harassed that he found it necessary to sit next to his window with a rifle, returning fire to mark a car that drove by his house shooting at it. He fled the state knowing that the police would come after him instead of the attackers. Reverend Newman, "Cuz," a soft-spoken ordained minister who could have very easily stayed in a safe church in Charleston or in some other city, gave up his precious calling so that he could drive thousands of miles to rallies and meetings in every part of South Carolina, organizing a fragile civil rights movement. He went to jail willingly and often, as did many in that era, to point out the patent injustice of the law and to pressure the larger white society to do the right thing. He too faced threats, made all the more real when his counterpart in Mississippi, NAACP field secretary Medgar Evers, died through assassination; at that point Newman began to make quiet arrangements for his family in case he did not live long enough to see them through to the end. In our town Rackley not only lost her teaching job, but she also went to jail frequently, as did her teen-aged daughters.

Thankfully these activist leaders prevailed, but they did not work alone. I also noted that Black people who were not necessarily visible "leaders" or activists often undertook constructive, resilient efforts to support the civil rights movement or to educate children and nurture them with human-affirming values. I could refer once again to Black parents' response to the Rosenwald program but also to the steadfast support many Black families, teachers, and community members gave to their own public schools, separate private schools, and HBCUs. In addition, we pointed out that Black parents who sacrificed their children during the first and subsequent waves of school desegregation were, in their own way, heroic.

Essential to the concept of constructive resilience is the idea that people laboring under strong oppression can work in understated ways to create a better society that reflects praiseworthy values. This can happen on either an individual or an institutional level. Good teachers as individuals are in a special place to promote such constructive resilience, through their work of uplifting young minds and spirits and counseling discipline, diligence, creativity, dignity, and other values, even as they teach book learning. Teachers deserve and receive a special call-out in this narrative, starting with reference to those who taught Mamie Garvin Field and my own father. The intermittent descriptions of my own teachers and summer tutors were representative of the legions of educators who continued to strive under challenging circumstances to educate Black children and youth.

Although Felton's teachers taught in the best of circumstances for a Rosenwald school, even that required doubled-up, dual classrooms with minimal help from student teacher assistants. Other Rosenwald schools provided basic physical facilities, when it was possible to build them, but still housed teachers with large class sizes and minimal salaries. Nevertheless, under constrained circumstances, many Black teachers shone. I provided a few examples from Felton, but also several of Wilkinson High School's teachers were representative of the genre. They offered spellbinding stories about Paris or about their lives, kept and treasured our good essays, coaxed out of our choir angelic voices, and gently chastised us when we didn't go on strike in support of civil rights as did other boycotting students.

Many Black teachers in segregated schools offered a level of compassion and genuine interest in their students that sometimes we noticed only when we did not have those Black teachers anymore. In a replay of Mamie Fields's early childhood experiences with white teachers in Charleston, those of us who "integrated" public schools and universities in the 1960s in the days before Black teachers were present sorely felt their absence, as must Black students in many situations today. I offered a limited number of examples of this special contribution by Black teachers, but these few examples were very much in keeping with the findings of authors such as Vanessa Siddle Walker, studying Caswell County in rural North Carolina, and James D. Anderson, studying Charleston's Black high schools. Tondra L. Loder-Jackson's study of teachers in Birmingham, Alabama, *Schoolhouse Activists,* is another relevant example. She found that Birmingham's teachers were in effect the support corps for the activist phase of the civil rights era but also transmitted to their students such values as upholding human rights and dignity. Although in recent years such efforts faltered, as educational tasks became more complicated because of increasing poverty concentration and lack of a unifying civil rights movement, the Black teachers she interviewed continued to try to instill positive values even as community institutions previously designed to support them—such as self-sufficient Black schools—fragmented.[3]

I also described constructive resilience at the organizational level, again with a focus on schools. I focused specifically on two HBCUs. During SC State's first seventy-five years, before giving up its agricultural program (and its farm) in 1971, a series of its leaders built a public institution respectful of and yet extending beyond agricultural and industrial education. President Miller founded SC

State as a constructive strategy to further Black education in the midst of white post-Reconstruction backlash. Presidents Wilkinson and Whittaker nudged it into higher education in spite of chronic repression and underfunding. President Turner's best qualities leaned in that constructive direction as well, particularly with his desire to train exemplary teachers, and President Nance cemented the school's transition into a modern, multiracial era. At Claflin, similarly, there was a series of constructive leaders and educators striving to offer Black students "modern" higher education, both spiritual and practical, and to produce teachers and other professionals, all in a context of relative racial inclusiveness. All such efforts succeeded in part because both institutions were resilient enough to survive.

The Mannings are one example of a Black family that contributed to the greater cause of constructive resilience, but they were only representative of many such families. They served the cause by educating their own children, teaching in the public school system, encouraging church parishioners to attend college, and supporting civil rights demonstrators, but they also tangibly furthered the cause of school desegregation and helped to educate generations of Black college students. At the same time, my family protected its own children and its own sense of self-worth by developing a resilient response to the casual subjugation inherent within Jim Crow and its subsequent iterations.

I actually did not describe this as fully as I could have. I detailed my parents' adaptive responses to discrimination, extending all the way to restaurants and travel, and offered family legacy stories about how they sent their daughters off to be educated in another town, but I have left out many other examples of my family's resilience and contributions. One story not yet shared: my Grandpa Manning ministered to a circuit church in Lake City, the town that so shamelessly harassed De Laine's family with death threats and gunfire. As noted previously, my grandfather preached stirring sermons urging people to educate their children and send them to college. He helped organize Sunday School classes that reiterated that message. He delivered his sermons in shiny, worn-out suits, and he drove to those churches in a battered car, preferring that his parishioners pay him modestly so that they could build brick churches. One of the parish families not only educated their child but sent him all the way through college (North Carolina A&T), which then led to the Massachusetts Institute of Technology doctoral program in physics.[4] Ron McNair became an astronaut; he was killed at age thirty-five in the explosion of the Challenger space shuttle, but in the meantime he inspired tens of thousands of young children, including my own two, to study science. The town of Lake City, to its credit, has erected a beautiful memorial plaza to its native son, with a fountain and statue. This moved my adult son, who fiercely admired McNair and once dreamed of becoming an astronaut because of him, to tears when he saw it.

The supportive local Black community, through its schools, churches, and the NAACP plus other organizations, did the best that it could monitor, protect, and inspire its own. The classical civil rights era was a time of great courage, and mission-driven action, rallies, conferences, inspiring speeches, moral certainty, and simple community building helped carry many people through difficult times. This narrative is intended to transmit a certain sense of rightfully earned pride. An oppressed people managed to triumph in spectacular ways.

As I recounted, several white people occasionally emerged as allies for this process. The fact that these were often lonely voices within the white population does not dim their importance. One of the first was T. Willard Lewis, the missionary who cofounded what became the majority-Black 1866 Conference of the Methodist Episcopal Church as well as Claflin. Other allies included various philanthropists as well as Claflin's third president, L. M. Dunton, whose dedication and fundraising efforts enabled the school to survive. J. B. Felton's statewide stewardship of the Rosenwald Program helped erect five hundred school buildings for Black students, and federal district court Judge J. Waties Waring's rulings gave hope that the law could become just.

Other white allies included Pres. Bennette Geer, Furman's progressive leader during the 1930s; Alice Spearman Wright, human relations proponent and friend of civil rights activists; and M. Hayes Mizell, informal historian and monitor of school desegregation. Although not as visible, some white allies defended the *Brown* decision when it first appeared or worked quietly with the SCCHR, the AFSC, or religious organizations to improve Black education or to enhance positive interracial relationships. A few white Orangeburg High School teachers taught with compassion and professionalism, and white Baha'is overlooked cultural norms to associate with their Black friends. White tutors drove down to South Carolina in 1964 to help prepare Black children for desegregation, and my own fellow SSOC students at Furman were allies as well. Unfortunately the majority of the white population, which tended to support the status quo, drowned out these voices. Geer lost his job; Wright and Waring sought out Black acquaintances for lack of white friends; and Mizell stands out as one of the few white voices of conscience during the "structural desegregation" era.

As to the question of how all of this felt, I have tried to give some insight into how various events personally affected such individuals as Fields, McCollom, and my father. My own impressions were of an individual's experiences, but they illustrated larger-scale issues. Though my circumstances, as a child of professional academics, were relatively favorable, my narrative can stand as a description of the psychological effects on Black children of a legitimized system of institutional white racism in public accommodations. My experiences in high school and at Furman, buttressed with testimony from Arthur Rose, Tyrone Dash, and Theodore Adams, and informed by personal memories of Pat Rose and Joe Vaughn, exemplify the fractured price of desegregation but also suggest possibilities for community, resilience, and recovery.

An important part of one question remains unanswered. I discussed who supported either Black education and/or school desegregation, but I did not say clearly whether their goals were met. Did desegregation efforts create equitable education for Black students, the main goal? The obvious answer is no, but gains occurred. Abolishing public schools segregated by law was a victory for social justice, and the *Brown* decision was a pivotal recognition of Black people as full US citizens. The decision's effects eventually unblocked mobility for Black people who could benefit from such openness, for example by attending true high schools or more easily entering professional programs such as law or medicine. Results were less obvious for those less able to benefit from increased access. No longer segregated by law, many public schools remained segregated by practice, with education for Black children under-resourced in fundamental ways. Trends that became obvious in the late 1960s and 1970s cemented educational inequality by race thereafter. Problems of inferior education for Black children, originally identified as an issue for southern states, turned out to affect educational systems in other regions as well.

Necessary changes that had to come, such as the abolition of a de jure dual system of segregated public education, did come. Political power that had to become more equitable did so, although political access is still tentative, with Black voters decidedly outnumbered. Public schools remain segregated by both race and class, but this is a broader problem for the nation as a whole. The battle to provide better schooling for all children and youth continues, but some efforts to uplift Black higher education have succeeded. Resilient Black communities that weathered the storm did survive, in various places and venues. Still, much work remains.

Moving Forward

I am not an expert in public school education, and I do not feel competent to address the huge, underlying problem of lack of equal access to public education. By necessity I have presented material through the lens of personal and family history, buttressed by research. I am technically not even a southerner anymore, having fled the South many decades ago, even though my heart remains attached to South Carolina, for many reasons.

I have however worked for many years as a professor in a field that has consistently forced me to see the results of racial disunity and prejudice. As a teenager I left a region that I thought was the main locus for racism only to land in Michigan, a state sorely affected by it as well. My chosen field of study, urban planning, seemed focused on the greater good, except for a racially oppressive mid-twentieth century program, urban renewal, almost ended in the 1970s. I soon found that my field supported white privilege through contemporary means as well, such as exclusionary zoning that made suburban locales inaccessible for all or city redevelopment policies that Black communities interpreted as exclusionary if not oppressive. Institutional racism affects our whole society, and the topic is inescapable for many fields of endeavor.

Because I have been thinking about this issue of racism for a long time, I can offer some comments about how we as a nation might move forward in this time of resurgent racism. I have taught mostly white Big Ten university students for several decades and worked directly with communities of color isolated and disenfranchised by racial oppression, such as majority-Black Michigan cities and neighborhoods in Detroit. This work taught me that what I once thought was a problem of the Deep South was not that at all. Almost all of my professional writing has addressed, at some level, issues of institutional and individual racism and their implications for cities. A good portion of my classroom teaching explored the challenge of racial injustice and its implications for professional practice in my field. Much of my private life is devoted to attempts to build bonds of unity between different races through discussion groups, formal race unity courses or programs, and elevated conversation.

The implications of this book for contemporary society are, perhaps, two-fold. The first is the need to understand the forces of destruction and their effects on everyday society. The second is the need to understand what constructive effort is necessary to overcome this history of racial division and suppression.

Racism is, quite simply, a hugely destructive force. In addition to my other readings, such as, very recently, Ibram X. Kendi's magnificent *Stamped from the Beginning* and Isabel Wilkerson's thoughtful *Caste*, at times I have had to go back to the visionary writings of Dr. King or to my own spiritual leaders to explore possible solutions, but these are saying much the same thing. Here is what I found upon rereading King's classic *Where Do We Go from Here: Chaos or Community?* Writing a year before his own assassination, King called racism "among the moral imperatives of our time," requiring us "to work all over the world with unshakable determination to wipe out the last vestiges of racism.

. . . We know full well that racism is still that hound of hell which dogs the tracks of our civilization. . . . Racism is no mere American phenomenon. Its vicious grasp knows no geographical boundaries."[5] He then talked about South Africa, but his words remind us as well that racism transcends region and state in this country. It transcends this country, having recently raised its ugly head in many other places around the world.

The biggest lesson I learned from writing this book that I did not realize before starting it is how deeply racism has affected the educational and there-fore the life chances of Black Americans. Because of training and reading in my own field of study, I knew very well that racism affected access to mortgage financing and to the houses themselves. I understood that the combination of disproportionate poverty and residential segregation affected Blacks' access to good health, living-wage employment, high-quality schools, functioning public services, personal safety, nourishing food, and other hallmarks of a good qual-ity of life. I realized that institutional racism haunts the criminal justice system. Even knowing these things, I found the evidence presented here of purposeful suppression of Black education, pursued with passion over several twentieth-century decades, shocking. The extent of southern segregationists' determina-tion to thwart even elementary school and certainly higher education for Blacks put into a new light the conditions and racial barriers urban professionals and academics have long observed in the northern cities to which southern Blacks fled. It is important to call this repressive history out now, in this time of pan-demic and post-pandemic, when some people mistakenly believe that the tables have turned and that Black people have gained some sort of privilege through affirmative action programs, targeted grants, and limited political success. On the contrary, the roots of racial suppression are so deep and so transformative that the race may never be able to catch up.

This is not a matter of trying to recover from slavery; again, before un-dertaking this research, I must admit that my thinking was trending in that direction. That was before I delved more deeply into what I had thought of as a Clarendon County problem, so carefully detailed in several books about the civil rights era and summarized in this one. That was before I learned how thoroughly oppressed Black education was in South Carolina and therefore in the rest of the South. That was before I realized that the conditions that I was seeing and studying in northern cities such as Detroit stemmed from this his-tory of marginalization and suppression that had led to migration, and that this migration only landed Black southerners in urban communities that imposed a different version of marginalization via residential and employment segregation and discrimination.

I had read many times about the wretched conditions that faced rural Black southerners, again with a focus on Clarendon County. I had wondered why Grandpa Manning had no diploma, although he carefully kept every significant piece of paper in a treasured scrapbook that is still in my possession, and why when he hung something on the wall that looked vaguely like a diploma Dad asked him to take it down. That was before I encountered the statistics, as recently as a year before writing these words, revealing that his son, my father, was one of only 303 Black South Carolinians awarded a public high school diploma in 1935 because the state and local school districts refused to finance high schools for Black students. I did the math, calculating in my own head the implications of multiplying so much educational oppression in one county or one state to a whole region and then a whole nation. Reparations for slavery would be only the beginning, leaving much unrepaired.

Dr. King said: "Racism can be that corrosive evil that will bring down the curtain on Western civilization." Without action, "some future historian will have to say that a great civilization died because it lacked the soul and commitment to make justice a reality for all men," including the poor.[6] This book's story, then, should help us all remember the challenge that is at hand. The extent to which we can overcome historical barriers such as those presented in this narrative and begin to build an egalitarian society is the extent to which we can survive. This simple personal, family, and local history only hinted at the depths of the problem.

But what should we do about this? Suppose that we do all understand the challenges and wish to overcome them. This leaves the question of how to overcome such deeply entrenched inequities and manifestations of racial prejudice, and how to move forward.

Again Dr. King provided advice. "Together we must learn to live as brothers or together we will be forced to perish as fools." In order to live together, we need to overcome the gap "between our scientific progress and moral progress. . . . The richer we have become materially, the poorer we have become morally and spiritually." He wrote that we all live in both internal and external realms. "The internal is that realm of spiritual ends expressed in art, literature, morals and religion. The external is that complex of devices, techniques, mechanisms and instrumentalities by means of which we live. Our problem today is that we have allowed the internal to become lost in the external. We have allowed the means by which we live to outdistance the ends for which we live."[7]

This advice to attend to the internal tracks very closely with the advice given to the worldwide Baha'i community. The Universal House of Justice said in 2020, in face of the rising incidents affecting Black Americans including violent police repression, the following: "Racism is a profound deviation from the standard of true morality. It deprives a portion of humanity of the opportunity to cultivate and express the full range of their capability and to live a meaningful and flourishing life, while blighting the progress of the rest of humankind." It then went on to say what would and would not work in overcoming this problem. "It must be supplanted by the establishment of just relationships among individuals, communities, and institutions of society that will uplift all and will not designate anyone as 'other.' The change required is not merely social and economic, but above all moral and spiritual." Furthermore, "the power to transform the world is effected by love, love originating from the relationship with the divine, love ablaze among members of a community, love extended without restriction to every human being."[8]

It is for this reason, recognition of the necessity of building just relationships founded on love, that I chose to include within this narrative descriptions of positive relationships. It would have been easy to write a book simply about the injustices suffered by my community, my family, myself. It would have been easy to make racism the exclusive focus of the book, and many books do this, giving us a healthy set of reference texts about this unfortunate human inclination. At some point, however, we need examples of other approaches, such as constructive resilience, featured in these pages. We need to highlight those few instances when we are able to find people who extend beyond racial identity to build friendships and to fight for social justice. Therefore I offered stories about T. Willard Lewis challenging white Charlestonians and casting his lot with Black Methodists; J. B. Felton helping to build schools for Black students through cooperative effort but still feeling unsatisfied; and L. M. Dunton devoting the better part of his life to raising up Claflin. The account of Judge and Mrs. Waring and their friendship with Septima Clark gives us courage. It was similarly necessary to tell you about my summer tutors and about Furman's SSOC. We spoke of Earl Middleton's fierce admiration of Alice Wright and willingness to work with her on better human relations, and of Modjeska Simkins, doing the same. We noted that "firsts" entered schools eager and willing to make white friends, although they met with rebuttal; Joe Vaughn was willing to cheerlead for his beloved Furman; SC State students protested Turner's firing of white faculty. We can take inspiration from such stories of past efforts and try to do our own part to overcome a historical legacy of racial division.

A major part of making such an effort, of course, is overcoming individual racial prejudice. We cannot expect pronouncements about love to cancel out ingrained racial prejudice. Hard work is necessary, purposeful effort, again as exemplified by Judge and Mrs. Waring who undertook their own study of racial oppression and then reached out to connect with Black friends. In modern times in the US, that could start with reading books about Black, Native American, and African history, or exploring the considerable written, auditory, and visual material that exists about US race relations. It requires diversifying friendship and work networks, mentoring young people who need guidance, and monitoring one's own sense of race-associated inferiority or superiority. It requires striving to become an anti-racist, but also to help build a stronger multiracial society.

Such relationship building still leaves unresolved problems of institutional racism. Overcoming individual prejudice and being willing to form interracial friendships does not erase the effects of generations-deep privilege or disadvantage. Larger efforts to improve society must continue, supported perhaps by increasing consciousness of injustices, similar to that rude awakening experienced by Judge Waring after he witnessed judicial injustice in the Woodard case, but accompanied by intelligent, effective social reform. Much of this will need to come at the state or federal levels, which can help resolve deep problems such as concentrated poverty, uneven school finance, or lack of political access. Other efforts will need to come from oppressed communities themselves, as they continue to educate and protect children, inspire youth, and affirm the inherent value of adults regardless of how the larger society views them.

Here is the issue, however. Institutional reform will not truly take place unless enough people support change not only in structures but also in their hearts. Otherwise, people will find ways to circumvent necessary reforms, as happened with school desegregation.

These are a few thoughts about broader implications, but this book at heart a simple story not designed to lecture readers. It aims to describe a legacy of constructive resilience that was independent of the existence, or absence, of school desegregation or school equality, or of wider social reform. Narration about such resilience highlights the nobility of a people who worked hard to survive and thrive despite dire circumstances. It is a love offering to my parents and by extension to my family and to my hometown, as well as to my peers, schools, and community. It is a small attempt to feature heroic people who lived in my childhood state and in a small town divided by railroad tracks, with white people on one side and Black on the other, at a time not so long ago. It is a gesture of support for those who aim to create healthy, nurturing communities characterized by triumph over adversity, nobility, and well-educated children and youth.

Life as Epilogue

After an interesting childhood and youth, described in pieces along with this book's more impersonal text, my own life evolved from the rugged years of a Jim Crow childhood and various experiences of school desegregation in both high school and college. My personal narrative about desegregation mostly ended once I transferred to Michigan State University (MSU) for the 1968–69 school year. That university choice was not random, so I will explain it and its implications.

In the spring of 1968, as I considered how to get out of the Deep South, two Black women from Michigan came to visit Greenville. They proved to have a strong influence on my life. Naomi Oden and Luella McKay were residents of Highland Park and Detroit. Both were Baha'is who had offered extraordinary service to that faith community during their lifetimes. They had come to Greenville to visit the Baha'is, and either Steve or Joe connected me with them. These women "adopted" me for one day. They decided to take me with them as they drove from Greenville to Atlanta for a short visit with a Baha'i who lived there. They picked me up at Furman, and we rode together for the two-hour drive to Atlanta and back again. Naomi was the more talkative, but both talked pretty much all the way there and back.

Hearing two middle-aged Black women talk easily about race and spirituality was a new experience. Wisdom rolled off their tongues as they offered a free-flowing commentary on the state of race relations and the need for spiritual awakening among all people, Black and white. Prominent in their discussion was Shoghi Effendi, leader of the worldwide Baha'i Faith from 1921 until he died in 1957.[1] Shoghi Effendi, who lived in Haifa, Israel, world center of the Baha'i Faith, was vitally interested in racial issues that affected North Americans, and he wrote many letters to American Baha'is explaining how to overcome racial prejudice and build a faith community characterized by racial unity.

Luella's and Naomi's words were not idle chatter but rather a one-day deep-dive lesson into the Baha'i teachings about racial unity, a dialogue based in large part upon their love for Shoghi Effendi's writings. These included, they told me, clear instructions concerning the responsibility of white people, such as to overcome their "inherent sense of superiority" and to consort with others without any racial prejudice. Shoghi Effendi also offered instructions for Black people, such as to become receptive to white people who were trying to overcome their own prejudice. He said that neither race was free from the hard work it would take to bring harmony.[2] I had never heard of a religion that offered such explicit suggestions for resolving racial disunity.

Although I was still skeptical and actually did not join the Baha'i Faith until three years later, their words fell on receptive ears. They were addressing the very things that I wanted to talk about in Furman's religion classes but could not, since in those classes we talked about Bible chapters but seldom addressed spiritual obligations during fractured times, and we never talked about race. These two women discussed the true nature of justice as a spiritual concept and the barriers that faced us in a society characterized by racial injustice. Their concept of justice included a strong concern for impoverished people, as in one of the verses that came from Baha'u'llah, the prophet-founder of the Baha'i Faith. Because Naomi would repeat this verse to me many times in the years to come, I remember it well. She emphasized the need for spirituality that uplifted those who had been "brought low in the land" by injustice and poverty and the importance of seeing them as "spiritual heirs" of the divine. At the same time, she would say, we should aim for the spiritual union of peoples of all races, nationalities, income levels, and creeds, as we created loving communities characterized by mutual respect.[3]

Somewhere in their stream of elevated conversation, on that special day, I expressed my mundane desire to transfer to somewhere up North, to a university with courses in Black or African studies. They immediately suggested MSU in East Lansing and mentioned that a few Baha'is attended school there. One of these was a poet named Richard Thomas, a Detroit native that Steve had mentioned often as well. I then remembered that MSU was among the schools that had sent me flyers when I was in eleventh and twelfth grade, touting their Honors College. I investigated MSU's multiple course offerings, seeing that these included several African languages and an African Studies Center, and started the paperwork for transfer to MSU.

Years later I realized that Steve and possibly other Baha'is had told Naomi and Luella that I was interested in the Baha'i Faith. The connection with MSU was an unanticipated outcome of this linkage. As matters unfolded thus, the

Greenville Baha'is had transferred me from one Baha'i community to another in Michigan, just as I transferred from one university to another. Their connections turned out to be helpful, because upon arrival I found MSU's size overwhelming. The number of students alone was three times Orangeburg's total population, and the huge dormitory complexes and sprawling land grant campus were very different from the cozy, sheltered insularity of Furman, Claflin, and SC State. It would have been easy to get lost in the crowd, but I arrived with one contact name. I immediately began working in the dormitory cafeteria at the lowest wage possible to earn spending and airplane flight money for home visits. This gave me connections with wonderful kitchen staff, who had a lot of fun doing the honest work of food service. I soon got in touch with Richard Thomas, a poet but also a Marine Corps veteran who had returned to college in his late twenties. By chance he and I had enrolled in the same Swahili class during my first MSU semester, and so my sole MSU contact walked into my life as a fellow classmate. Richard remembered conversations about me with Steve and Naomi, and he introduced me to the MSU Black student community and Baha'is in the Lansing metropolitan area.

MSU turned out to be a good place for me, even though any illusions I had about the North as the promised land soon vanished. My plane arrived in August 1968, a year after the civil disorders of 1967 had burned down a good portion of Detroit, ninety miles away. The embers of emotions were still smoldering from that contentious summer. In addition it soon became clear that the state itself was bifurcated, with huge racial and cultural differences between the Upper Peninsula and out-state sections compared to Lower Peninsular cities such as Lansing and Detroit. Race relations were better than in the Deep South but still flawed; the history of racial discrimination and segregation in housing and employment was sobering. Even so, MSU was a great place for me, with several hundred Black students, a few established Black faculty, and a variety of international students. I felt freer living in a place that did not have a recent history of "white only" and "colored" signs. I felt safer living in a state where racial epithets were not common parlance and happy to attend school not far from Detroit, epicenter of the magnificent Motown. This was all a temporary respite, to be sure; I intended to go back South after college or maybe after graduate school, but in the meantime I could breathe more easily.

On campus it was possible to sample myriad courses ranging from Swahili to philosophy and anthropology, with many gifted professors along the way. The sociology professors were especially memorable. I liked a Black professor named Ruth Simms Hamilton so much that I ended up taking four courses from her. Her Urban Sociology course led me eventually to my life's career as an urban planning professor. Another wonderful professor was Sal Restivo, a young sociologist who was as savvy about current events as one could hope for in a professor. John Useem, a seasoned sociologist, opened up my vision of the world as a locus of multiple cultural phenomena, and historian Norman Pollack offered keen insights into American history and society that have stayed with me. Robert L. Green, a Black education professor, was like an elder brother for activist Black students on campus. He gave us a tangible connection with the civil rights movement since he had worked directly with Dr. King and SCLC on school desegregation issues, and he became the first director of the new MSU Center for Urban Affairs established while I was a student. The MSU Honors College provided special course sections, a sheltering study lounge, and information about potential graduate school fellowships.

As an MSU undergraduate, I was able to engage not only with excellent professors but also with communities of Black students and of Baha'is and to begin to find some balance between my interests in Black studies and in religion. Black MSU students had formed the Black Student Alliance (BSA), and I participated in their activities, including a sit-in at a dormitory cafeteria (not my own) as we demanded more course offerings on the urban crisis and in Black studies.

The deeper I engaged with the BSA and the allied Office of Black Affairs, the more I realized that something was missing in the typical route of Black activism: key spiritual values, such as love for all humanity, respect for women, and dedication to the peaceful transformation of society. Many of my Black MSU peers seemed to lack vision about possible solutions for the world's ills or to veer toward supporting armed resistance. Also alarming were some of their personal lives. Some became isolationist Nation of Islam adherents, at which point women became marginal in a way that was disturbing. Others became radical political proponents but did not know how to translate that rhetoric into productive lives. One committed suicide as a dramatic illustration of this problem, others turned to alcohol, and another dropped out and somehow lost her way. These were the "activists"; other less political Black students were able to balance their lives or zone out entirely with football games and boozy parties, but that was a perilous journey I chose not to take.

All the while Richard Thomas consorted with and even led Black students as BSA cochair but maintained his firm grounding in the Baha'i Faith. We soon became study partners as well as closer than that. He was notable among our peers for his maturity, and not just because of his age and veteran status but also because he could defuse conflict and bring diverse views together in agreement before you even realized what he was doing. These were all qualities that the

Baha'i Faith had honed within him but characteristics of his personality as well. He was also articulate, affable, and grounded in Black history, as Orangeburg activists were but with Detroit-bred charm and a softer edge. His personality reminded me of Rev. I. V. Manning, Grandpa, the happy, visionary, articulate extrovert. Four months after graduation, I married Richard. I was very young, twenty, and he was thirty-two, but we were happy together and willing to work as we continued our education. He was and is my best friend. He had no interest in living in the South, and we eventually found faculty jobs at MSU; my original plans to return to South Carolina after college thereby changed, but for a very good reason.

Soon after we married, I realized that I wanted to become a Baha'i. I was already close to this faith, due in large part to the many meetings to which Richard had taken me, but the Black student movement on campus had forced me to decide upon a pathway for the rest of my life. I became more grateful for the guidance about racial unity that the Baha'i Faith offered, and it answered many of the questions that had dogged me about the Bible and about religion in general, concerning life after death, the role of prayer, the equality of men and women, and values. Embracing this faith, along with marrying a wonderful adherent, allowed me to heal spiritually and emotionally.

During my senior year, MSU's Honors College helped me apply for several fellowships for graduate school, and I received three fellowships to attend any graduate school I wanted. The most generous was a four-year full fellowship for doctoral work from the Danforth Foundation. Richard and I decided to go to Ann Arbor's University of Michigan together, where he entered a doctoral program in history and I entered one in Urban and Regional Planning. He received his doctorate in 1976 after writing his dissertation on the history of Detroit's Black community. I received mine in 1977 after writing "Blacks on the South Carolina Sea Islands," a dissertation about the impact of tourism on the same Gullah people that Mamie Fields, Septima Clark, and my mother had taught. Mom put me in touch with families that she still knew many years after teaching high school on Johns Island. That research met a felt need for Black Sea Islanders, who asked me to study the economic and land-loss effects of forthcoming Kiawah Island development on nearby Black residents; they asked the development company to finance the study and then to provide limited reparations and jobs.[4]

When we graduated with doctoral degrees, Richard and I already had two beautiful children who have now grown up into two capable adult professionals and given us four bright grandchildren. We both taught on the MSU faculty

Family members ca. 1972, Hartsville, South Carolina. H. V. Manning
holding baby Kemba Thomas, Michelle Manning, Mrs. Fannie Manning,
June Manning Thomas, Ethel Manning. Richard Thomas, photographer.
Family album photo.

for most of our careers. As Richard approached retirement, I switched to my
doctoral alma mater to join the University of Michigan's urban and regional
planning faculty in 2007.

We both loved writing. Richard specialized in Black history and the history of US race relations, highlighting "the other tradition" of the interracial
struggle for social justice. He developed this approach, referenced in this book,
based upon Baha'i concepts of racial unity. My writing has centered on the urban planning profession and its uneven history with racial justice. This includes
a history of Detroit's redevelopment decisions and their impact on Black communities as well as other work on social injustice in racially segregated postin-
dustrial cities. This work has used my youthful experiences with segregation as
a spur to examine the need for social justice in northern cities. I also determined
early in my career to help correct a major gap in the urban planning literature,
which was the challenge of racial justice.[5] At first little writing existed about

the intersections of race and urban planning, but this field has now burgeoned. Another goal was to help create a national interest group of minority planning faculty who could support one another and minority communities; that interest group has now had a major impact on the planning academy, via the Association of Collegiate Schools of Planning. Governing board membership and leadership roles with both the interest group and its parent Association allowed me to support national efforts to advance racial diversity within the urban planning academy, for both faculty and students.[6]

One book different from these pursuits has roots in the one-day trip to Atlanta with Naomi and Luella in 1968, the trip that led me to Michigan and to my future life. *Planning Progress: Lessons from Shoghi Effendi*, published in 1999, is a short history of that leader's plans for the systematic evolution of the worldwide Baha'i community. I wrote it to deepen my understanding of Shoghi Effendi as well as to explore the role of spirituality in my own field of urban planning. Richard and I have offered much volunteer service to the Baha'i Faith, such as by hosting talks open to the public, meetings, and study circles in our home or elsewhere and serving on local and regional administrative bodies, but our scholarship has benefited from this association as well.

Early in my marriage, in 1972, my mother retired from Claflin's faculty. She was only fifty-seven; at first I could not understand why she retired so early, but she told me that teaching was not fun anymore and that the students had changed in some way. This was news to me; I had not realized it was fun for her or that life had shifted in her classroom. She then became increasingly active in church affairs, and for two years in the mid-1980s she served as president of the newly biracial SC Conference of the United Methodist Women (UMW). Later in life, thus, she was able to lead a key statewide church organization and form friendships with both white and Black Methodist women, gaining wider recognition for her natural leadership skills.

A local reporter asked her, upon her election as UMW president, about her retirement; her response was instructive. She said, "I like staying in the background. It's very *comfortable*. My husband, he is the public person." Furthermore, "by 1972 we finally had enough qualified teachers for me to quit, and he needed me at home."[7] This reminded me that supporting Dad at home and parenting my younger sister were real jobs for Mom. It also reminded me that both SC State and Claflin, in that era, were favoring faculty applicants with earned PhDs and pressing current faculty to go back to school for that terminal degree. Mom had no time for that. In 1986 Claflin gave her an honorary doctorate anyway, for her many services to Claflin and to the UMW. They conferred this at the same time that they gave an honorary doctorate to Senator Thurmond, who had somehow redeemed himself by introducing legislation to support HBCUs, and by creating a small foundation to assist underprivileged students in the state.

Keeping in mind Mom's words about teaching being fun, I have always fully thrown myself into teaching my university classes, enjoying this immensely, and seeing the act of guiding young students as the most meaningful part of my academic career. In this effort my role models have been not only Mom but also my teachers at Felton, Wilkinson High School, and selectively at Orangeburg High School, as well as Furman, MSU, and the University of Michigan. Because of my field's connection with professional practice, many of my urban planning students and I, at both universities, have worked with small urban communities throughout Michigan, helping them assess conditions and create neighborhood plans. It was a particular joy to carry out such work in Detroit's majority-Black neighborhoods.

I could never repay my parents adequately for their loving care, and then for good measure I married a Detroit man and we stayed in Michigan, necessitating their limited contact with their only two grandchildren. My parents adored Richard, however, and virtually adopted him as a son. Our own son, Ali, attended HBCU Morehouse College in Atlanta for his undergraduate education before attending medical school at the University of Michigan. While at Morehouse he was able to visit his grandparents frequently, during holidays, and to form lasting bonds. My parents thought very highly of their only grandson and appreciated this connection. Dr. Ali Manning Thomas is now a hospitalist physician who also does diversity training/recruitment in the Seattle area. Our daughter, Kemba Saran Thomas Braynon, did not have the same opportunities as a youth to connect with these grandparents, but when she did, such contact was memorable. She is now a registered architect based in Michigan and specializing in historic preservation; she builds and rehabilitates buildings just like her grandfather Rev. H. V. Manning and her great-grandfather Rev. I. V. Manning. Her latest project is a civil rights museum in Selma, Alabama.

Richard and I cared for my invalid mother in our East Lansing home for the better part of five years, as she descended fully into Alzheimer's disease. Richard was a full helpmate in this difficult, honorable mission. Michelle, also a helpmate, took care of her for one year, in Miami. Mom passed away in 2002 in Michigan. My dad passed away in 1997, after trying to take care of her as best he could, until his heart gave out from the stress. Both lie buried in Hartsville, Darlington County, next to Rev. I. V. and Fannie Manning, Dad's parents. Michelle moved back to Orangeburg in 2009, having married a wonderful man who has also since passed away. She moved there to work for Claflin, raising money for the school through its development office; in this way our family was able to continue serving Claflin. She works in Tingley Memorial Hall, as did Dad and Mom.

Well, there is a life and a family update, summarized just enough to lead into the next two experiences. These experiences touch upon the legacy of events narrated in this book.

The first one happened by chance, in the fall of 2018. Because my academic work included urban planning history, I was not surprised to receive an invitation to participate in a panel for the Urban History Association (UHA) that would meet in Columbia, South Carolina. UHA meets every two years and draws not only historians who are interested in urban studies but also urban studies and planning scholars who are interested in history. Someone on the conference planning committee knew that I was a South Carolina native and suggested me for a keynote panel on the Orangeburg Massacre, as an example of local history. The organizers had no idea that I had any connection with Orangeburg; they simply picked me as an urban planning historian who grew up in South Carolina.

As they sent details about the panel, I looked to see its other members. These included two notable women, Henrie Monteith Treadwell, Simkins's niece and the first woman to integrate USC, as well as Heather Thompson, a University of Michigan colleague who had recently won the Pulitzer Prize for her book *Blood in the Water.* Despite such luminaries, the most amazing person listed was Cleveland Sellers. I had not seen Sellers for fifty years, another side effect of fleeing South Carolina in my youth. There it was, on my computer screen: he would serve as a fellow panelist.

I already knew what had become of him; occasionally I would hear about his life after the massacre. He described some of that in his book *The River of No Return,* but that book is more than forty years old. I knew that he had eventually earned a doctorate, lived out of state for a while, and then worked at USC as both faculty member and director of the USC African American Studies Program. He also served as president of Voorhees College in his hometown of Denmark for seven years, stepping down in 2015. Occasionally people still held memorial services for the victims of the massacre in Orangeburg, and his name would emerge as associated with those events. These bare facts I knew vaguely, but little else.

Seldom do I write out the text of talks, since my job has offered lots of practice in public speaking, but I did not trust myself to give an off-the-cuff talk on desegregation and the massacre. The fact that Sellers would be there made me all the more careful. I wrote out a ten-minute talk and prepared a basic Power-Point. When I arrived at the venue, there he was, in the flesh. It was wonderful to see him alive and well, having accomplished so much in his life. I asked if he remembered me; he said, "Of course I remember you; you are President Manning's daughter. You integrated the local high school." So I was not as invisible as I felt as a teenager! Afterward we took photographs together to remember the moment.

During his portion of the panel, Sellers summarized the history of the massacre as a pivotal civil rights event and gave an account of decades-long attempts to gain justice or compensation for massacre victims. He showed a deeply affecting video that included personal narratives of physical survivors, some of them still carrying bullets in their bodies or paralyzed, and in that way, we could see evidence of sacrifices made. This was entirely new for me; I had never had a chance to see the faces of the survivors so many years afterward and to hear their stories. Sellers had helped keep the massacre at the forefront of public consciousness. After a few years living away, he had returned to the state to educate students and the public about Black studies and racial injustice. He made a space for educating students at both mainstream USC and HBCU Voorhees.

Part of the personal healing process for Sellers was to gain an official pardon twenty-five years after his imprisonment as supposed instigator leading to the massacre. Another was to apply for and receive, forty years after he earned but did not receive it, the Boy Scouts of America official Eagle Scout award. His marriage with Sandy did not last, but he married a second time and devoted much energy to parenting three children that resulted from that union.[8] His youngest son, Bakari Sellers, became the youngest state legislator in South Carolina's history, elected at age twenty-two, and Bakari now serves as a regular CNN commentator; thus continues the Sellers legacy of politically aware service.

The second experience took place only because of the work done in preparation for writing this book. Starting in 2017, I made many research trips to explore various archival collections in Columbia, Charleston, and Orangeburg. I also traveled to Greenville's Furman, although much of their archival material was online. Furman had contacted me before that for an interview as they put together material for the fifty-year commemoration of Furman's desegregation. That 2015 commemoration led to a very helpful webpage, complete with feature articles, as well as a beautiful soft-cover, glossy folio that contains several articles, some of which I used as sources for this book.[9]

Although these sources were helpful, it was important to visit Furman's archival collection on site. Nothing can match meeting with a knowledgeable archivist in their own facility, where they can talk to you about your query and immediately pull up documents only available on paper. Jeffrey Makala introduced me to many such materials concerning Furman's desegregation, but he also updated me about an important initiative. Furman's Office of the Provost had set up a task force on slavery injustice. He showed me display cases with historical memorabilia, demonstrating that Furman's namesake and earliest leaders accepted and promoted slavery, and he gave me a copy of the resulting report. Befittingly the task force named the report after Abraham, a formerly enslaved man who served for many years as a servant for the family of James C. Furman, son of Richard Furman, the university's proslavery namesake. This report, *Seeking Abraham,* is not unlike efforts by more prominent universities to investigate their proslavery past.[10]

I had attended Furman for only one year and then left, so my ties were tenuous. Nevertheless, I had given a talk on urban studies at Furman in 1989; that trip allowed me to visit with my former roommate Lillian, a public-school teacher who was serving on Greenville's city council, and to see how Furman had progressed. Perhaps because of archivist Makala, Furman invited me to come back and give an evening talk in connection with the inaugural Joseph Vaughn Day Commemoration, to take place January 29, 2020, in celebration of Joe's enrollment. The emailed invitation came from a young Black woman, Deborah Allen, director of the Center for Inclusive Communities at Furman. The name of her office was in itself significant. As she explained to me when we met, Furman had expanded to 20 percent minority students among its undergraduates, including 6 percent Black, and it now included Black faculty among other staff members, including herself. I already knew that it had long ago separated from the SCBC, becoming a private university.

That visit was unforgettable. Richard joined me as we flew from Michigan, checked into a hotel, and drove to the campus, scarcely recognizable after so many years. Anticipated was a noontime march from Furman's library building to the chapel. The weather was chilly, and so we arrived early on the library steps but then went inside to keep warm. When we came back out again, we could hardly believe what we were seeing. On one portion of the steps stood a small Black gospel choir composed of students running through a dress rehearsal, and a large cluster of others, of all races, stood nearby. More and more people arrived, in waves, adding to a convivial spirit as we all stood on the steps waiting for the march. I was amazed; where did all these people come from, twenty-nine years after Joe's death? Why were they all here? It soon became evident that this was going to be a large crowd happy to celebrate Joe's life. The small choir sang spirited music to cheer us up for the walk, and then what felt like hundreds of people began to walk toward the chapel. The march enveloped us with a wave of happiness, conviviality, and determination rolled up into one.

It all felt like a dream or a movie set, totally unreal. It was hard for me to walk, choking back tears as I was with each step.

Why was I so emotional during that march and then the service? Because of a strange mixture of joy and sadness. The joy came from seeing so many people honor Joe's contributions to Furman. It came from pride in Joe's great life. It came from seeing a student who was a first to integrate his school honored in a way not possible for other first children and youth, who had met only jeers and epithets in still-resentful small towns and cities. The reverse was also true, therefore; underneath the joy I felt sadness at the pain many of us had suffered, without such reparation. I felt personal loss because fleeing the South had meant fleeing Furman, Greenville, and the chance to get to know my Furman and Orangeburg friends better, to see them evolve into the adults they became. Leaving South Carolina was the best choice for me; I could never regret the resulting life's work and wonderful family, all blessings for which I am grateful. Nevertheless, how utterly sad to consider the promising potential if I had been able to stay.

The march was just the beginning on that grand day. All went smoothly as orchestrated by the working group headed by Allen's office that planned the inaugural ceremony. At the large chapel, we received beautiful glossy programs for the service, with Joe's picture as he stood on the library steps in 1965, in a pose that the trustees determined would become manifest in a commissioned statue to be located (and erected in 2021) on the same spot as the pose. Chapel seats were filling up fast, and so Richard let me walk ahead so I could be sure to get a seat; he and others had to stand outside or in the back. Furman's president welcomed all, including two or three dozen members of Joe's family. Joe's young cousin talked about his remarkable impact on the Greenville Black community, the local school system in which he taught, and his own family. The chair of Furman's trustees promised that Furman would always hold this commemoration, every year, and that the board would implement additional recommendations from the task force's *Seeking Abraham* report. That report offered hard truths and strong recommendations, such as changing the names of some buildings and roads, as well as changing investment, policy, and scholarship strategies to further social justice, but Furman would do this.

Rodney Acker, who graduated from Furman in 1973, long after Joe graduated, but who knew him well, read a prayer from the Baha'i Faith. Rodney was the first Black athlete at Furman, and he too had become a Baha'i and lived out his life in the Greenville community. I thought about Joe's bravery. How hard it must have been to be the first but still write that 1967 article announcing his new faith to other Furman students. Here was Rodney, many years later, reading a prayer at Joe's commemoration on behalf of the Baha'i community. Rodney came to my evening talk as well, and four of us—Rodney, Ricky Abercrombie, Richard, and myself—went out to dinner afterward, trading memories. Ricky gave us an update on his own family members that had become Baha'is only because Ricky as a bad-boy Sterling High School student had amazed his own family by straightening out his life. By giving talks at that high school, Ricky transformed local youth as many embraced his faith, including Joe. We talked about the wonder of it all, our gathering to see the honor that Furman bestowed upon our friend Joe.[11]

I can think of no better way to end this book than to cite from the City of Greenville's proclamation, first read before the large crowd attending that January 29 commemoration. Here are some passages from that proclamation establishing Joseph Vaughn Day:

WHEREAS Furman University's Seeking Abraham Report (2018) has found that the University was complicit in its early history with slavery and its legacy; and

WHEREAS the sacrificial labor and support of African-American people has been crucial to the existence of the University and the Greenville community throughout its history; and

WHEREAS the University is taking steps to reckon with and repair its history with respect to race, and to educate students who will have the opportunity to heal injustices on a daily basis; and

WHEREAS the Board of Trustees voted on December 8, 1964, to reaffirm open admission leading to the enrollment of Henry Adair, William Bowling, and James Kibler as graduate students in education, and the enrollment of Joseph Vaughn as the first African American undergraduate on January 29, 1965;

WHEREAS Joseph Vaughn continued his fight for deeply held principles, including his leadership and dialogues about the Vietnam War and race, his change of belief to the Baha'i Faith, and his organization of a rally to support students at South Carolina State University following the Orangeburg Massacre and to honor Martin Luther King Jr., following the assassination; and

WHEREAS his example paved the way for the admission of African American women Lillian Brock Fleming, Sarah Reece, and June Manning Thomas to be admitted in the fall of 1967; and the desegregation of Furman Athletics by Rodney Acker in 1969; and

WHEREAS all members of the community should learn from the

courage of Joseph Vaughn the importance of seizing educational opportunity in speaking out for equity and justice; and

WHEREAS doing so will build a sense of belonging and beloved community that is deeply needed in our world today;

NOW THEREFORE,

Be it resolved that the city of Greenville officially honors the memory of Joseph Vaughn and declares Joseph Vaughn Day as the 29th day of January 2020, and every successive 29th of January, joining Furman University in its historical work of introspection, commemoration, and healing.

NOTES

Introduction

1. Efforts used to ensure dual school systems in Michigan are described in Highsmith, *Demolition Means Progress.*

2. Lau, *Democracy Rising.*

3. See 2021 rankings, "Best Colleges: Claflin University," *US News and World Report,* https://www.usnews.com/best-colleges/claflin-university-3424/overall-rankings (accessed March 13, 2021).

4. "Derrick Bell (1930–2011)," *Harvard Law Today,* https://today.law.harvard .edu/derrick-bell-1930–2011/?redirect=1 (accessed 13 March 2021). See also Hughes, Noblit, and Cleveland, "Derrick Bell"; Bell, "Burden of *Brown* on Blacks"; Bell, "Serving Two Masters."

5. Information about Johns Island in C. S. Brown, *Ready from Within,* 104.

6. See, e.g., Levine, *Freedom's Children;* Beals, *Warriors Don't Cry;* Devlin, *Girl Stands at the Door.*

7. Constitution of the State of South Carolina Ratified in Convention, December 4, 1895.

8. Sorensen, "Constructive Resistance."

9. Schock, "Practice and Study of Civil Resistance," 277.

10. Sorensen, "Constructive Resistance," 52; Mantena, "Gandhi and the Means-Ends Question in Politics," 8.

11. Sorensen, "Constructive Resistance," 57.

12. Universal House of Justice to Baha'i students in Iran, September 9, 2007; to believers in Iran, March 5, 2009; and similar letters dated June 23, 2009; March 21, 2010; March 21, 2011; May 14, 2011; and August 27, 2013. https://www.bahai.org /library/authoritative-texts/the-universal-house-of-justice/messages/.

13. Fields, *Lemon Swamp,* 41.

14. Ibid.

15. Drago, *Initiative, Paternalism, and Race Relations;* R. S. Baker, *Paradoxes of Desegregation.*

16. Drago, *Initiative, Paternalism, and Race Relations.*

17. Rollock and Dixson, "Critical Race Theory," 3.

18. McIntosh, "White Privilege and Male Privilege"; Leonardo, "Color of Supremacy."

19. Hughes, Noblit, and Cleveland, "Derrick Bell"; Feagin and Barnett, "Success and Failure."

20. The "other tradition" discussed in R. W. Thomas, *Understanding Interracial*

Unity; R. W. Thomas, *Racial Unity.* Antiracism discussed in Kendi, *Stamped from the Beginning.*

21. Yarbrough, *Passion for Justice;* Gergel, *Unexampled Courage.*

1: Black Education as a Response to Jim Crow

1. Anderson, *Education of Blacks,* 16.
2. Gordon, *Sketches,* 82–86; Hine, *South Carolina State University,* 64; Rachal, "Gideonites and Freedmen."
3. Rachal, "Gideonites and Freedmen," 459; Gordon, *Sketches,* 87–89.
4. John Alvord, cited in Anderson, *Education of Blacks,* 15.
5. Du Bois, *Souls of Black Folk,* 15.
6. Anderson, *Education of Blacks,* 19.
7. Gordon, *Sketches,* 99, 102, quote on 103.
8. Du Bois, *Souls of Black Folk,* 15.
9. Anderson, *Education of Blacks,* 23.
10. Ibid., 26.
11. Edgar, *South Carolina,* 420; Constitution of the State of South Carolina (1895); Charron, "Septima Poinsette Clark," 241.
12. Shuler, *Blood and Bone,* 57.
13. Edgar, *South Carolina,* 463, quote on 489.
14. Gordon, *Sketches,* 107.
15. Quoted in Charron, "Septima Poinsette Clark," 241.
16. Newby, *Black Carolinians,* 84, 96–99; Fitchett, "Role of Claflin College," 58.
17. Anderson, *Education of Blacks,* 187–88; Fitchett, "Role of Claflin College," 58–59; Daniel, "Public Education," 189–90. Table and source cited in Edgar, *South Carolina,* 490.
18. Anderson, *Education of Blacks,* 31.
19. Du Bois, *Souls of Black Folk.*
20. Anderson, *Education of Blacks,* 66, 72, 83, 86, 193–96.
21. Gore, *On a Hilltop High.*
22. Ibid., 33. See also Brawley, *Two Centuries of Methodist Concern.*
23. Fields's mother remembered this incident of leading Black congregants out of church. Fields, *Lemon Swamp,* 32–33.
24. Gore, *On a Hilltop High,* 35.
25. A. Webster and T. W. Lewis to "Dear Brother," December 1, 1869, cited in Gore, *On a Hilltop High,* 40; Mitchell, "Making of a Modern Education," 270.
26. Gordon, *Sketches,* 96.
27. Gore, *On a Hilltop High,* 170.
28. Ibid., 106.
29. Mitchell, "Making of a Modern Education," 276. By "modern," Mitchell refers to the more old-fashioned tradition of focusing on oral recitation of the classics rather than flexible inquiry.
30. Gore, *On a Hilltop High,* 116.
31. Sources offer different perspectives of this split. See Hine, *South Carolina State University,* 8–9, and, for much more detail, Gore, *On a Hilltop High,* 116–24. See also

Fitchett, "Role of Claflin College," 50–51, and Brawley, *Two Centuries of Methodist Concern*, 208–10.

32. Hine, *South Carolina State University*, 4–5, 35.

33. Ibid., 38–41, 52 (quote).

34. Fitchett, "Role of Claflin College," 53–54.

35. Anderson, *Education of Blacks*, 245, cites data from the US Commissioner of Education.

36. Hine, *South Carolina State University*, 36, 56, 75, 79.

37. Ibid., 19–20, 22–25; Fitchett, "Role of Claflin College," 51.

38. Drago, *Initiative, Paternalism, and Race Relations*, 4–5, confirms that her fears were justified.

39. Fields, *Lemon Swamp*, 100.

40. Gullah language was a combination of several African languages that enslaved Africans, thrown together on these isolated islands, developed into their own form of communication.

41. Fields, *Lemon Swamp*, 125–26.

42. Ibid., 227–29.

43. Walker, "Valued Segregated Schools."

44. Walker, *Their Highest Potential*; C. S. Brown, *Ready from Within*, 104. See also Charron, *Freedom's Teacher*, 50–54.

45. Quote from Hubert Vernon Manning, short autobiographical narrative in author's possession, 1, variable paging.

46. Black southern ministers in this era were not required to hold theological, bachelor's, or even high school degrees. Manning, "Christian Education," 36–40. See also Mays and Nicholson, *The Negro's Church*, 40–47.

47. Manning, autobiographical narrative, 6.

48. Ibid., 5–8.

49. Ibid., 10.

50. Franklin, "Place of Carter G. Woodson"; Givens, "'There Would Be No Lynching.'"

51. Fitchett, "Role of Claflin College," 62; Fitchett, "Occupational Preferences."

52. Hubert V. Manning, untitled talk that begins "Text: Mark 3:33–35 And They Said unto Him," n.d. Dr. Hubert V. Manning Collection, Archives and Special Collections, Claflin University (hereafter Manning Claflin), box 2, "Miscellaneous."

53. Manning, autobiographical narrative, 16.

54. Ibid., 14.

55. Ethel Manning, letter to Rev. I. V. Manning, May 27, 1946. Author's possession.

56. Newby, *Black Carolinians*, 201–8.

57. Manning, "Christian Education," 71–74.

58. Ibid., 75.

59. Calculation of ratios using data from ibid., 44–46. His analysis examined the six most rural and six most urban counties.

60. Ibid., 48, 59.

61. Ibid., 78–79.

62. Gravely, "Civil Right."

63. Gore, *On a Hilltop High,* 105–6, 165–68; Anderson, *Education of Blacks,* 107–9.

2: Struggling for Equal Education

1. For insights into barbershops, see Middleton, *Knowing Who I Am.*

2. Webber, *College Soda Shop.* This has anecdotes from 1941–60.

3. Now called "Trinity United Methodist Church." Facts from US Department of the Interior National Park Service, National Register of Historic Places Registration form (pdf), pp. 6–7.

4. The label "clinic" appears next to Felton faculty names in SC State annual reports of that era.

5. Walker, *Their Highest Potential.*

6. Gorman and Stickell, "Partners in Progress."

7. Weathers, "Rosenwald School Building," E-8.

8. For more detail on philanthropic organizations, see Weathers, "Rosenwald School Building," E-6; Anderson, *Education of Blacks,* chap. 4.

9. Bell, "*Brown v. Board of Education.*"

10. Quoted in Anderson, *Education of Blacks,* 154.

11. Ibid., 158.

12. Gorman and Stickell, "Partners in Progress," 16 (first quote), 15 (second quote).

13. Ibid., 16 (first quote), 12 (second quote).

14. Ibid., 18 (first quote), 17 (second quote). See also Anderson, *Education of Blacks,* 170.

15. Aaronson and Mazumder, "Impact of Rosenwald Schools."

16. Hine, *South Carolina State University,* 117. Hines notes in a footnote, 420, that the state contributed through legislative appropriations $1.7 million to the Rosenwald schools.

17. Gorman and Stickell, "Partners in Progress," 20; emphasis added.

18. Weathers, "Rosenwald School Building," E-24.

19. Gordon, *Sketches,* 108.

20. Anderson, *Education of Blacks,* 179

21. The report noted that a large fraction of Black children attended private nonprofit schools rather than the public schools. South Carolina Department of Education (SCDE), "A Survey of School Buildings Grounds and Equipment in South Carolina," Division of School House Planning, assisted by State Planning Board, 1937. Data from unpaginated front matter, map of enrollment, https://dc.statelibrary .sc.gov/bitstream/handle/10827/6070/DOE_Survey_of_School_Buildings_Grounds _and_Equipment_1937.pdf?sequence=1&isAllowed=y (accessed March 8, 2021).

22. SCDE, "Survey of School Buildings," summary statistics, 174–79, with more details, e.g., 42, 84.

23. Ibid., 3, 41–42, 76–77, 63–64.

24. Cited in Fultz, "Charleston," 637.

25. The public school system for Black students included Shaw Memorial School; Morris Street School, founded in 1867 and renamed later as Simonton in 1891; and

Charleston Colored Industrial School, opened in 1911 and renamed Burke Industrial School in 1920. Ibid., 636–37.

26. W. T. B. Williams, "Negro Schools of Charleston, SC," April 1, 1904, 2–3. Rockefeller Archive Center, General Education Board records, series 1.2, box 200, folder 1899.

27. Edgar, *South Carolina,* 468.

28. Fultz, "Charleston," 637, 640–41. See also C. S. Brown, *Ready from Within,* 99, 110; Newby, *Black Carolinians,* 158–59.

29. Fultz, "Charleston," 639. See also Charron, *Freedom's Teacher,* 89–96.

30. Fultz, "Charleston," 636.

31. R. S. Baker, *Paradoxes of Desegregation,* 40–43.

32. Ibid., 47, 44.

33. Lau, "Mr. NAACP."

34. Modjeska Simpkins to "Fellow-Citizens," April 15, 1943; emphasis added. Modjeska Monteith Simkins Papers, South Carolina Political Collections, University of South Carolina (hereafter Simkins USC), box 2, "Topical, NAACP, general, 1932–1950."

35. Charron, *Freedom's Teacher,* 164–65. The 1940 ruling in *Virginia, Alston et al. v. School Board of City of Norfolk et al.,* reached the US Supreme Court.

36. R. S. Baker, *Paradoxes of Desegregation,* 52.

37. Ibid., 58–62.

38. Ibid., 61.

39. Cole, *Campus Color Line;* Mays, *Born to Rebel.*

40. Boyce, "Top Brass."

41. Mays, *Born to Rebel,* 196.

42. Gore, *On a Hilltop High,* 169–74.

43. Ibid., 184–88, 192–93.

44. Buttressing known family history are several interviews repeating these facts, such as "28 Years with Claflin," *Claflin College Alumni Bulletin* 10, no. 3 (1984): 1–13.

45. Gore, *On a Hilltop High,* 191.

46. "Mrs. Ethel Braynon Manning: Our First Lady for 28 Years," *Claflin College Alumni Bulletin* 10, no. 3 (1984): 14.

47. "28 Years with Claflin," 4.

48. Ibid.

49. Ibid., 5.

50. Gore, *On a Hilltop High,* 105.

51. Ibid.; Glover, *Men of Vision;* Johnson, *Torchbearers;* "28 Years with Claflin."

52. The Morrill Act of 1890 designated certain HBCUs as having land-grant status; the original nineteen, along with two current HBCUs designated under the Morrill Act of 1862, are listed at "Council of 1890s Institutions," APLU, https://www.aplu.org/members/councils/1890-universities/council-of-1890s-institutions.html (accessed March 13, 2021).

53. Cole, *Campus Color Line,* explains in chap. 1 that the pressures on private Black schools were also large.

54. Hine, *South Carolina State University,* 51, 56.

55. Ibid., 66.

56. President of the Colored Normal Industrial, Agricultural and Mechanical College of South Carolina, "34th Annual Report, Covering the Year September 1929 to September 1930," 7, 9, 17–19, 24; Hine, *South Carolina State University.*

57. Hine, *South Carolina State University,* 122–23.

58. Ibid., 106–23.

59. Ibid., 58; and "Trinity United Methodist Church" pdf source, 6.

60. For 1934–35 per-student funding at SC State was $138, while it was $307 for the Citadel, $277 for Clemson, $257 for USC, and $231 per Winthrop. Ibid., 134. Bond discussed on 136–37.

61. Ibid., 159, 165.

62. Ibid., 170.

63. President of the Colored Normal Industrial, Agricultural and Mechanical College of South Carolina, "Annual Report for Period September 1943 to September 1944," 18, 22.

64. "Annual Report Number for Period September 1944 to September 1945," *State Agricultural and Mechanical College Bulletin* 35, no. 1 (1946): 26–27. Information about perks for trustee members is available in several places in Hine, *South Carolina State University,* e.g., 181.

65. State A & M, "Annual Report 1944–45," 28, 35.

66. Devlin, *Girl Stands at the Door.*

67. R. S. Baker, *Paradoxes of Desegregation,* 66–71.

68. Hine, *South Carolina State University,* 196; R. S. Baker, *Paradoxes of Desegregation,* 72–74.

69. Hine, *South Carolina State University,* 184–85.

70. W. H. Calcott, October 4, 1945, memo to Board of Trustees, State Agricultural and Mechanical College, appendix 3 of State A&M, "Annual Report 1944–45," 41.

71. Ibid., 42, 45–46.

72. A strong account of the law school trial and Whittaker's role is available in Hine, *South Carolina State University,* 190–92. Also see Moore and Anderson, "Thorn in the Side."

73. Hine, *South Carolina State University,* 194.

74. "Annual Report Number for Period September 1946 to September, 1947," *State Agricultural and Mechanical College Bulletin,* 38, no. 1 (1948): 11, 12 (emphasis added). Later in the same document, in a supplement covering June 1 to October 15, 1947, Whittaker reports that the law school opened.

75. State A&M, "Annual Report 1946–47," 31.

76. State A&M, "Annual Report 1944–45," 39.

77. R. S. Baker, *Paradoxes of Desegregation,* 84–85.

78. Moore and Anderson, "Thorn in the Side," 80 (for numbers), 79 (for list of graduates of the school), 87 (for impact).

79. Hine, *South Carolina State University,* 208.

80. Ibid., 125, 207–8.

81. Newspaper article cited in Hine, *South Carolina State University,* 208n154.

82. "Annual Report Number for the Period October 1955 to October 1956," *South Carolina State College Bulletin* 46 no. 1 (1957): 17; emphasis added.

83. "Annual Report Number for the Period October 1960 to October 1961," *South Carolina State College Bulletin*, 52 no. 1 (1962): 17, 21.

84. Boyce, "Top Brass."

85. Walker, "Valued Segregated Schools."

3: A Neighboring County Arises

1. Byrnes's biographer cited in Burton, Burton, and Appleford, "Seeds in Unlikely Soil," 190. It is also possible that from the Supreme Court's perspective, South Carolina's *Briggs* had several disadvantages compared to Kansas's *Brown,* such as location in the heavily segregated Deep South. Kluger, *Simple Justice,* 531–34.

2. Kluger used a description of the circumstances surrounding *Briggs v. Elliott* as the opening chapter for *Simple Justice,* his book analyzing *Brown.* See also Gona, *Dawn of Desegregation.* Also noteworthy is Burton, Burton, and Appleford, "Seeds in Unlikely Soil."

3. SCDE, "Survey of School Buildings," 97–98, 113–14, 145–46. I explain the 6-0-1 funding system in chap. 1. See also Gona, *Dawn of Desegregation,* 8.

4. Gona, *Dawn of Desegregation,* 10–11; Burton, Burton, and Appleford, "Seeds in Unlikely Soil," 177–79.

5. Gona, *Dawn of Desegregation,* 6–9.

6. Kluger, *Simple Justice,* 301.

7. Gona, *Dawn of Desegregation,* 145–47; Kluger, *Simple Justice,* 345.

8. Compare, e.g., Kluger, *Simple Justice;* Edgar, *South Carolina;* Burton, Burton, and Appleford, "Seeds in Unlikely Soil"; and Gona, *Dawn of Desegregation.*

9. The AME Church began in Philadelphia in 1787. "Our History, " African Methodist Episcopal Church, https://www.ame-church.com/our-church/our-history/ (accessed February 17, 2021).

10. Gona, *Dawn of Desegregation,* 23.

11. Ibid., 26, Kluger, *Simple Justice,* 14.

12. Ibid., 17–18.

13. Gona, *Dawn of Desegregation,* 44, as well as passages in Kluger, *Simple Justice,* and Burton, Burton, and Appleford, "Seeds in Unlikely Soil."

14. "Handkerchief head" is a derogatory term for informant that Reverend De Laine used on several occasions.

15. The Fourteenth Amendment (1868) supposedly granted equal rights of citizenship to all persons born or naturalized in the United States.

16. Gona, *Dawn of Desegregation,* 192.

17. Ibid., 138 (quote), 190–94.

18. Arlonial De Laine Bradford, interview with Millicent Brown, June 9, 2009, Summerton, South Carolina, 14. "Somebody Had to Do It" Collection, at Avery Research Center for African American History and Culture, Lowcountry Digital History Initiative, https://ldhi.library.cofc.edu/exhibits/show/somebody_had_to_do_it /oral_histories (hereafter "Somebody" Avery).

19. Gona, *Dawn of Desegregation,* 134. The fine was later reduced to $2,700, still a considerable sum.

20. Quotes from one-page summary of events by Joseph A. De Laine, "August 1962—Some Reminiscence of My Life: Vacation Reflections." John Henry McCray Collection, South Caroliniana Library, University of South Carolina (hereafter McCray USC), "Politics/Persons/DeLaine, Joseph," microfilm roll 9. Now also available via online USC Collections.

21. Also counted by Gona as among these few White people of redeemable quality is a White sheriff in nearby Manning, South Carolina, that De Laine had supported politically. Gona, *Dawn of Desegregation,* 100–102, 104–5.

22. Ibid., 193.

23. Burton, Burton, and Appleford, "Seeds in Unlikely Soil," 195.

24. Most of this account is from Gona, but see also De Laine, "August 1962— Some Reminiscence of My Life."

25. Joseph A. De Laine, letter to John McCray, February 21, 1955. McCray USC, "Politics/Persons/De Laine, Joseph," microfilm roll 9.

26. Gona calls *Briggs* the first time that "a group of American citizens had petitioned a United States federal court to abolish segregation in public schools with the claim that it violated the equal protection clause of the Fourteenth Amendment" (*Dawn of Desegregation,* 143). For a summary of precursor school desegregation efforts, see Devlin, *Girl Stands at the Door.*

27. Gona, *Dawn of Desegregation,* 143–47; Kruger, *Simple Justice,* 365.

28. For statements about the "right" thing to do, see "Inaugural Address of the Honorable Governor James F. Byrnes as Governor of South Carolina," January 16, 1951, 2. South Carolina State Library Digital Collections. For summary of legislation and accomplishments, see "Address of Governor James F. Byrnes to the South Carolina Education Association in Columbia, S.C.," March 25, 1954, South Carolina State Library Digital Collections. See also South Carolina Department of Education, State Educational Finance Commission, "South Carolina's Educational Revolution: A Report of Progress in South Carolina," ca. 1955.

29. "Address of Governor," 3, 5.

30. Edgar, *South Carolina,* 523.

31. "Inaugural Address," 2.

32. "Endanger" quote from "Inaugural Address," 3; promise to close schools in "Address of Governor," 7; "prejudiced," ibid., 8.

33. "Inaugural Address," 3.

34. "Address of Governor," 8–9.

35. Newby, *Black Carolinians,* 309–13.

36. Edgar, *South Carolina,* 485–7. Data on Black migration from South Carolina at Civil Rights and Labor History Consortium, University of Washington, https://depts .washington.edu/moving1/map_black_migration.shtml (accessed June 16, 2021).

37. For photographs of both sets of older schools and the newer Orangeburg High School, see Atkinson, *Orangeburg.*

4: Defending White Schools

1. Hall, "Long Civil Rights Movement."

2. "Address of Governor," 9.

3. Kilpatrick, "School Integration," 1. William D. Workman Collection, South Carolina Political Collections, University of South Carolina (hereafter Workman USC), box 27, "Education 1950–1962 Desegregation, Various Schools."

4. Workman, *Case for the South*. Prince Edward County case described at https://virginiahistory.org/learn/historical-book/chapter/closing-prince-edward-countys -schools

5. Kendi, *Stamped from the Beginning*.

6. Hicks, "Judge No Longer 'Lost to History.'"

7. Crespino, *Strom Thurmond's America*.

8. "Statement by Sen. Strom Thurmond (D-SC) Prepared for Use at the Meeting of States Right League in Sumter, South Carolina, August 4, 1955," 3. Workman USC, box 31, "Integration/Civil Rights, General, 1946–1956."

9. "Declaration of Constitutional Principles," released Monday, March 12, 1956, as reprinted by Association of Citizens' Councils, 1–2. Workman USC, box 31, "Integration/Civil Rights, Citizens' Councils, S.C. 1955–56."

10. In Workman USC, box 31, "Integration/Civil Rights, General, 1946–1956." Thurmond's role described in Edgar, *South Carolina*, 528.

11. "Address by Senator Strom Thurmond (D-SC) before the Virginia State Bar Association at White Sulphur Springs, West Virginia, August 5, 1955," 5, Workman USC, box 28, "Education, Speeches, Strom Thurmond Speech."

12. Thomas R Waring, "Three Addresses." Workman USC, box 33, "Integration/Civil Rights, Race Relations 1959."

13. Waring, "Southern Case," 42.

14. Ibid., 160, 162.

15. Ibid., 163.

16. Ibid., 170, 174.

17. Ibid., 211.

18. Ibid., 234.

19. "Report on Integration" transcript, September 29, 1957, 23. William D. Workman Collection, William L. Clements Library, University of Michigan (hereafter Workman UM), box 22.

20. Mrs. George Winton, handwritten letter to W. D. Workman Jr., September 30, 1957. Workman UM, box 22, folder 17. See similar letters in box 22, folders 15, 16, and 17.

21. Ernest F. Hollings, letter to W. D. Workman Jr., October 4, 1957. Workman UM, box 22, folder 18.

22. W. D. Workman Jr., *Observer Bureau*, clipping stamped July 25, 1954. Workman USC, box 31, "Integration/Civil Rights, General, 1946–1956." Definitions of South Carolina's Lowcountry differ, but generally this designation includes counties in the southeast portion of the state, especially those surrounding Charleston County.

23. John H. McCray, "Need for Changing: Moot, Feeble and Warped," *Baltimore Afro-American*, January 14, 1956; "He Proves Our Case," *Baltimore Afro-American*, January 14, 1956.

24. R. S. Baker, *Paradoxes of Desegregation*, 94.

25. "Interim Report of South Carolina School Committee, December 14, 1955," 4–5. Ernest F. Hollings Collection, South Carolina Political Collections, University of South Carolina, box 20, "Public, Gubernatorial L, topic Segregation, Gressette committee, 1954–59."

26. R. S. Baker, *Paradoxes of Desegregation*, 113–14. The Elloree case concerning Black schoolteachers was *Bryan v. Austin*. Case materials in Workman USC, box 31, "Integration/Civil Rights General 1946–56."

27. Ballantyne, *New Politics in the Old South*, 16.

28. Hine, *South Carolina State University*, 225–29.

29. Boyce, "Top Brass"; Hine, "Civil Rights and Campus Wrongs."

30. White, "White Citizens' Councils," 262.

31. Ibid. See also Gamarekian, "Ugly Battle of Orangeburg," and Hine, "Civil Rights and Campus Wrongs."

32. N.A., "Organization of a Local Citizens' Council," received October 7, 1955. Workman USC, box 31, "Integration/Civil Rights, Citizen Councils S.C. 1955–56." See also "The Association of Citizens' Councils of South Carolina: The First Half-year," June 19, 1956. Workman USC, box 31, "Integration/Civil Rights, Citizen Councils S.C. 1955–56."

33. Gamarekian, "Ugly Battle of Orangeburg," 32.

34. Ibid., 34.

35. For highlights of several Orangeburg leaders, see Lare, *Champions*. Also see several books by Williams: *Freedom and Justice; Out-of-the-Box in Dixie;* and Dubose and Williams, *Orangeburg*.

36. Williams, *Freedom and Justice;* Williams, *Out-of-the-Box in Dixie.*

37. The three officers were Reverend McCollom; James Sulton, treasurer; and John E. Brunson, secretary. Narrative from Brunson cited in Williams, *Out-of-the-Box in Dixie*, 99.

38. McCollom, "Peace, Peace." The interview date is 1982, but Reverend McCollom died April 16, 1980. Introductory page, Rev. Matthew D McCollom Collection, Archives and Special Collections, Claflin University (hereafter McCollom Claflin).

39. "To: Public School Officials of Orangeburg, South Carolina, District 5. A Petition," scrapbook. McCollom Claflin.

40. Modjeska Simkins, interview with Jacqueline Hall, July 23–31, 1976. Simkins USC, box 1, "Oral History" (hereafter Simkins, "Oral History").

41. White, "White Citizens' Councils," 266–67; Hine, "Civil Rights and Campus Wrongs," 315. For a discussion of the boycott list and a photograph of the list, see Sulton, "List."

42. Hine, "Civil Rights and Campus Wrongs," 317–20. See former SC State student narratives: Moore, "Part I: Expulsion"; C. H. Brown, "Effigy of a President"; and Pyatt, "Summer of Tears," 72.

43. Hine, "Civil Rights and Campus Wrongs," 319.

44. Crespino, *Strom Thurmond's America,* 132–33; Edgar, *South Carolina,* 545–46; White, "Dorothy Hamby."

45. Gergel, *Unexampled Courage,* 132.

46. J. Waties Waring, "Dissenting Opinion, *Briggs v. Elliott,*" Documented Rights, https://www.archives.gov/exhibits/documented-rights/exhibit/section5/detail/briggs-dissent-transcript.html (accessed January 30, 2021).

47. Septima Clark, letter to Elizabeth Waring, July 23, 1951. J. Waties and Elizabeth Waring Collection, Avery Research Institute (hereafter Waring Avery), folder 1–1, "Letters from S. Clark and R. Cornwall, 1950–51."

48. Septima Clark, letter to Elizabeth Waring, February 12, 1951. Waring Avery, folder 1–1, "Letters from S. Clark and R. Cornwall, 1950–51."

49. Septima Clark, letter to J. Waties and Elizabeth Waring, May 9, 1962. Waring Avery, folder 1–2, "Letters from S. Clark and R. Cornwall, 1952–64."

50. William D. Workman Jr., letter to James M. Dabbs, January 3, 1956. Workman USC, box 27, "Education 1950–62 Desegregation Various Schools." He wrote similar letters to others.

51. James M. Dabbs, letter to William D. Workman Jr., January 6, 1956, and attached "Statement of My Position on the Race Issue." Workman USC, box 27, "Education 1950–62 Desegregation Various Schools." "James Dabbs, 74, Liberal in South," *New York Times,* May 31, 1970, https://www.nytimes.com/1970/05/31/archives/james-dabbs-74-liberal-in-south-exhead-of-regional-council-gained.html.

52. Mrs. James M. Dabbs, open letter to Gov. James F. Byrnes, May 19, 1954. Workman USC, box 27, "Education 1950–62 Desegregation Various Schools."

53. T. E. Tindall, "Reflections of a White Elementary School Principal in South Carolina on the Issue of Desegregation." South Carolina Council on Human Relations, South Caroliniana Library, University of South Carolina (hereafter SCCHR USC), box 20, "Education 1956–60."

54. Septima Clark, letter to J. Waties and Elizabeth Waring, November 30, 1952. Waring Avery, folder 1–2, "Letters from S. Clark and R. Cornwall, 1952–64." The League of Women Voters opposed the state's initiative to remove the provision for free public education from state law, which required a referendum in October 1952; Black, "Harriet Simons."

55. Black, "Harriet Simons," 185.

56. "Is it Not Permissible to Debate Controversy?" *Gamecock,* December 2, 1955. SCCHR USC, box 20, "Education 1954–55."

57. Klibaner, "Travail of Southern Radicals."

58. Dunbar, "Southern Regional Council." The predecessor of the Southern Regional Council, the Commission on Interracial Co-operation, formed in 1919 and included a South Carolina chapter; ibid., 108.

59. Synnott, "Alice Buck Norwood Spearman Wright," 206.

60. Overview/background of archival materials, SCCHR USC; "South Carolina Council on Human Relations record," USC, https://archives.library.sc.edu/repositories/3/resources/56 (accessed February 20, 2020).

61. Venters, *No Jim Crow Church,* 142–44.

62. Shoghi Effendi, *Advent of Divine Justice.*

5: Living There and Then

1. Gona, *Dawn of Desegregation;* Simkins, "Oral History," 49.

2. Publication of the petitioners' names is mentioned in Lau, *Democracy Rising,* 215.

3. R. S. Baker, *Paradoxes of Desegregation,* 96.

4. Many Black people used Black travelers' guides during those years, although I do not remember my parents' using one.

5. For descriptions of socioeconomic differences and colorism among Black people in Orangeburg, see Mack, *Parlor Ladies.*

6. On Byrd and Hinton, see especially Lau, *Democracy Rising.*

7. See her letter to Gov. Olin D. Johnson, April 17, 1944, on frontispiece of Robbins, *Modjeska Monteith Simkins;* Jones-Branch, "Modjeska Monteith Simkins."

8. Simkins, "Oral History," 60.

9. Ibid., 61–62.

10. Ibid., 71–72.

11. Chicago letter from Fred L. Jones, letter to "Mrs. A. W." Simkins, October 14, 1955; Philadelphia letter from Emma J. De Shield, letter to Modjeska Simkins, October 14, 1955. Both in Simkins USC, box 2, "Topical, NAACP, General, October to December 1955."

12. Simkins, "Oral History," 77–78.

13. Modjeska Simkins to "Officers and Members of Local Branches of NAACP," n.d. 1958; Gloster Current, memo, May 9, 1958; Ruby Hurley, letter to Gloster Current, May 23, 1958; memo to Robert Carter from Gloster Current, May 21, 1958; minutes of the 1958 Annual Meeting of the South Carolina Conference of Branches, NAACP. All these in NAACP, Part 27, Selected Branch Files, 1956–65, series A, reel 13, microfilm accessed at the University of Michigan. For relevant letters between Simkins and Wilkins, see Modjeska Simkins, March 24, 1958, letter to Wilkins; Simkins, March 24, 1958, additional letter to Wilkins; and Wilkins, April 3, 1958, response letter to Simkins—all of these in NAACP, part 3, series D, 1956–65 Educational Equality South Carolina, reel 8, microfilm. See also Simkins, "Oral History," 82–84.

14. "Newman, no less an adversary to the white establishment than Simkins, who was a more in-your-face leader, had a different style and philosophy as a strategist. . . . Newman, a leader who angered more slowly, used his wit, intelligence, philosophy, morality, and practicality in dealing with the white political establishment. Both leaders were effective." Logan, "I. DeQuincey Newman," 20.

15. Comments from Newman's archivist Herbert J. Hartsook, oral communication with the author, fall 2017. See "Biographical Note" for Isaiah DeQuincey Newman Papers, South Carolina Political Collections, University of South Carolina Libraires (hereafter Newman USC). For a book-length account of Newman's life, see Logan, *Spirit of an Activist.*

16. Logan, "I. DeQuincey Newman," 15–17.

17. Logan and McRant, "Making the Impossible Possible," 49.

18. See chronology in Logan, *Spirit of an Activist,* xx–xxiii.

19. M. E. Brown, "NAACP Year," 68; Clyburn, prologue.

20. McCollom, "Peace, Peace," 272.

21. Ibid., 273.

22. Ibid., 275.

23. "Annual Report, December 7, 1961," 11–13. Newman USC, folder "Topical, NAACP, reports."

24. Logan, *Spirit of an Activist*. James Thomas, a fellow minister, said Newman "was an excellent preacher and even-tempered enough to share tough talk with his congregation and others while maintaining great composure and sense of purpose"; ibid., 153.

25. See Rackley's account of the arrest in Rackley Blackwell, "Gloria Rackley Blackwell," 281.

26. Date recorded in the *Torch*, October 10, 1963, vol. 1, no. 7.

6: Struggling to Learn

1. I. DeQuincey Newman, "South Carolina 100 Years after the Emancipation Proclamation, Annual Report 1963 of I. DeQuincey Newman, Field Secretary for South Carolina National Association for the Advancement of Colored People," 13–14. Newman USC, folder "NAACP, reports, 1962, August 20–February 5, 1964." See also "Annual Report," December 7, 1961. Newman USC, folder "NAACP, reports, 1961–January 30, 1961." Cox, "Integration with [Relative] Dignity," cites protest letters sent to Governor Donald Russell, 280. See Harvey Gantt's account in the same book, 352–58.

2. Meadows, "Chapters Never Written"; Devlin, *Girl Stands at the Door*.

3. In 1967 the White head of the Methodist Church's national education office told a potential donor: "Claflin College . . . of which Dr. Hubert V. Manning is president . . . has little or no support from white people in South Carolina and yet is the best college for Negro youth in that state." John O. Gross, letter to Dr. and Mrs. Guy H. Williams, October 21, 1967. Manning Claflin, box 2, "H. V. Manning—Correspondence."

4. Dad's interpretation of the gist of this 1 Kings chapter, as summarized in his talk, was: "Arise, Elijah, get up from under the Juniper Tree, there are seven thousand in Israel who have not bent their knees to Baal."

5. Hubert V. Manning, "Chapel Address, Tuesday, January 20, 1970." Manning Claflin, box 2, "Speeches."

6. Hubert V. Manning, untitled talk that begins "Text: Mark 3:33–35 And They Said unto Him," n.d. Manning Claflin, box 2, "Miscellaneous."

7. Hine, *South Carolina State University*, 307.

8. "NAACP Conference Program, October 22–25, 1959, in Greenville SC," Papers of the NAACP, part 27, Selected Branch Files 1956–65, series A: The South, reel 13, University of Michigan. See also "Statewide Conference of Religious Leaders, South Carolina NAACP, Held June 13–15, Claflin College and Trinity Methodist Church," Ibid., Reel 14; and I. DeQuincey Newman to Gloster Current, March 17, 1962, letter with attached "Annual Honor Guard Dinner of the South Carolina Conference of Branches," Ibid., Reel 14.

9. Hine, "Civil Rights and Campus Wrongs," 320; see also 322–23.

10. See photographs in Williams, *Out-of-the-Box in Dixie,* 174–77, 188–89; Claflin gymnasium and bandstand pictures appear on 178–79, 214.

11. A full copy of the Torch, 1963–64, is in Claflin University archives.

12. "Seven times" is from personal conversation with Frances Edwards, ca. May 2021.

13. For confirmation see Rackley Blackwell, "Gloria Rackley Blackwell," 284.

14. James S. Thomas, interview by Chuck Thomas, April 13, 2005, in freestanding notebook titled "Interview with Bishop James and Ruth Thomas," Claflin University Archives.

15. Dr. H. V. Manning, "Charting a Course for Church Action in Civil Rights," talk delivered at the Southeastern Regional Convention of the NAACP, Greenville, SC, February 16, 1961. Manning Claflin, box 2, "Miscellaneous."

16. Edward J. Odom Jr., letter to Dr. H. V. Manning, February 21, 1961, personal copy of the letter obtained from Bobby Donaldson, July 31, 2017, email to the author.

17. The ruling was *Edwards et al. v. South Carolina,* March 2, 1963.

18. *1963–64 Wilkinsonian,* available in Salley Archives, Orangeburg Historical Society, Orangeburg, South Carolina.

19. Dr. H. E. Caldwell, July 7, 1963, letter to Mr. S. Clyde Fair, mayor, in Harlowe E. Caldwell files, Claflin University Archives (hereafter Claflin Caldwell). Memo is located in same files. Caldwell was a local dentist for many years. At the time of this letter, he was president of the Orangeburg NAACP branch.

20. Matthew J. Perry, June 13, 1963, letter to Mr. Arthur Rose. J. Arthur Brown Collection, Avery Research Center, box 1, folder 2.

21. See especially issues of the *Torch* from August 28, September 6, September 17, October 24, and October 31; issues continued through May 1964. Photocopies in Williams, *Out-of-the-Box in Dixie,* 218–41.

22. "Orangeburg Branch of NAACP Presents Roy Wilkins, Executive Secretary, NAACP," November 13, 1963, at Trinity Methodist Church. Claflin Caldwell.

23. *Torch,* September 6, 1963, 1.

24. Branch, *Parting the Waters,* 427.

25. "No More Mourning," *Torch,* September 26, 1963, 1–2.

26. Rackley Blackwell, "Gloria Rackley Blackwell," 285.

27. *Adams et al. v. School District No. 5 Orangeburg et al.,* Workman USC, box 27 "Education, School Desegregation Adams et al. v. Orangeburg," 9.

28. Dudziak, *Cold War Civil Rights.*

29. The 1964 Orangeburg tutorial project was probably a joint effort between the American Friends Service Committee and SCLC. It included white youths who volunteered in 1965 but remembered the previous summer as well. See interviews in the Stanford Digital Repository of Earl Coblyn, 1965 (https://purl.stanford.edu/xto69tc7953), and of an anonymous white female interviewed by Sarah L. Oates, KZSU Project, 1965, Orangeburg, https://purl.stanford.edu/rd292zg2112 (accessed March 16, 2021).

30. The three boys and ten girls were Theodore Adams; Evelyn, Jacqueline, and Tyrone Dash, siblings; Leona Ferguson; Barbara Fields; Rosetta Gooden; June

Manning; Tyrone Robinson; Alice Smith; Brenda Smiley, Ann Marie Thomas; and Heidi Williams.

31. Interview with Arthur Rose Jr., February 4, 2009, not yet posted, "Somebody" Avery. Pat Rose recording also not yet available due to formatting problems.

32. Tyrone Dash, "The Courage Necessary for Civil Rights," talk at the College of Charleston, February 16, 2021. https://www.youtube.com/watch?v=5weiyPIG p9M&t=14s (accessed April 8, 2021).

33. Interview with Theodore Adams, April 8, 2009, "Somebody" Avery.

7: Struggling to Desegregate

1. Synnott, "Alice Buck Norwood Spearman Wright," 200.

2. Wright, Oral History, August 8, 1976. Interview G-0065–2. Southern Oral History Program Collection (#4007), Southern Historical Collection, Wilson Library, University of North Carolina at Chapel Hill.

3. Middleton, *Knowing Who I Am,* 80–81. See confirmation in Septima Clark's assessment of Wright, in Oral History Interview with Septima Poinsette Clark, July 25, 1976. Interview G-0016. Southern Oral History Program Collection (#4007).

4. T. E. Tindall, "Reflections of a White Elementary School Principal in South Carolina on the Issue of Desegregation," 1960, as well as other similar statements in the same folder. SCCHR USC, box 20, "Program, Education General 1956–60."

5. Wright, Oral History, 61.

6. Synnott, "Alice Buck Norwood Spearman Wright," 205.

7. Wright, Oral History, 76, 78 (quote), 79–82; O'Neill, "Memory, History."

8. Middleton, *Knowing Who I Am,* 82.

9. See, e.g., "Higher Education Discussion Group." SCCHR USC, box 20, "Programming Educational: General, 1956–60."

10. Alice Spearman and Elizabeth Ledeen, letter to Mrs. Thomas J. Tobias, March 31, 1964. SCCHR USC, box 20, "Programme, Education 1964." Spearman, letter to Sara Lowrey, July 2, 1964, ibid. Michael P. Wood, Memorandum to Co-sponsoring Organizations, July 15, 1965. SCCHR USC, box 20, "Programme, Education General 1965." Elizabeth Ledeen, letter to unnamed, June 24, 1965, ibid.; "Some Guidelines for Local Councils on Human Relations," August 9, 1965, ibid.

11. See "SPEED-UP Newsletters." SCCHR USC, box 22. Alice Spearman, grant proposal, April 29, 1966. SCCHR USC, box 22, "SPEED-UP Grant Proposals." SCCHR USC, box 21, "SPEED-UP, Program, General, 1967–1970 Ending/Demise."

12. Wright, Oral History, 92.

13. Ibid., 101; Middleton, *Knowing Who I Am,* 81; Synnott "Alice Buck Norwood Spearman Wright," 214. See also Collection Description, SCCHR USC, https://archives.library.sc.edu/repositories/3/resources/56 (accessed March 1, 2021).

14. Program, Frogmore, April 1965. SCCHR USC, box 20, "Programme, Education, General 1965."

15. Dunbar, "Southern Regional Council"; Synnott, "Alice Buck Norwood Spearman Wright," 206, 211; Curry, "Voices from the Civil Rights Movement."

16. M. Hayes Mizell, untitled two-page summary of his life, March 1964. M. Hayes Mizell Papers, South Caroliniana Library, University of South Carolina

(hereafter Mizell USC), box 113, "Writing: 1962–64." "M. Hayes Mizell Papers," Mizell USC. Courtney Siceloff, memo to agencies sponsoring the school desegregation project (Bernice Robinson, SCLC; Mr. Hagans, National Sharecroppers Fund; Walter E Solomon, PEA; Charles Davis, AFSC; J. T. McCain, CORE; I, DeQuincy Newman, NAACP; Alice Spearman, SCCHR; Richard Miles, VEP; C. C. Lewis, PTA), March 2, 1966. Mizell USC, box 20, "Program, Education, 1966, 1 of 2."

17. Terence L. Johnson, "African American Civil Rights and Educational Equality Organizing in South Carolina," American Friends Service Committee Archives, https://www.afsc.org/sites/default/files/documents/African%20American%20Civil%20Rights%20and%20Educational%20Equality.pdf (assessed March 3, 2021).

18. Greenville Education Committee," brief history. SCCHR USC, box 20, "Programme Education, 1966."

19. Alice Spearman, letter to Sara Lowrey, July 2, 1964. SCCHR USC, box 20, "Program, Education General, 1964"; "Greenville Education Committee," SCCHR USC box 20, "Program, Education General, 1966, 2 of 2"; "South Carolina Conference on School Desegregation," Penn Conference Center, Frogmore, April 23–25, 1965, program in SCCHR USC, box 20, "Program, Education, 1965."

20. School Desegregation Project of (name your community), "Instructions to Friendly Visitors," April 8, 1965, AFSC document in SCCHR USC, box 20, "Program, Education, 1965."

21. "M. Hayes Mizell Papers," 6.

22. M. Hayes Mizell, "School Desegregation in South Carolina, 1966: A Critique," December 1966, 14–15. December. South Carolina Community Relations Program, American Friends Service Committee. Mizell USC, box 10, "Education: Desegregation: CRP: School Desegregation Program Task Force."

23. Ibid., 15–16.

24. M. Hayes Mizell, "Testimony Prepared for Sub Committee on Education Labor and Public Welfare Committee, United States Senate," August 15, 1967, 8. Mizell USC, box 111, "Speeches: 1967."

25. See, e.g., his 1966 report published as Mizell, "School Desegregation in South Carolina"; and Jenkins and Mizell, "Divisive Issue."

26. M. Hayes Mizell, memo to Barbara Moffett, Will Hartzler, Constance Curry, Pam Coe, June 29, 1967. Mizell USC, box 11, "Education: Desegregation: South Carolina Community Relations Program, 1967–1974." Title IV of the Civil Rights Act of 1964 authorized grants for institutions of higher learning applying to offer training institutions for public school systems undergoing desegregation. Claflin's Buxton applied for and received such a grant, as did USC.

27. Mizell, memo to Moffett et al., June 29, 1967.

28. Ibid.

29. M. Hayes Mizell, memo to Barbara Moffett, Will Hartzler, Constance Curry, and Pam Coe, March 15, 1967. Mizell USC, box 11, "Education: Desegregation: US Commission on Civil Rights, SC State Advisory Committee: 1966–1967."

30. M. Hayes Mizell, memo to Barbara Moffett, Will Hartzler, Constance Curry, and Pam Coe, February 7, 1967. Mizell USC, box 11, "Education: Desegregation: South Carolina Community Relations Program, 1967–1974."

31. Gauerke and Green, *If the Schools Are Closed.*

32. Bill Rone, "SC Private School Memo," September 13, 1964. USC Workman, box 27, "Education, Private Schools, 1959–1976."

33. Leifermann, "Not Yet Still Means Never," 69.

34. "Strom Thurmond Reports," vol. 13, no. 21, June 4, 1967. USC Workman, box 27, "Education, Private Schools, 1959–1976."

35. Discussion of Furman's summer programs in *Furman Magazine,* winter 1965, 2; spring 1965, 21; summer 1968, 4–7. See also the *Furman Paladin,* April 29, 1966, 1.

36. Mary Beth and Suzanne described in "John Crabtree Oral History (2004)," interview by Courtney Tollison, Furman University Oral Histories no. 28. https://scholarexchange.furman.edu/oral-histories/28 (accessed March 1, 2021).

37. O'Neill, "Memory, History."

38. When Thurmond died his grown children did not deny Essie Mae Washington-Williams's public claim, made after decades of her own silence, that she was Thurmond's Black daughter. It had been an open secret among Black people in Orangeburg for years that Thurmond had fathered a child with a teenaged Black housekeeper when he himself was a young man. He paid for this daughter's SC State tuition and visited her on campus as well as received occasional visits from her, in his office, for many years. Crespino, *Strom Thurmond's America,* 306–11.

39. Crespino, *Strom Thurmond's America,* 199.

8: Struggling to Survive

1. Southern Regional Council, "Desegregation in Higher Education," 1, 2, 5, 6; "SCCHR Report on the Enrollment of Negro Students in Recently Desegregated Colleges of the State, First Semester 1964–65," 1. SCCHR USC, box 20, "Program, Education, 1963."

2. Cox, "Integration with [Relative] Dignity."

3. Oral history interview with James Redfern, February 22, 1974, 3. Interview A-0273. Southern Oral History Program Collection (#4007), Southern Historical Collection, Wilson Library, University of North Carolina at Chapel Hill.

4. O'Neill et al., *Seeking Abraham,* 13.

5. Tollison, "In Pursuit of Excellence," 23–48.

6. Henderson, "'Building Intelligent and Active Public Minds,'" 40.

7. Ibid; Neumann, "'We Cannot Expect,'" 122–41.

8. Neumann, "'We Cannot Expect.'"

9. Ibid., 133–40.

10. Brian Neumann, "Progress, Pragmatism, and Power: Furman's Struggle over Desegregation," 2, https://www.furman.edu/diversity-inclusion/commemorating-desegregation/wp-content/uploads/sites/169/2020/01/BrianNeumann.pdf (accessed March 2, 2021).

11. Ralph B. Kolb, letter to President, Furman University, December 14, 1961. Furman University vertical files, "I: Integration." See also, in same folder, John Wesner Jr., letter to John Plyler, December 25, 1961, and William Lancaster, letter to John Plyler, December 18, 1961.

12. Neumann, "Progress, Pragmatism, and Power," 3.

13. Larry Estridge, videotaped oral history with Courtney Tollison, Furman University oral histories, https://scholarexchange.furman.edu/oral-histories/34/ (accessed March 2, 2021).

14. J. Wilbert Wood, letter to Robert W. Major, December 16, 1964. Furman University vertical files, "I: Integration."

15. John L. Plyler, letter to J. Wilbert Wood, November 23, 1964. Furman University vertical files, "I: Integration." See also John L. Plyler, scrapbook 7, 1962–65. Clipping is Lucille Green, "Many Records Broken at Baptist Convention," *Greenville (SC) News,* November 13, 1964.

16. Quote in Courtney Tollison, "A Majority of One," *Furman Magazine,* summer 2008, 20, as cited in Brian Neumann, "This Is 'Him': The Life of Joseph Allen Vaughn," https://www.furman.edu/diversity-inclusion/commemorating-desegregation /wp-content/uploads/sites/169/2020/01/ThisisHim.pdf (accessed March 2, 2021).

17. Joe died in 1991 at the age of forty-five. Neumann, "This Is 'Him,'" 3.

18. First quote from Estridge, oral history; other quotes from John Duggan, August 30, 2004, videotaped oral history with Courtney Tollison, Furman University Oral Histories, https://scholarexchange.furman.edu/oral-histories/31/ (accessed March 15, 2021).

19. Joseph Vaughn, "Why I Am a Baha'i, Not a Christian," *Furman Paladin,* February 10, 1967, 6, 8.

20. Neumann, "Progress, Pragmatism, and Power," 6; Estridge and Duggan oral histories; Jack Sullivan, "The 60s Remembered," *Furman Magazine,* summer 1990; "Ethicist to Lecture," *Furman Paladin,* September 29, 1967, 1; December 8, 1967, 1.

21. Michelle Simpkins, "Furman's First Black Students Look Back," *Furman Paladin,* February 8, 1985.

22. Ibid. See also Neumann, "This Is 'Him.'"

23. Estridge oral history.

24. *Furman Paladin,* October 27, 1967.

25. Jack Sullivan, *Furman Paladin,* October 27, 1967, 3 (covers two movements); November 3, 1967, 2; November 10, 1967, 2; November 17, 1967, 2; December 8, 1967, 2–3.

26. *Furman Paladin,* November 10, 1967, 1 (quote). The speaker's organization, The Clergy and Laymen Concerned about Vietnam (CALCV), founded in 1965, had some connections with the civil rights movement; included among its members was Dr. Martin Luther King. https://kinginstitute.stanford.edu/encyclopedia/clergy-and -laymen-concerned-about-vietnam-calcav (accessed March 3, 2021).

27. George Johnson, "Black Power Discussed," *Furman Paladin,* February 29, 1968, 4. See also February 5, 1968, 1, 2; March 8, 1968, 2.

28. Sellers with Terrell, *River of No Return.* Sellers discusses Sandy in several places.

29. Carmichael and Hamilton, *Black Power,* 81.

30. Duggan oral history.

31. See, particularly, the interviews in Lare, *Champions of Civil and Human Rights.*

32. Boyce, "Top Brass."

33. Hine, *South Carolina State University*, 285.

34. Hine, *South Carolina State University*, 294.

35. Gore, *On a Hilltop High*, 221.

36. Hine, *South Carolina State University*, 301–7.

37. Ibid., 309–10.

38. For a discussion of some of the discomfort surrounding BACC's presence at SC State, see Hine, *South Carolina State University*, 308–9. For a contrasting view and a Black reading list, see Cleveland Sellers, interview by Jack Bass, February 8 and March 12, 2001, in Dubose and Williams, *Orangeburg 1968*, 145.

39. Sellers, *River of No Return*, 206–7; Shuler, *Blood and Bone*, 76.

40. Nelson and Bass, *Orangeburg Massacre;* Dubose and Williams, *Orangeburg 1968*. See also Watters and Rougeau, *Events at Orangeburg.*

41. Student numbers come from Hine, *South Carolina State University*, 337, and Gore, *On a Hilltop High*, 226.

42. Shuler, *Blood and Bone*, 74–75. Shuler identifies Oscar Butler as dean of men (72), but Hine lists him as director of student activities (Hine, *South Carolina State University*, 311).

43. Shuler, *Blood and Bone*, 73–76, 132 ("angry"); see also John Stroman, interviewed by Damon Fordham, February 8, 2001, in Dubose and Williams, *Orangeburg 1968*, 166–70.

44. Sellers, interview by Bass, in Dubose and Williams, *Orangeburg 1968*, 145–46.

45. Hine, *South Carolina State University*, 312; Dubose and Williams, *Orangeburg 1968*, 148.

46. Shuler, *Blood and Bone*, 123.

47. The requests appear in both Shuler, *Blood and Bone*, 80–81, and in Gore, *On a Hilltop High*, 229. The wording differs in the two versions.

48. Twenty-eight were wounded; one person wounded in the stomach went home instead of the hospital, and some counts missed him. For the number of officers, see Shuler, *Blood and Bone*, 83.

49. Hine, *South Carolina State University*, 317.

50. Gore, *On a Hilltop High*, 231; Shuler, *Blood and Bone*, 85–86.

51. Quotes from Sellers in Dubose and Williams, *Orangeburg 1968*, 139.

52. Hine, *South Carolina State University*, 321.

53. George Johnson, "'Sympathetic Marchers' Protest Student Killings," *Furman Paladin*, February 16, 1968.

9: Keeping up a Struggle

1. "The Orangeburg Declaration, Orangeburg Branch NAACP with Full Support of National NAACP," February 11, 1968. NAACP papers, part 29, Branch Department Files, series A, 1965–72, Field Staff Files reel 09.

2. NAACP press release, "NAACP News for immediate release," August 1, 1968. NAACP papers, part 29, Branch Department Files, series A, 1965–72, Field Staff Files reel 09.

3. For a timeline see Logan, *Spirit of An Activist*, xvii–xxvii. Newman became executive president of Statewide Home Foundation in 1969, commissioner of the State

Housing Authority in 1971, and director of the Governor's Office of Rural Development in 1975. In 1982 South Carolinians elected him to the South Carolina Senate as the first Black person elected to that body since Reconstruction. More information about the transition to Williams can be found in NAACP papers, part 29, Branch Department Files, series A, 1965–72, Field Staff Files reel 09, for example in letters from Gloster Current to Isaac Williams, February 18, 1971, and March 30, 1971.

4. Isaac Williams, "Annual Report on the South Carolina Conference of Branches, NAACP," November 19, 1971. NAACP papers, part 29, Branch Department Files, series A, 1965–72, Field Staff Files reel 09. The report on education appears on pages 2–3.

5. Life of Isaac Williams in the South Carolina African American History Calendar at https://scafricanamerican.com/honorees/isaac-w-williams/ (accessed March 11, 2021).

6. Bell, "School Litigation Strategies."

7. Ibid. See also Baum, *Brown in Baltimore,* which tells a parallel tale.

8. M. Hayes Mizell, "The Crisis of the White Folks," February 25, 1968, 3, 5, 7. Mizell USC, box 111, "Speeches: 1968."

9. M. Hayes Mizell, letter to George McMillan, February 26, 1968. Mizell USC, box 9, "Education: Desegregation CRP: School Desegregation Program, South Carolina, General."

10. M. Hayes Mizell, "Desegregation and the Southern Negro Educators," opening statement before the NEA Conference on Equality of Educational Opportunity, Washington, DC, February 14–16, 1968, 5. Mizell USC, box 111, "Speeches: 1968."

11. Mizell, "South Has Genuflected," 19.

12. Burton and Reece, "The Palmetto Revolution," 87.

13. Mary Timmons, in Tonya Brown, "Lamar Riots Remembered 50 Years Later," ABC15 News, March 5, 2020, at https://wpde.com/news/local/lamar-riots-remembered-50-years-later. See also Herb Frazier, "Lamar Riots," *South Carolina Encyclopedia,* https://www.scencyclopedia.org/sce/entries/lamar-riots/ (accessed March 11, 2021).

14. Phyllis McClure, memo to Alan Black, Winifred Green, Curtis Harris, et al., September 8, 1969. Mizell USC, box 17, "Education: Educational Coalition: Desegregation: Monitoring Projects."

15. M. Hayes Mizell, September 15, 1974, memo and report to Winifred Green. Mizell USC, box 6, "Administration: South Carolina Community Relations Program, Reports, 1974–1976."

16. Mizell, "Desegregation in South Carolina." 4.

17. Ibid., 10.

18. Ibid., 10–11.

19. Burton and Reece, "Palmetto Revolution."

20. Dufford, *My Tour through the Asylum.*

21. Bell, "Burden of *Brown* on Blacks," 29, 32, 36.

22. B. D. Baker, "America's Most Financially Disadvantaged School Districts."

23. Edgar, *South Carolina,* 555.

24. Vaden, "Before the Corridor of Shame," 228–31.

25. Cohn, "Equity Effects."

26. Vaden, "Before the Corridor of Shame," 232–34.

27. Allen, "Forgotten *Brown* Case."

28. Ibid., 449; Morgan, "What Is Left to Argue."

29. Allen, "Forgotten *Brown* Case," 458.

30. Public School Review data, https://www.publicschoolreview.com/scott-s
-branch-high-school-profile (accessed March 15, 2021).

31. Allen, "Forgotten *Brown* Case," 459–60.

32. Public School Review data, https://www.publicschoolreview.com/holly-hill
-elementary-school-profile/29059 (accessed March 6, 2021).

33. Tran, Aziz, and Reinhardt, "Rage against the Machine," 177.

34. Documentary information at "BBC Documentary Highlights Life as a Teenager at SC High School," WIS News, October 17, 2016, https://www.wistv.com/story
/33407818/bbc-documentary-highlights-life-as-a-teenager-at-sc-high-school/. Public
School Review data, https://www.publicschoolreview.com/orangeburg-wilkinson-high
-school-profile (accessed March 6, 2021).

35. Towncharts educational data for South Carolina, https://www.towncharts.
com/South-Carolina/South-Carolina-state-Education-data.html (accessed March 6,
2021).

36. "Claflin University: A Brief Historical Reference." 2020–21 edition, https://
issuu.com/claflinuniversity1869/docs/claflin_university_2020_history_book (accessed
March 6, 2021).

Conclusion: Moving to the Future

1. For an excellent study of similar desegregation difficulties in a border state, see
Baum, *Brown in Baltimore*.

2. Edgar, *South Carolina,* 532–35.

3. Loder-Jackson, *Schoolhouse Activists;* Suh et al., "Experiences of African
American Teachers."

4. John Stevenson, "BHM Remembers: Dr. Ronald McNair," BHM2021, October 21, 2015, https://www.Blackhistorymonth.org.uk/article/section/science-and
-medicine/bhm-remembers-robert-mcnair/ (accessed March 17, 2021).

5. King, *Where Do We Go from Here,* 173.

6. Ibid., 176.

7. Ibid., 171.

8. Universal House of Justice, letter to the Baha'is of the United States, July
22, 2020. https://www.bahai.org/library/authoritative-texts/the-universal-house-of
-justice/messages/20200722_001/1#870410250.

Life as Epilogue

1. Shoghi Effendi was the great-grandson of the cofounder of the Baha'i Faith,
Baha'u'llah. After his death leadership of the worldwide Baha'i community passed
first to a council of respected elders and then to an elected Universal House of Justice,
composed of nine members and headquartered in Haifa, Israel.

2. Shoghi Effendi, *Advent of Divine Justice.*

3. They were referring to a quote by Baha'u'llah, but he was citing a passage from the Quran: "And We desire to show favor to those who were brought low in the land, and to make them spiritual leaders among men, and to make of them Our heirs." Baha'u'llah, *Kitab-i-Iqan,* 134. Baha'u'llah (1817–1892) was raised in the Muslim faith in Persia but founded an independent world religion that responded to the need for rejuvenation of spiritual belief and social teachings.

4. J. M. Thomas, "Blacks on the South Carolina Sea Islands."

5. J. M. Thomas, *Redevelopment and Race;* Thomas and Bekkering, *Mapping Detroit;* Thomas and Ritzdorf, *Urban Planning and the African American Community.*

6. The network is the Planners of Color Interest Group (POCIG), a special group nestled with the parent organization the Association of Collegiate Schools of Planning (ACSP). I helped cofound POCIG in 2007 and served as its cochair from 2008 until 2011. It has sponsored pipeline initiatives, support for untenured planning faculty of color, research on diversity matters, and other activities. "POCIG Initiatives," ACSP, https://www.acsp.org/page/POCIG_Initiatives (accessed March 13, 2021). I also served as president of ACSP, a member association for US planning schools, from 2013–15; key work in that role included promoting the diversity of the urban planning academy's faculty.

7. Catherine Bundy, "Mrs. Manning Pressed into Service," *Times and Democrat,* n.d., clipping in Manning Claflin, box 2, "Miscellaneous."

8. Sellers, oral interview in Du Bois and Williams, *Orangeburg 1968.*

9. "50 Years Commemorating Desegregation at Furman, 1865–2015."

10. O'Neill et al., *Seeking Abraham.* A summary is available of some USC and other South Carolina universities' efforts, some initiated by students. Evan Kurtzler, Sarah Conlon, Jamie Diane Wilson, and Joann Zeise, "Revealing Slavery's Legacy at a Public University in the South," NCPH, October 27, 2014, https://ncph.org/history-at-work/revealing-slaverys-legacy-part-1/.

11. Abercrombie, *Crossing the Line.*

BIBLIOGRAPHY

Archival Collections

Avery Research Center for African American History and Culture, Charleston, SC
    J. Arthur Brown Collection
    J. Waties and Elizabeth Waring Collection
    Millicent Brown Collection
    "Somebody Had to Do It" Collection
Claflin University, HV Manning Library, Archives and Special Collections, Orangeburg, SC
    Harlowe E. Caldwell files
    Hubert V. Manning Collection
    James S. Thomas Notebook
    Matthew D. McCollom Papers
    The *Torch* newsletter records
Furman University Archives, Greenville, SC
    Furman Magazine and *Paladin,* online
    John L. Plyler, scrapbooks
    yearbooks
    vertical files, desegregation
Historical Collection, Miller F Whittaker Library, South Carolina State University, Orangeburg, SC
    Annual reports, SCSU, 1929–67
    Cecil Williams photographs
Papers of the NAACP, Selected Branch Files, microfilm, University of Michigan Libraries, Ann Arbor
Salley Archives, Orangeburg Historical Society, Orangeburg, SC
    Yearbooks, Wilkinson and Orangeburg High Schools
    Vertical files
South Carolina Political Collections, University of South Carolina, Columbia
    Ernest F. Hollings Collection
    Isaiah DeQuincey Newman Papers
    Modjeska Monteith Simkins Papers
    William D. Workman Collection
South Caroliniana Library, University of South Carolina, Columbia
    John Henry McCray Collection
    M. Hayes Mizell Collection
    South Carolina Council on Human Relations Collection
William L. Clements Library, University of Michigan, Ann Arbor
    William D. Workman Collection, 1957

Secondary Sources

Aaronson, Daniel, and Bhashkar Mazumder. "The Impact of Rosenwald Schools on Black Achievement." *Journal of Political Economy* 119, no. 5 (2011): 821–88.

Abercrombie, Richard. *Crossing the Line: A Memoir of Race, Religion, and Change.* Wilmette, IL: Bellwood, 2019.

Allen, Delia B. "The Forgotten *Brown* Case: *Briggs v. Elliott* and Its Legacy in South Carolina." *Peabody Journal of Education* 94, no. 4 (2019): 442–67.

Anderson, James D. *The Education of Blacks in the South, 1860–1935.* Chapel Hill: University of North Carolina Press, 1988.

Atkinson, Gene. *Orangeburg.* Charleston: Arcadia, 2001.

Baha'u'llah. *Kitab-i-Iqan: The Book of Certitude.* Wilmette, IL: Baha'i Publishing Trust, 2003.

Baker, Bruce D. "America's Most Financially Disadvantaged School Districts and How They Got That Way: How State and Local Governance Causes School Funding Disparities." Center for American Progress, July 2014. https://cdn.americanprogress .org/wp-content/uploads/2014/07/BakerSchoolDistricts.pdf.

Baker, R. Scott. *Paradoxes of Desegregation: African American Struggles for Educational Equity in Charleston, South Carolina, 1926–1972.* Columbia: University of South Carolina Press, 2006.

Ballantyne, David T. *New Politics in the Old South: Ernest F. Hollings in the Civil Rights Era.* Columbia: University of South Carolina Press, 2016.

Baum, Howell S. *Brown in Baltimore: School Desegregation and the Limits of Liberalism.* Ithaca: Cornell University Press, 2010.

Beals, Melba Pattillo. *Warriors Don't Cry.* New York: Pocket Books, 1994.

Bell, Derrick A., Jr. "*Brown v. Board of Education* and the Interest-Convergence Dilemma." *Harvard Law Review* 93, no. 3 (1980): 518–33.

———. "The Burden of *Brown* on Blacks: History-Based Observations on a Landmark Decision." *North Carolina Central Law Review* 7 (1975): 25–38.

———. "School Litigation Strategies for the 1970's: New Phases in the Continuing Quest for Quality Schools." *Wisconsin Law Review* 1970, no. 2 (1970): 257–97.

———. "Serving Two Masters: Integration Ideals and Client Interests in School Desegregation Litigation." *Yale Law Journal* 85, no. 4 (1976): 470–516.

Black, Jennifer. "Harriet Simons: Women, Race, Politics, and the League of Women Voters of South Carolina." In *South Carolina Women: Their Lives and Times,* vol. 3, ed. Marjorie Julian Spruill, Valinda W. Littlefield, and Joan Marie Johnson, 179–99. Athens: University of Georgia Press, 2012.

Boyce, Travis D. "Top Brass Polishing Other People's Brass: Evaluating Aspects of the Marred Legacy of an African American College President." *Journal of Pan African Studies* 6, no. 7 (2014): 238–60.

Branch, Taylor. *Parting the Waters: America in the King Years 1954–63.* New York: Simon & Schuster, 2007.

Brawley, James P. *Two Centuries of Methodist Concern: Bondage, Freedom, and Education of Black People.* New York: Vantage, 1974.

Brown, Charles H. "Effigy of a President." In Lare, *Champions of Civil and Human Rights in South Carolina,* 57–66.

Brown, Cynthia S, ed. *Ready from Within: Septima Clark and the Civil Rights Movement.* Trenton, NJ: Africa World Press.

Brown, Millicent E. "The NAACP Year: Newman as South Carolina Field Director." In Logan, *The Spirit of an Activist: The Life and Work of I. DeQuincey Newman,* 63–83.

Burton, Orville Vernon, Beatrice Burton, and Simon Appleford. "Seeds in Unlikely Soil: The *Briggs v. Elliott* School Segregation Case." In *Toward the Meeting of the Waters: Currents of the Civil Rights Movement of South Carolina During the Twentieth Century,* ed. Winfred B. Moore Jr. and Orville Vernon Burton, 176–200. Columbia: University of South Carolina Press, 2008.

Burton, Vernon, and Lewie Reece. "The Palmetto Revolution: School Desegregation in South Carolina." In *With All Deliberate Speed: Implementing Brown v. Board of Education,* ed. Brian J. Daugherity and Charles C. Bolton, 59–91. Fayetteville: University of Arkansas Press, 2008.

Carmichael, Stokely, and Charles Hamilton. *Black Power: The Politics of Liberation in America,* New York: Random House, 1967.

Charron, Katherine Mellen. *Freedom's Teacher: The Life of Septima Clark.* Chapel Hill: University of North Carolina Press, 2009.

———. "Septima Poinsette Clark: The Evolution of an Educational Stateswoman." In *South Carolina Women: Their Lives and Times* vol. 3, ed. Marjorie Julian Spruill, Valinda W. Littlefield, and Joan Marie Johnson, 240–61. Athens: University of Georgia Press, 2012.

Clyburn, James E. Prologue to Logan, *Spirit of an Activist,* 1–3.

Cohn, Elchanan. "Equity Effects of the Educational Finance Act in South Carolina." *Economics of Education Review* 3, no. 4 (1984): 333–39.

Cole, Eddie R. *The Campus Color Line: College Presidents and the Struggle for Black Freedom.* Princeton, NJ: Princeton University Press, 2020.

Cox, M. Ron. "Integration with [Relative] Dignity: The Desegregation of Clemson College and George McMillan's Article at 40." In *Toward the Meeting of the Waters: Currents in the Civil Rights Movement of South Carolina during the Twentieth Century,* ed. Winfred B. Moore Jr. and Orville Vernon Burton, 274–85. Columbia: University of South Carolina Press, 2008.

Crespino, Joseph. *Strom Thurmond's America: A History.* New York: Hill & Wang, 2012.

Curry, Constance. "Voices from the Civil Rights Movement in South Carolina." In *Toward the Meeting of the Waters: Currents in the Civil Rights Movement of South Carolina during the Twentieth Century,* ed. Winfred B. Moore Jr. and Orville Vernon Burton, 342–48. Columbia: University of South Carolina Press, 2008.

Daniel, J. McT. "Public Education." In University of South Carolina, *South Carolina, Economic and Social Conditions in 1944,* vol. 1., 177–205. Spartanburg, SC: Reprint Company, 1975.

Devlin, Rachel. *A Girl Stands at the Door: The Generation of Young Women Who Desegregated America's Schools.* New York: Basic Books, 2018.

Drago, Edmund L. *Initiative, Paternalism, and Race Relations: Charleston's Avery Normal Institute.* Athens: University of Georgia Press, 1990.

Du Bois, W. E. B. *The Souls of Black Folks.* Amazon Classics Edition. N.d.

Dubose, Sonny, and Cecil Williams. *Orangeburg 1968: A Place and Time Remembered.* Orangeburg, SC: Cecil Williams, 2008.

Dudziak, Mary L. *Cold War Civil Rights: Race and the Image of American Democracy.* Princeton, NJ: Princeton University Press, 2011.

Dufford, William E. *My Tour through the Asylum: A Southern Integrationist's Memoir.* Columbia: University of South Carolina Press, 2017.

Dunbar, Leslie W. "The Southern Regional Council." *Annals of the American Academy of Political and Social Science* 357, no. 1 (1965): 108–12.

Edgar, Walter B. *South Carolina: A History.* Columbia: University of South Carolina Press, 1998.

Emmons, Caroline, Dwonna Naomi Goldstone, Stefanie Decker, Maxine D. Jones, Bobby L. Lovett, Marvin W. Dulaney, Clarissa Myrick-Harris, et al. *Southern Black Women in the Modern Civil Rights Movement.* College Station: Texas A&M University Press, 2013.

Fanon, Frantz. *The Wretched of the Earth.* New York: Grove/Atlantic, 2007.

Feagin, Joe R., and Bernice McNair Barnett. "Success and Failure: How Systemic Racism Trumped the Brown v. Board of Education Decision." *University of Illinois Law Review* 2004, no. 5 (2004): 1099–1130.

Fields, Mamie G., with Karen Fields. *"Lemon Swamp and Other Places: A Carolina Memoir.* New York: Free Press, 1983.

Fitchett, E. Horace. "The Occupational Preferences and Opportunities for Negro College Students." *Journal of Negro Education* 7 (1938): 498–513.

———. "The Role of Claflin College in Negro Life in South Carolina." *Journal of Negro Education* 12, no. 1 (1943): 42–68.

Franklin, John Hope. "The Place of Carter G. Woodson in American Historiography." *Negro History Bulletin* 13, no. 8 (1950): 174–76.

Fultz, Michael. "Charleston, 1919–1920: The Final Battle in the Emergence of the South's Urban African American Teaching Corps." *Journal of Urban History* 27, no. 5 (2001): 633–49.

Gamarekian, Edward. "The Ugly Battle of Orangeburg." *Reporter,* January 24, 1958, 32–34.

Gantt, Harvey. "Harvey B. Gantt." In *Toward the Meeting of the Waters: Currents in the Civil Rights Movement of South Carolina during the Twentieth Century,* ed. Winfred B. Moore Jr. and Orville Vernon Burton, 352–58. Columbia: University of South Carolina Press, 2008.

Gauerke, Warren E., and Donald R. Green. *If the Schools Are Closed: A Critical Analysis of the Private School Plan.* Atlanta: Southern Regional Council, 1959.

Gergel, Richard. *Unexampled Courage: The Blinding of Sgt. Isaac Woodard and the Awakening of President Harry S. Truman and Judge J. Waties Waring.* New York: Sarah Crichton Books, 2019.

Givens, Jarvis R. "'There Would Be No Lynching if It Did Not Start in the School-room': Carter G. Woodson and the Occasion of Negro History Week, 1926–1950." *American Educational Research Journal* 56, no. 4 (2019): 1457–94.

Glover, Vivian. *Men of Vision: Claflin and Her Presidents.* Orangeburg, SC: Bill Wise Printers, 1995.

Gona, Ophelia De Laine. *Dawn of Desegregation: J. A. De Laine and* Briggs v. Elliott. Columbia: University of South Carolina Press, 2012.

Gordon, Asa H. *Sketches of Negro Life and History in South Carolina.* Columbia: University of South Carolina Press, 1971.

Gore, Blinzy L. *On a Hilltop High: The Origin and History Claflin College to 1984.* Spartanburg, SC: Reprint Company, 1993.

Gorman, Bob, and Lois Stickell. "Partners in Progress: Joseph B. Felton, the African American Community, and the Rosenwald School Program." *Carologue* 18, no. 3 (2002): 14–20.

Gravely, William. "The Civil Right Not to Be Lynched: State Law, Government, and Citizen Response to the Killing of Willie Earle (1947)." In *Toward the Meeting of the Waters: Currents in the Civil Rights Movement of South Carolina during the Twentieth Century,* ed. Winfred B. Moore Jr. and Orville Vernon Burton, 93–118. Columbia: University of South Carolina Press, 2008.

Hall, Jacquelyn Dowd. "The Long Civil Rights Movement and the Political Uses of the Past." *Journal of American History* 91, no. 4 (2005): 1233–63.

Henderson, A. Scott. "'Building Intelligent and Active Public Minds': Education and Social Reform in Greenville County during the 1930S." *South Carolina Historical Magazine* 106, no. 1 (2005): 34–58.

Hicks, Brian. "Judge No Longer 'Lost to History.'" *Charleston (SC) Post and Courier,* April 4, 2104. https://www.postandcourier.com/archives/judge-no-longer-lost-to-history/article_d67efdd0–4c6e-579d-a514-555113d53652.html.

Highsmith, Andrew R. *Demolition Means Progress: Flint, Michigan, and the Fate of the American Metropolis.* Chicago: University of Chicago Press, 2015.

Hine, William C. "Civil Rights and Campus Wrongs: South Carolina State College Students Protest, 1955–1968." *South Carolina Historical Magazine* 97, no. 4 (1996): 310–31.

———. *South Carolina State University: A Black Land-Grant College in Jim Crow America.* Columbia: University of South Carolina Press, 2018.

Hughes, Sherick, George Noblit, and Darrell Cleveland. "Derrick Bell's Post-*Brown* Moves toward Critical Race Theory." *Race Ethnicity and Education* 16, no. 4 (2013): 442–69.

Jenkins, H. Harrison, and M. Hayes Mizell. "A Divisive Issue, Freedom of Choice" (1968). N.p.: ERIC Clearinghouse.

Johnson, Vermelle. *Torchbearers: The Story of Claflin University's First Ladies.* Orangeburg, SC: Claflin University Press, 2014.

Jones-Branch, Cherise. "Modjeska Monteith Simkins: I Cannot Be Bought and Will Not Be Sold." In *South Carolina Women: Their Lives and Times,* vol. 3, ed. Marjorie Julian Spruill, Valinda W. Littlefield, and Joan Marie Johnson, 221–39. Athens: University of Georgia Press, 2012.

Kendi, Ibram X. *Stamped from the Beginning: The Definitive History of Racist Ideas in America.* New York: Nation Books, 2016.

Kilpatrick, James Jackson. "School Integration—Four Years After: The South vs. the High Court's 1954 Ruling." *Human Events,* May 12, 1958, 1–4.

King, Martin Luther, Jr. *Where Do We Go from Here: Chaos or Community?* Boston: Beacon, 1968.

Klibaner, Irwin. "The Travail of Southern Radicals: The Southern Conference Educational Fund, 1946–1976." *Journal of Southern History* 49, no. 2 (1983): 179–202.

Kluger, Richard. *Simple Justice: The History of* Brown v. Board of Education *and Black America's Struggle for Equality.* New York: Vintage, 2011.

Lare, Marvin Ira, ed. *Champions of Civil and Human Rights in South Carolina,* vol. 1, *Dawn of the Movement Era, 1955–1967.* Columbia: University of South Carolina Press, 2016.

Lau, Peter F. *Democracy Rising: South Carolina and the Fight for Black Equality since 1865.* Lexington: University Press of Kentucky, 2006.

———. "Mr. NAACP: Levi Byrd and the Remaking the NAACP in State and Nation, 1917–1960." In *Toward the Meeting of the Waters: Currents in the Civil Rights Movement of South Carolina during the Twentieth Century,* ed. Winfred B. Moore Jr. and Orville Vernon Burton, 146–55. Columbia: University of South Carolina Press, 2008.

Leifermann, Henry P. "Not Yet Still Means Never: Orangeburg, South Carolina." *New South,* Fall 1969, 68–73.

Leonardo, Zeus. "The Color of Supremacy: Beyond the Discourse of 'White Privilege.'" *Educational Philosophy and Theory* 36, no. 2 (2004): 137–52.

Levine, Ellen. *Freedom's Children: Young Civil Rights Activists Tell Their Own Stories. 1993.* New York: Puffin, 2003.

Loder-Jackson, Tondra L. *Schoolhouse Activists: African American Educators and the Long Birmingham Civil Rights Movement.* Albany: SUNY Press, 2015.

Logan, Sadye L. M. "I. DeQuincey Newman: The Servant Leader." In Logan, *Spirit of an Activist,* 8–45.

———, ed. *The Spirit of an Activist: The Life and Work of I. DeQuincey Newman.* Columbia: University of South Carolina Press, 2014.

Logan, Sadye L. M., and Josephine A. McRant. "Making the Impossible Possible: Building Alliance between Religion and Politics." In Logan, *Spirit of an Activist,* 47–62.

Mack, Kibibi Voloria C. *Parlor Ladies and Ebony Drudges: African American Women, Class, and Work in a South Carolina Community.* Knoxville: University of Tennessee Press, 1999.

Manning, Hubert Vernon. "Christian Education and Socio-economic Needs of Negroes in South Carolina." MA thesis, Boston University, 1947.

Mantena, Karuna. "Gandhi and the Means-ends Question in Politics." *Occasional Papers of the School of Social Sciences* 46 (2012): 1–25.

Mays, Benjamin E. *Born to rebel: An autobiography.* University of Georgia Press, 2003.

Mays, Benjamin E., and Joseph Nicholson. *The Negro's Church*. New York: Institute of Social and Religious Research, 1933.

McCollom, Matthew. "Peace, Peace, Where There Is No Peace." In Lare, *Champions of Civil and Human Rights in South Carolina*, 269–75.

McIntosh, Peggy. "White Privilege and Male Privilege: A Personal Account of Coming to See Correspondence through Work in Women's Studies," 7–18, in *Race, Class, and Gender: An Anthology*, ed. M. Andersen and P. H. Collins. Belmont, CA: Wadsworth, 1992.

Meadows, Karen. "Chapters Never Written, Voices Never Heard: Children as Social Agents During the Era of School Desegregation. The Narratives of Ruby Bridges, Millicent Brown, and Josephine Boyd Bradley." PhD dissertation, University of North Carolina at Greensboro, 2005.

Middleton, Earl, with Joy W. Barnes. *Knowing Who I Am: A Black Entrepreneur's Memoir of Struggle and Victory in the American South*. Columbia: University of South Carolina Press, 2008.

Mitchell, David T. "The Making of a Modern Education: Methodists and Claflin University, 1869–1913." *Methodist History* 55. no. 4 (2017): 265–77.

Mizell, M. Hayes. "Desegregation in South Carolina," remarks presented November 11, 1974. Distributed by ERIC Clearinghouse, 1974

———. "School Desegregation in South Carolina." *Integrated Education* 4, no. 6 (1966): 30–50.

———. "The South Has Genuflected and Held onto Tokenism." In "A Divisive Issue: Freedom of Choice," special issue. *Southern Education Report* 3, no. 6 (1968): 19–21.

Moore, Alfred D., III, and Christian K. Anderson. "A Thorn in the Side of Segregation: The Short Life, Long Odds, and Legacy of the Law School at South Carolina State College." *American Educational History Journal* 45, no. 1 (2018): 71–89.

Moore, Fred Henderson. "Part I: Expulsion." In Lare, *Champions of Civil and Human Rights in South Carolina*, 25–43.

Morgan, Denise C. "What Is Left to Argue in Desegregation Law: The Right to Minimally Adequate Education." *Harvard BlackLetter Journal* 8 (1991): 99–133.

Nelson, Jack, and Jack Bass. *The Orangeburg Massacre*. New York: Ballantine Books, 1970.

Neumann, Brian. "'We Cannot Expect to Rebuild the World Overnight': Race, Reform, and Reaction at Furman University, 1933–1955." *South Carolina Historical Magazine* 16, no. 2 (2015), 122–41.

Newby, Idus A. *Black Carolinians: A History of Blacks in South Carolina from 1895 to 1968*. Columbia: University of South Carolina Press, 1973.

O'Neill, Stephen. "Memory, History, and the Desegregation of Greenville, South Carolina." In *Toward the Meeting of the Waters: Currents in the Civil Rights Movement of South Carolina during the Twentieth Century*, ed. Winfred B. Moore Jr. and Orville Vernon Burton, 286–300. Columbia: University of South Carolina Press, 2008.

O'Neill, Stephen, et al. *Seeking Abraham: A Report of Furman University's Task Force on Slavery and Justice*. Greenville, SC: Furman University, 2018.

Pyatt, Alice. "A Summer of Tears." In Lare, *Champions of Civil and Human Rights in South Carolina,* 67–77.

Rachal, John R. "Gideonites and Freedmen: Adult Literacy Education at Port Royal, 1862–1865." *Journal of Negro Education* 55, no. 4 (1986): 453–69.

Rackley Blackwell, Gloria. "Gloria Rackley Blackwell and Her Daughters Jamelle Rackley-Riley and Lurma Rackley, Part 1: Roots of a Storm." In Lare, *Champions of Civil and Human Rights in South Carolina,* 276–86.

Robbins, Becci. *Modjeska Monteith Simkins: A South Carolina Revolutionary.* Columbia: South Carolina Progressive Network, 2018.

Rollock, Nicola, and Adrienne D. Dixson. "Critical Race Theory." In *The Wiley Blackwell Encyclopedia of Gender and Sexuality Studies,* ed. Nancy A. Naples et al., 1–6. Malden, MA: Wiley-Blackwell, 2016.

Schock, Kurt. "The Practice and Study of Civil Resistance." *Journal of Peace Research* 50, no. 3 (2013): 277–90.

Sellers, Cleveland, with Robert Terrell. *The River of No Return: The Autobiography of a Black Militant and the Life and Death of SNCC.* 1973. Jackson: University Press of Mississippi, 1990.

Shoghi Effendi. *The Advent of Divine Justice.* Wilmette, IL: Baha'i Publishing Trust, 1969.

Shuler, Jack. *Blood and Bone: Truth and Reconciliation in a Southern Town.* Columbia: University of South Carolina Press, 2012.

Sørensen, Majken Jul. "Constructive Resistance: Conceptualising and Mapping the Terrain." *Journal of Resistance Studies* 2, no. 1 (2016): 49–78

South Carolina Historic Properties Record (website), Trinity Methodist Episcopal Church, National Register of Historic Places, accessed July 19, 2021, http://schpr .sc.gov/index.php/Detail/properties/12731.

Suh, Yonghee, Brian J. Daugherity, Jihea Maddamsetti, and Angela Branyon. "Experiences of African American Teachers in Desegregated PK–12 Schools: A Systematic Literature Review." *Schools* 17, no. 2 (2020): 271–93.

Sulton, James E. "The List." In Lare, *Champions of Civil and Human Rights in South Carolina,* 44–56.

Synnott, Marcia G. "Alice Buck Norwood Spearman Wright: A Civil Rights Activist." In *South Carolina Women: Their Lives and Times,* vol. 3, ed. Marjorie Julian Spruill, Valinda W. Littlefield, and Joan Marie Johnson, 200–220. Athens: University of Georgia Press, 2012.

Thomas, June Manning. "Blacks on the South Carolina Sea Islands: Planning for Tourist and Land Development." PhD dissertation, University of Michigan, 1977.

———. *Redevelopment and Race: Planning a Finer City in Postwar Detroit.* 2nd ed. Detroit: Wayne State University Press, 2013.

Thomas, June Manning, and Henco Bekkering, eds. *Mapping Detroit: Land, Community, and Shaping a City.* Detroit: Wayne State University Press, 2015.

Thomas, June Manning, and Marsha Ritzdorf, eds. *Urban Planning and the African American Community: In the Shadows.* Thousand Oaks, CA: Sage, 1997.

Thomas, Richard W. *Racial Unity: An Imperative for Social Progress*. Ottawa: Baha'i Studies Publications, 1993.

———. *Understanding Interracial Unity: A Study of US Race Relations*. Thousand Oaks, CA: Sage, 1996.

Tollison, Courtney. "In Pursuit of Excellence: Desegregation and Southern Baptist Politics at Furman University." *History of Higher Education Annual* 23 (2005): 23–48.

Tran, Henry, Mazen Aziz, and Sara Frakes Reinhardt. "Rage against the Machine: The Legacy of Education Leaders' Valiant Struggle for Social Justice in *Abbeville v. South Carolina*." *Journal of School Leadership* 31, no. 3 (2021): 166–88. https://doi.org/10.1177/1052684619899612.

Vaden, Luci. "Before the Corridor of Shame: The African American Fight for Equal Education after Jim Crow." PhD dissertation, University of South Carolina, 2014.

Venters, Louis. *No Jim Crow Church: The Origins of South Carolina's Baha'i Community*. Gainesville: University Press of Florida, 2015.

Walker, Vanessa Siddle. *Their Highest Potential: An African American School Community in the Segregated South*. Chapel Hill: University of North Carolina Press, 1996.

———. "Valued Segregated Schools for African American Children in the South, 1935–1969: A Review of Common Themes and Characteristics." *Review of Educational Research* 70, no. 3 (2000): 253–85.

Waring, Thomas R. "The Southern Case against Desegregation." *Harper's,* January 1, 1956, 39–45.

Watters, Pat, and Weldon Rougeau. *Events at Orangeburg: A Report Based on Study and Interviews in Orangeburg, South Carolina, in the Aftermath of Tragedy*. Atlanta: Southern Regional Council, 1968.

Weathers, Lindsay C. M. "The Rosenwald School Building Program in South Carolina, 1917–1932." Submission to the National Register of Historic Places, National Park Services, US Dept. Interior, Washington, DC (2008), E-8.

Webber, Clemmie. *The College Soda Shop: An Education for Life*. Orangeburg, SC: Cecil Williams, 2005.

White, John W. "Dorothy Hamby: The Rise of Two-Party Politics in South Carolina." In *South Carolina Women: Their Lives and Times,* vol. 3, ed. Marjorie Julian Spruill, Valinda W. Littlefield, and Joan Marie Johnson, 322–45. Athens: University of Georgia Press, 2012.

———. "The White Citizens' Councils of Orangeburg County, South Carolina." In *Toward the Meeting of the Waters: Currents in the Civil Rights Movement of South Carolina during the Twentieth Century,* ed. Winfred B. Moore and Orville Vernon Burton, 261–73. Columbia: University of South Carolina Press, 2008.

Williams, Cecil J. *Freedom and Justice: Four Decades of the Civil Rights Struggle as Seen by a Black Photographer of the Deep South*. Macon, GA: Mercer University Press, 1995.

———. *Out-of-the-Box in Dixie: Cecil Williams' Photography of the South Carolina Events that Changed America*. Orangeburg, SC: Cecil J. Williams, 2007.

Workman, William Douglas. *The Case for the South*. New York: Devin-Adair, 1960.

X, Malcolm, and Alex Haley. *The Autobiography of Malcolm X*. New York: Grove, 1965.

Yarbrough, Tinsley E. *A Passion for Justice: J. Waties Waring and Civil Rights*. New York: Oxford University Press, 2001.

INDEX

Please note that italicized page numbers in this index refer to illustrations.